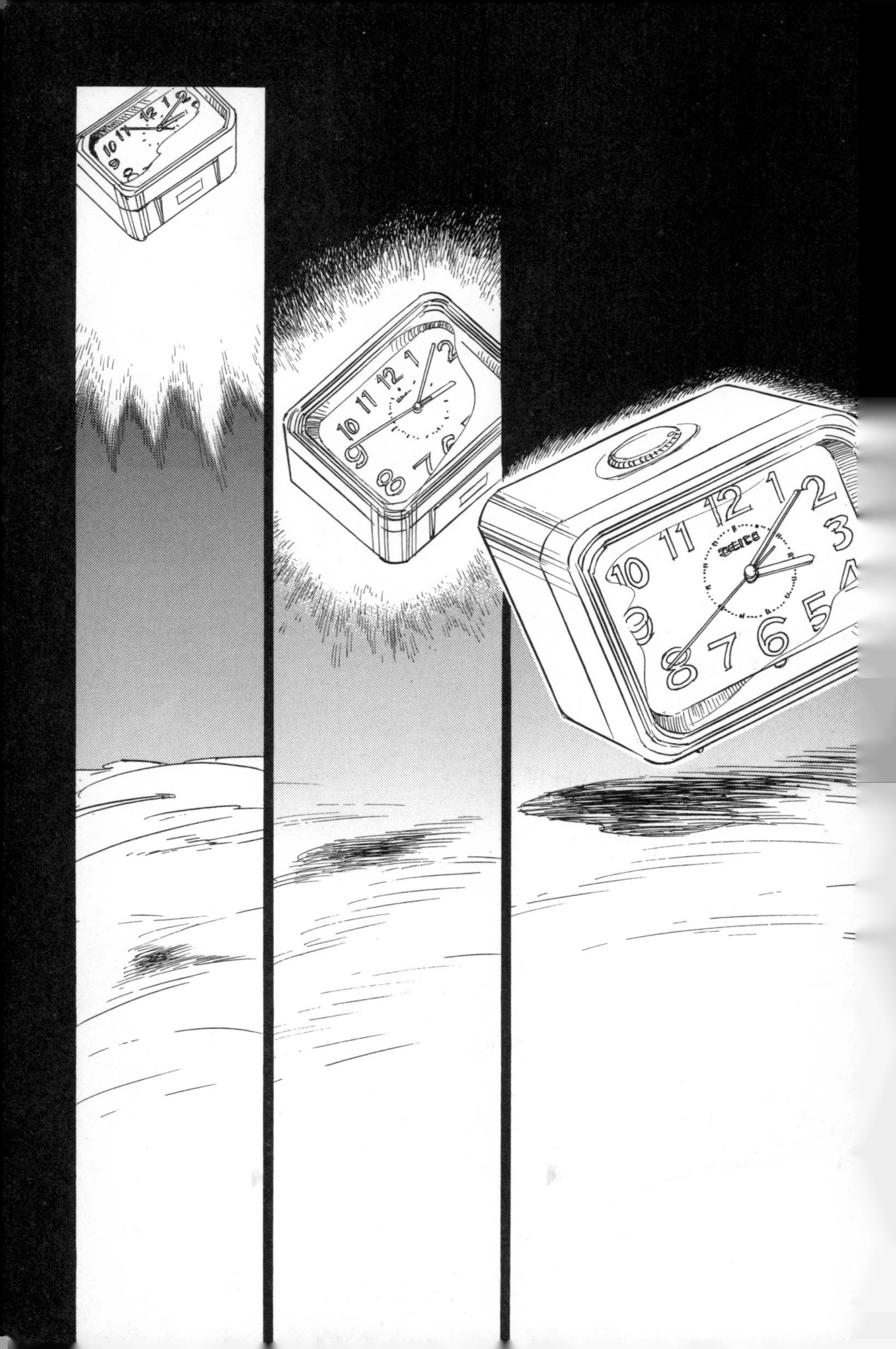

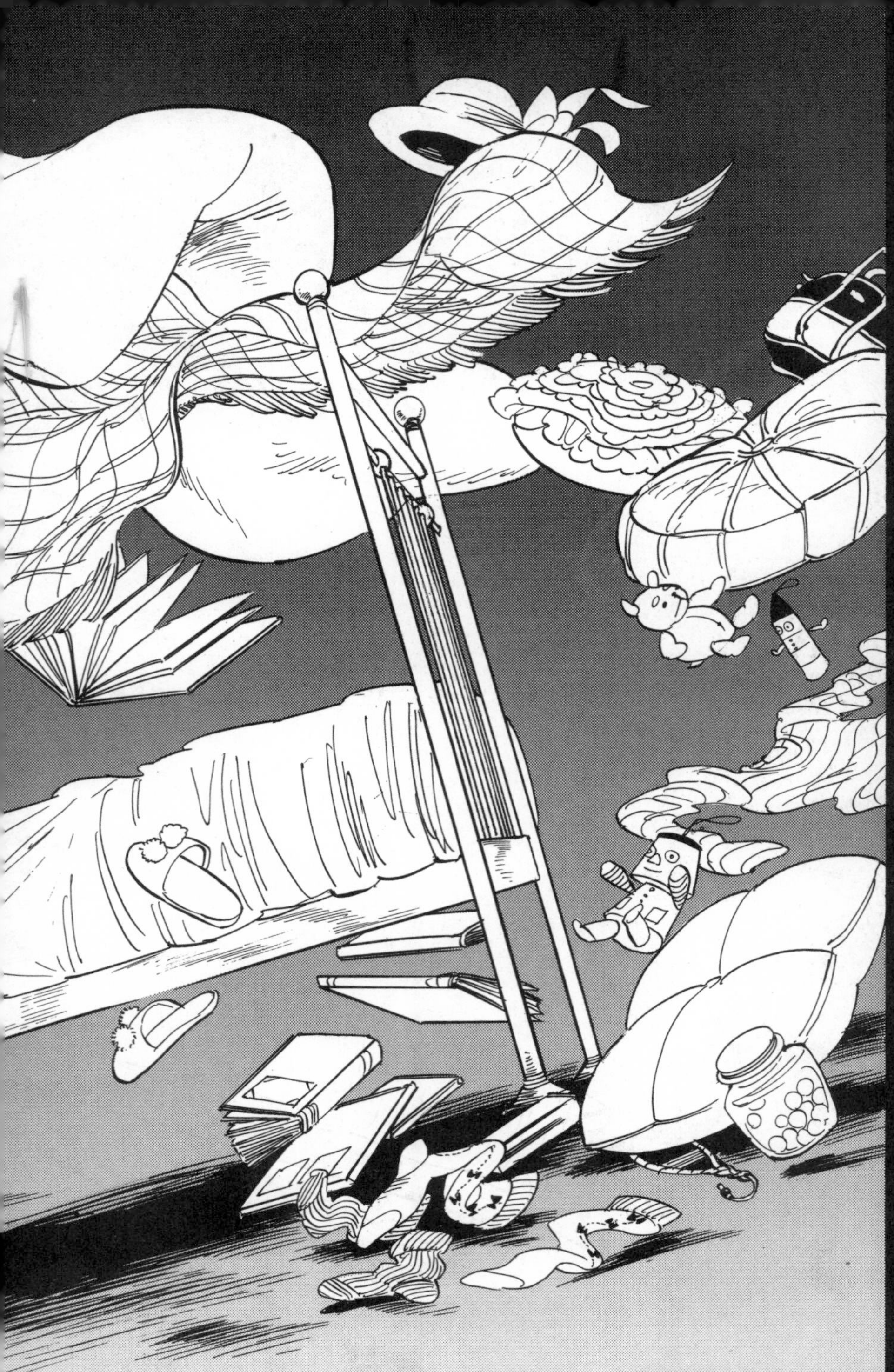

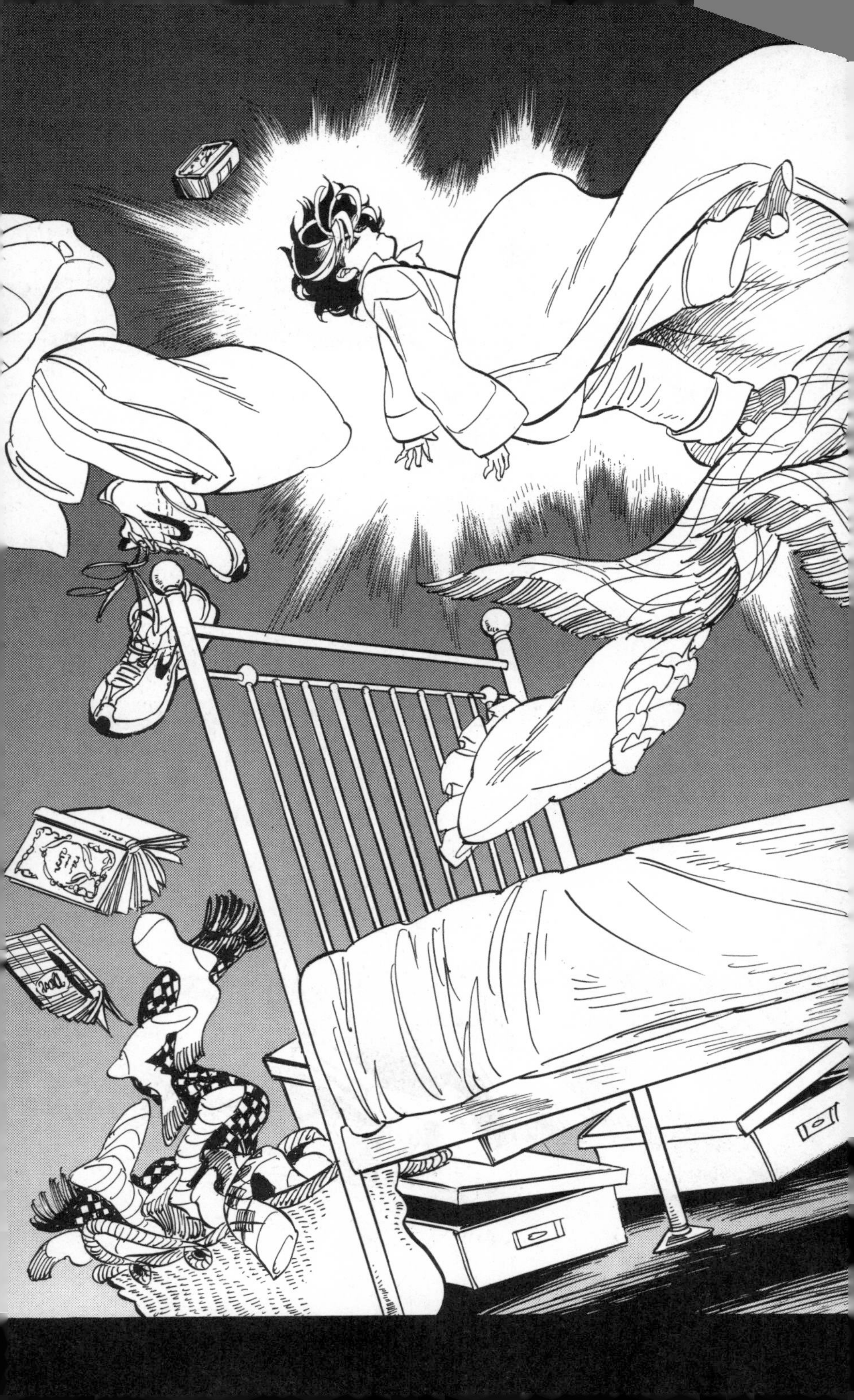

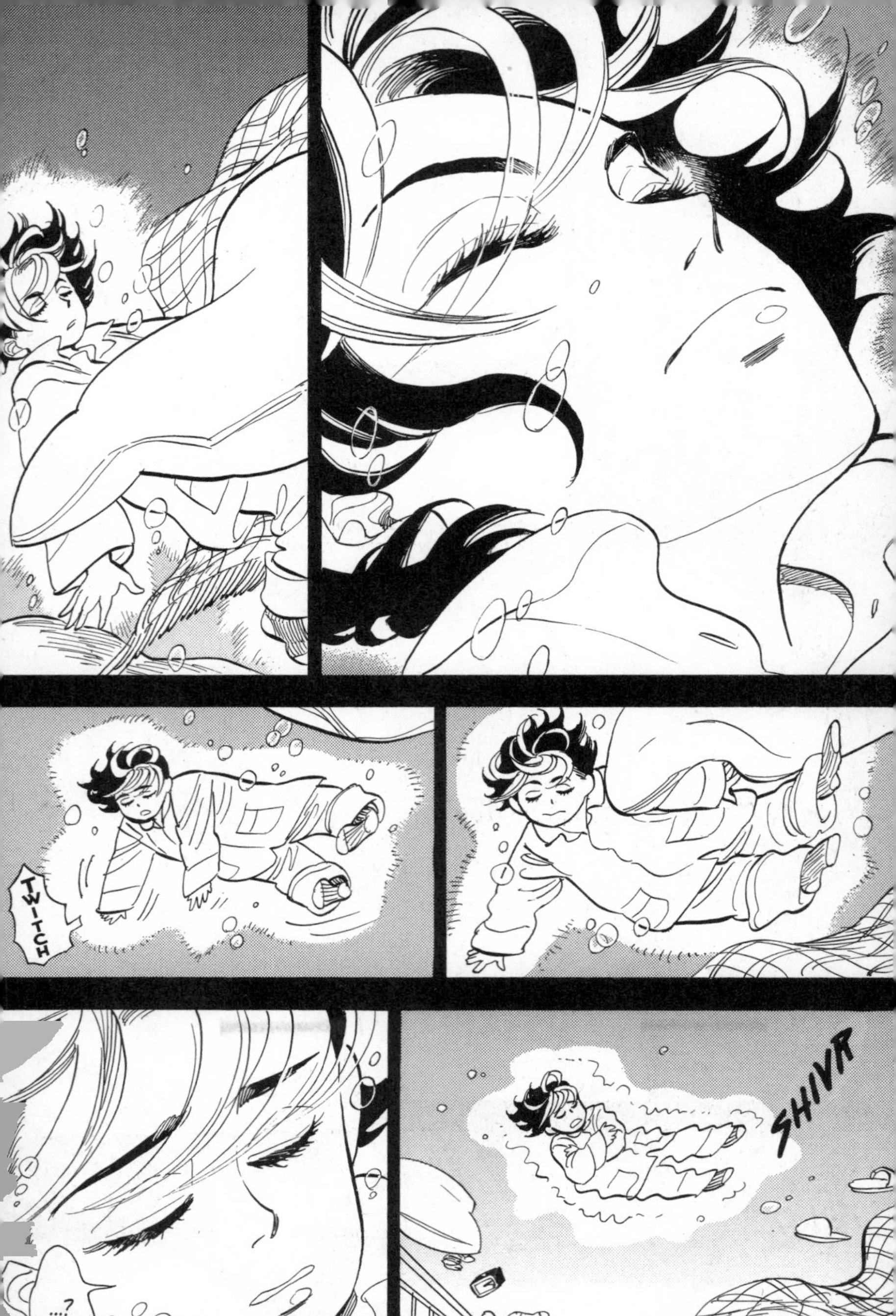
TWITCH
SHIVR
...?

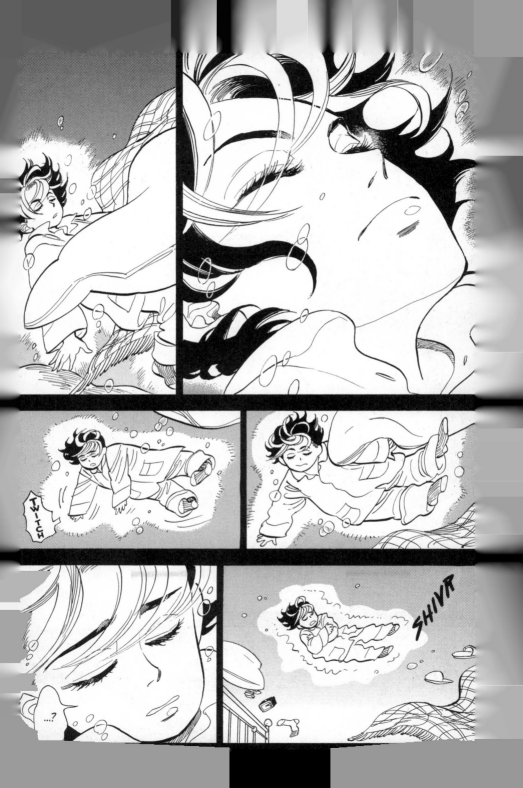

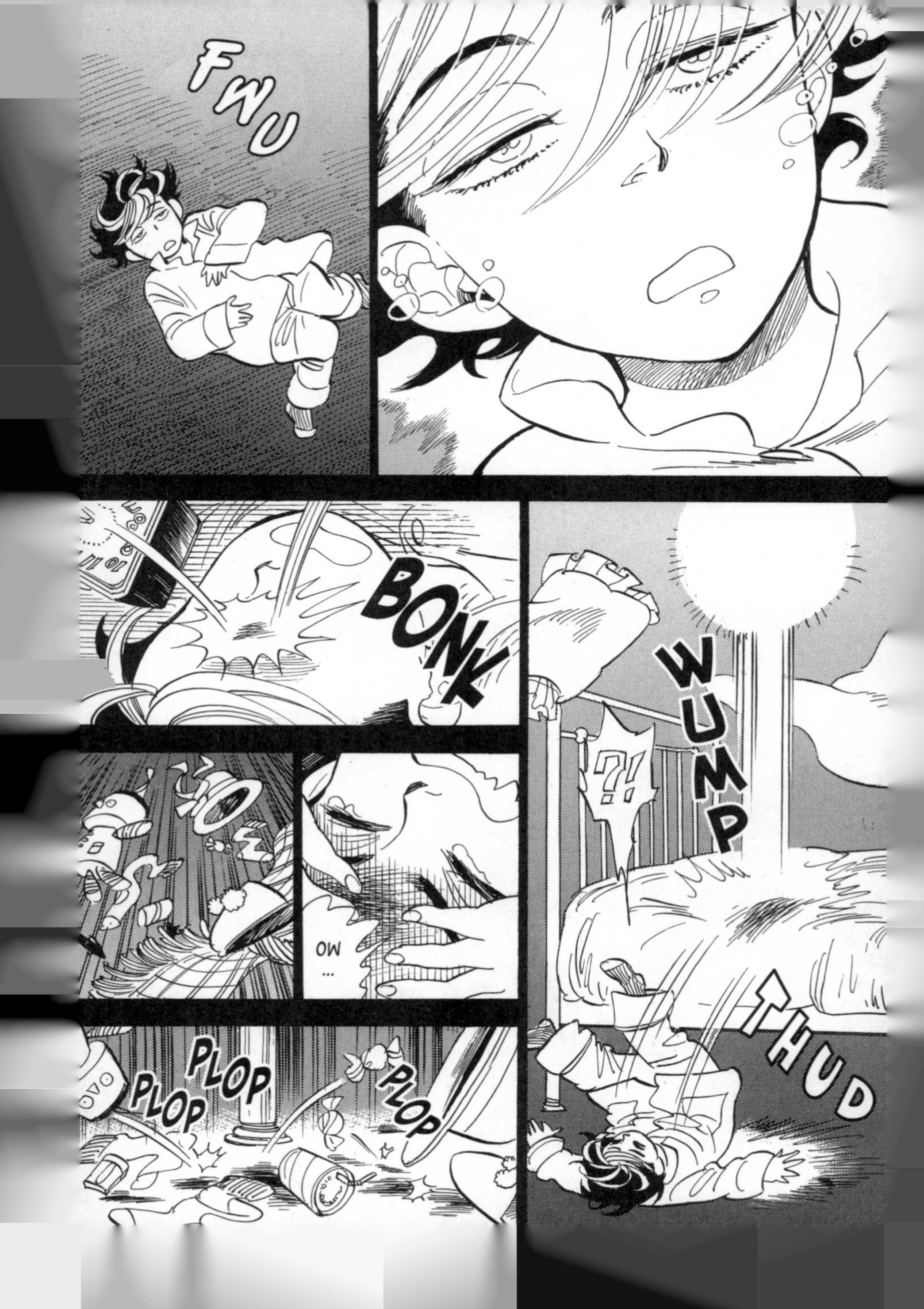
FWU
WUMP
?!
THUD
BONK
OW...
PLOP
PLOP
PLOP

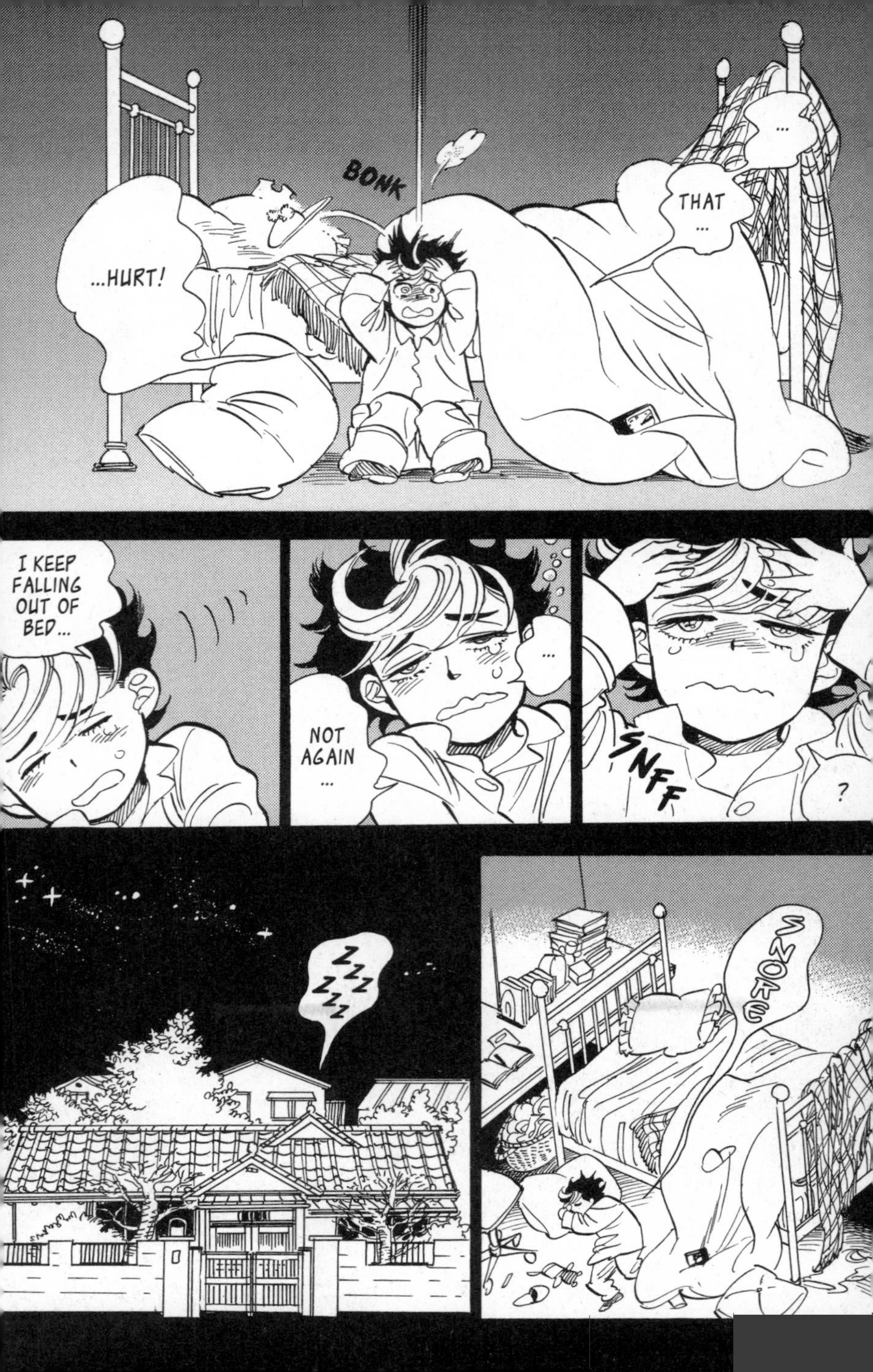
...
THAT ...
BONK
...HURT!
?
SNFF
...
NOT AGAIN ...
I KEEP FALLING OUT OF BED...
SNORE
Z Z Z Z Z

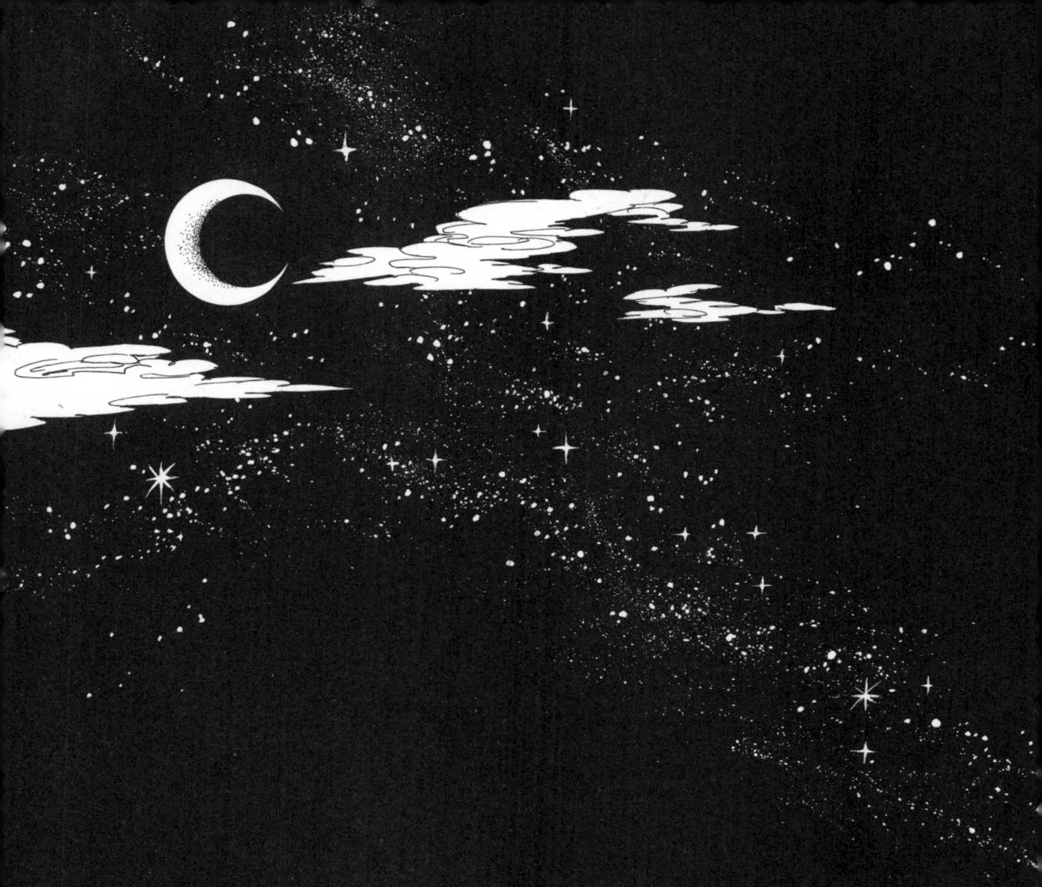

Ran and the Gray World 1

Story and Art by **Aki Irie**

Contents

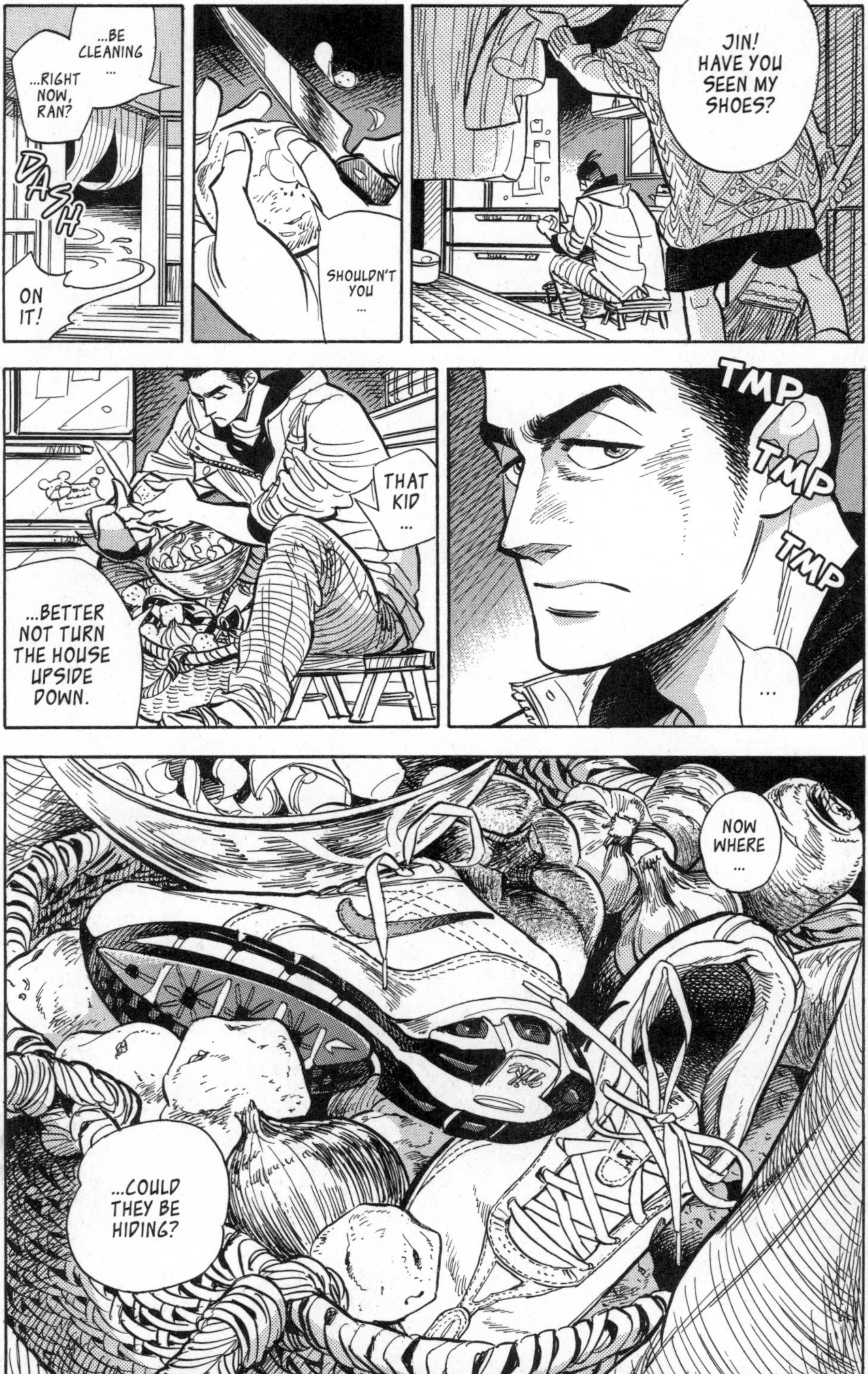
JIN! HAVE YOU SEEN MY SHOES?
SHOULDN'T YOU ...
...BE CLEANING ...
...RIGHT NOW, RAN?
DASH
ON IT!
TMP
TMP
TMP
...
THAT KID ...
...BETTER NOT TURN THE HOUSE UPSIDE DOWN.
NOW WHERE ...
...COULD THEY BE HIDING?

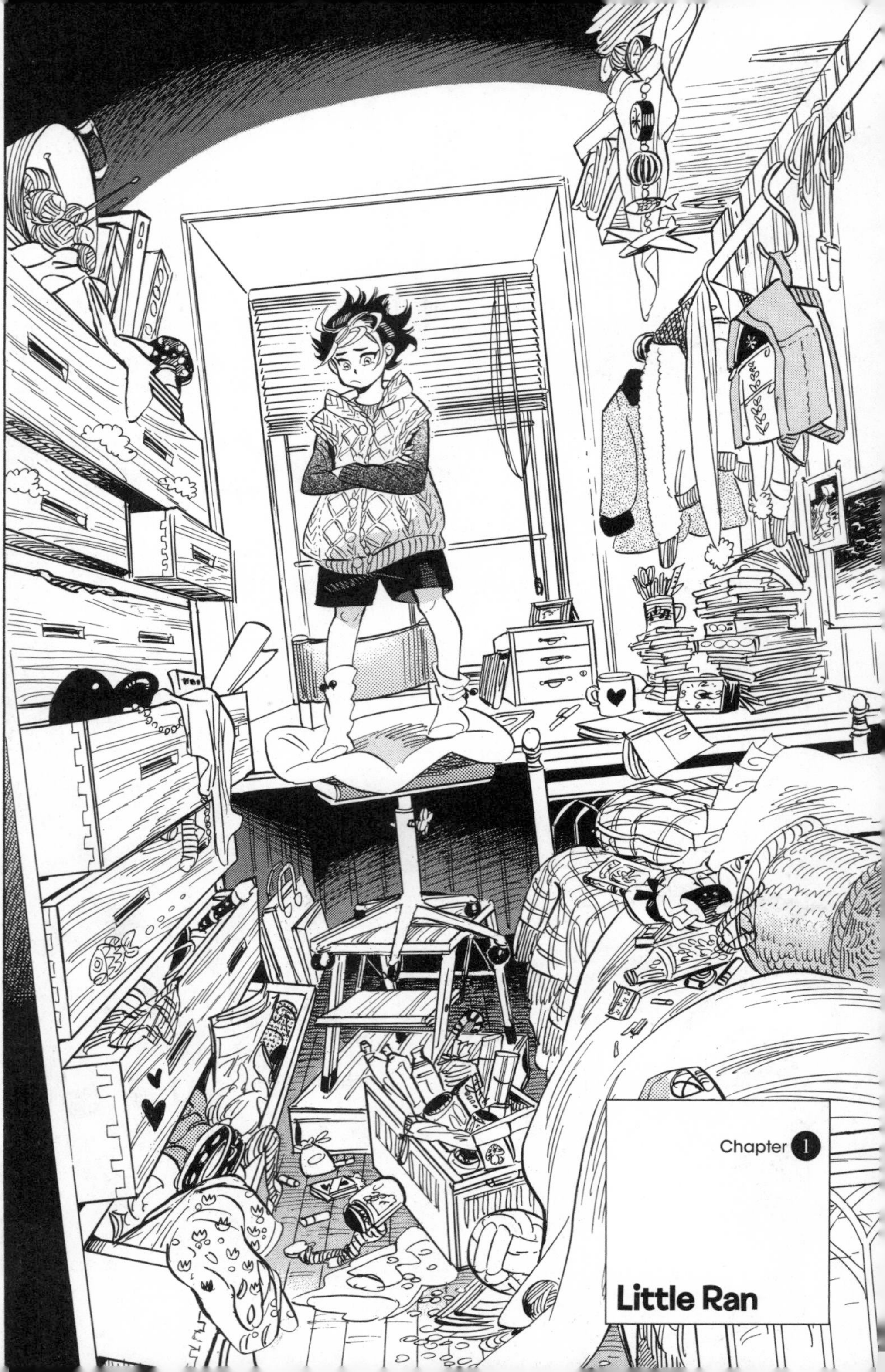

Chapter 1

Little Ran

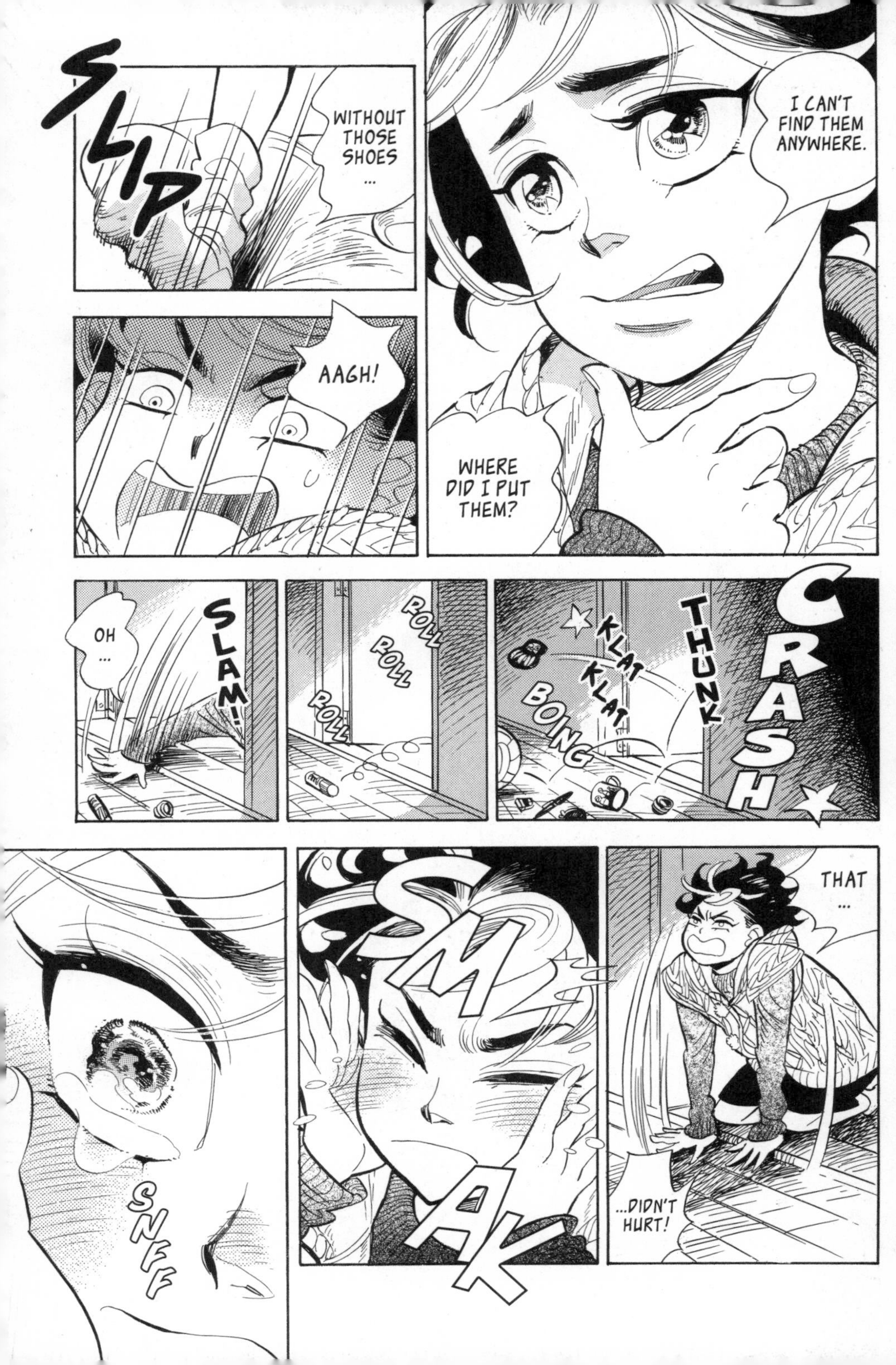
I CAN'T FIND THEM ANYWHERE.
WHERE DID I PUT THEM?
SLIP
WITHOUT THOSE SHOES ...
AAGH!
CRASH
THUNK
KLAT KLAT
BOING
ROLL ROLL ROLL
OH ...
SLAM!
THAT ...
...DIDN'T HURT!
SMAK
SNFF

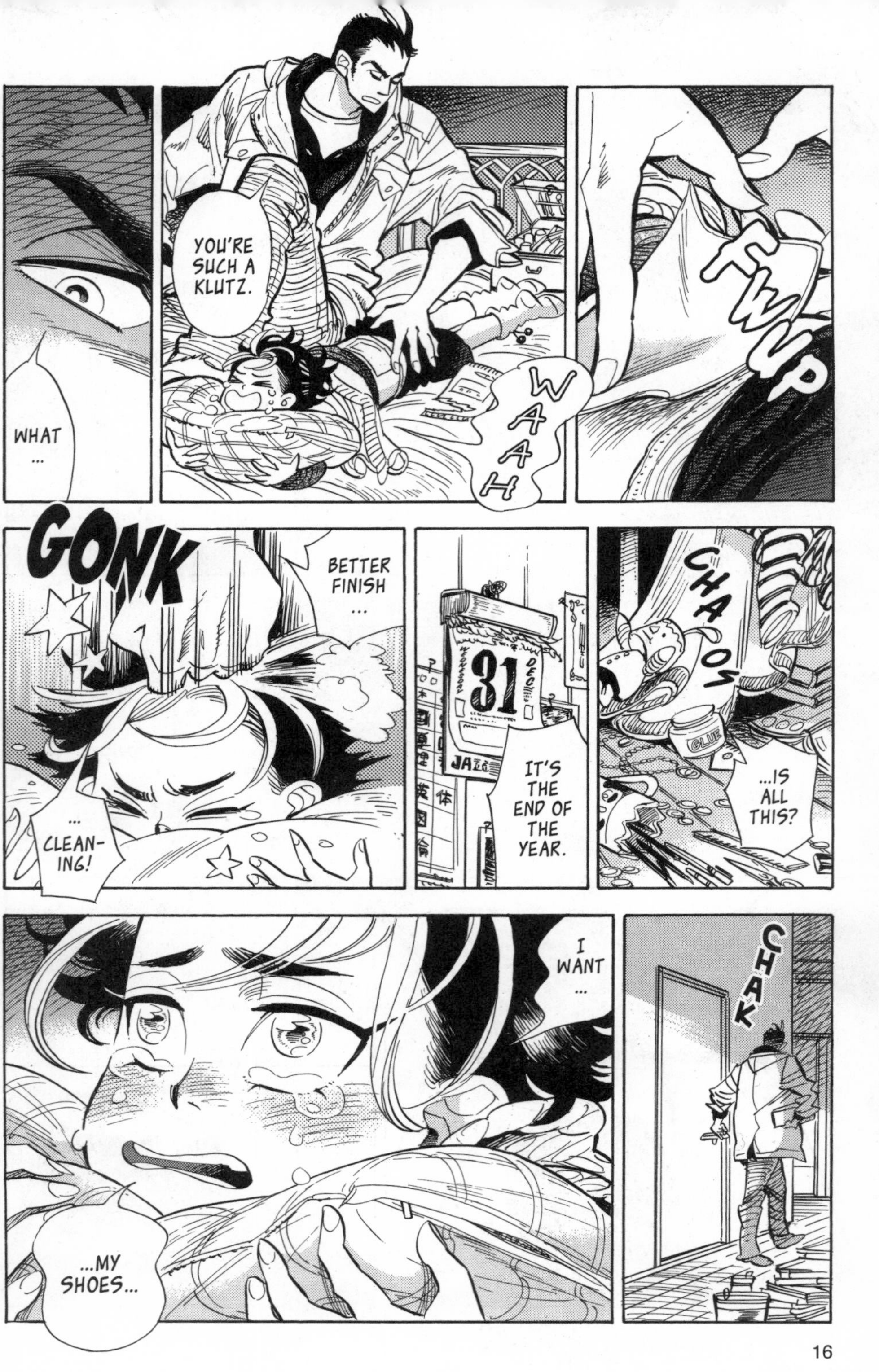
FWUP
YOU'RE SUCH A KLUTZ.
WAAH
WHAT ...
CHAOS
...IS ALL THIS?
IT'S THE END OF THE YEAR.
BETTER FINISH ...
GONK
... CLEANING!
CHAK
I WANT ...
...MY SHOES...

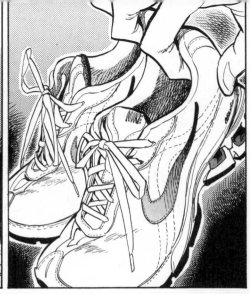

IF SHE...

...GOES THROUGH EVERYTHING, SHE'LL FIND THEM.

SHNK

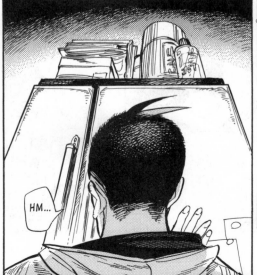

HM...

...

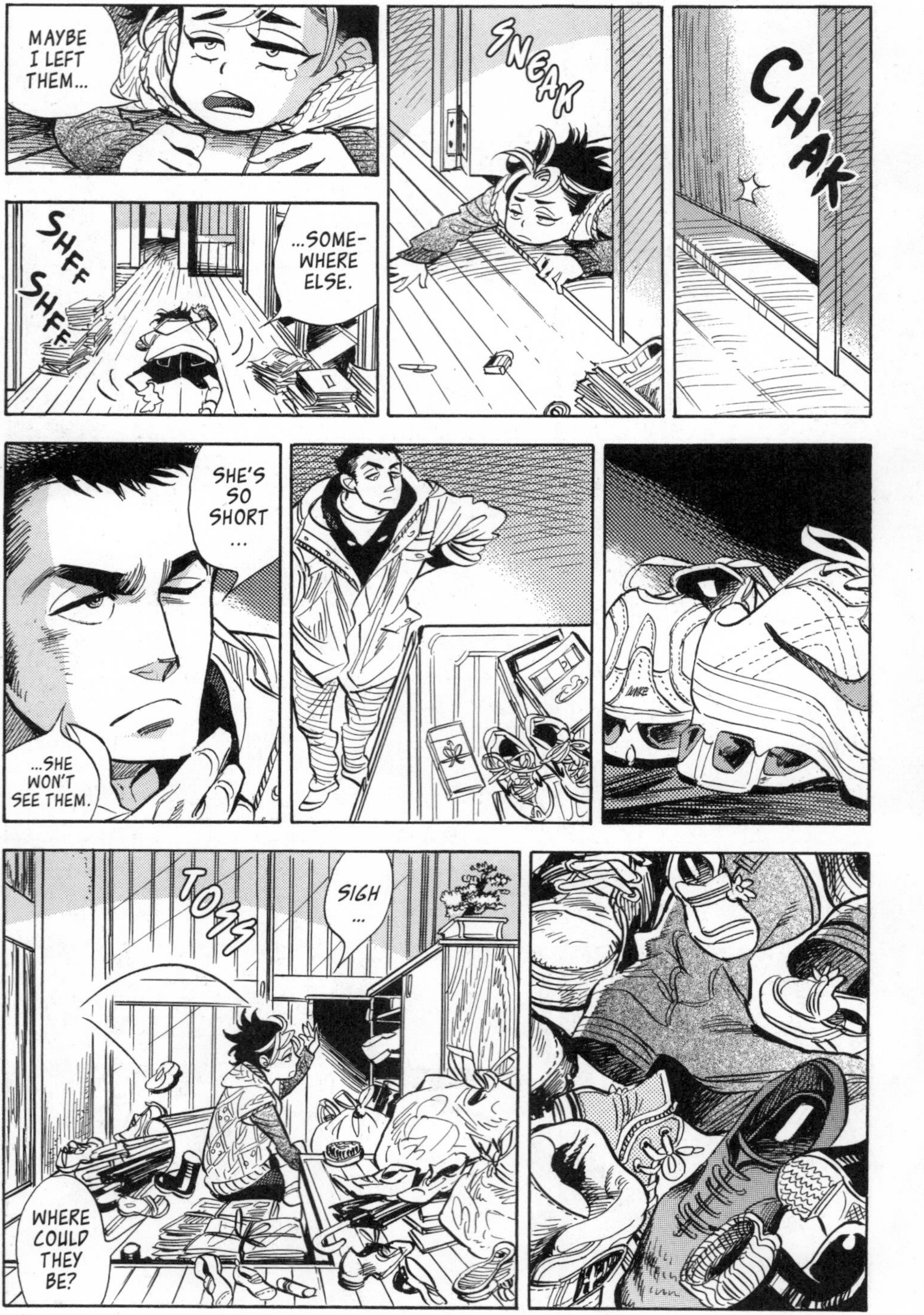
CHAK
SNEAK
MAYBE I LEFT THEM...
...SOME-WHERE ELSE.
SHFF SHFF
SHE'S SO SHORT...
...SHE WON'T SEE THEM.
SIGH...
TOSS
WHERE COULD THEY BE?

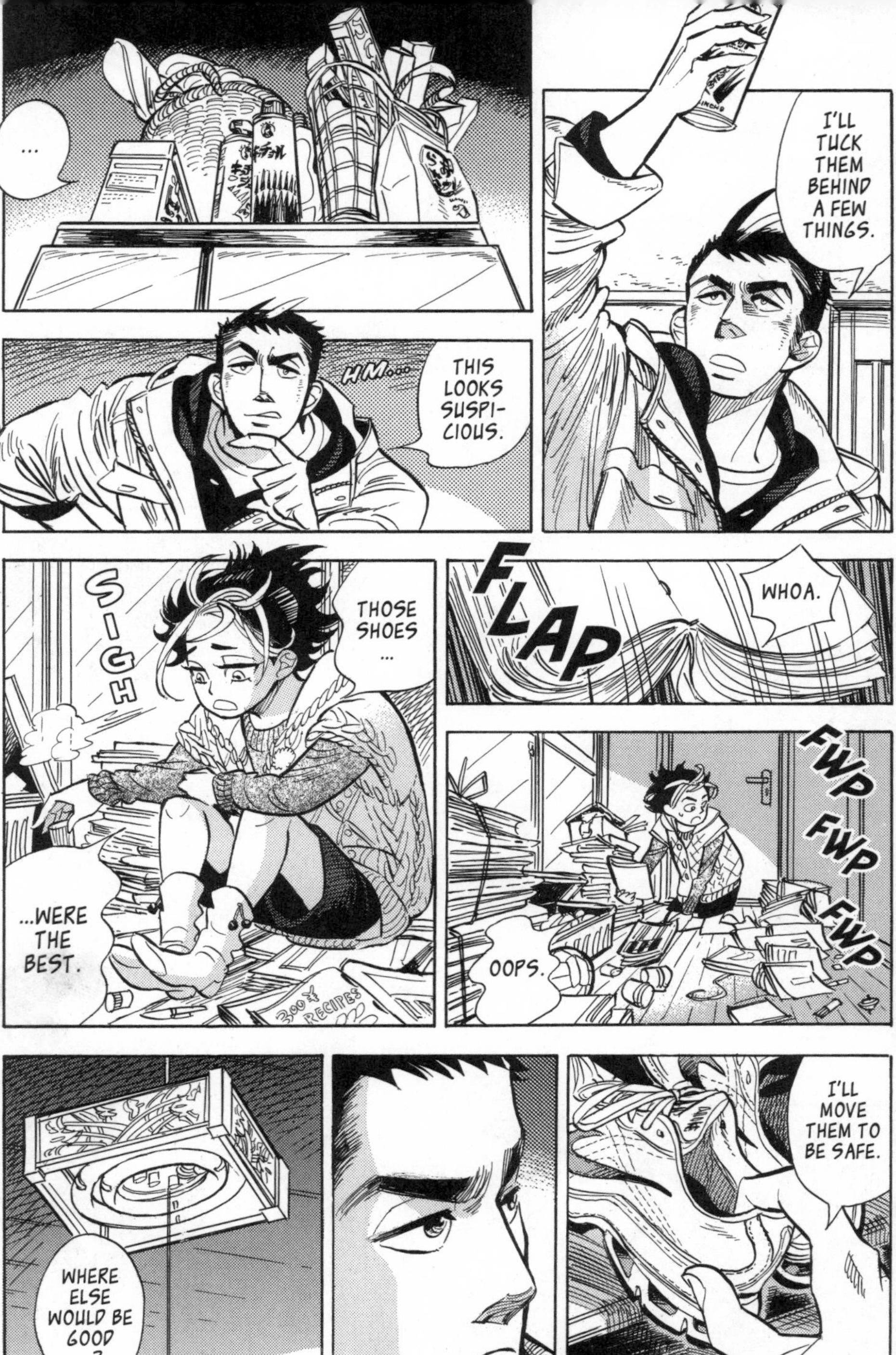
I'LL TUCK THEM BEHIND A FEW THINGS.
...
HM...
THIS LOOKS SUSPICIOUS.
WHOA.
FLAP
FWP FWP FWP
OOPS.
THOSE SHOES ...
SIGH
...WERE THE BEST.
300 RECIPES
I'LL MOVE THEM TO BE SAFE.
WHERE ELSE WOULD BE GOOD ...?

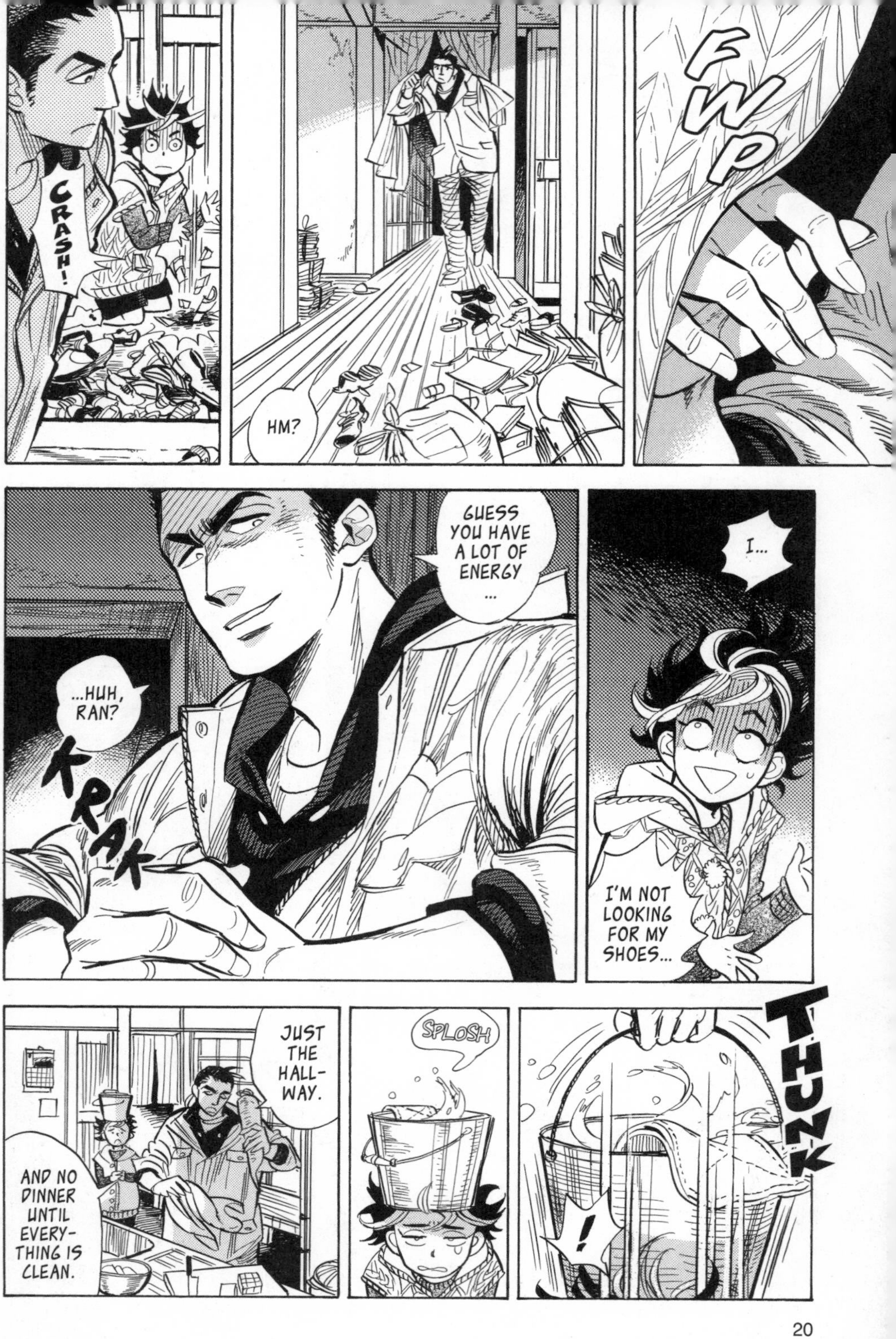
FWP
HM?
CRASH!
I...
I'M NOT LOOKING FOR MY SHOES...
GUESS YOU HAVE A LOT OF ENERGY ...
...HUH, RAN?
KRAK
THUNK
!
SPLOSH
JUST THE HALL-WAY.
AND NO DINNER UNTIL EVERY-THING IS CLEAN.

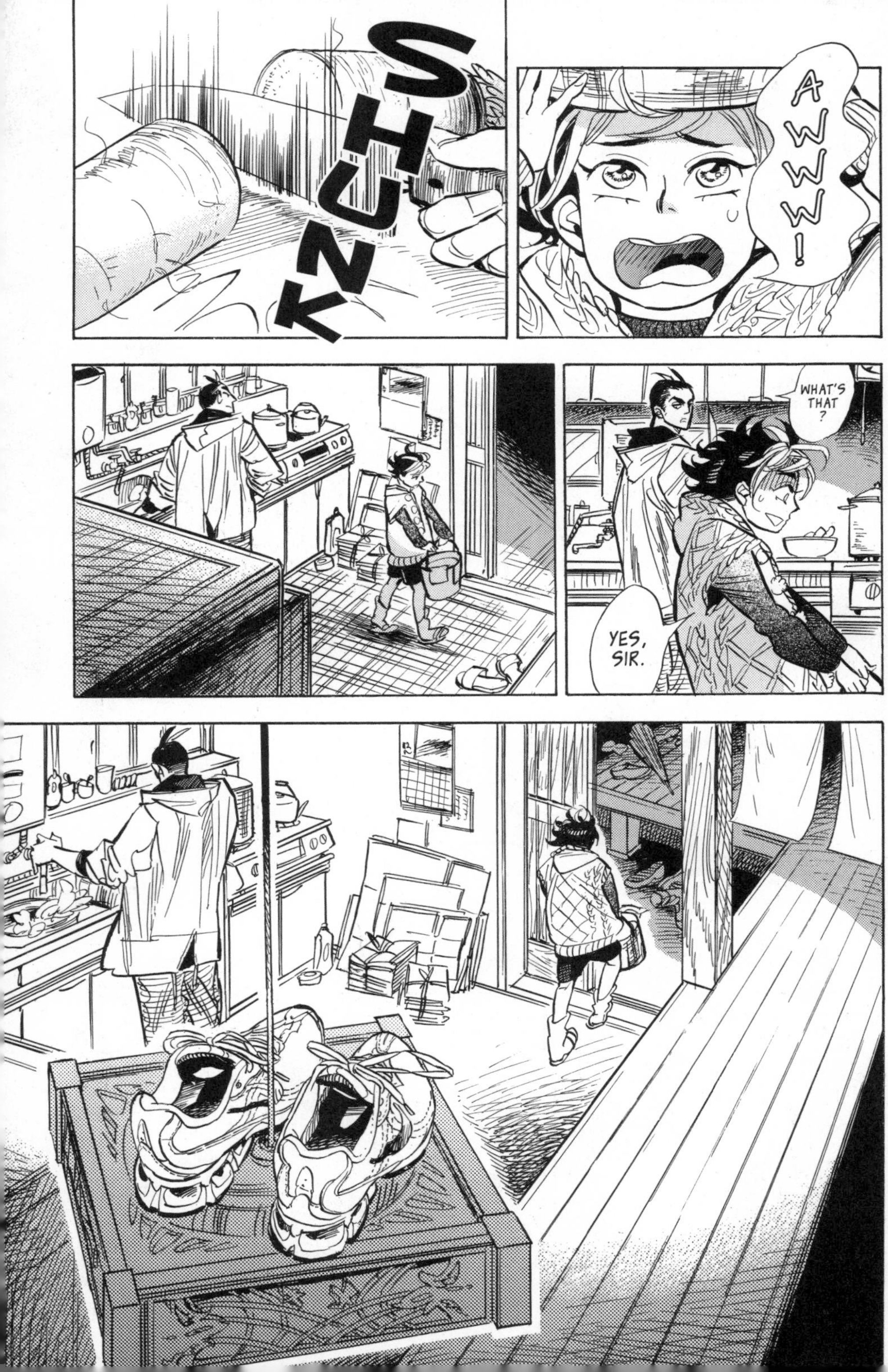
AWWW!
SHUNK
WHAT'S THAT?
YES, SIR.

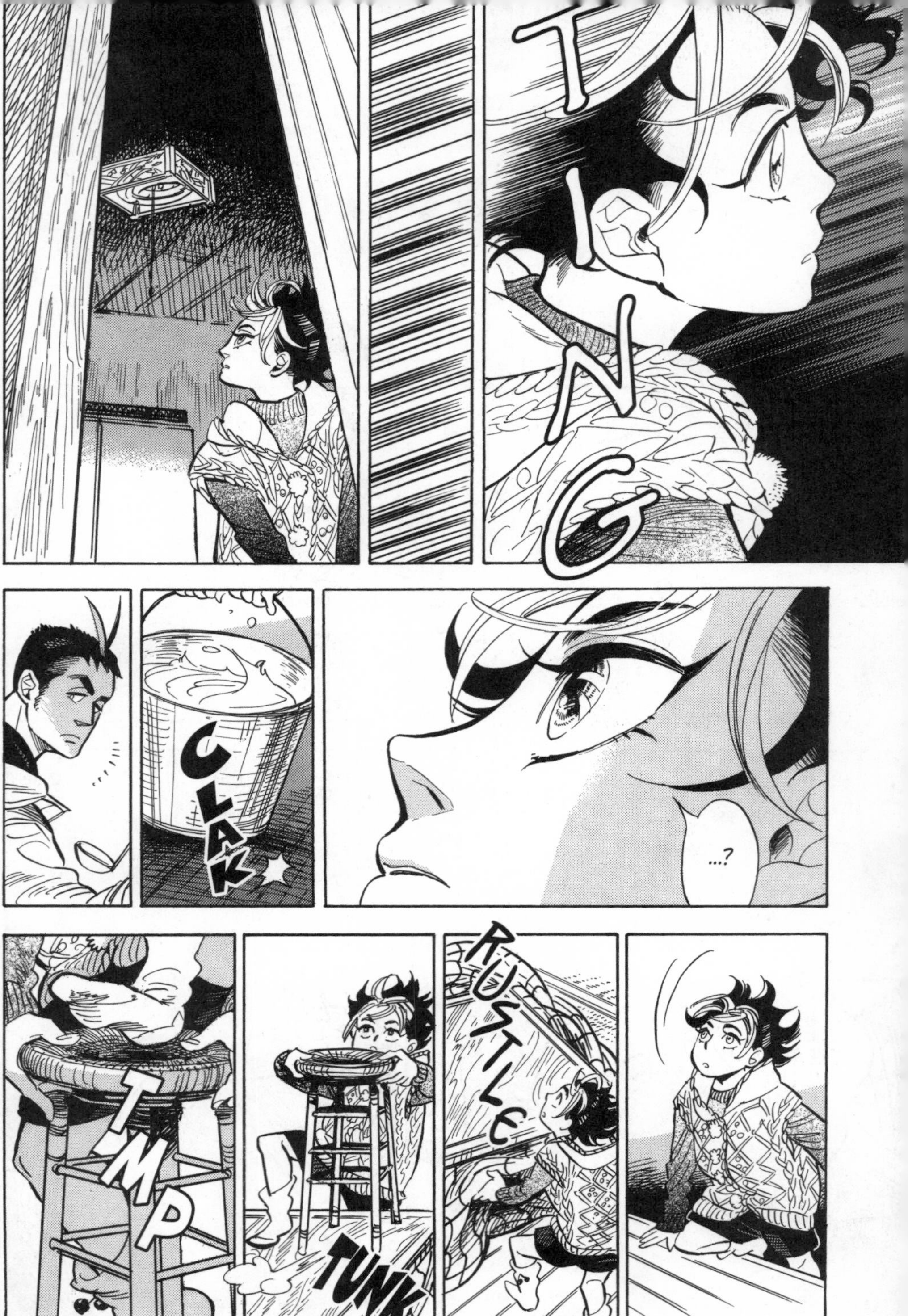
TING
...?
CLAK
RUSTLE
TUNK
TMP

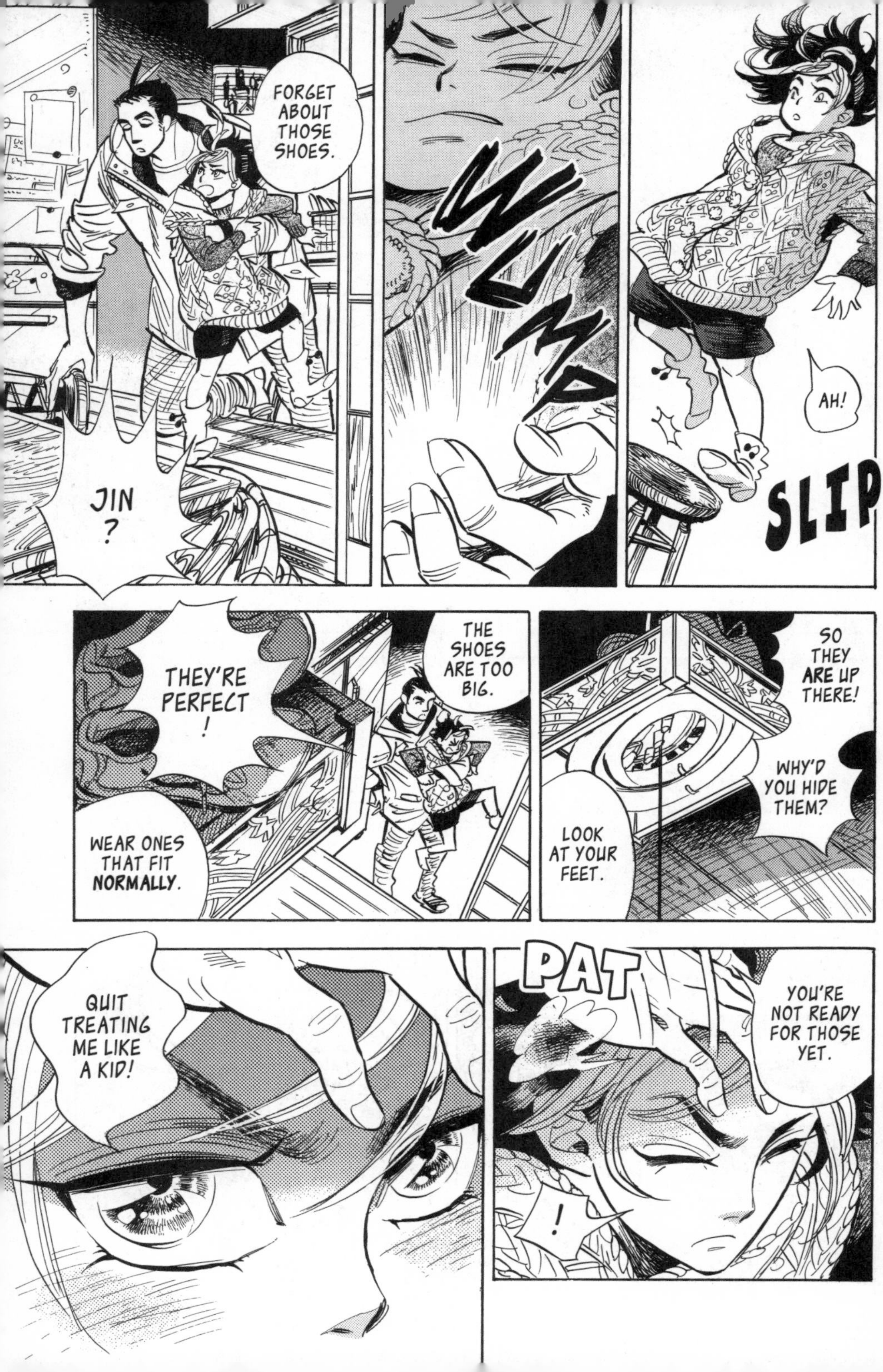
AH!
SLIP
WUMP
FORGET ABOUT THOSE SHOES.
JIN?
SO THEY **ARE** UP THERE!
WHY'D YOU HIDE THEM?
LOOK AT YOUR FEET.
THE SHOES ARE TOO BIG.
THEY'RE PERFECT!
WEAR ONES THAT FIT **NORMALLY**.
PAT
YOU'RE NOT READY FOR THOSE YET.
!
QUIT TREATING ME LIKE A KID!

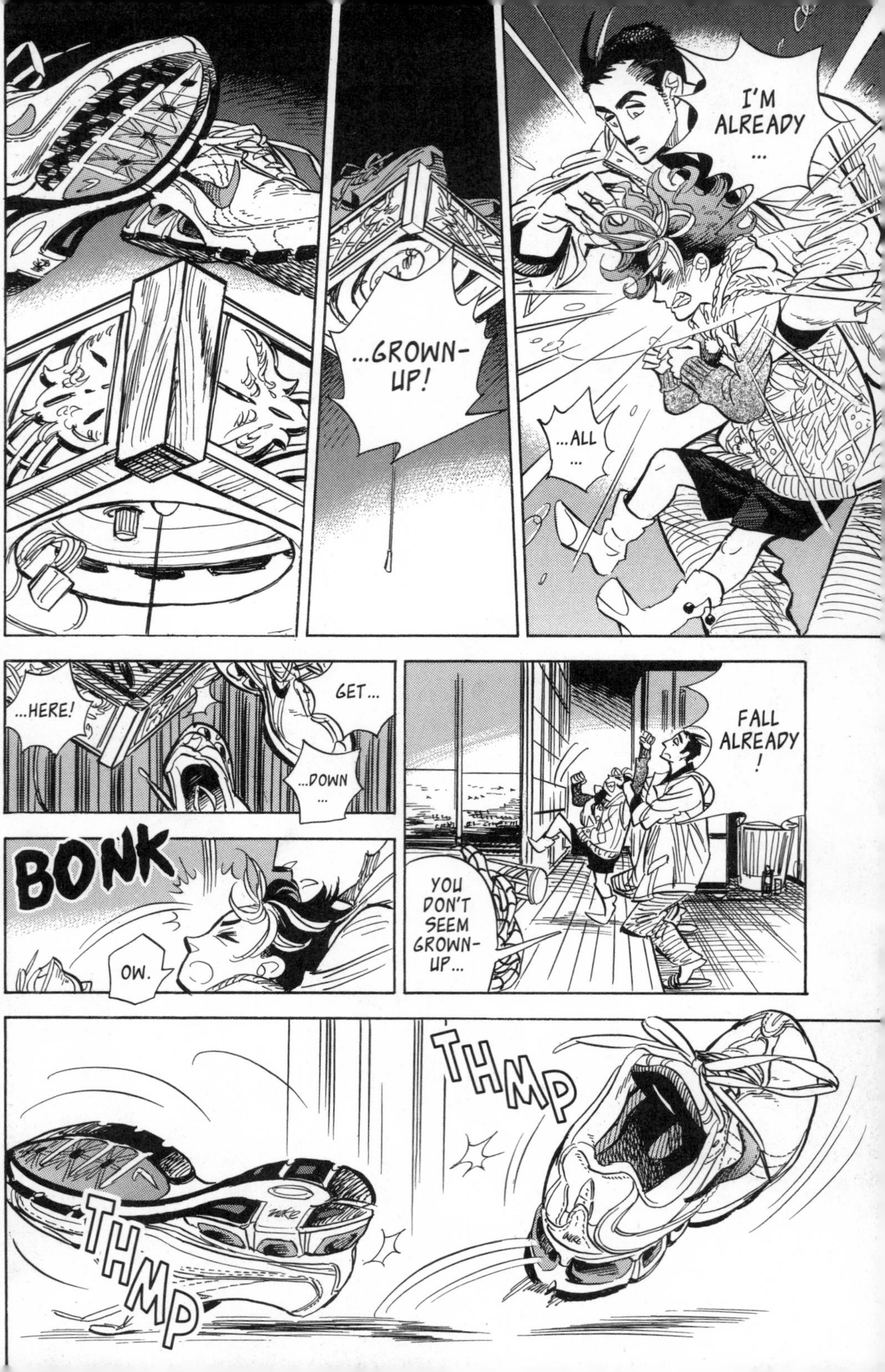
I'M ALREADY ...
...ALL ...
...GROWN-UP!
FALL ALREADY!
YOU DON'T SEEM GROWN-UP...
GET...
...DOWN ...
...HERE!
BONK
OW.
THMP
THMP

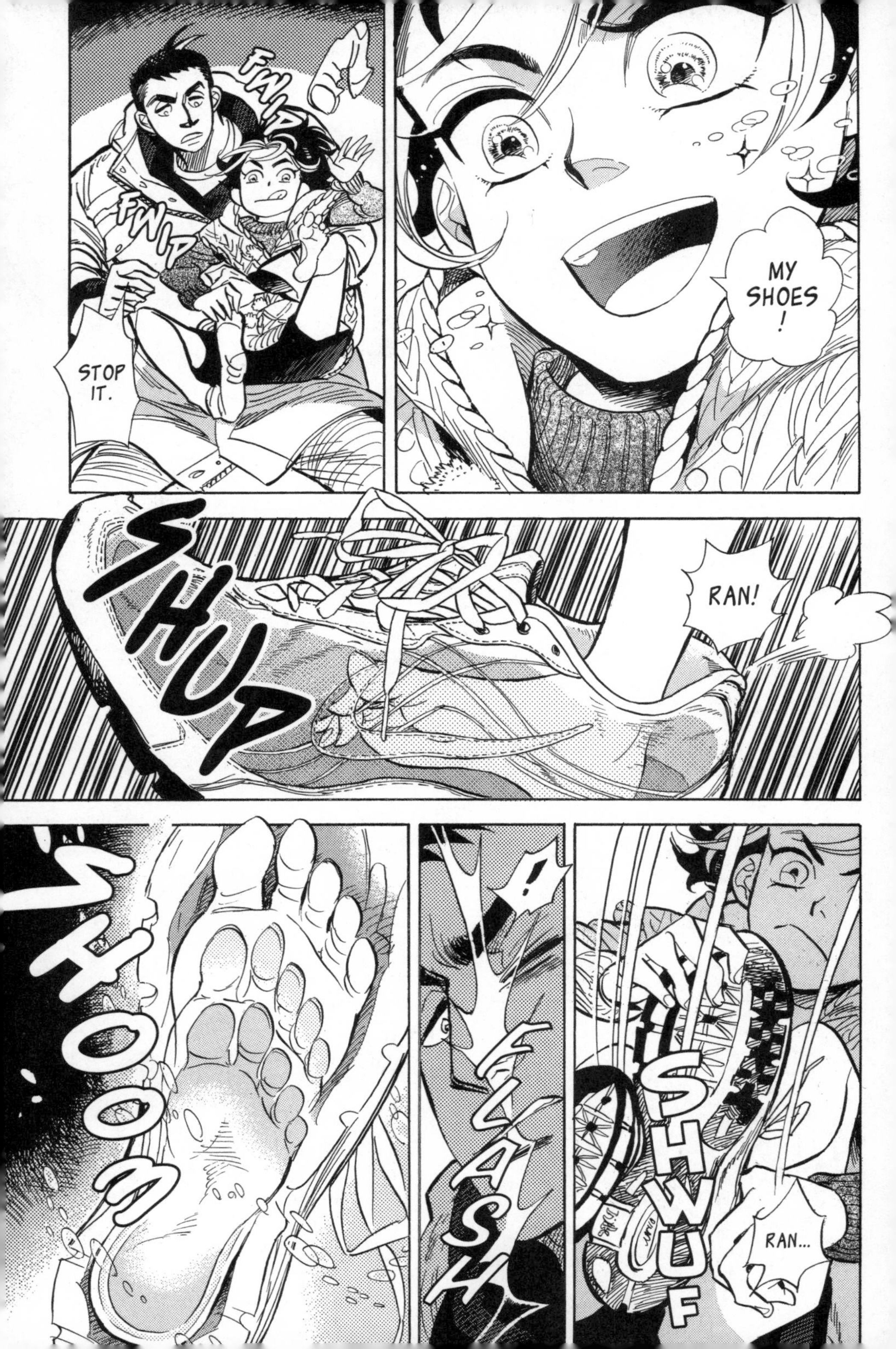
MY SHOES!
FWAP
FWIP
STOP IT.
RAN!
SHUP
RAN...
SHWUF
!
FLASH
SHOOM

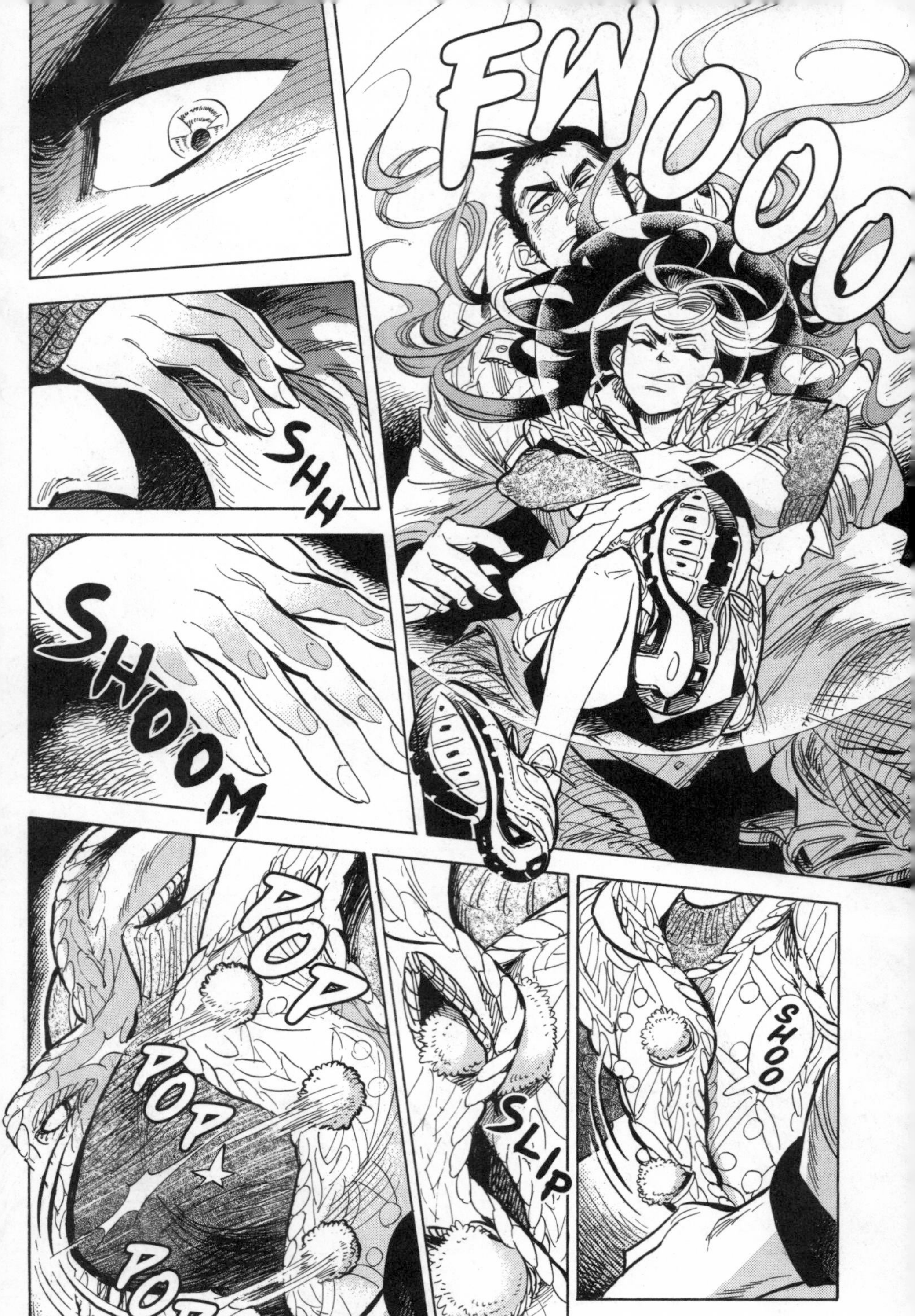
FWOOOO
SHH
SHOOM
SHOO
SLIP
POP
POP
POP
POP

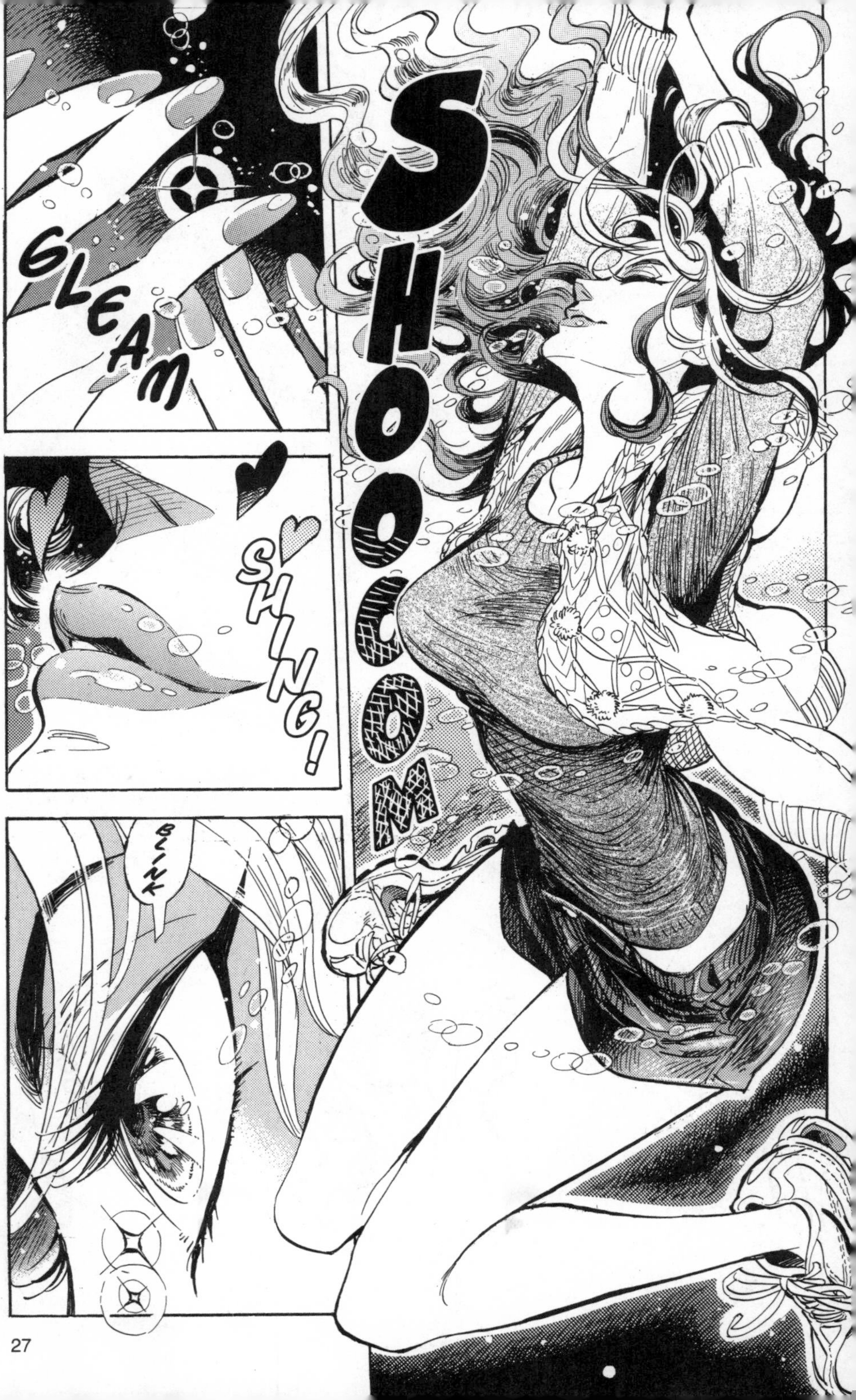
SHOOOOOM
GLEAM
SHING!
BLINK

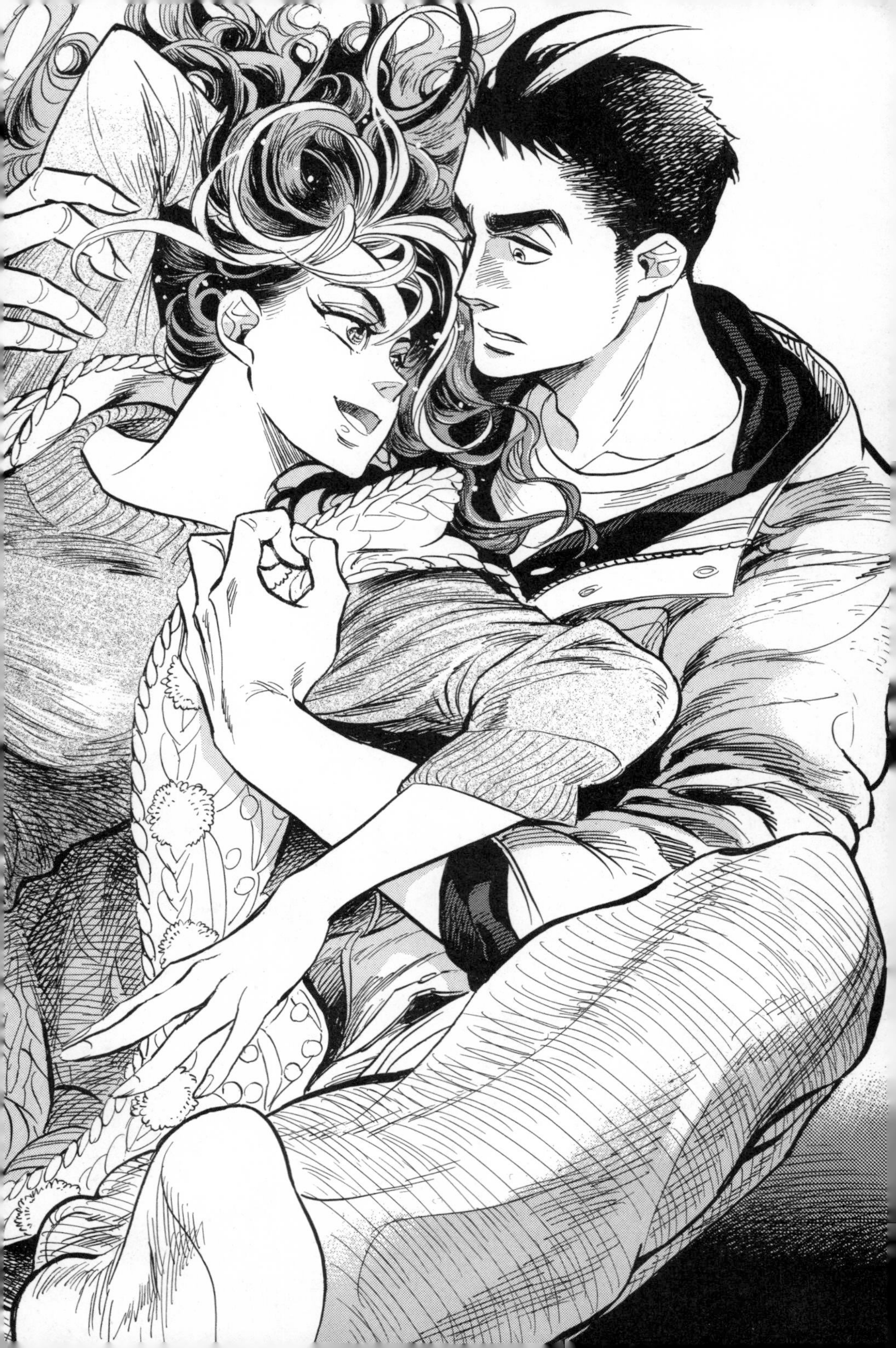

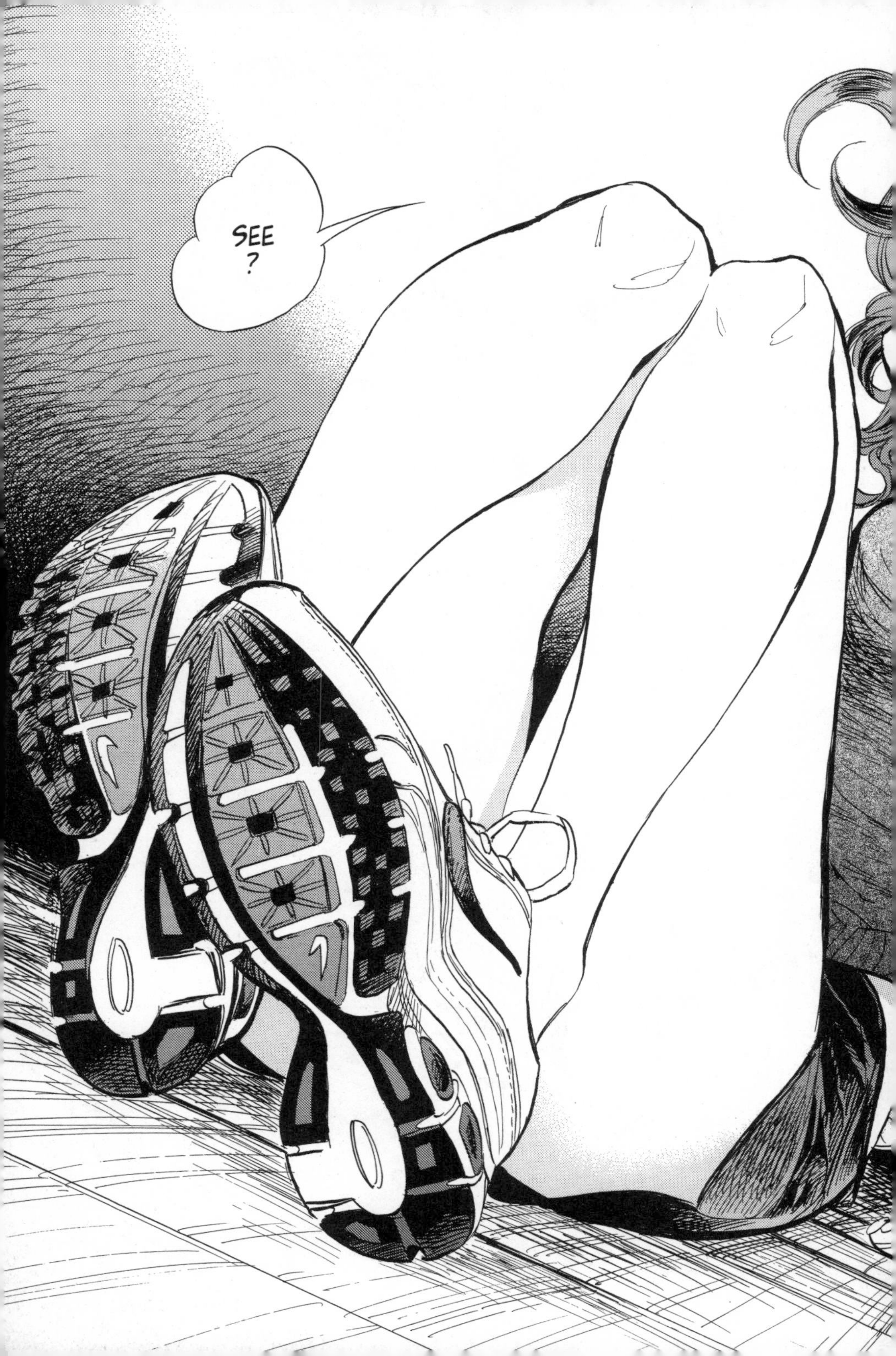
SEE?

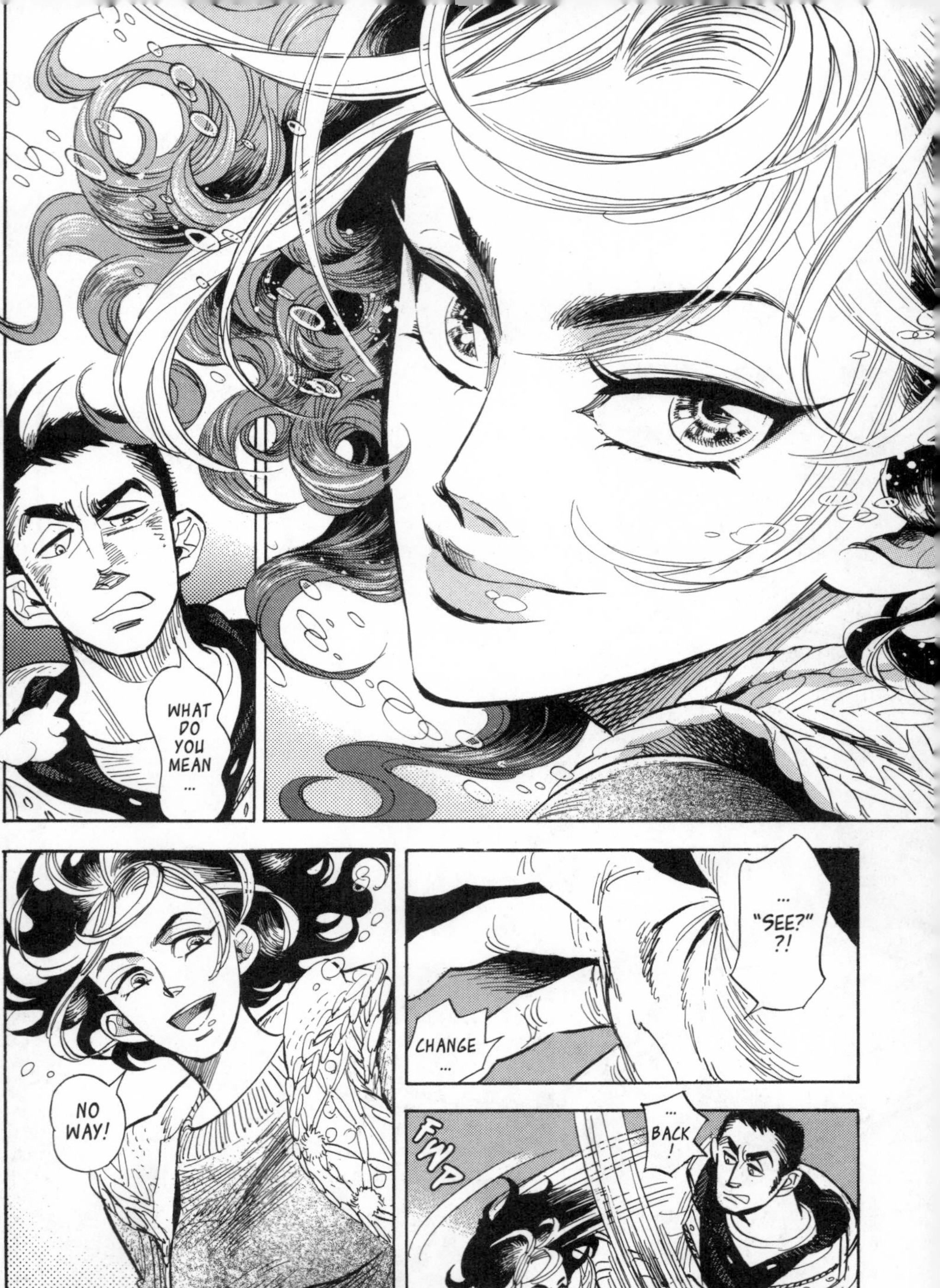
WHAT DO YOU MEAN ...
... "SEE?" ?!
CHANGE ...
... BACK!
FWP
NO WAY!

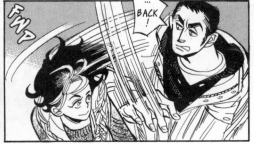

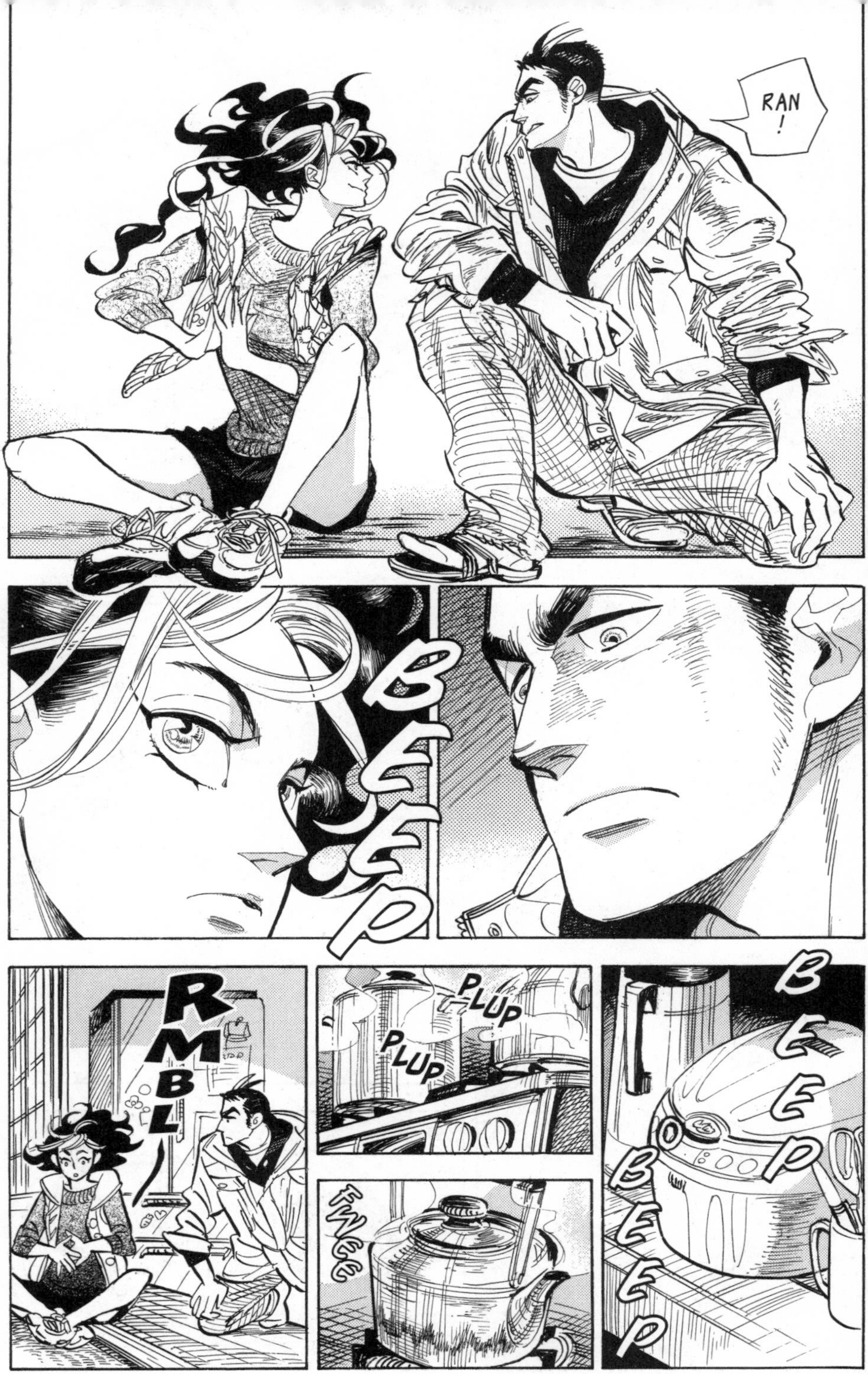
RAN!
BEEEP
BEEP
BEEP
PLUP
PLUP
TWEE
RMBL!

YOU THINK YOU'RE EATING?

CLANG

WHAT'S FOR...

CHAK

...DINNER ?

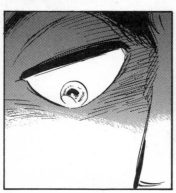

YOU KNOW ...

TING

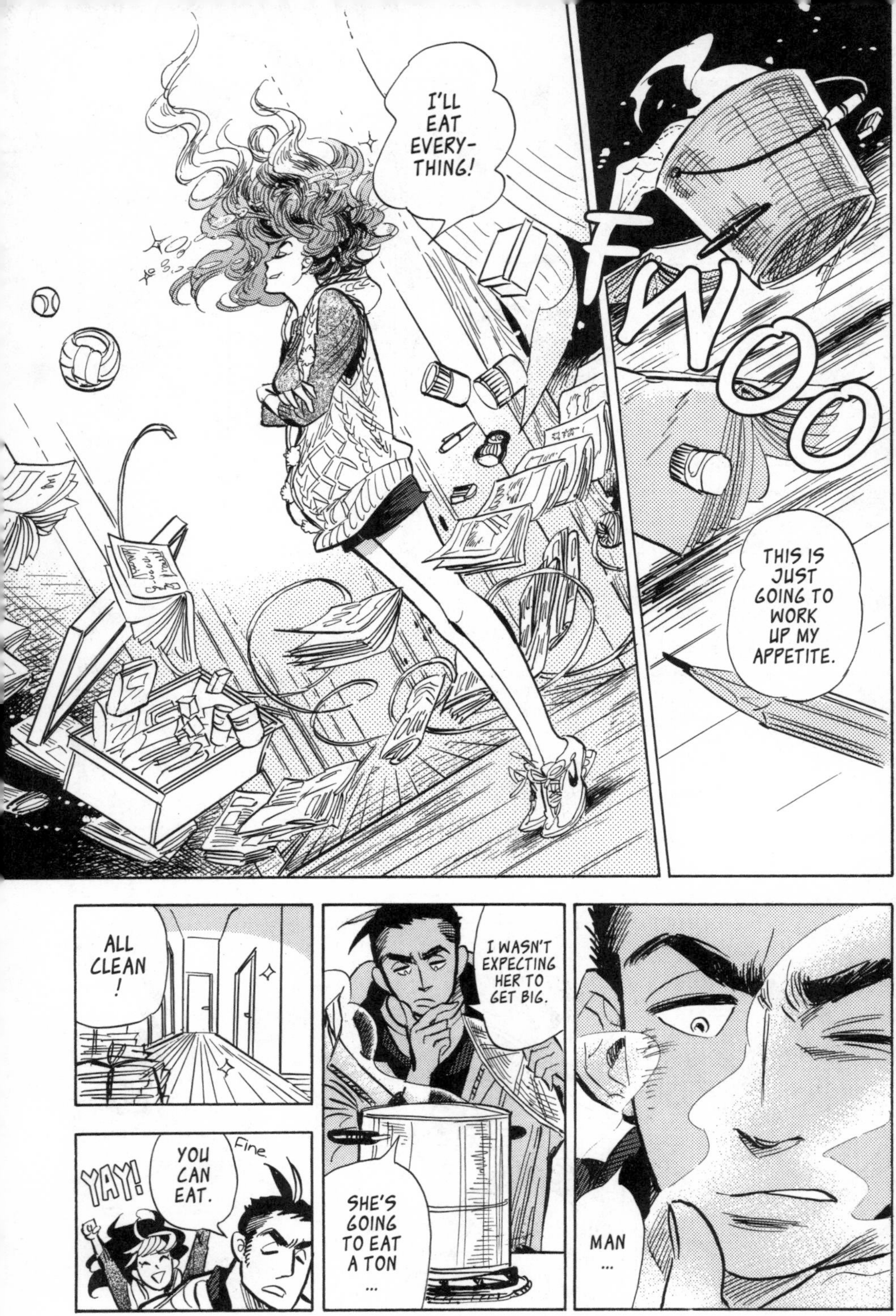
FWOOO
THIS IS JUST GOING TO WORK UP MY APPETITE.
I'LL EAT EVERYTHING!
MAN ...
I WASN'T EXPECTING HER TO GET BIG.
SHE'S GOING TO EAT A TON ...
ALL CLEAN!
Fine.
YOU CAN EAT.
YAY!

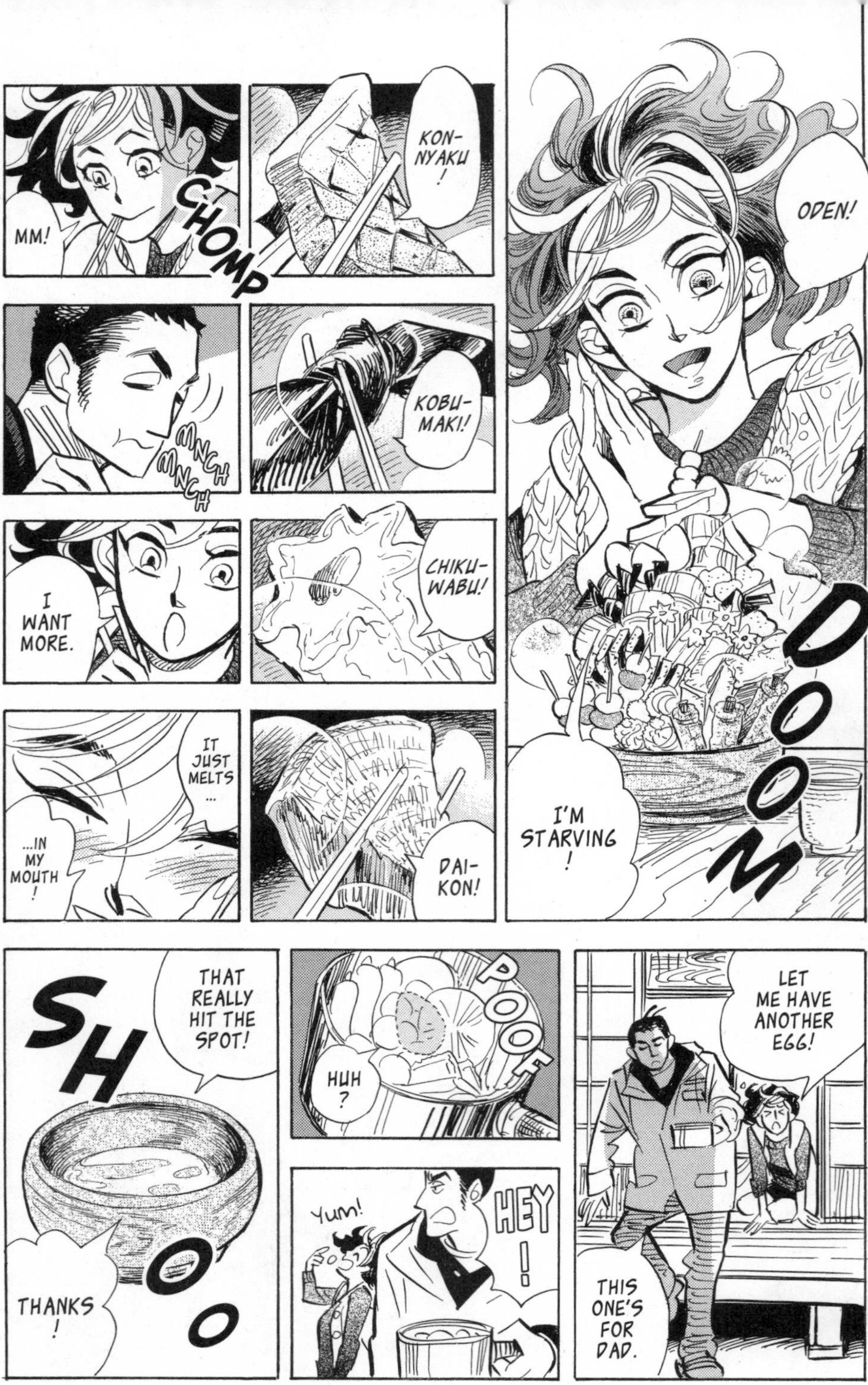
ODEN!
DOOOOM
I'M STARVING!
KON-NYAKU!
MM!
CHOMP
KOBU-MAKI!
MNCH MNCH
CHIKU-WABU!
I WANT MORE.
DAI-KON!
IT JUST MELTS...
...IN MY MOUTH!
LET ME HAVE ANOTHER EGG!
THIS ONE'S FOR DAD.
POOF
HUH?
HEY!
Yum!
THAT REALLY HIT THE SPOT!
SHOOO
THANKS!

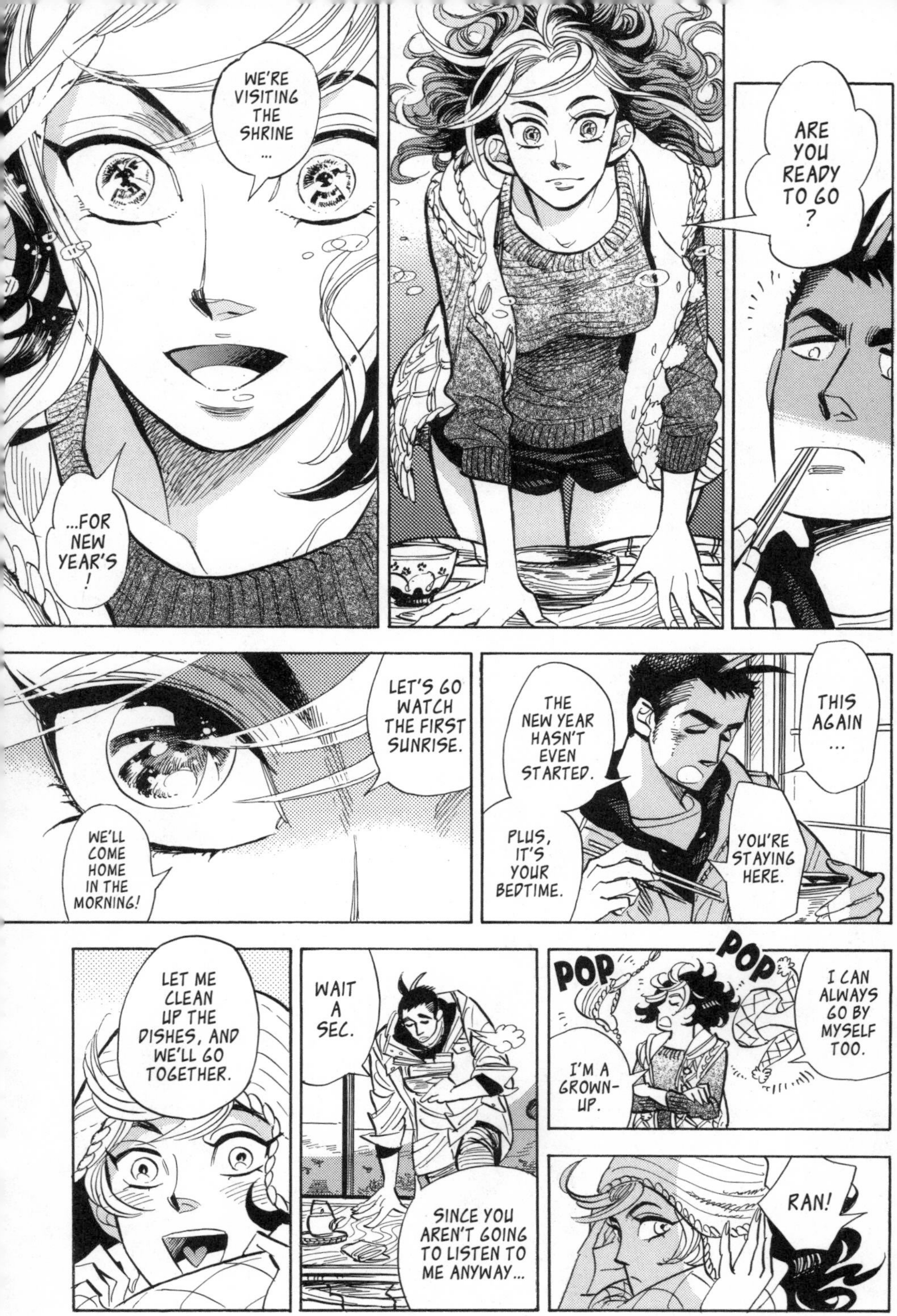
ARE YOU READY TO GO?
WE'RE VISITING THE SHRINE...
...FOR NEW YEAR'S!
THIS AGAIN...
THE NEW YEAR HASN'T EVEN STARTED.
YOU'RE STAYING HERE.
PLUS, IT'S YOUR BEDTIME.
LET'S GO WATCH THE FIRST SUNRISE.
WE'LL COME HOME IN THE MORNING!
I CAN ALWAYS GO BY MYSELF TOO.
POP
POP
I'M A GROWN-UP.
RAN!
WAIT A SEC.
SINCE YOU AREN'T GOING TO LISTEN TO ME ANYWAY...
LET ME CLEAN UP THE DISHES, AND WE'LL GO TOGETHER.

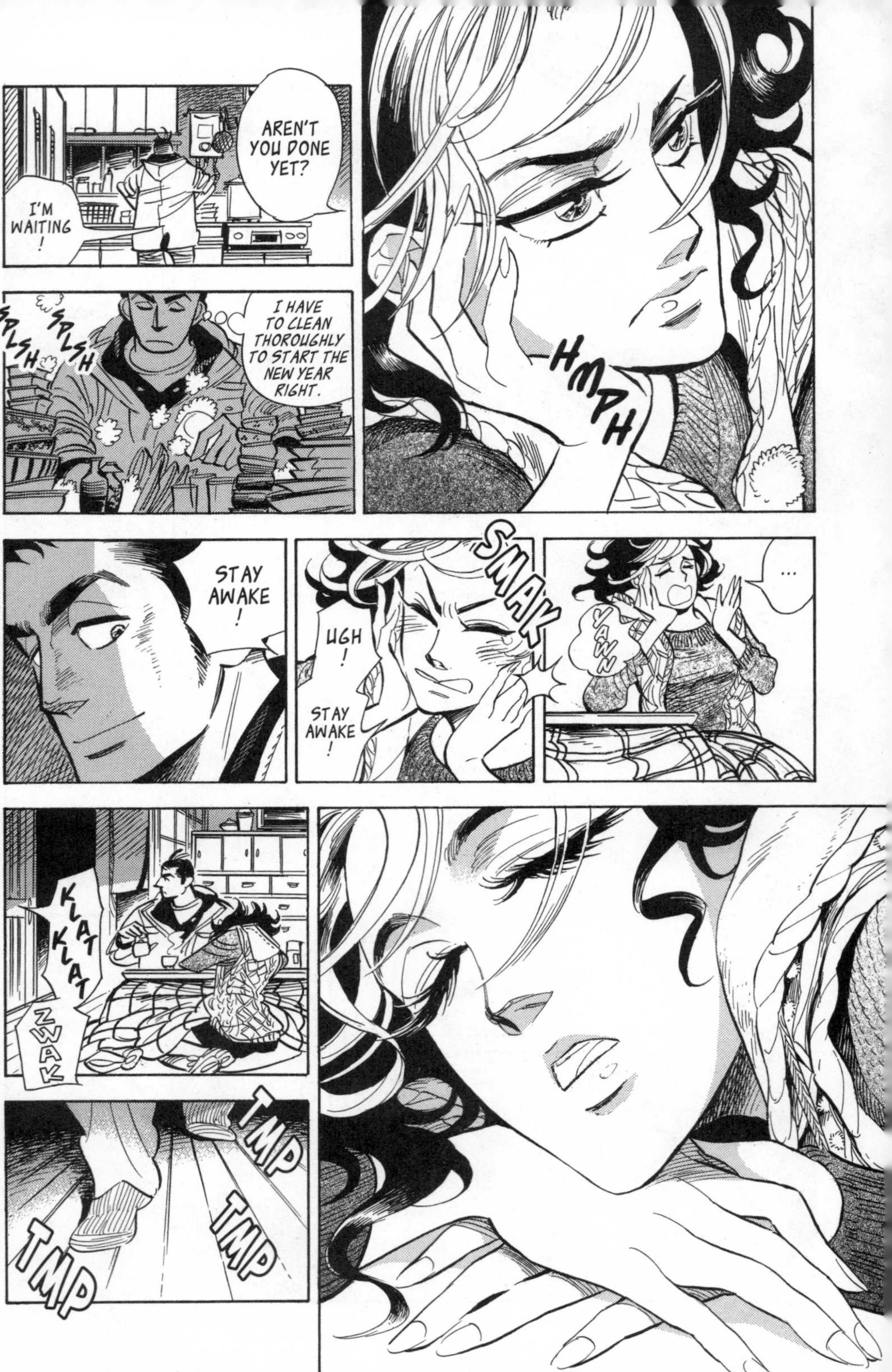
HMPH
AREN'T YOU DONE YET?
I'M WAITING!
SPLSH
SPLSH
I HAVE TO CLEAN THOROUGHLY TO START THE NEW YEAR RIGHT.
...
YAWN
SMAK
UGH!
STAY AWAKE!
STAY AWAKE!
KLAT KLAT
ZWAK
TMP
TMP
TMP

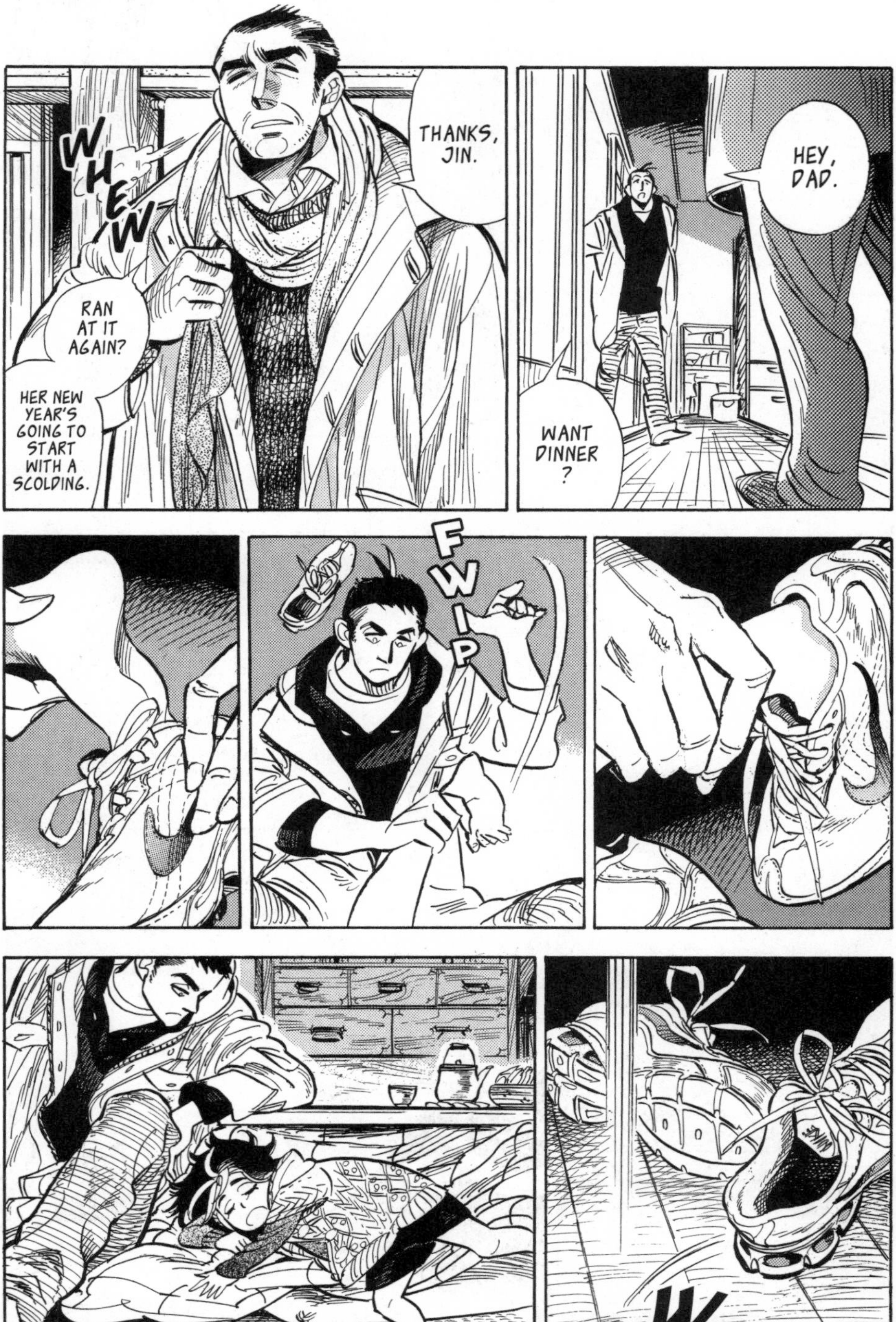
HEY, DAD.
WANT DINNER?
THANKS, JIN.
WHEW
RAN AT IT AGAIN?
HER NEW YEAR'S GOING TO START WITH A SCOLDING.
FWIP
WHMP

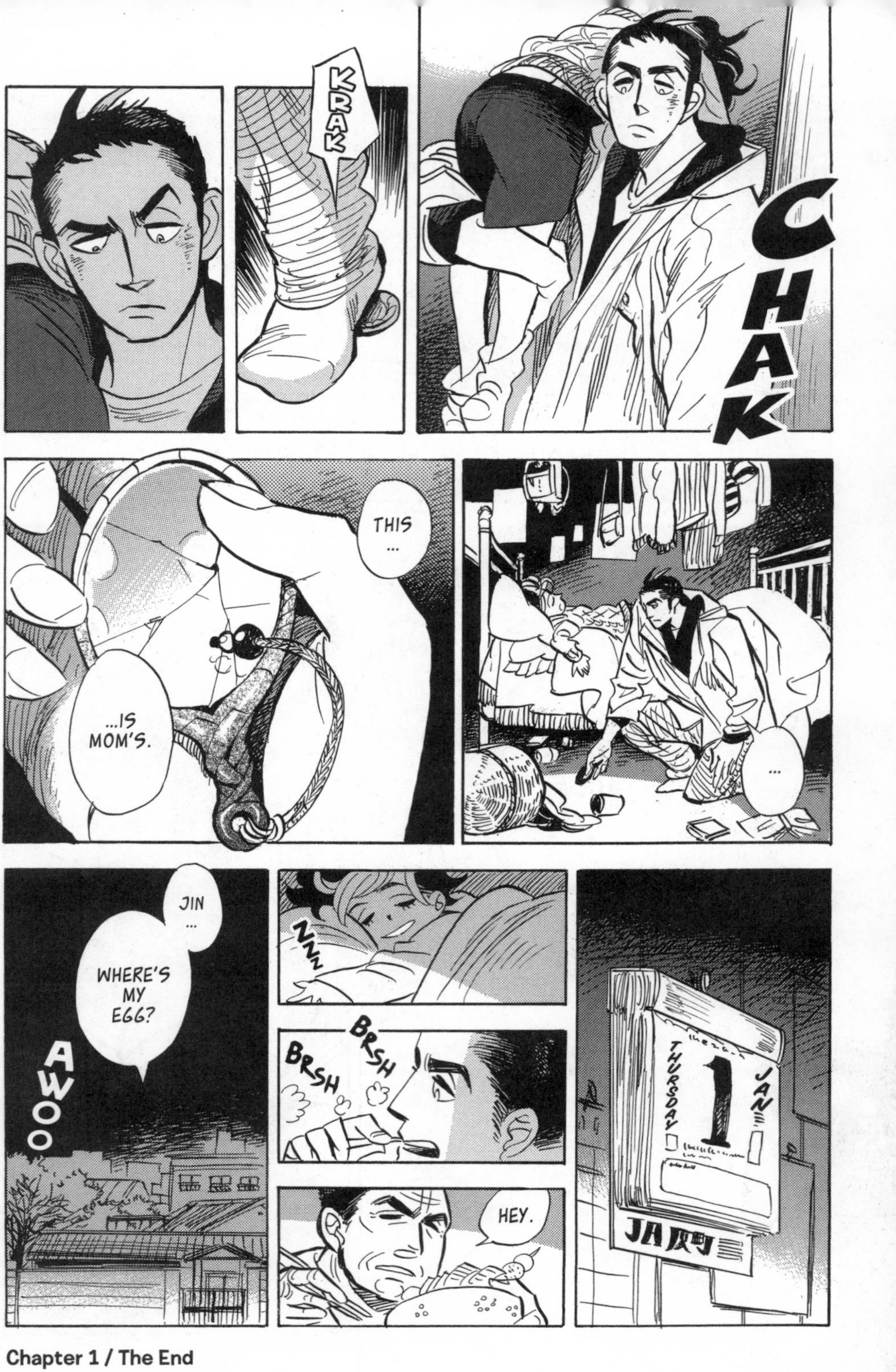
CHAK
KRAK
...
THIS ...
...IS MOM'S.
JAN
1
THURSDAY
ZZZ
BRSH
BRSH
HEY.
JIN ...
WHERE'S MY EGG?
AWOO

Chapter 1 / The End

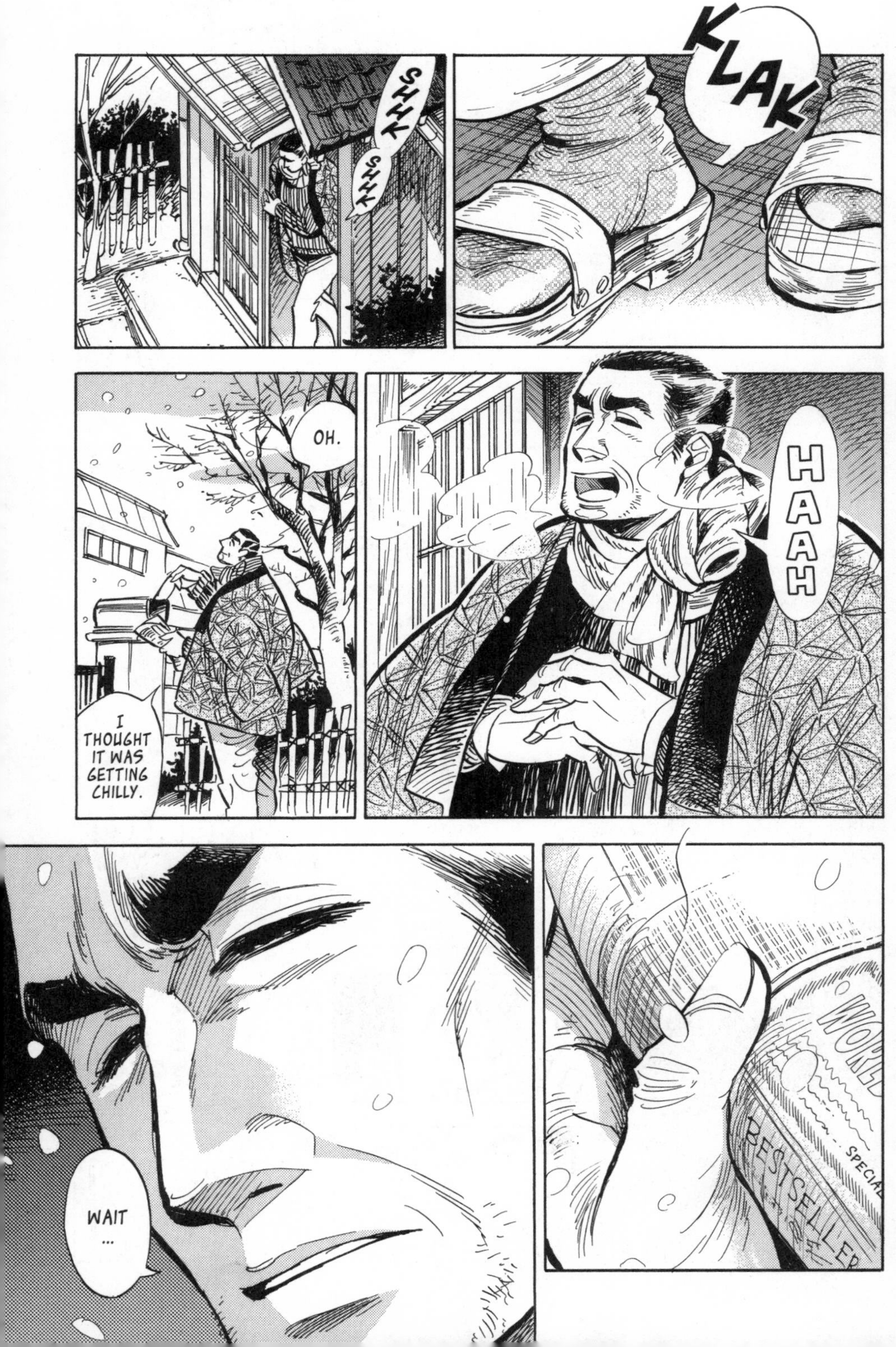
KLAK
SHHK SHHK
HAAAH
OH.
I THOUGHT IT WAS GETTING CHILLY.
WORLD
SPECIAL
BESTSELLER
WAIT ...

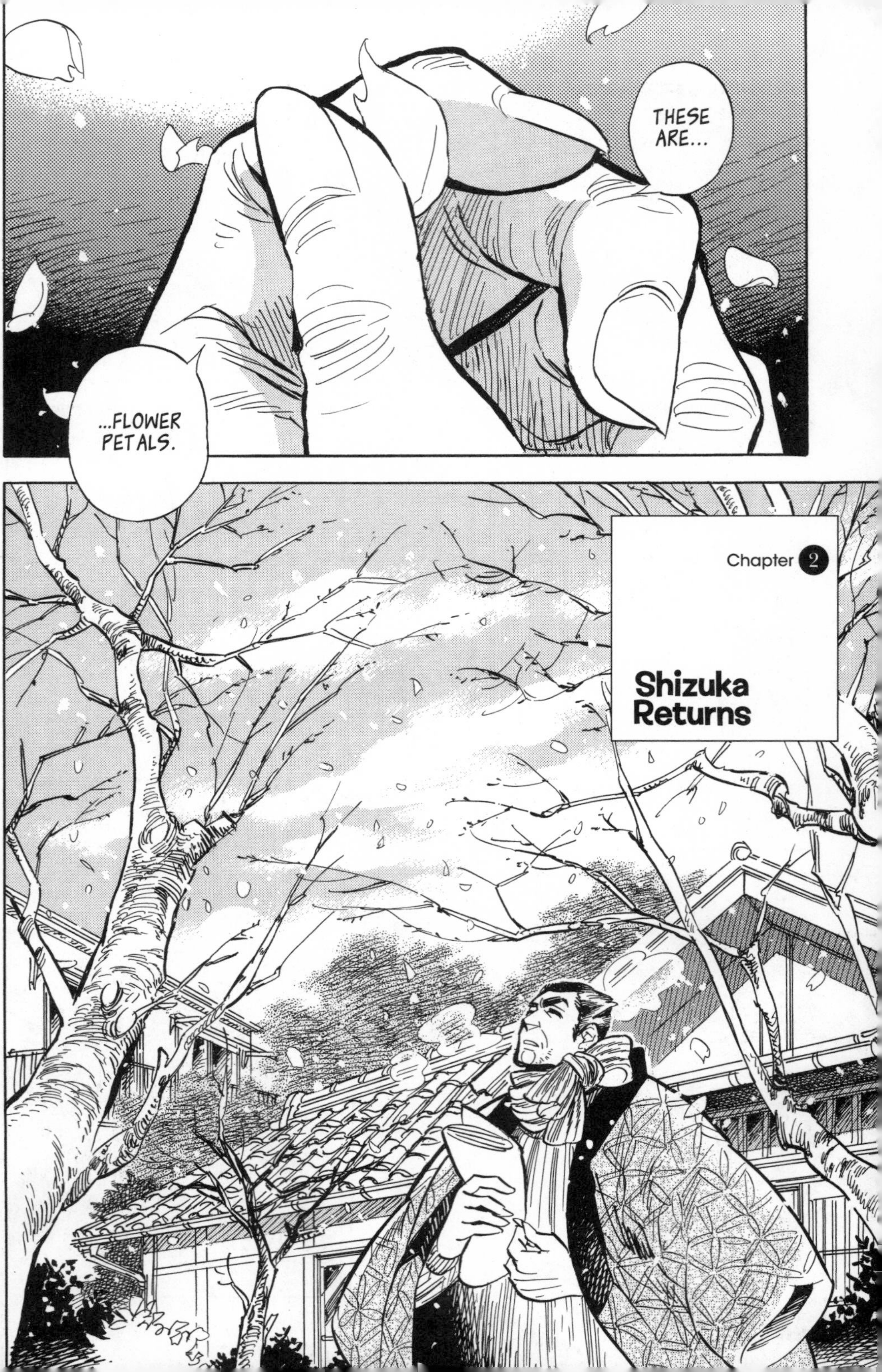
THESE ARE...
...FLOWER PETALS.
Chapter 2
Shizuka Returns

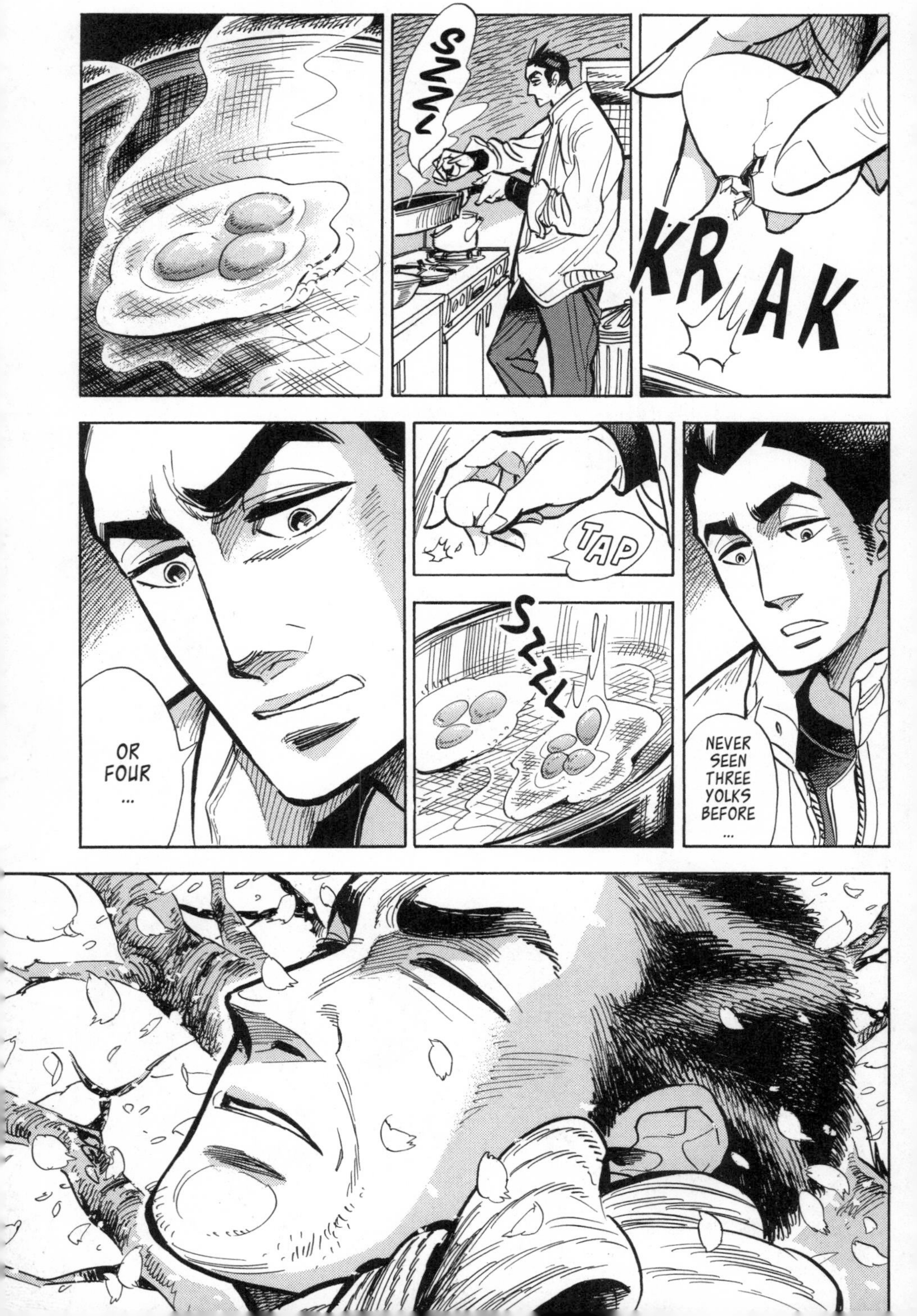
KRAK
SNNNN
NEVER SEEN THREE YOLKS BEFORE ...
TAP
SZZZ
OR FOUR ...

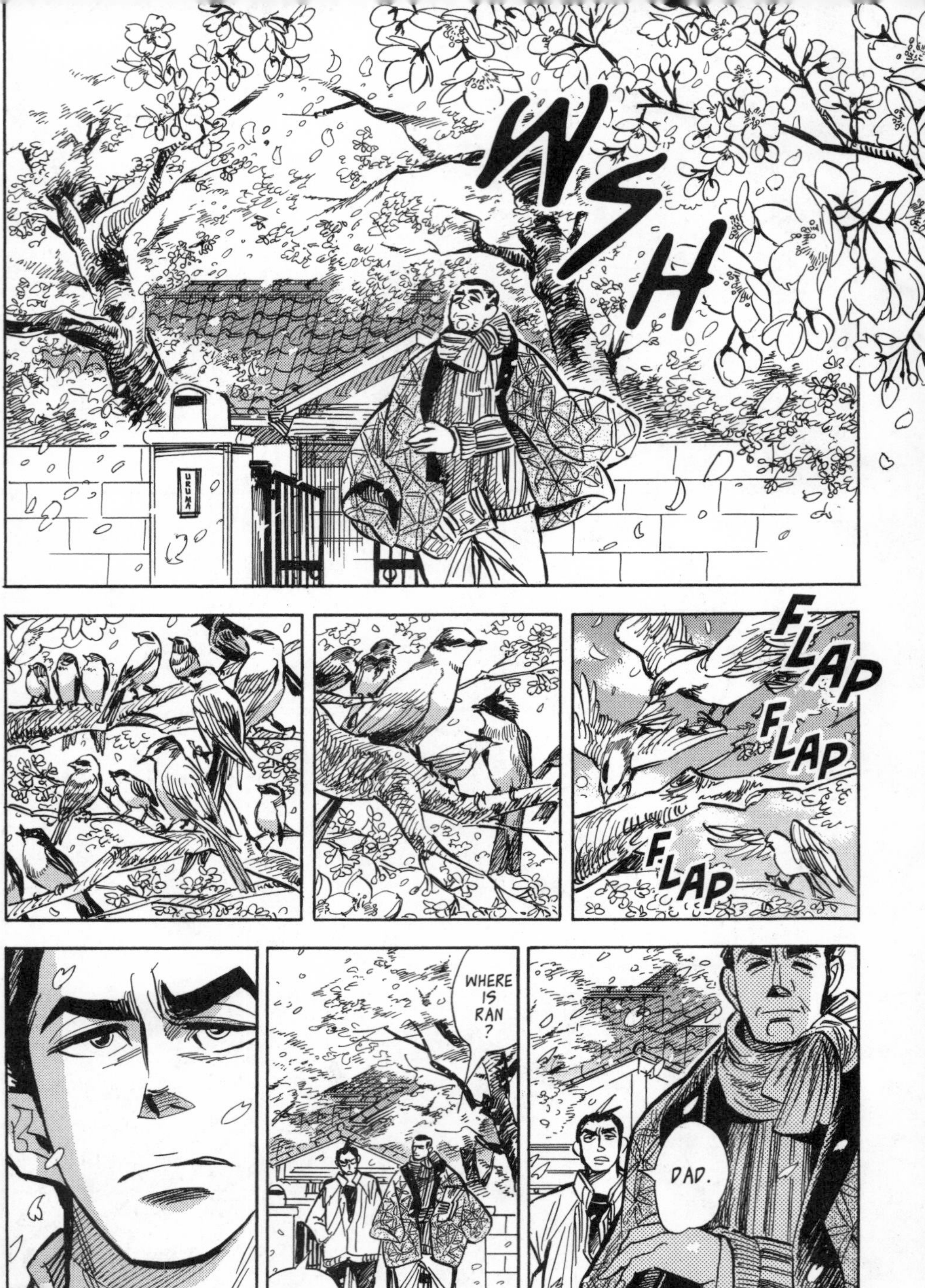
WSH
URUMA
FLAP
FLAP
FLAP
DAD.
WHERE IS RAN?
STILL ASLEEP.

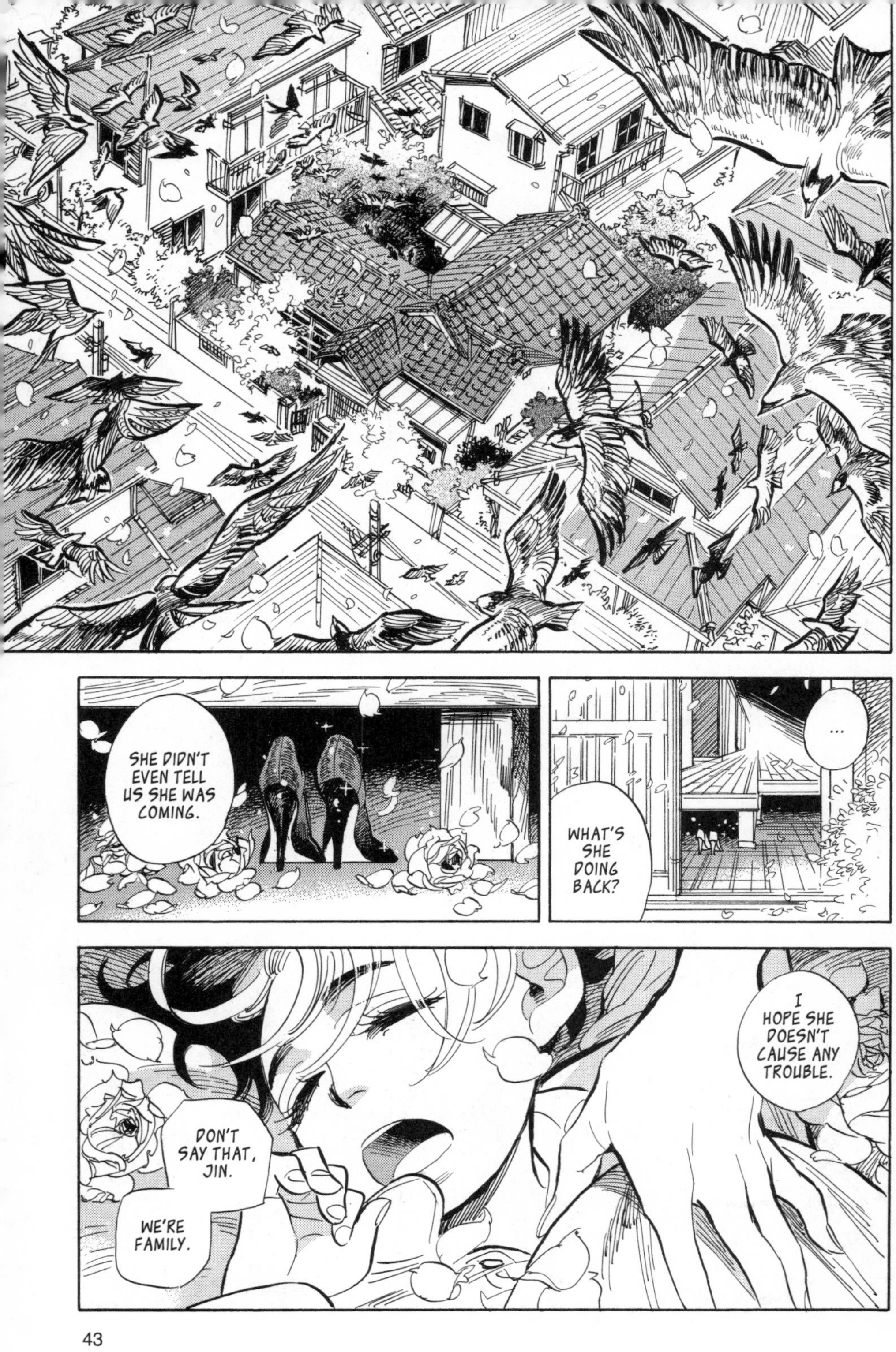
...
WHAT'S SHE DOING BACK?
SHE DIDN'T EVEN TELL US SHE WAS COMING.
I HOPE SHE DOESN'T CAUSE ANY TROUBLE.
DON'T SAY THAT, JIN.
WE'RE FAMILY.

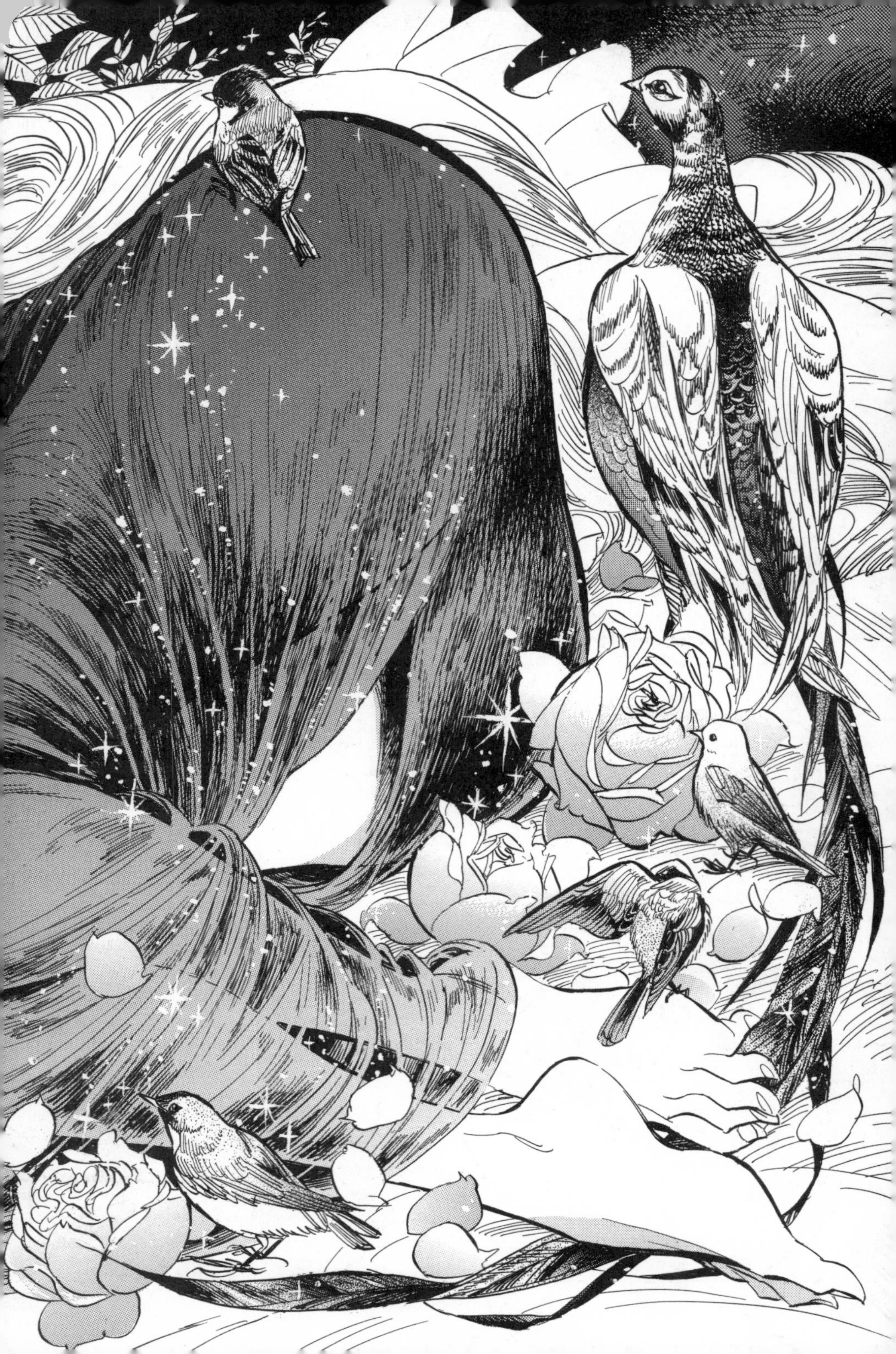

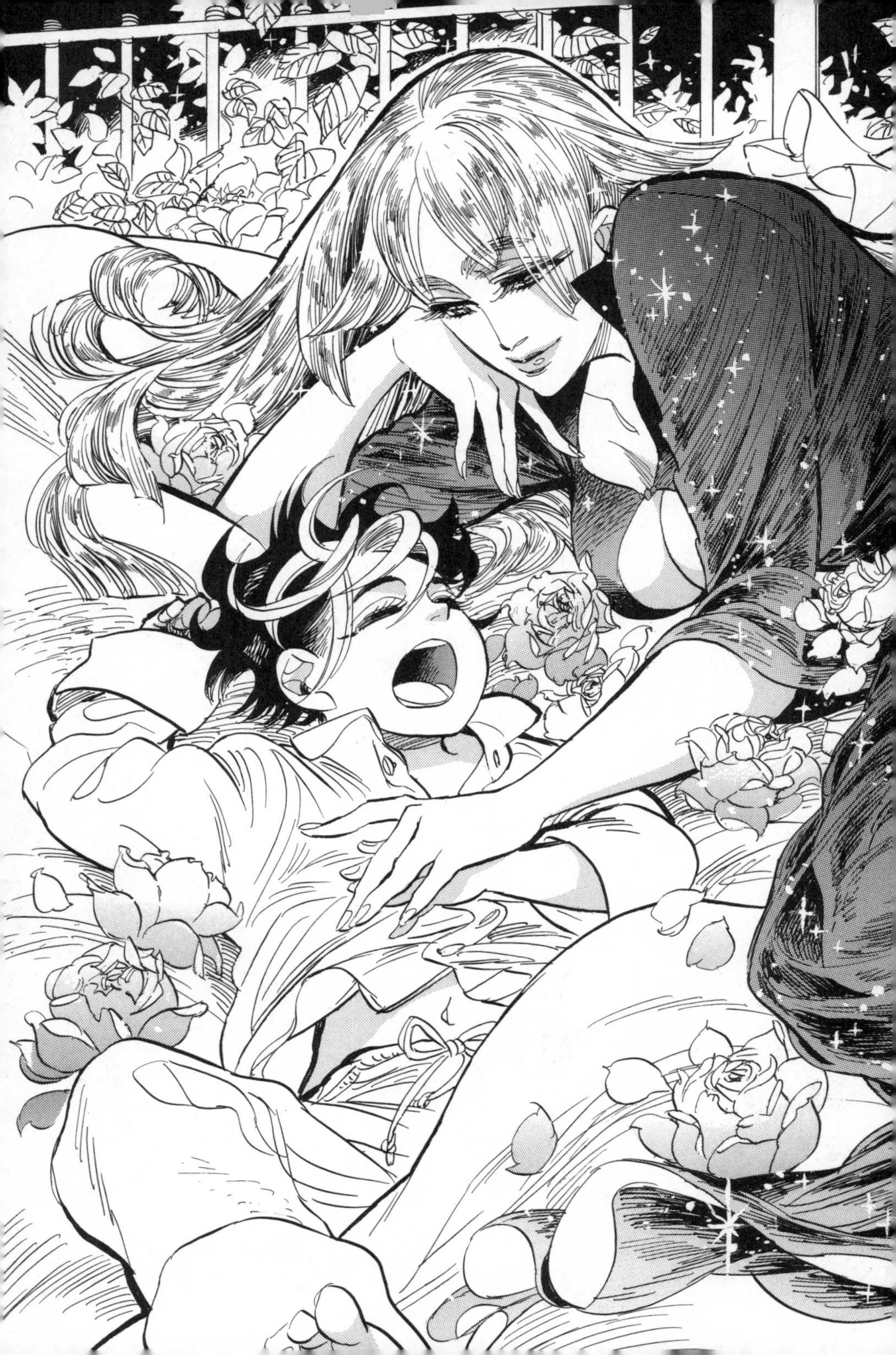

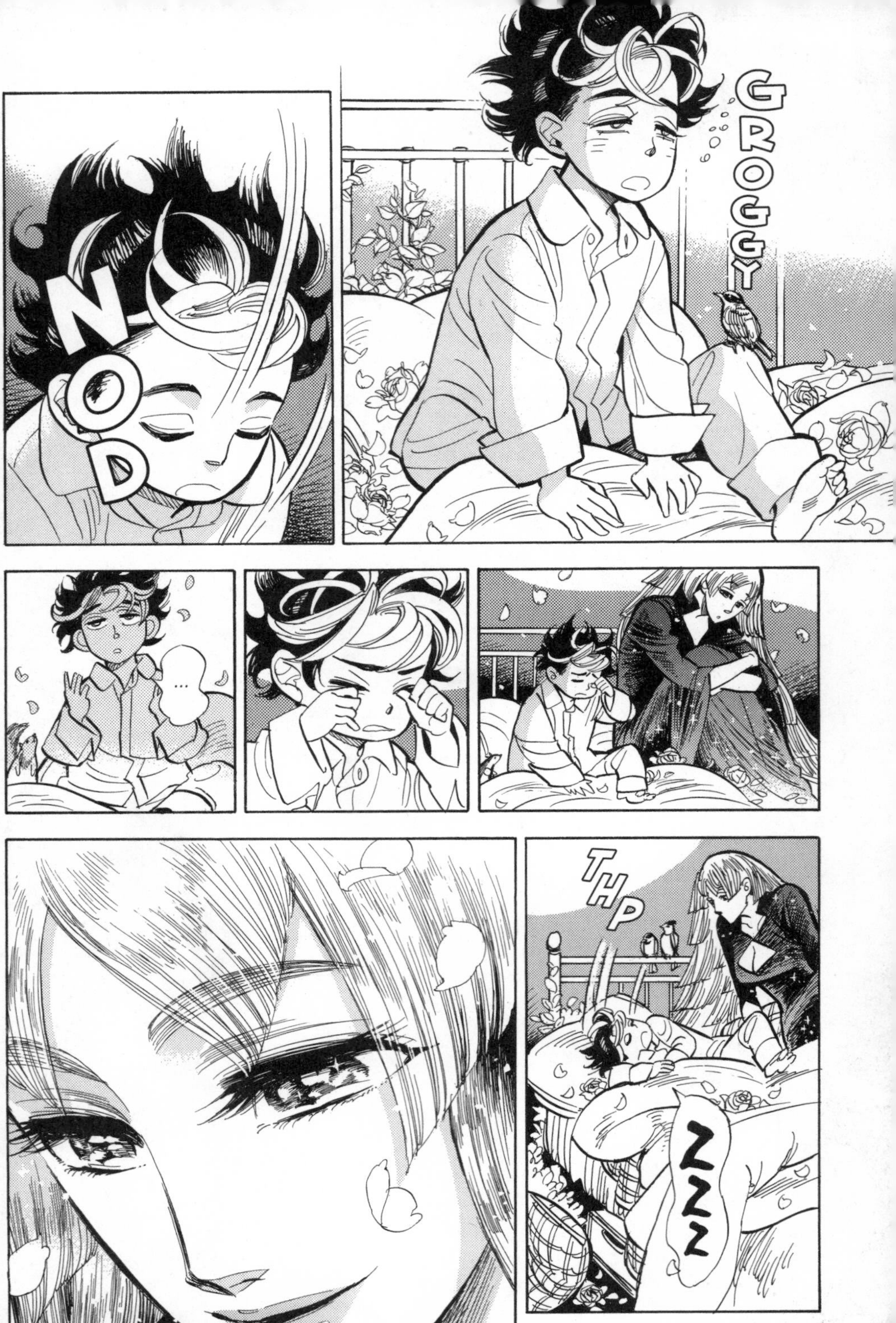
GROGGY
NOD
...
THP
ZZZ

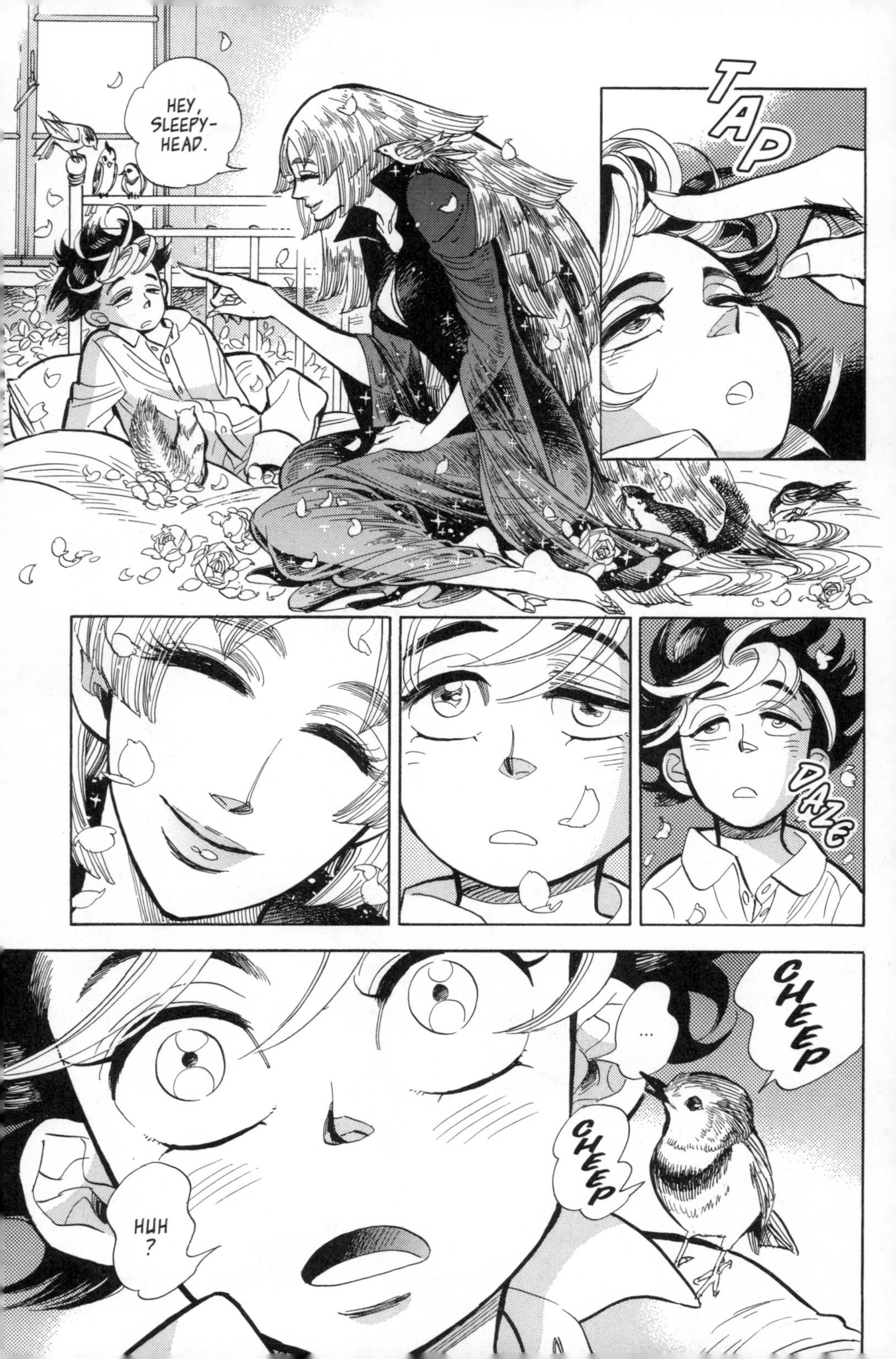
TAP
HEY, SLEEPY-HEAD.
DAZE
CHEEP
...
CHEEP
HUH?

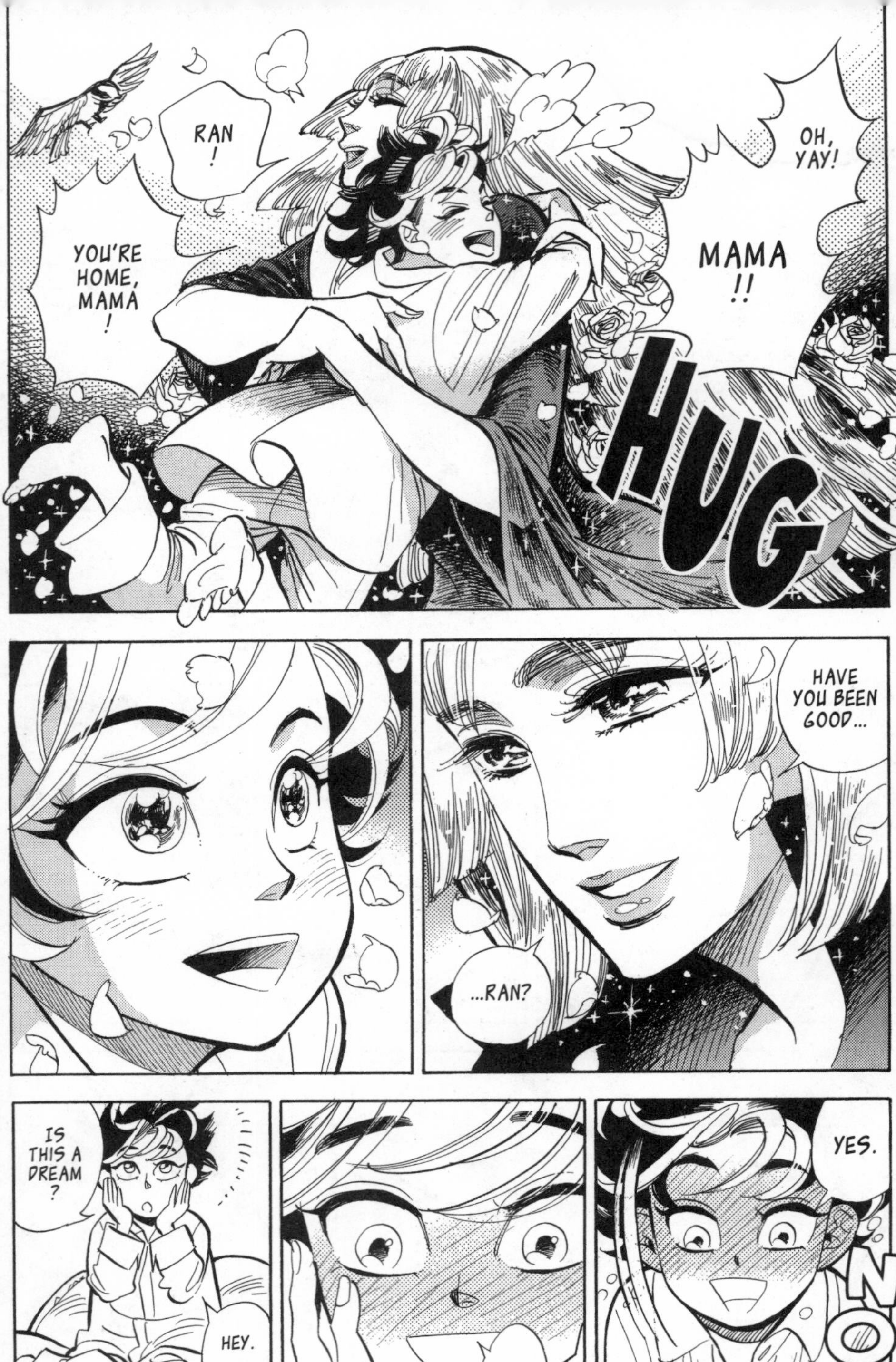
OH, YAY!
RAN!
MAMA!!
YOU'RE HOME, MAMA!
HUG
HAVE YOU BEEN GOOD...
...RAN?
YES.
NOD
...
IS THIS A DREAM?
HEY.

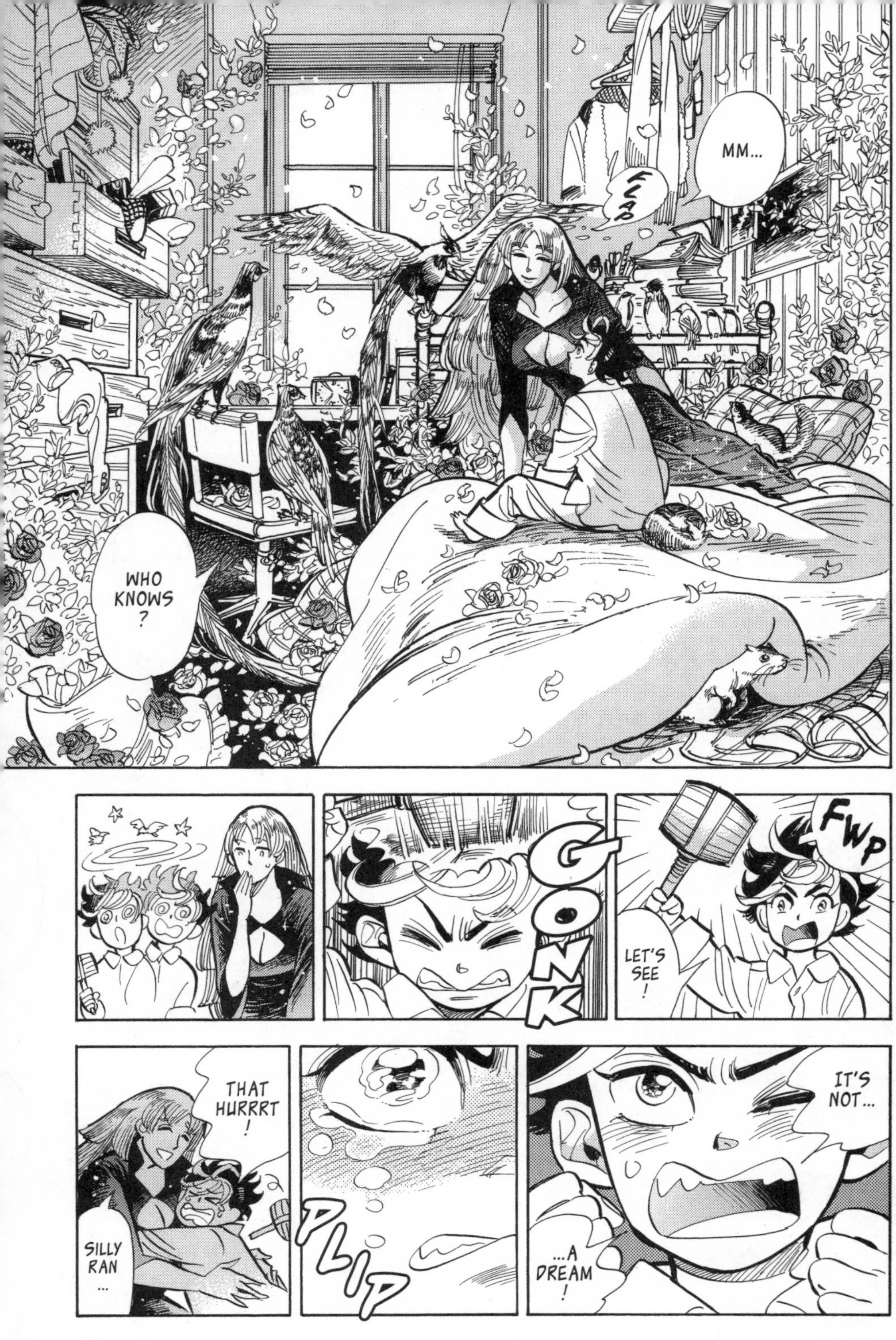

MM...
FLAP
WHO KNOWS ?
FWP
LET'S SEE !
GONK
IT'S NOT...
...A DREAM !
PLIP
THAT HURRRT !
SILLY RAN ...

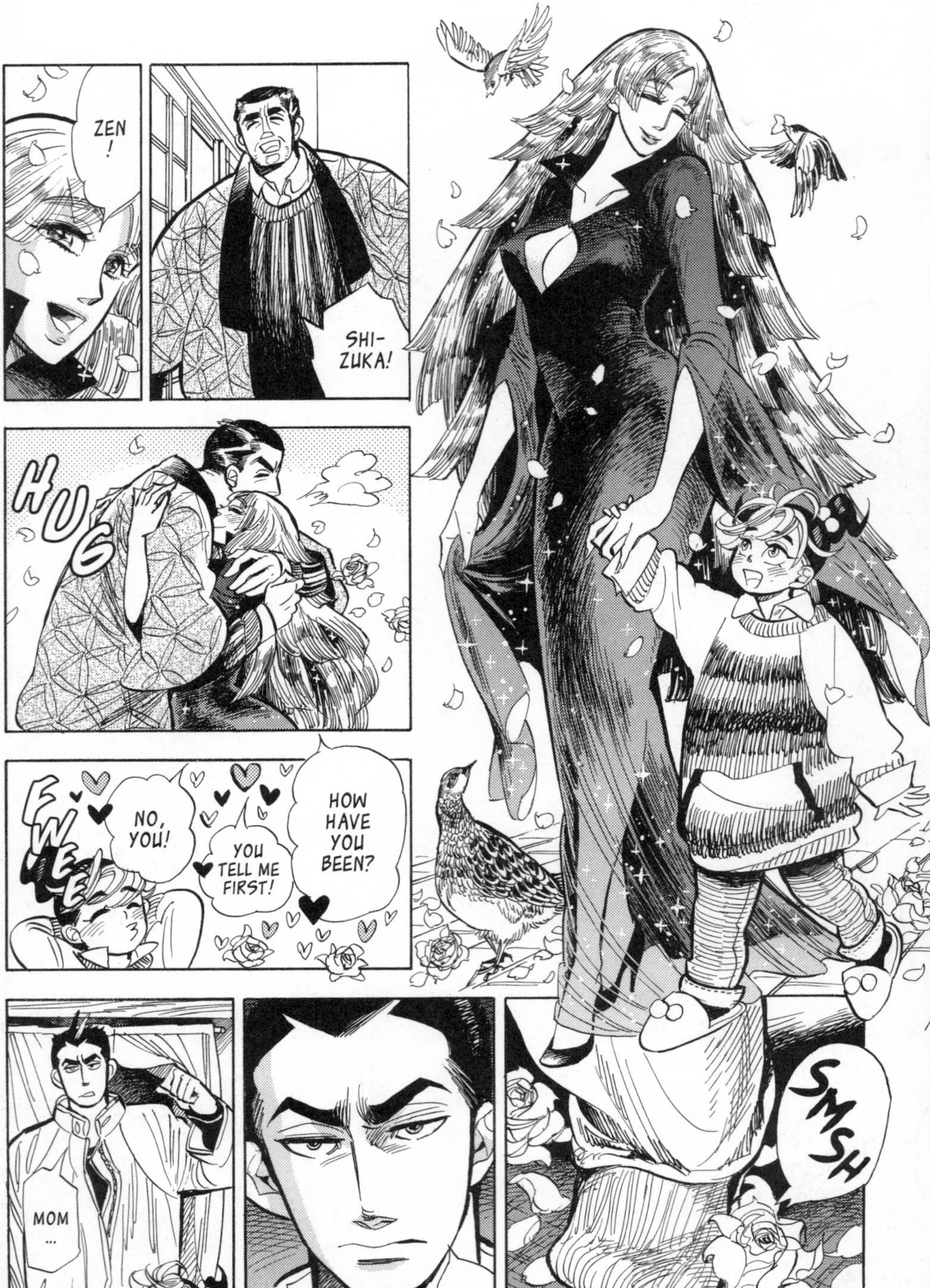

SHI-ZUKA!
ZEN!
HUG
HOW HAVE YOU BEEN?
YOU TELL ME FIRST!
NO, YOU!
FWEE
SMSH
...
MOM ...

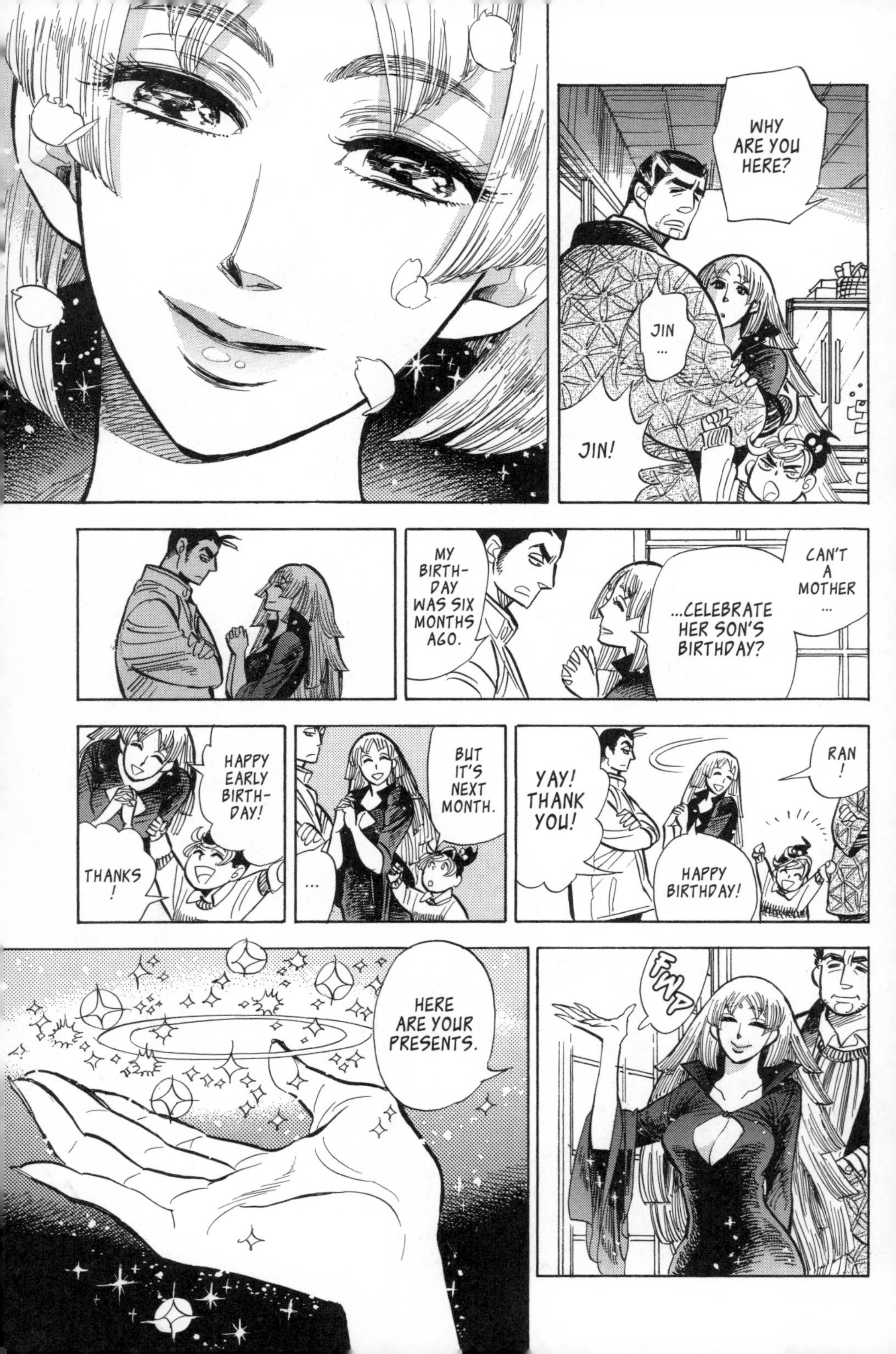
WHY ARE YOU HERE?
JIN ...
JIN!
CAN'T A MOTHER ...
...CELEBRATE HER SON'S BIRTHDAY?
MY BIRTHDAY WAS SIX MONTHS AGO.
RAN!
YAY! THANK YOU!
HAPPY BIRTHDAY!
BUT IT'S NEXT MONTH.
...
HAPPY EARLY BIRTHDAY!
THANKS!
FWAP
HERE ARE YOUR PRESENTS.

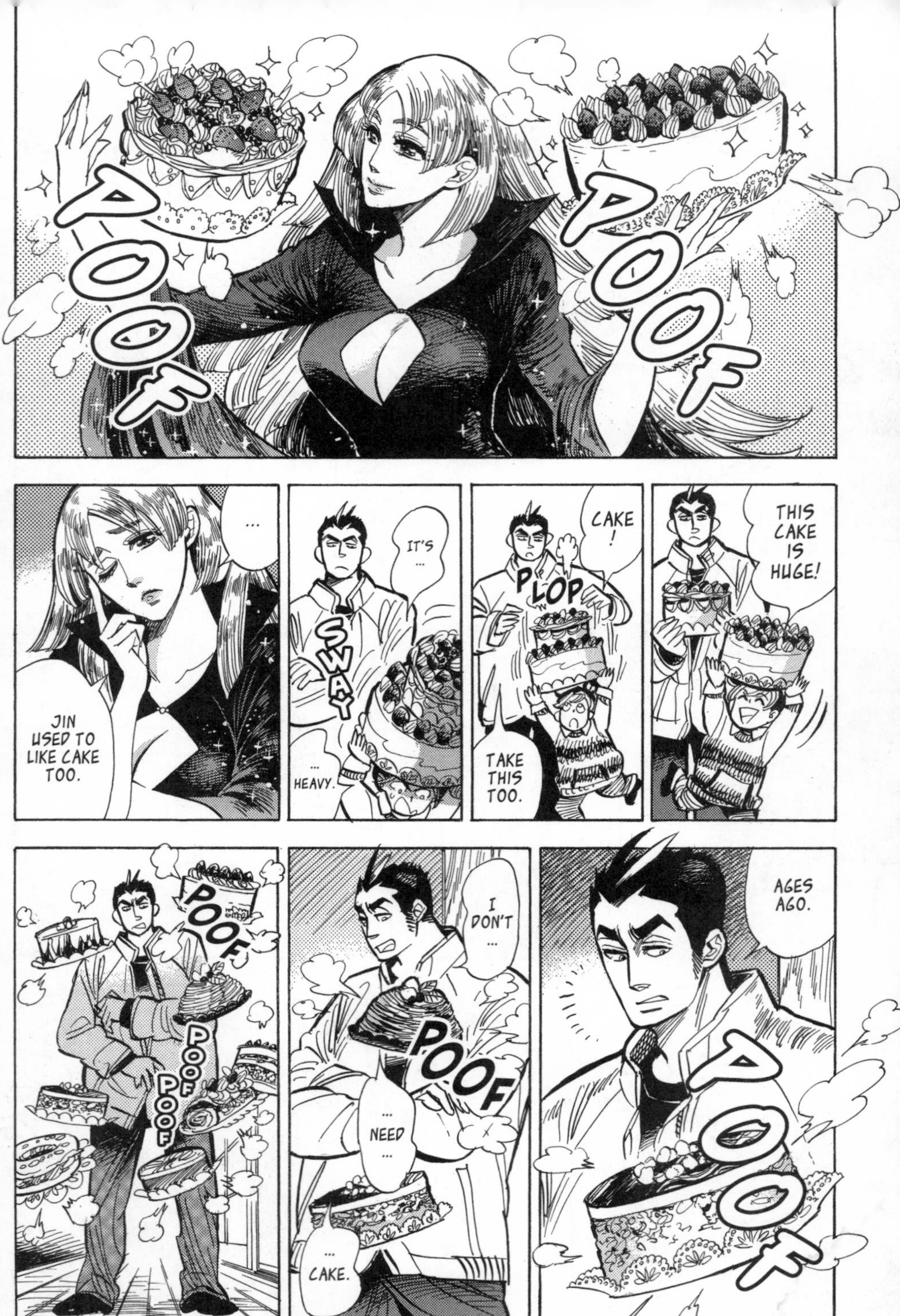
POOF
POOF
THIS CAKE IS HUGE!
CAKE!
PLOP
TAKE THIS TOO.
IT'S...
SWAY
...HEAVY.
...
JIN USED TO LIKE CAKE TOO.
AGES AGO.
POOF
I DON'T...
POOF
...NEED...
...CAKE.
POOF
POOF
POOF

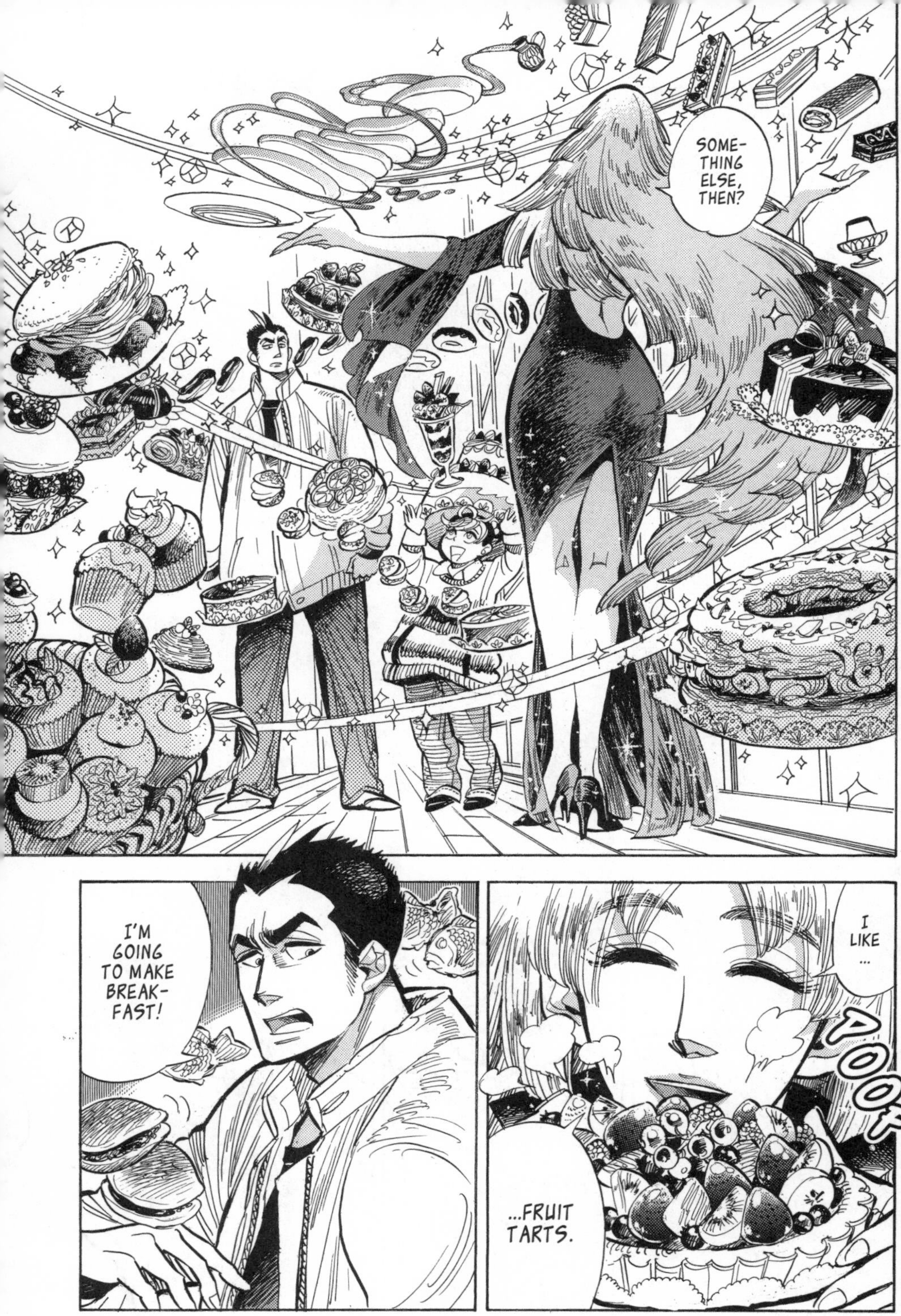
SOME-THING ELSE, THEN?
I LIKE ...
POOF
...FRUIT TARTS.
I'M GOING TO MAKE BREAK-FAST!

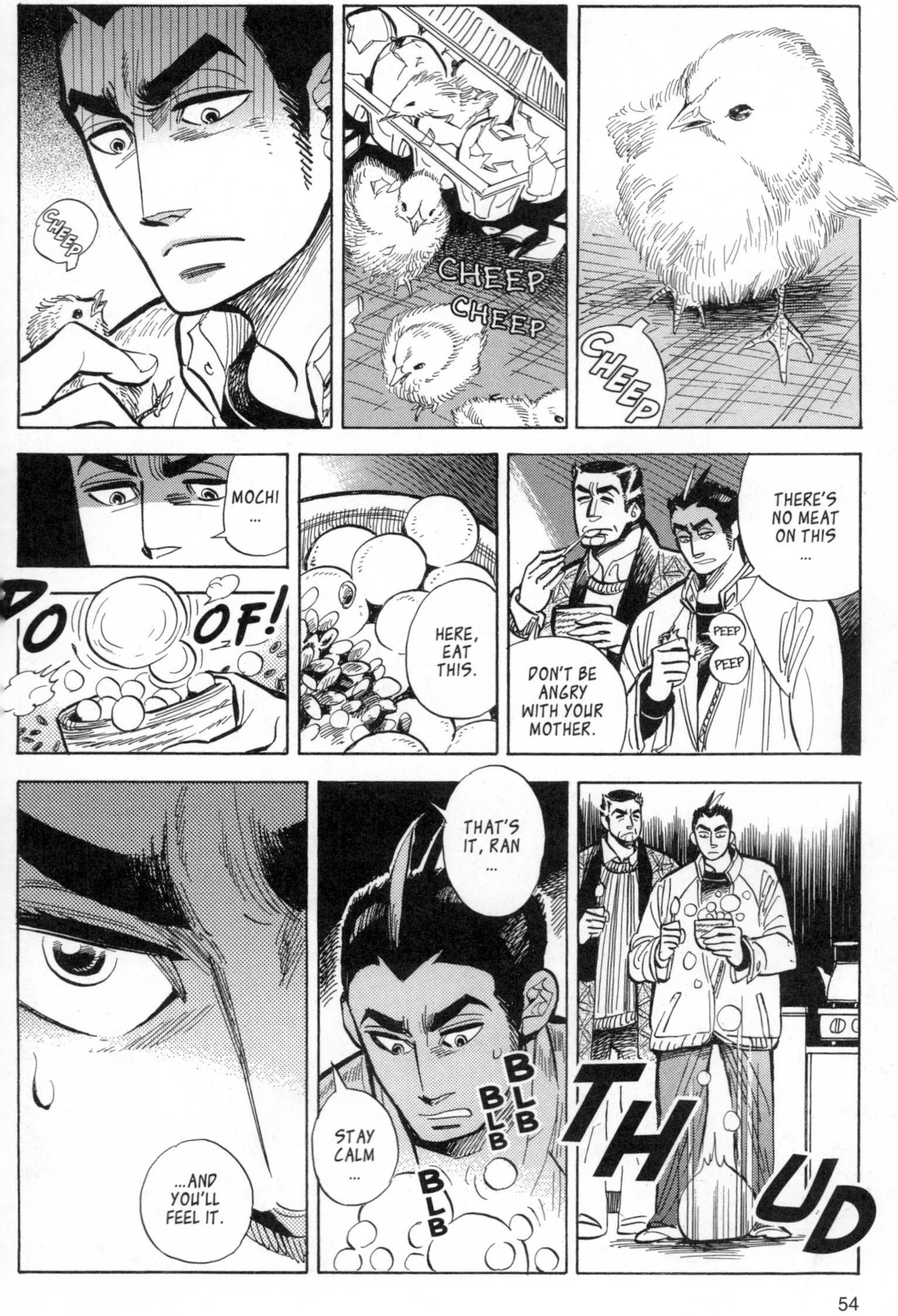
CHEEP
CHEEP
CHEEP
CHEEP
THERE'S NO MEAT ON THIS ...
PEEP
PEEP
DON'T BE ANGRY WITH YOUR MOTHER.
HERE, EAT THIS.
MOCHI ...
DOOF!
THUD
THAT'S IT, RAN ...
BLB
BLB
BLB
STAY CALM ...
BLB
...AND YOU'LL FEEL IT.

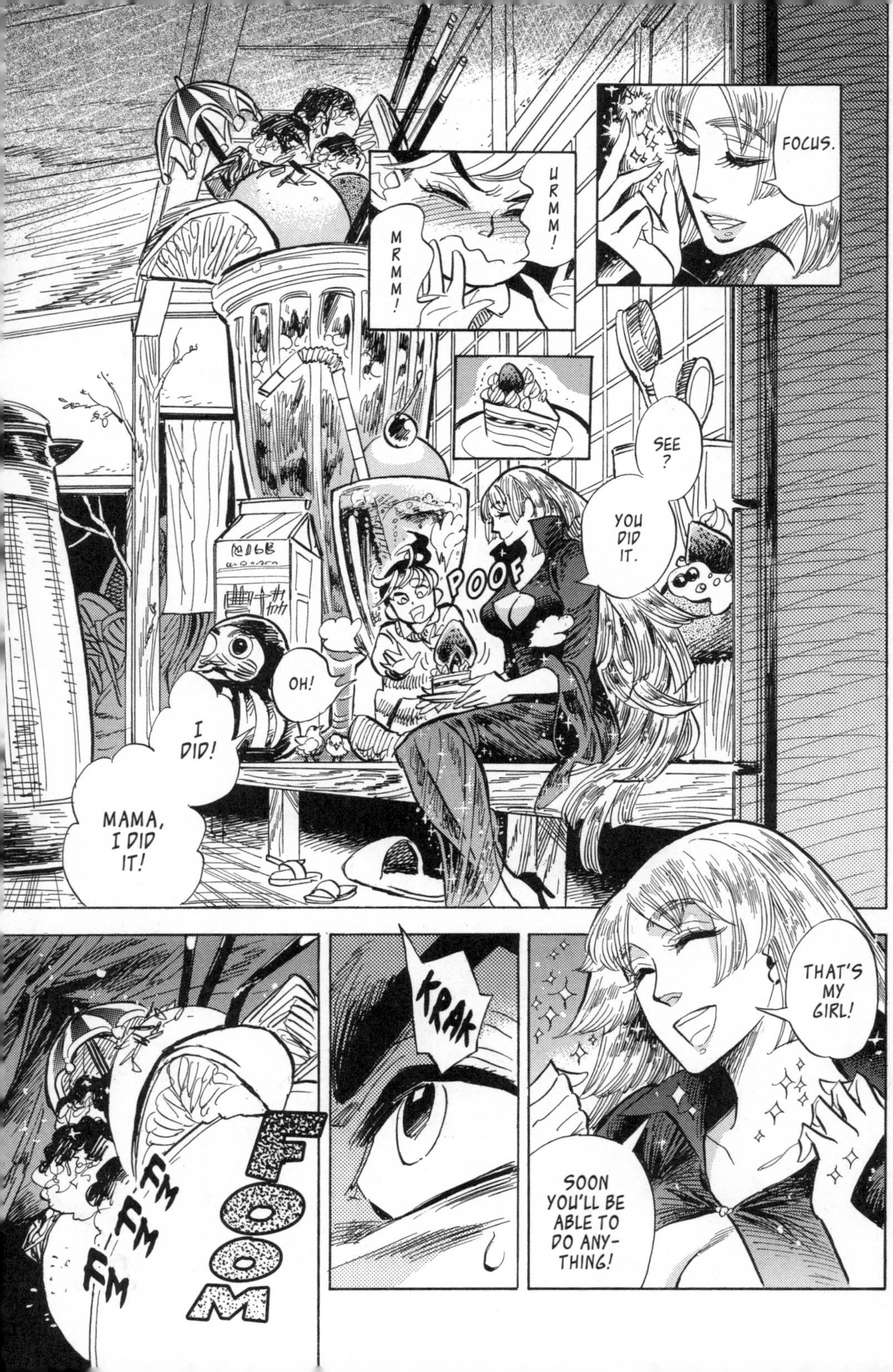
FOCUS.
URMMM!
MRMM!
SEE?
YOU DID IT.
POOF
OH!
I DID!
MAMA, I DID IT!
THAT'S MY GIRL!
SOON YOU'LL BE ABLE TO DO ANY-THING!
KRAK
FOOOM
FM FM FM

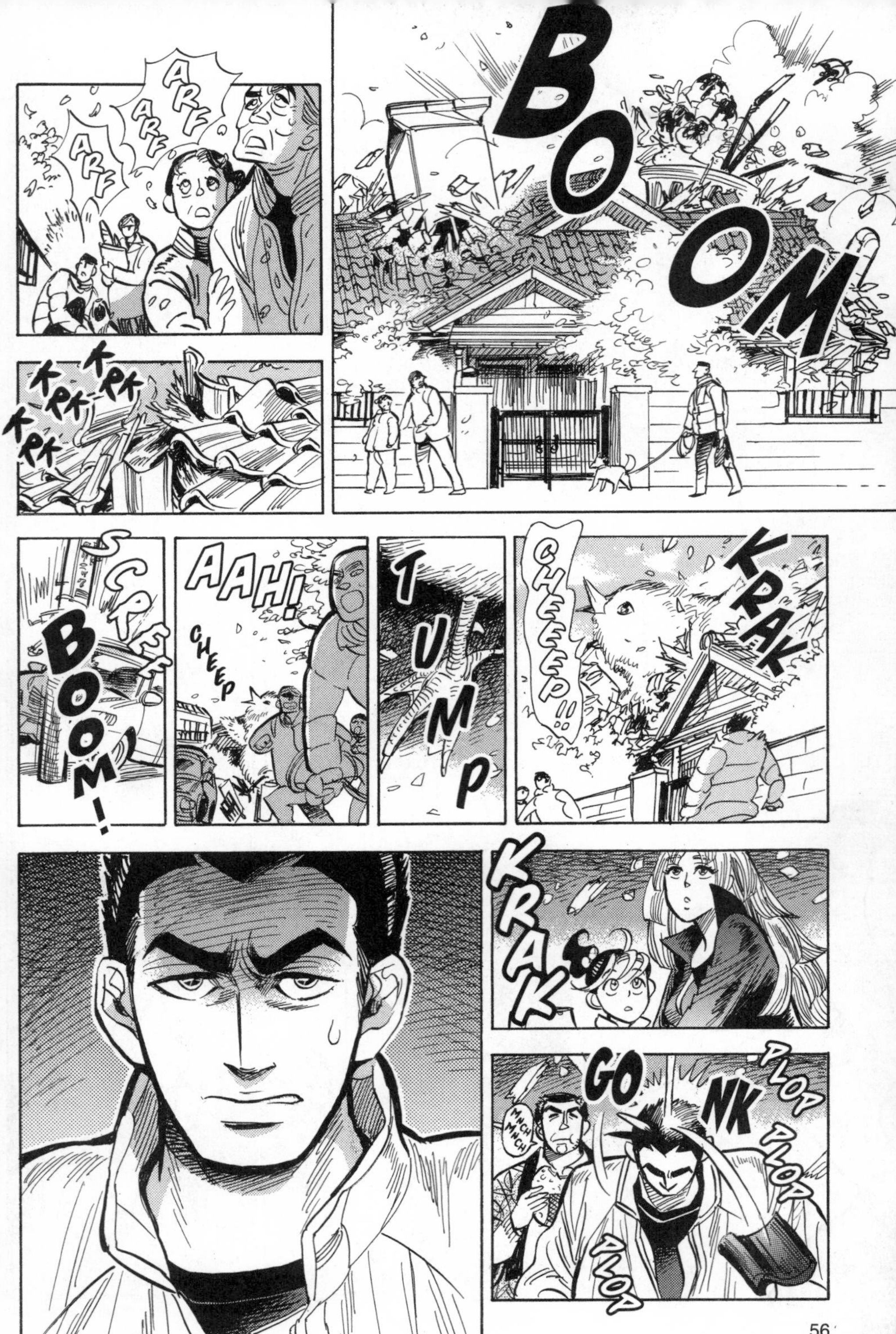
BOOM
ARF
ARF
ARF
KRK
KRK
KRK
KRK
KRAK
CHEEEP!!
TUMP
AAH!
CHEEP
SCREE
BOOOM!
KRAK
KRAK
GONK
PLOP
PLOP
PLOP
PLOP
MNCH MNCH

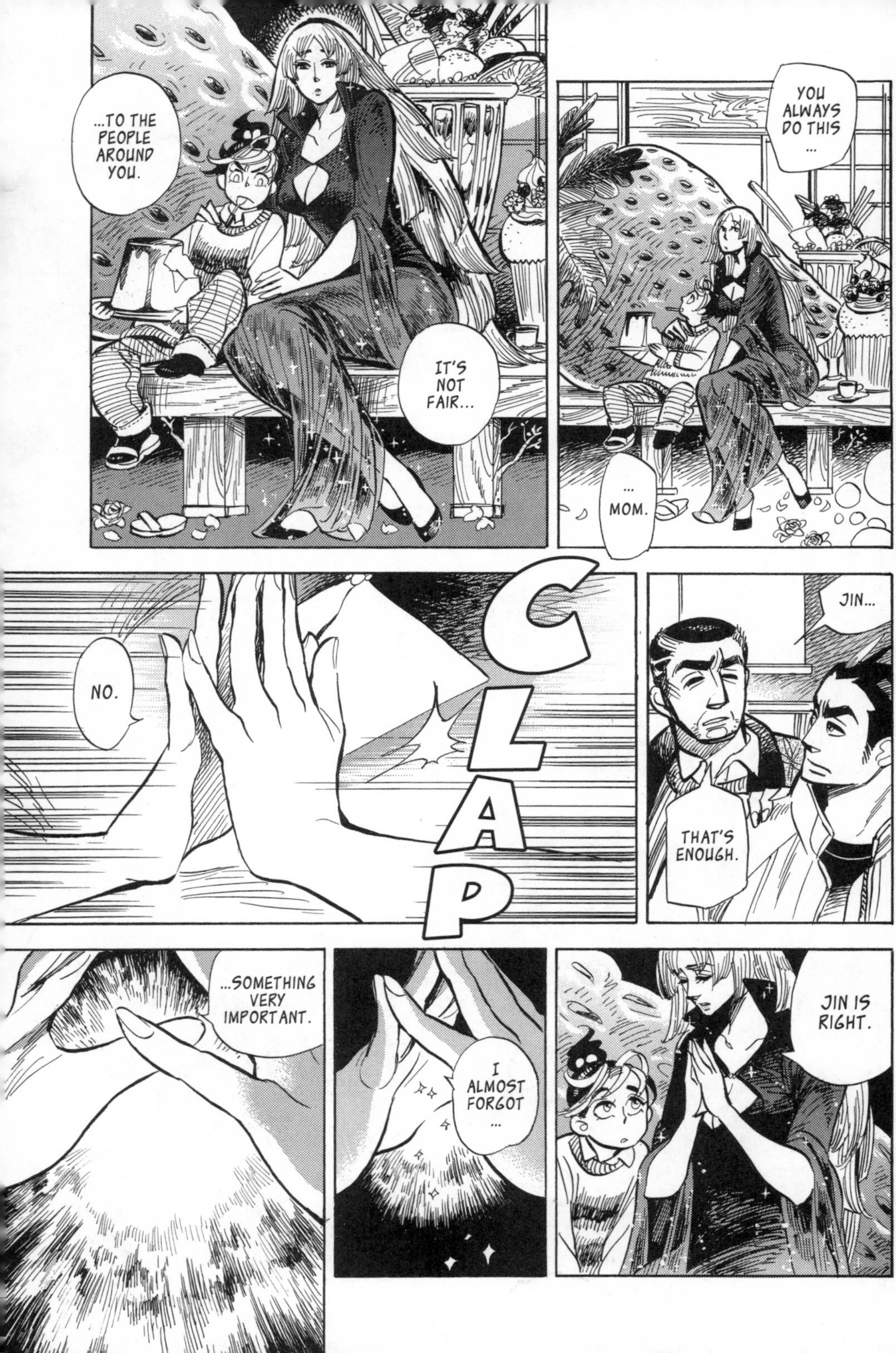
YOU ALWAYS DO THIS ...
... MOM.
...TO THE PEOPLE AROUND YOU.
IT'S NOT FAIR...
JIN...
THAT'S ENOUGH.
CLAP
NO.
JIN IS RIGHT.
I ALMOST FORGOT ...
...SOMETHING VERY IMPORTANT.

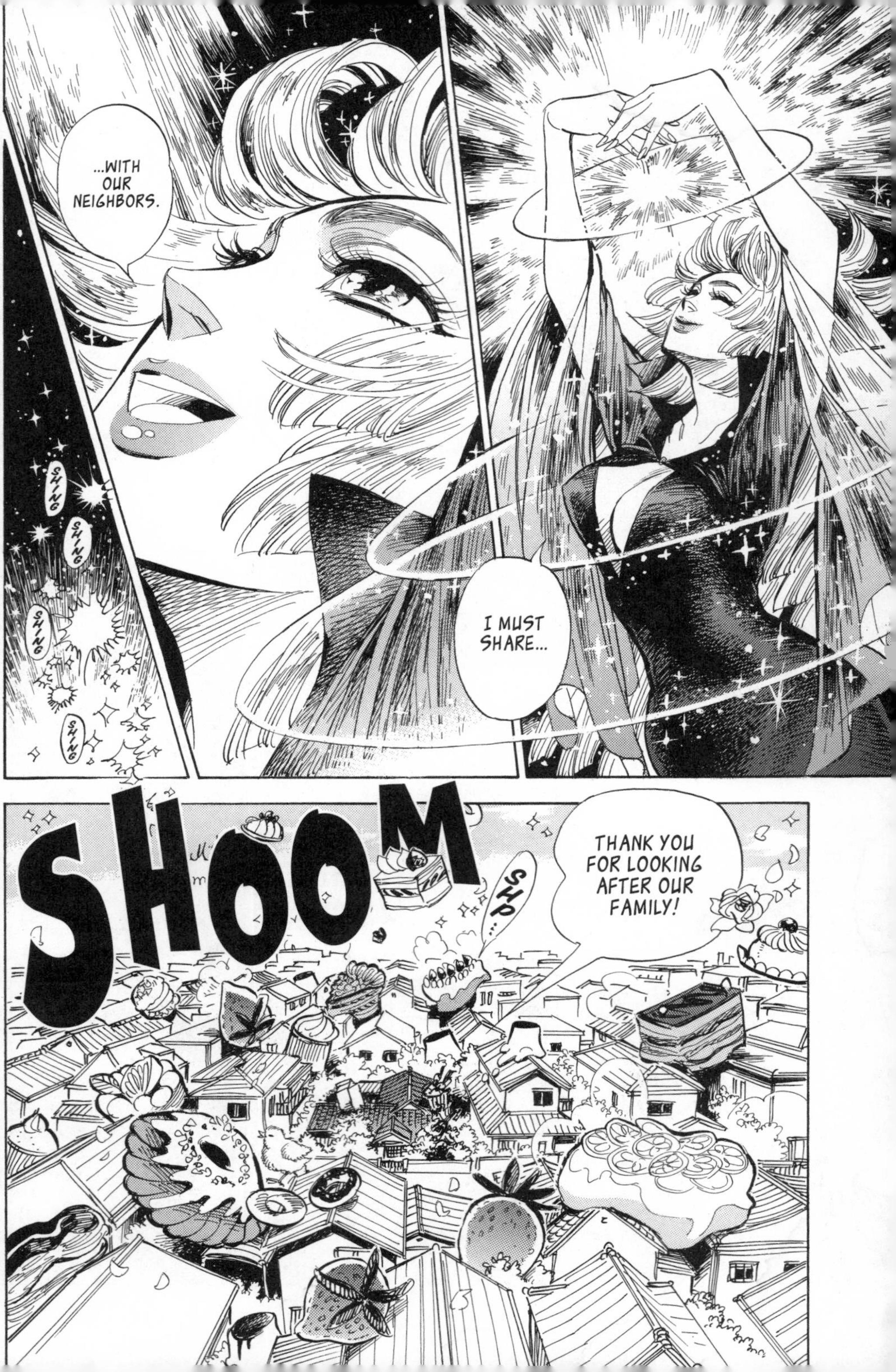
I MUST SHARE...
...WITH OUR NEIGHBORS.
SHING
SHING
SHING
SHING
THANK YOU FOR LOOKING AFTER OUR FAMILY!
SHP...
SHOOM

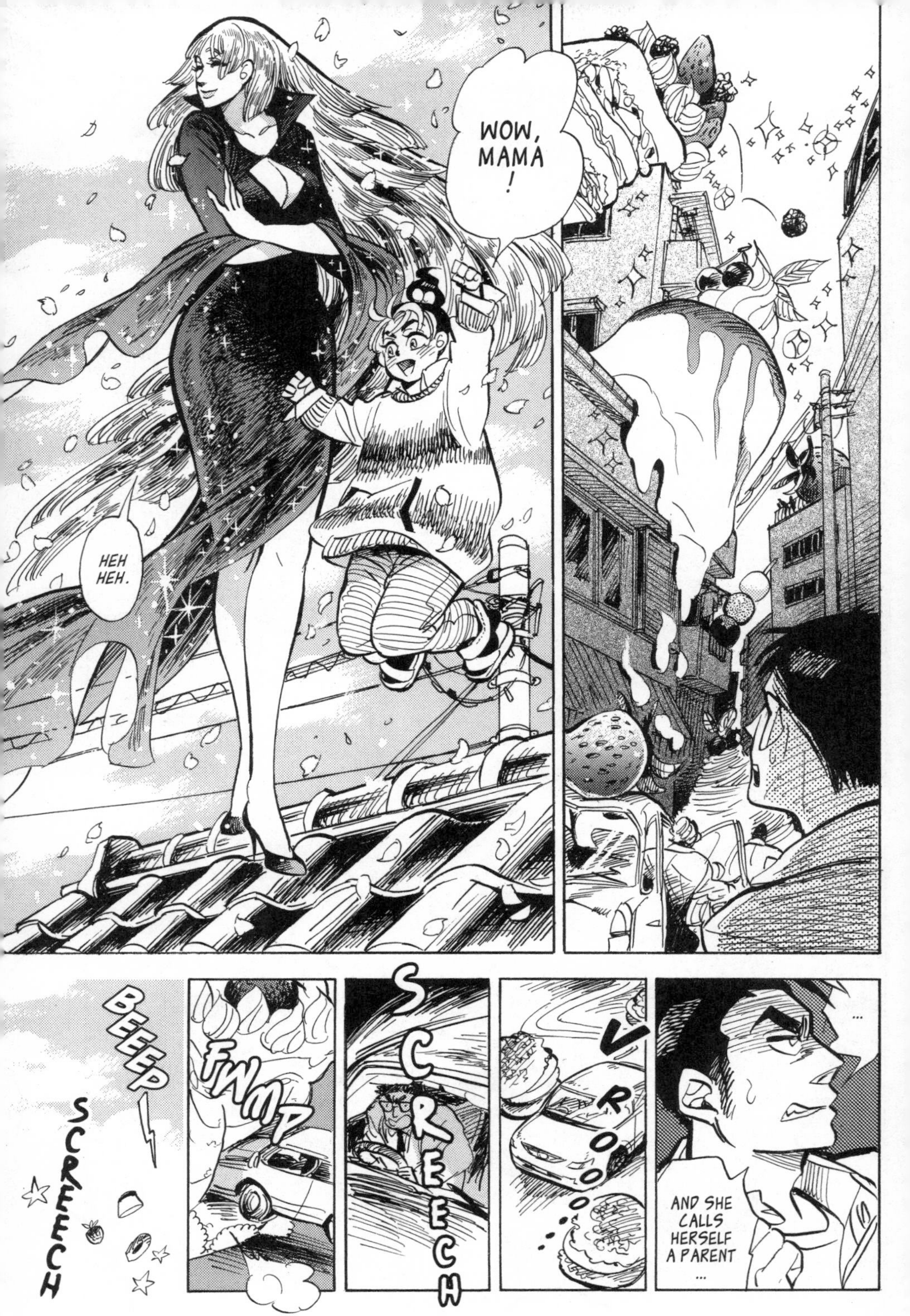
WOW, MAMA!
HEH HEH.
...
AND SHE CALLS HERSELF A PARENT ...
VROOO...
SCREECH
FWMP
BEEEP
SCREEECH

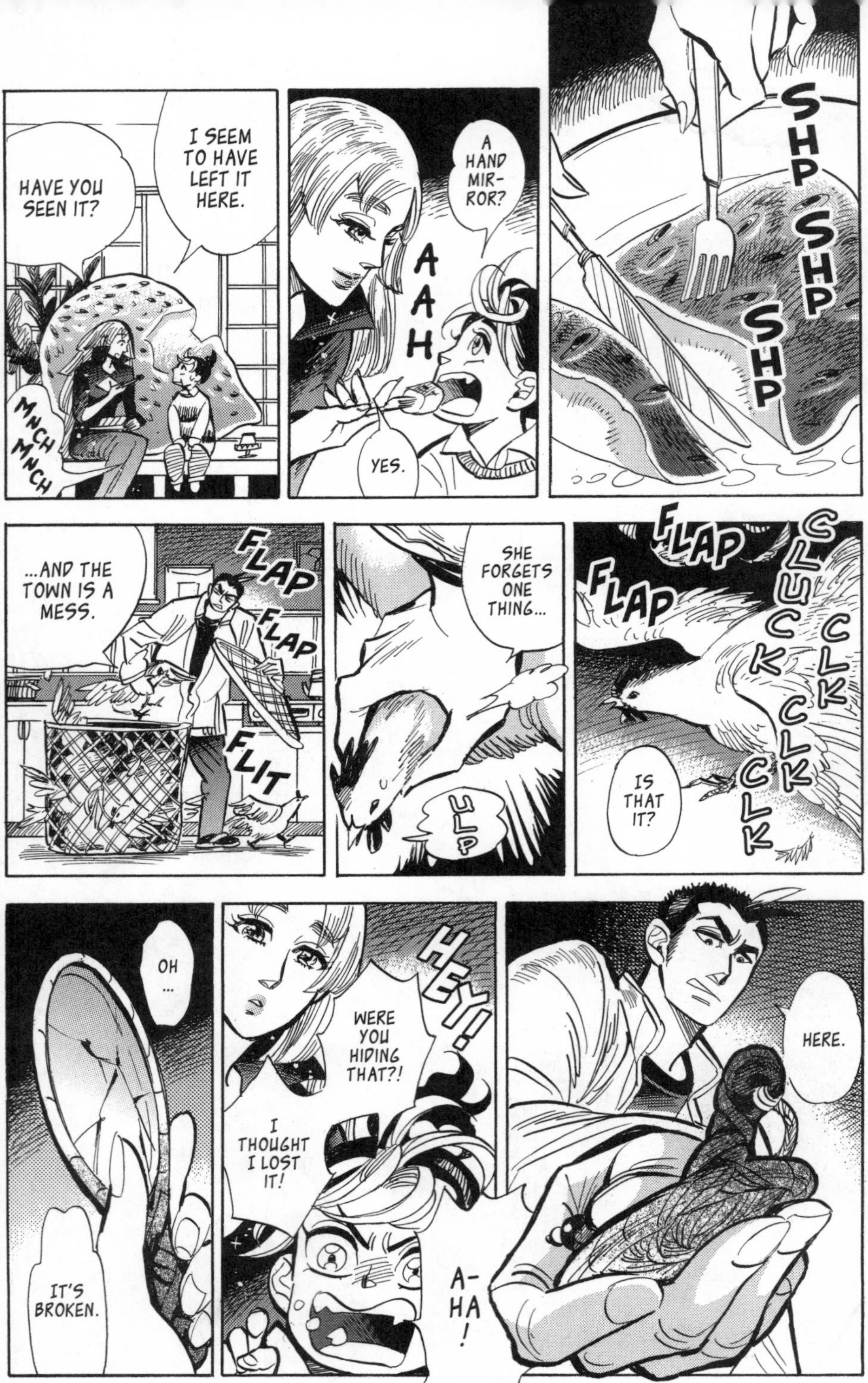
SHP SHP SHP SHP
A HAND MIRROR?
AAH
YES.
I SEEM TO HAVE LEFT IT HERE.
HAVE YOU SEEN IT?
MNCH MNCH
FLAP FLAP
CLUCK CLK CLK CLK CLK
IS THAT IT?
SHE FORGETS ONE THING...
ULP
...AND THE TOWN IS A MESS.
FLAP FLAP
FLIT
HERE.
HEY!
WERE YOU HIDING THAT?!
I THOUGHT I LOST IT!
A-HA!
OH...
IT'S BROKEN.

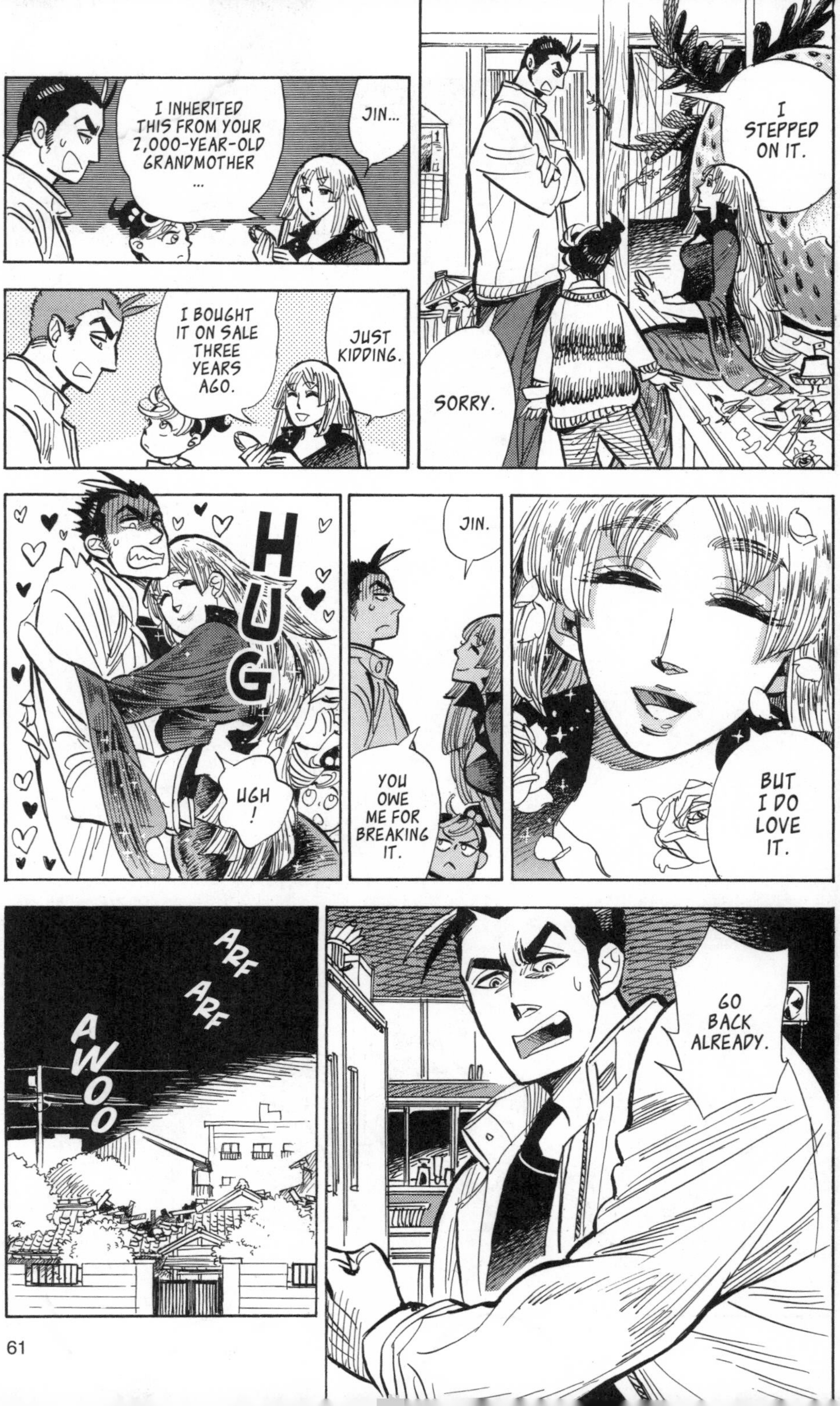
I STEPPED ON IT.
SORRY.
JIN...
I INHERITED THIS FROM YOUR 2,000-YEAR-OLD GRANDMOTHER ...
JUST KIDDING.
I BOUGHT IT ON SALE THREE YEARS AGO.
BUT I DO LOVE IT.
JIN.
YOU OWE ME FOR BREAKING IT.
HUG
UGH!
GO BACK ALREADY.
ARF
ARF
AWOO

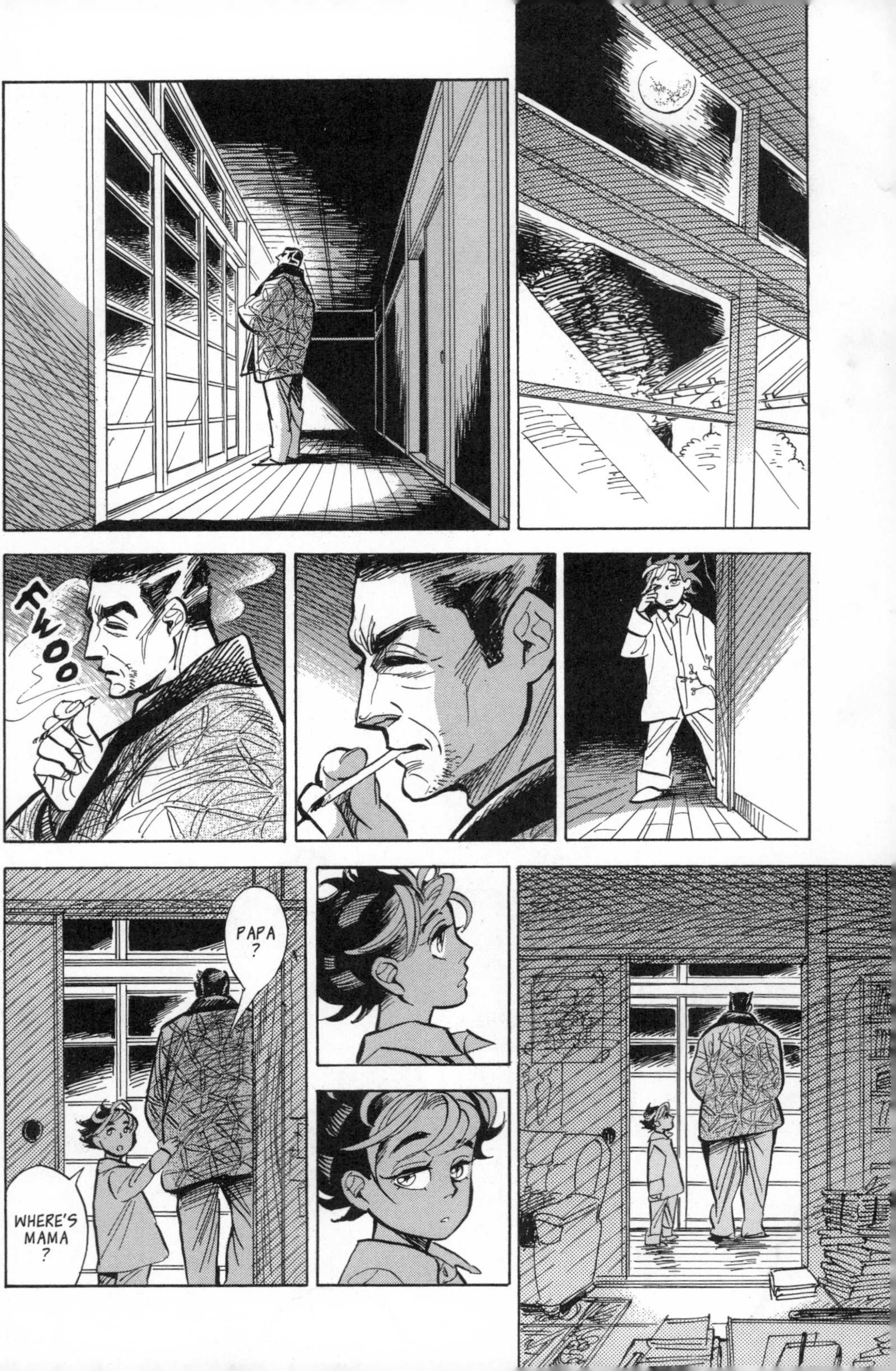
FWOO
PAPA?
WHERE'S MAMA?

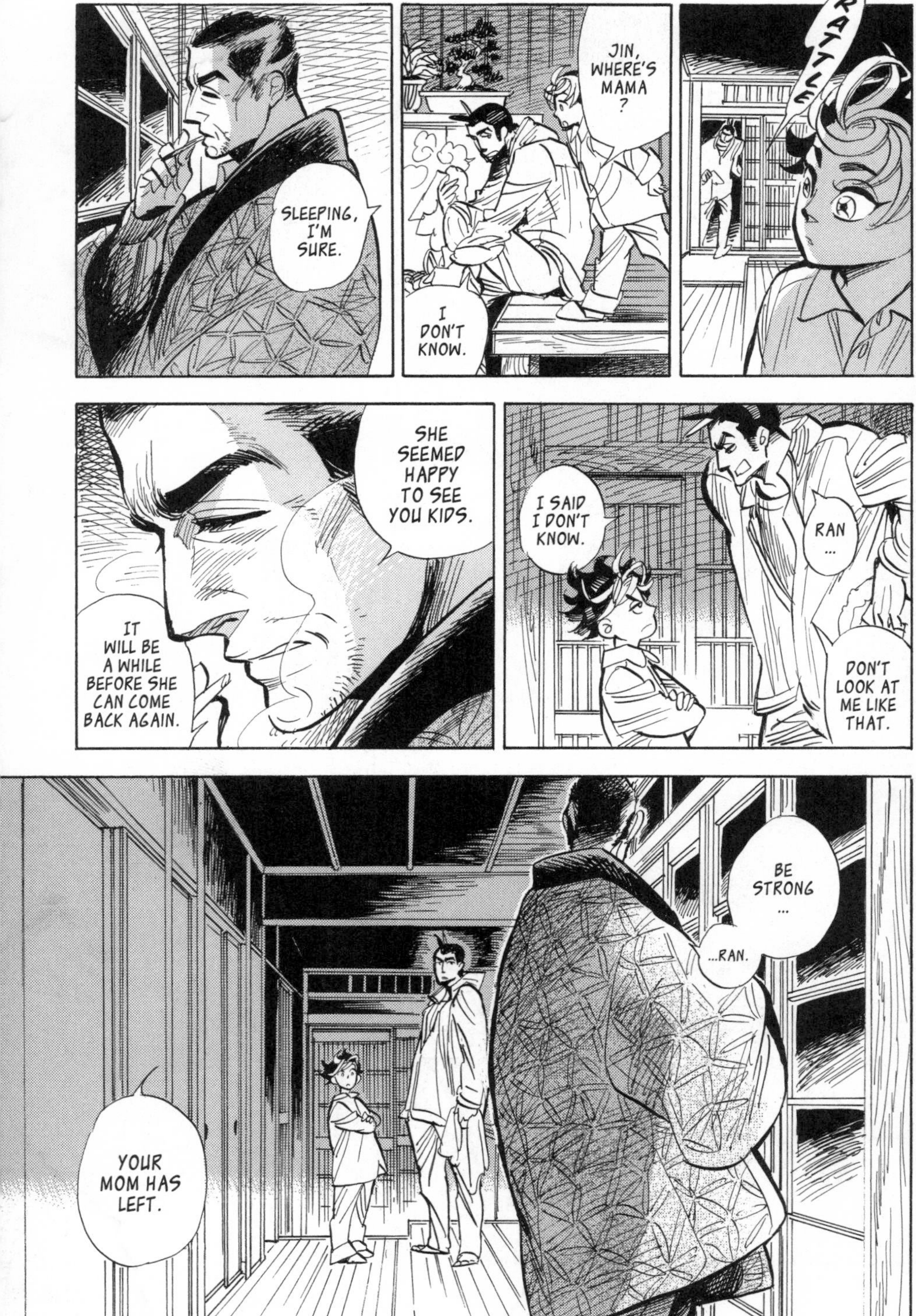
RATTLE
JIN, WHERE'S MAMA?
I DON'T KNOW.
SLEEPING, I'M SURE.
RAN ...
I SAID I DON'T KNOW.
DON'T LOOK AT ME LIKE THAT.
SHE SEEMED HAPPY TO SEE YOU KIDS.
IT WILL BE A WHILE BEFORE SHE CAN COME BACK AGAIN.
BE STRONG ...
...RAN.
YOUR MOM HAS LEFT.

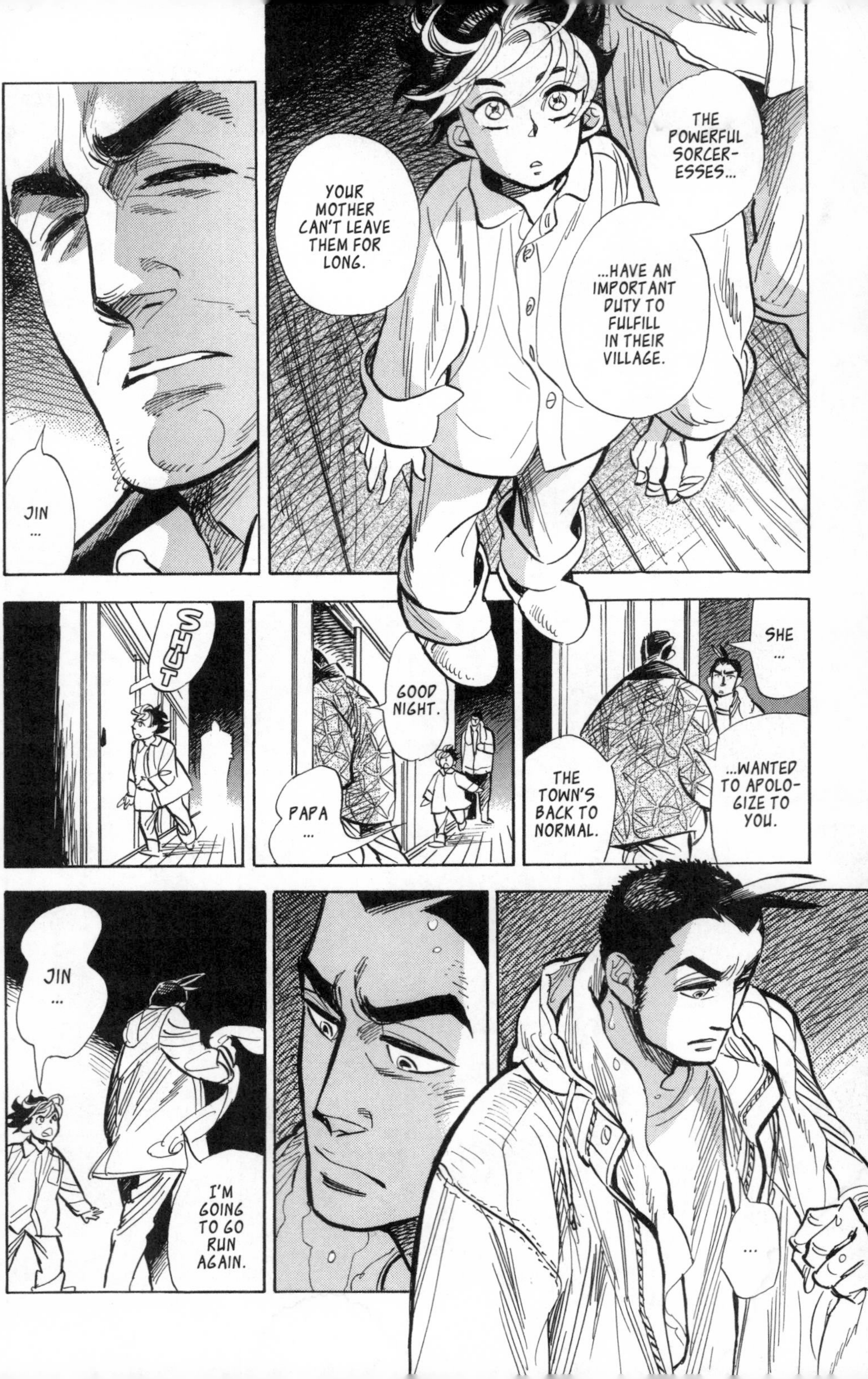
THE POWERFUL SORCERESSES...
...HAVE AN IMPORTANT DUTY TO FULFILL IN THEIR VILLAGE.
YOUR MOTHER CAN'T LEAVE THEM FOR LONG.
JIN ...
SHE ...
...WANTED TO APOLOGIZE TO YOU.
THE TOWN'S BACK TO NORMAL.
GOOD NIGHT.
PAPA ...
SHUT
...
JIN ...
I'M GOING TO GO RUN AGAIN.

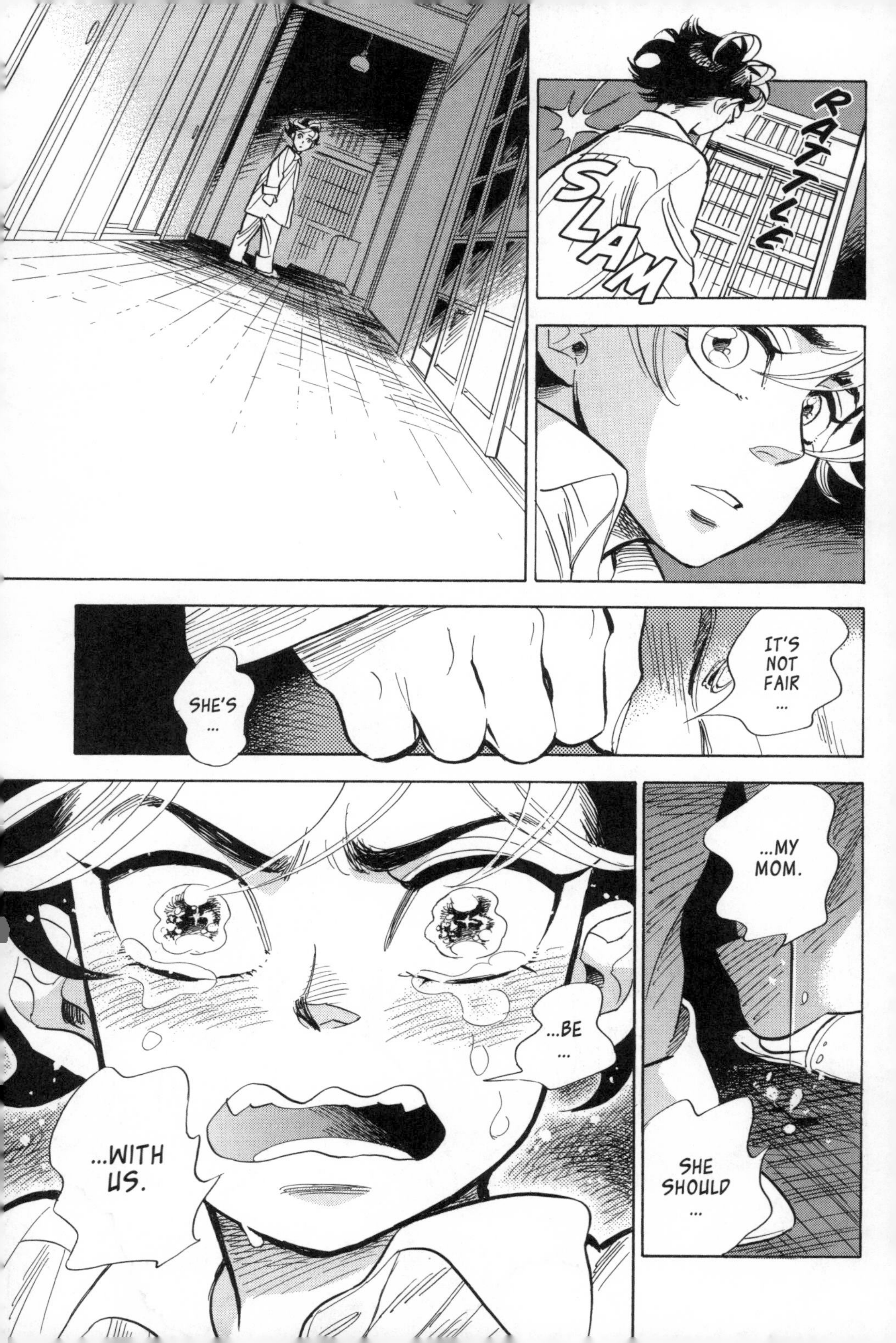
RATTLE
SLAM
IT'S NOT FAIR ...
SHE'S ...
...MY MOM.
SHE SHOULD ...
...BE ...
...WITH US.

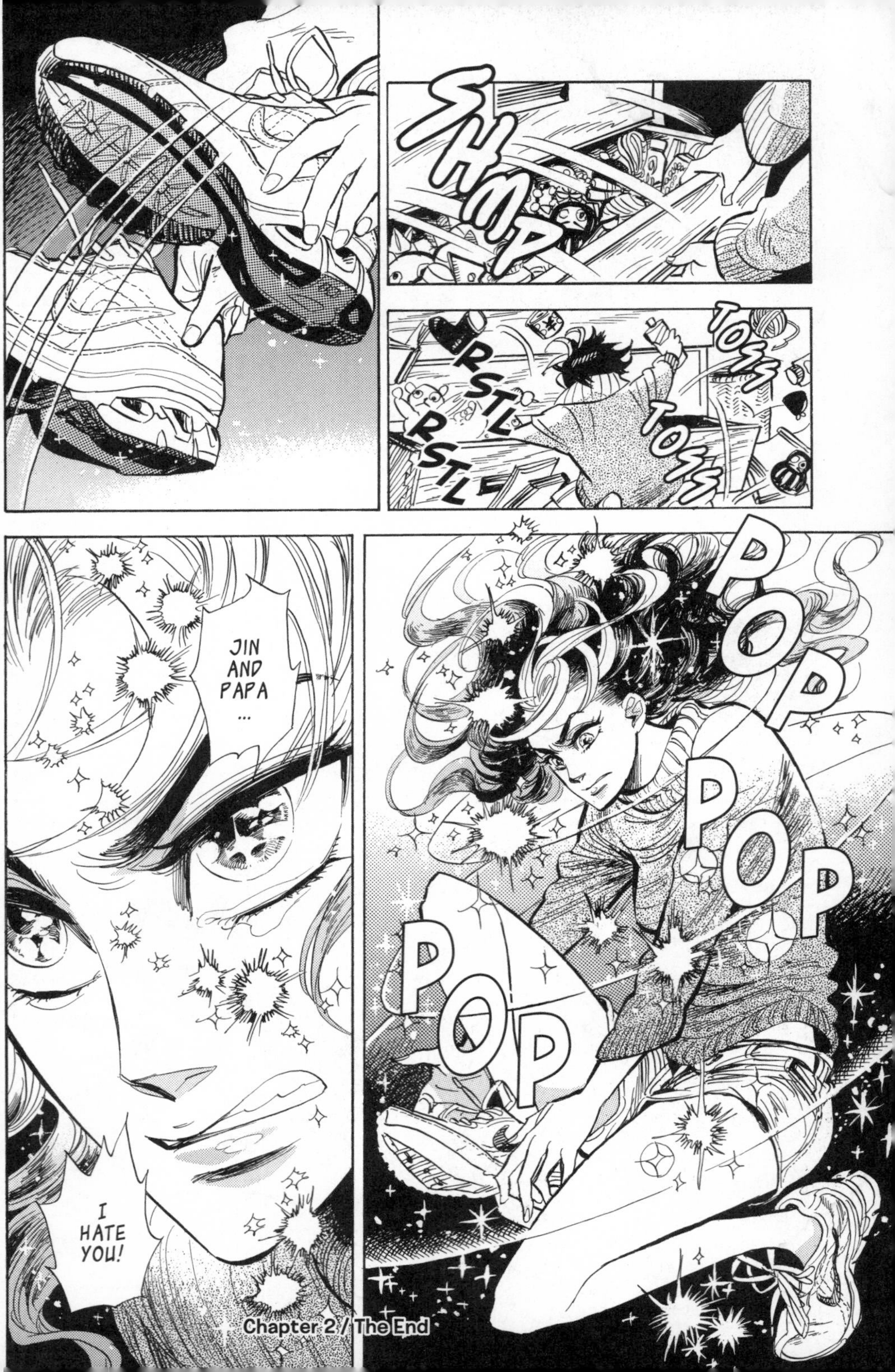
SHMP
TOSS
TOSS
RSTL
RSTL
POP
POP
POP
POP
JIN AND PAPA ...
I HATE YOU!

Chapter 2 / The End

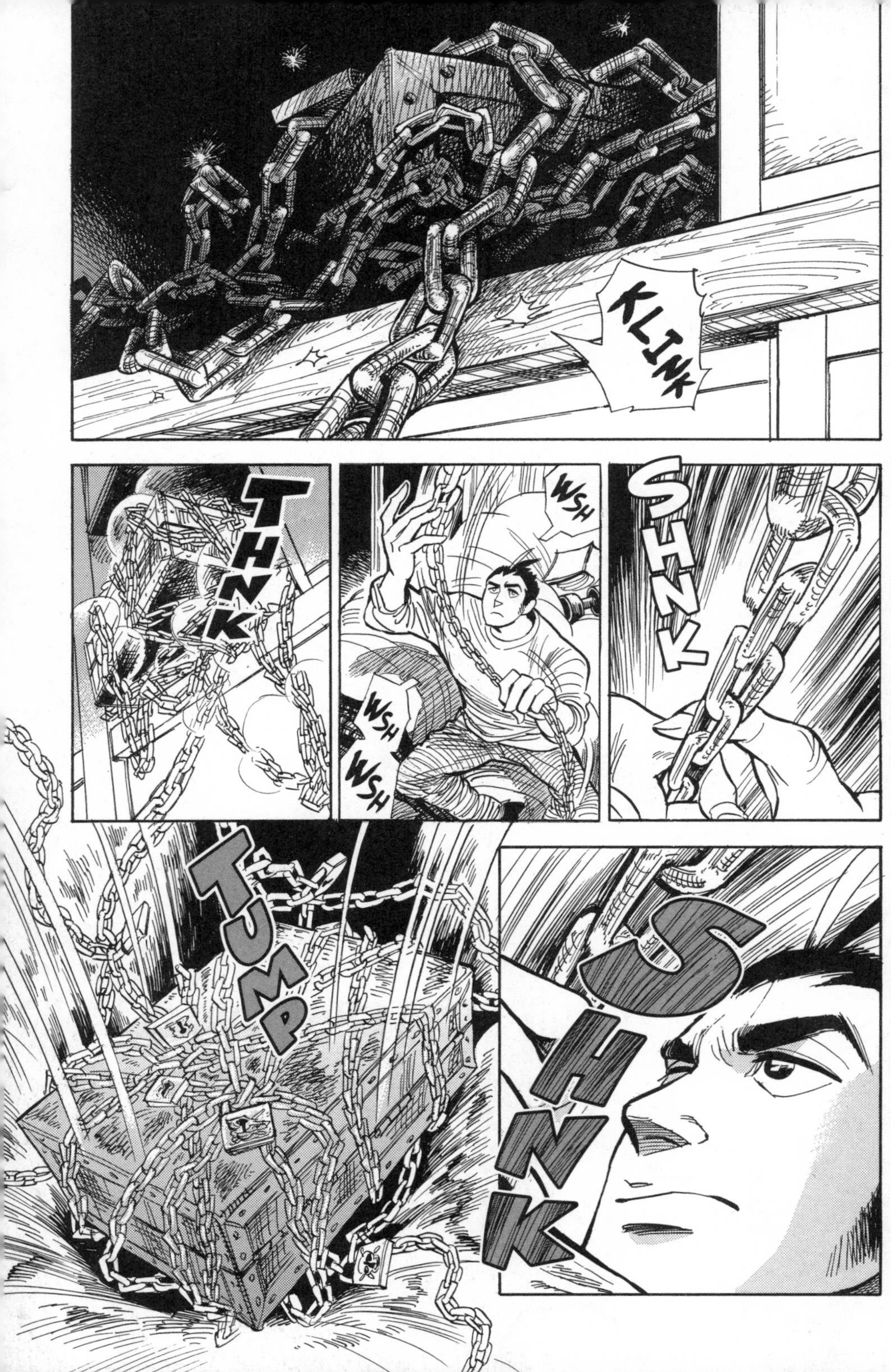
KLINK
SHNK
WSH
WSH
WSH
THNK
SHNK
TUMP

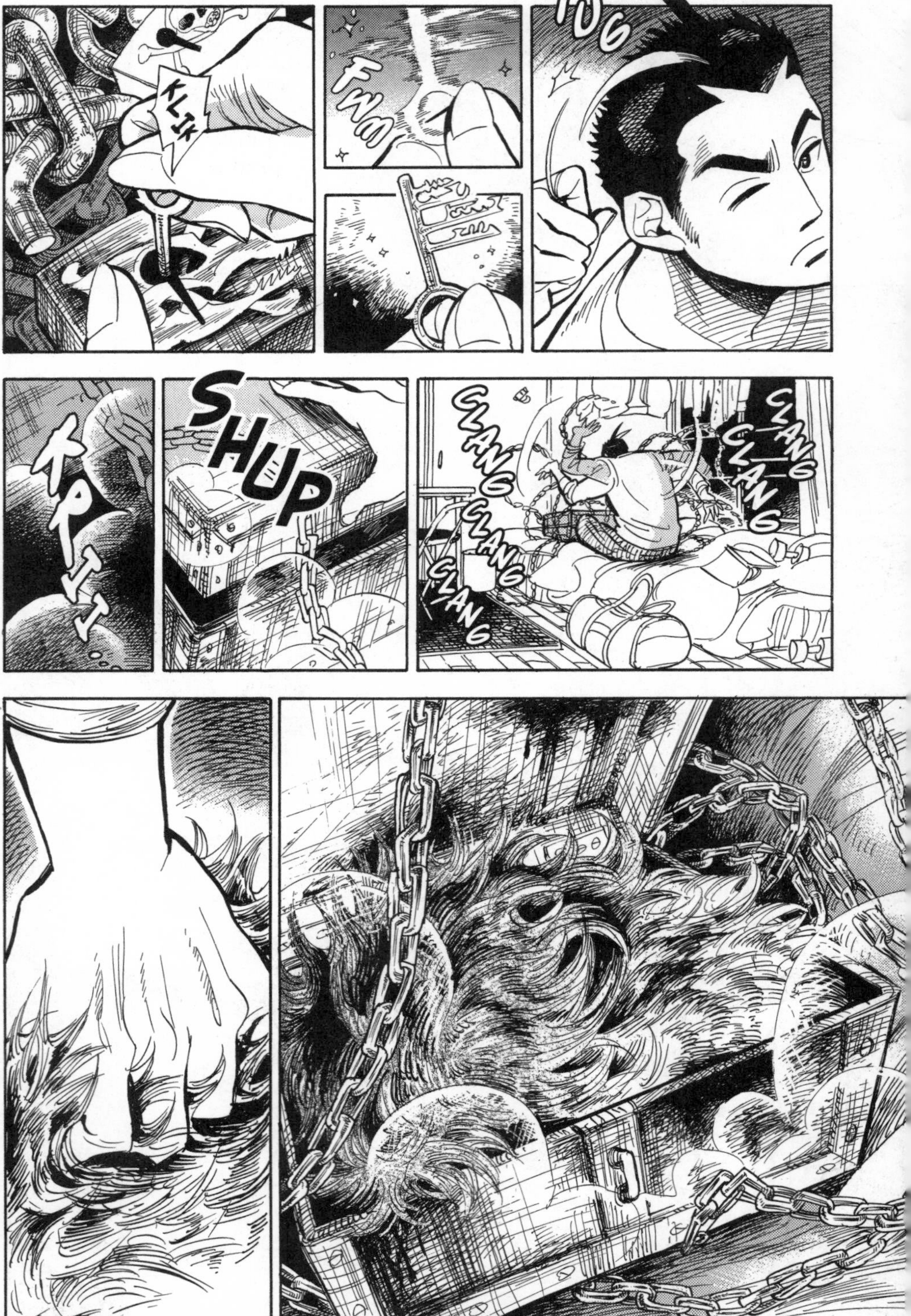
TUG
FWM
KLIK
CLANG
CLANG
CLANG
CLANG
CLANG
CLANG
CLANG
SHUP
KRII

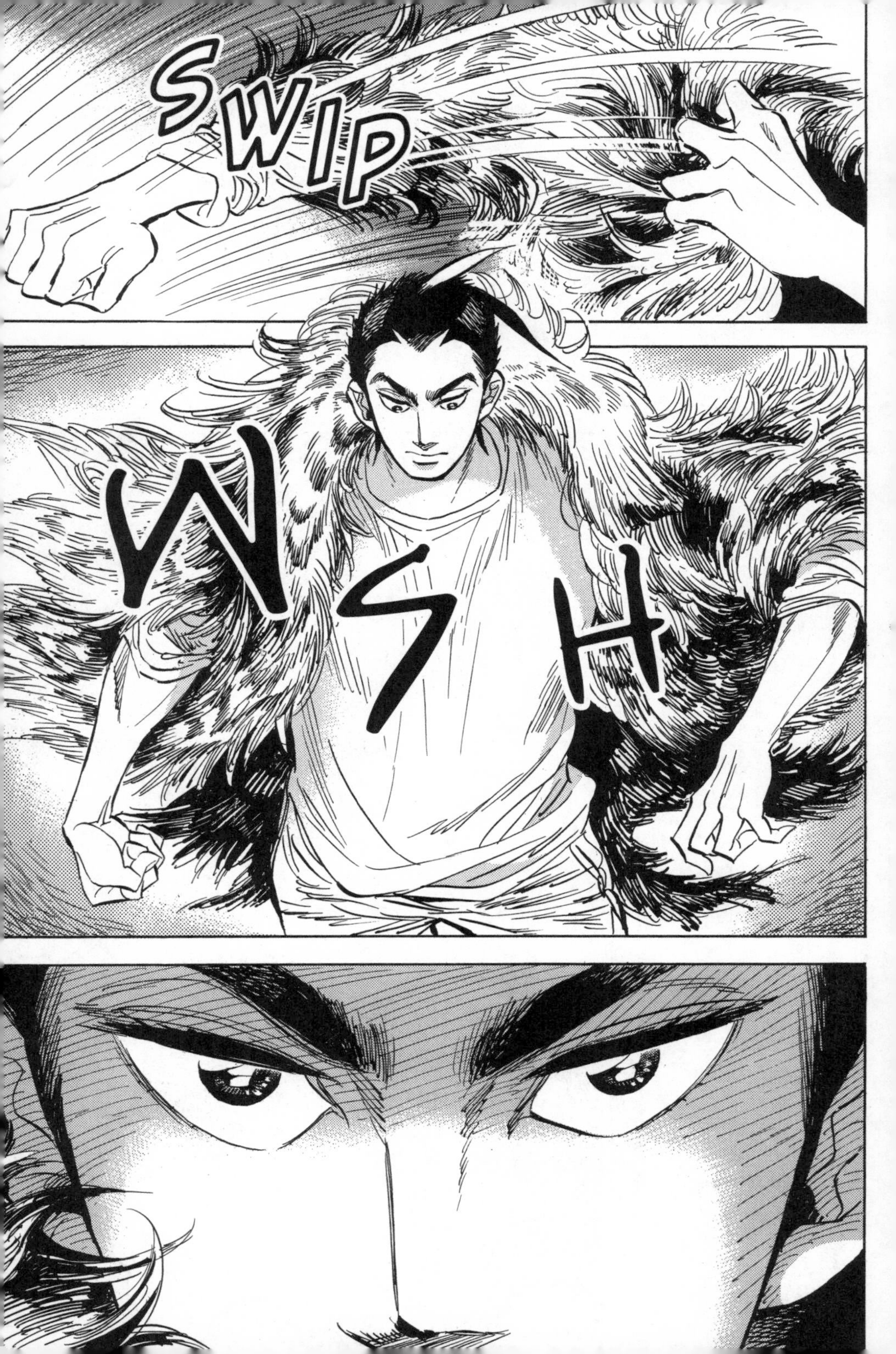
SWIP
WSH

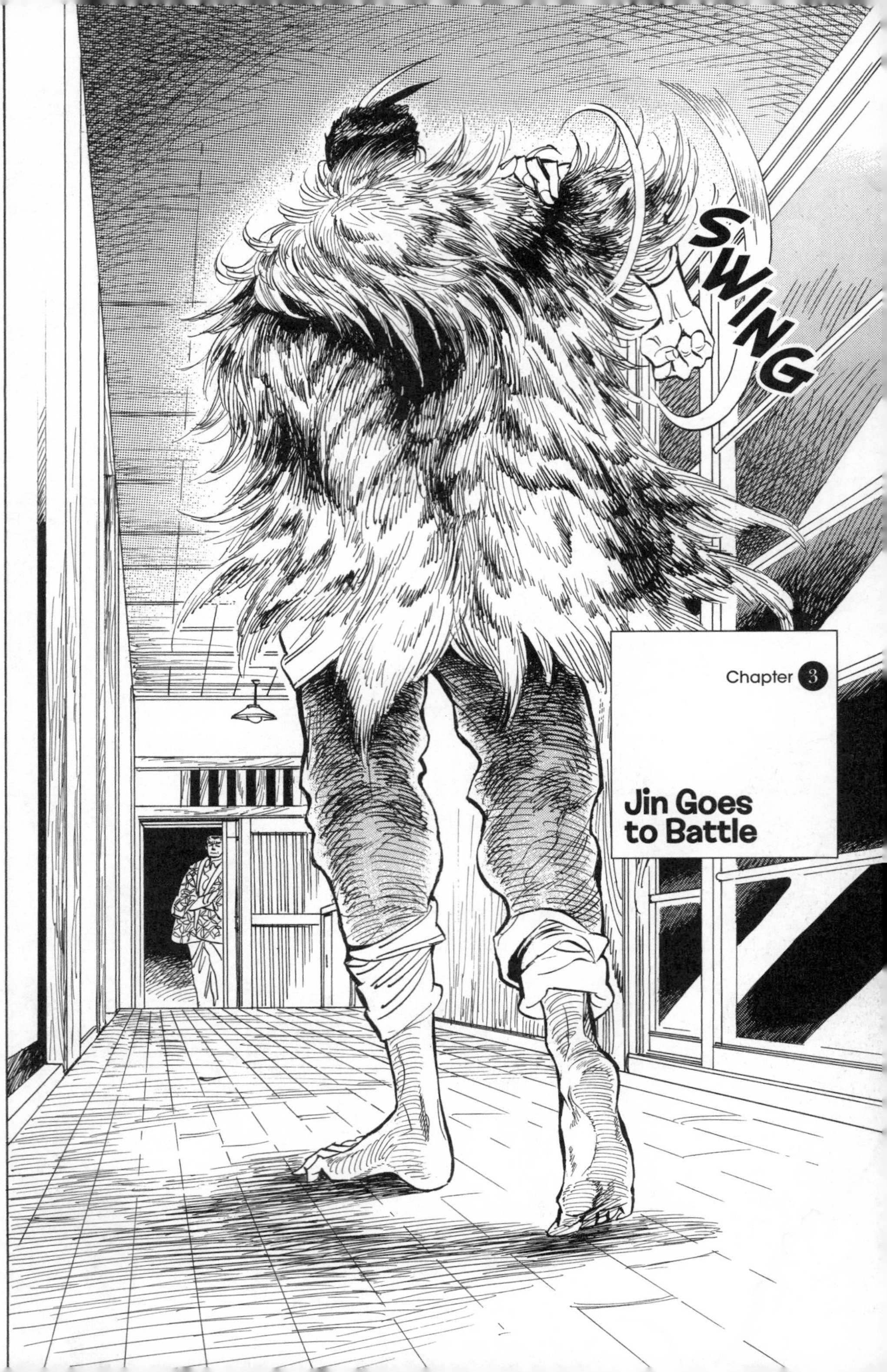
SWING
Chapter 3
Jin Goes to Battle

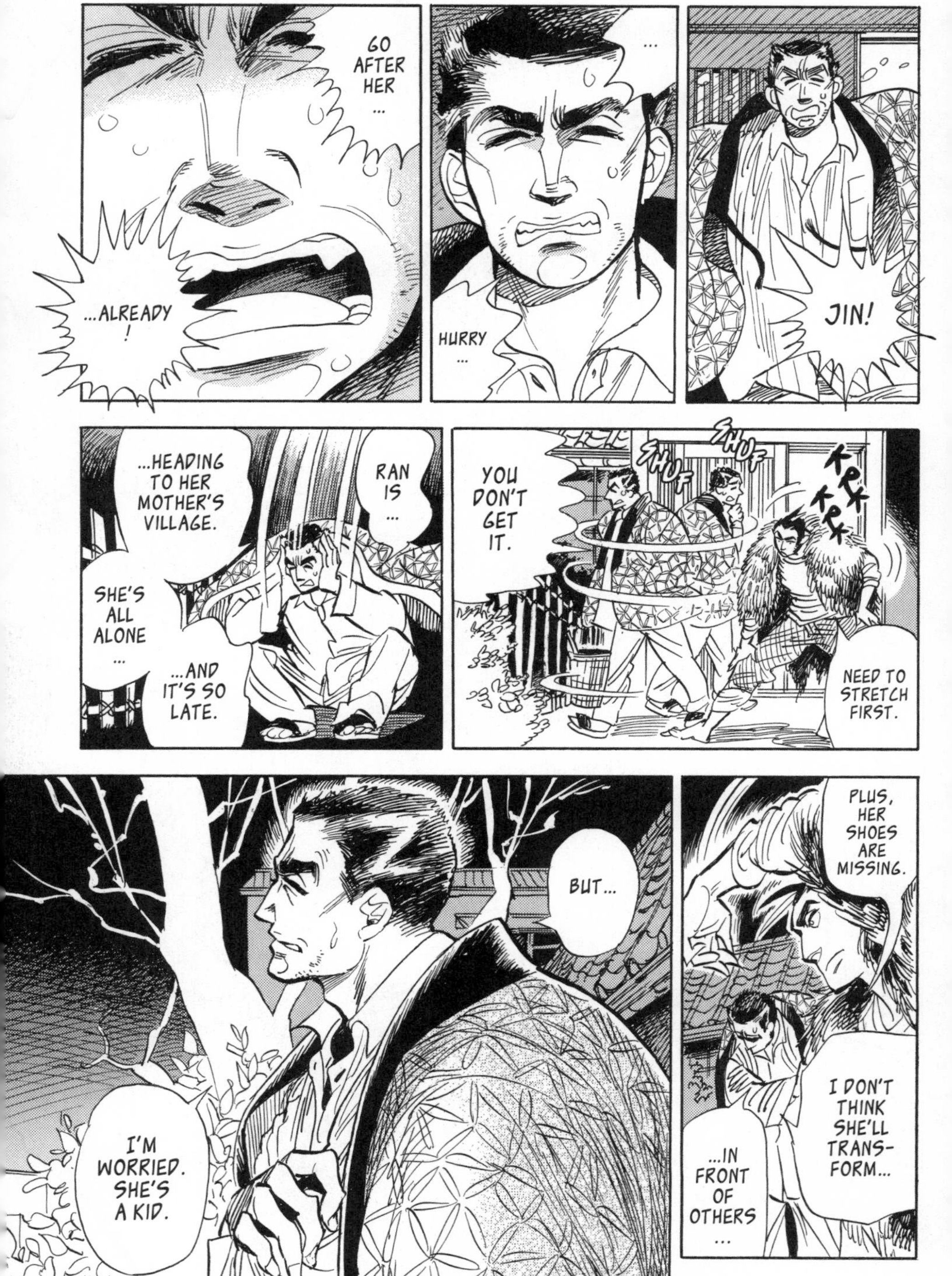
JIN!
...
HURRY ...
GO AFTER HER ...
...ALREADY !
SHUF SHUF
KRK KRK KRK
YOU DON'T GET IT.
NEED TO STRETCH FIRST.
RAN IS ...
...HEADING TO HER MOTHER'S VILLAGE.
SHE'S ALL ALONE ...
...AND IT'S SO LATE.
PLUS, HER SHOES ARE MISSING.
I DON'T THINK SHE'LL TRANS-FORM...
...IN FRONT OF OTHERS ...
BUT...
I'M WORRIED. SHE'S A KID.

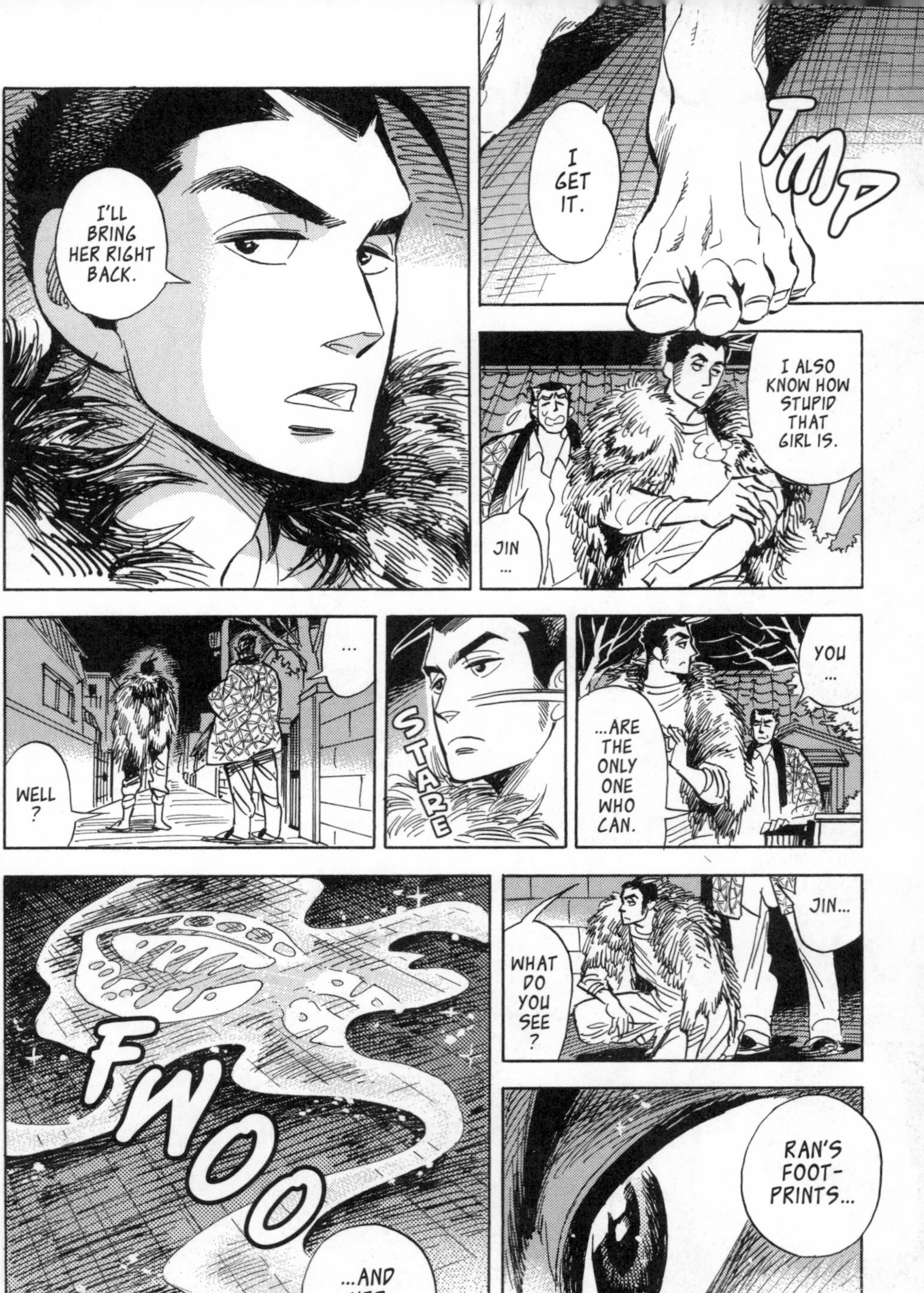
TMP
I GET IT.
I ALSO KNOW HOW STUPID THAT GIRL IS.
JIN ...
I'LL BRING HER RIGHT BACK.
YOU ...
...ARE THE ONLY ONE WHO CAN.
STARE
...
WELL ?
JIN...
WHAT DO YOU SEE ?
RAN'S FOOT-PRINTS...
FWOOO
...AND HER SCENT.

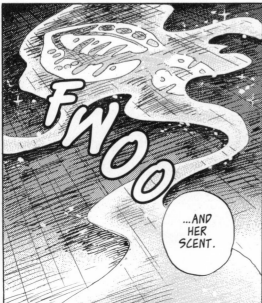

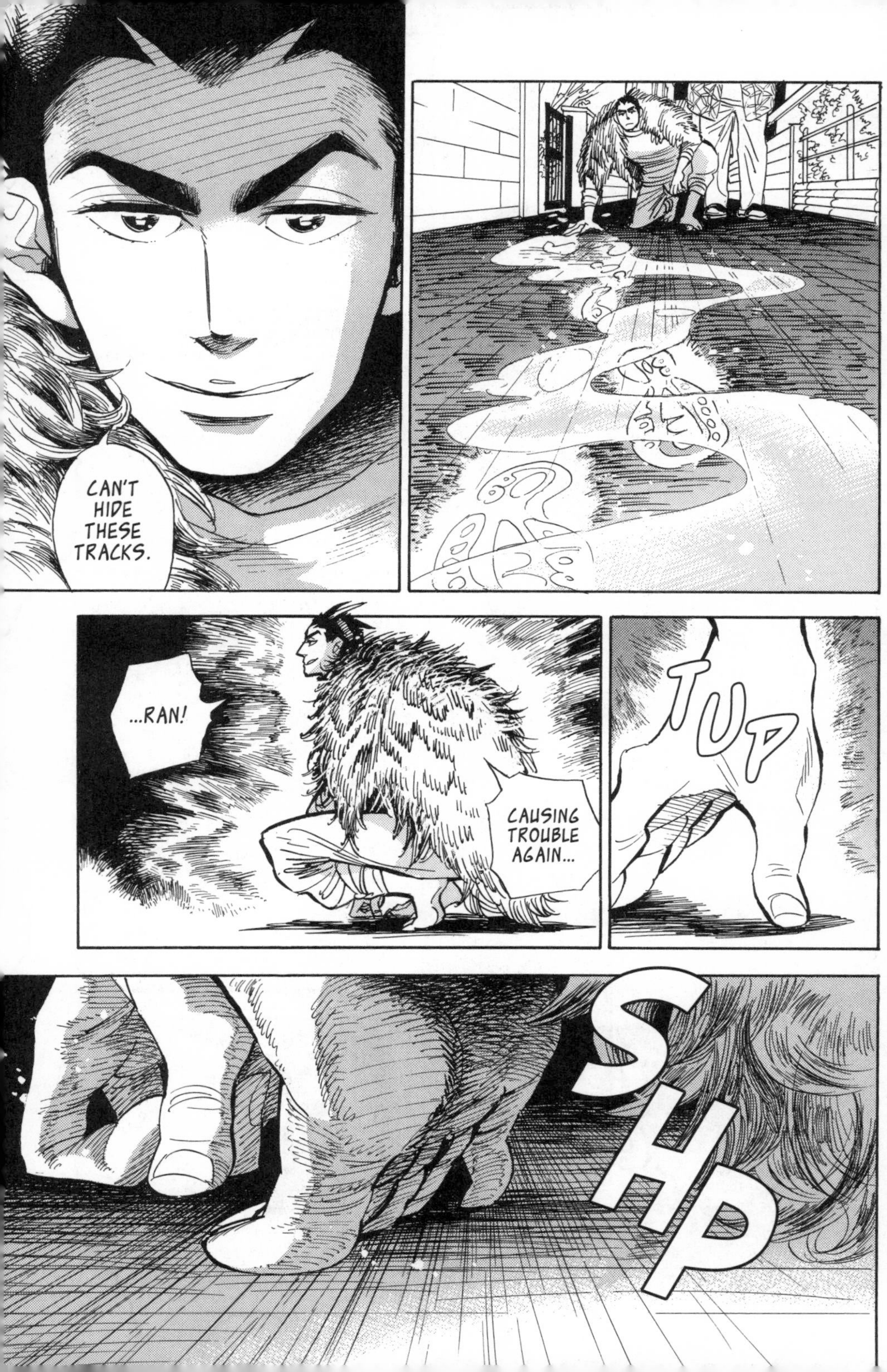
CAN'T HIDE THESE TRACKS.
TUP
CAUSING TROUBLE AGAIN...
...RAN!
SHP

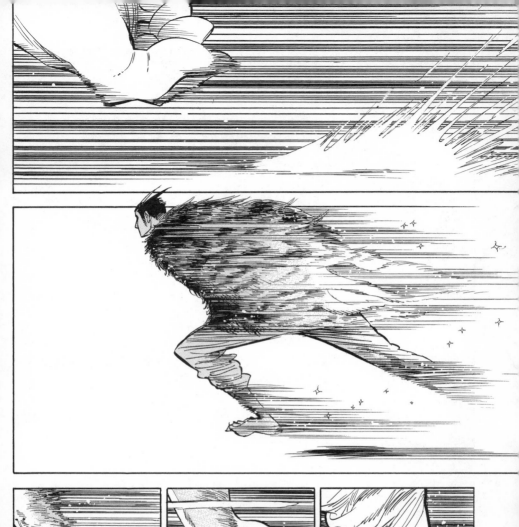

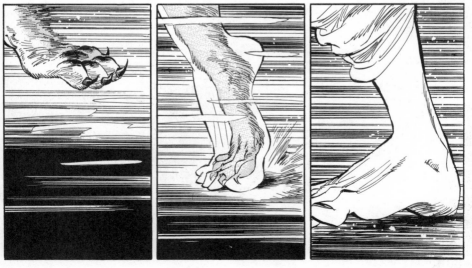

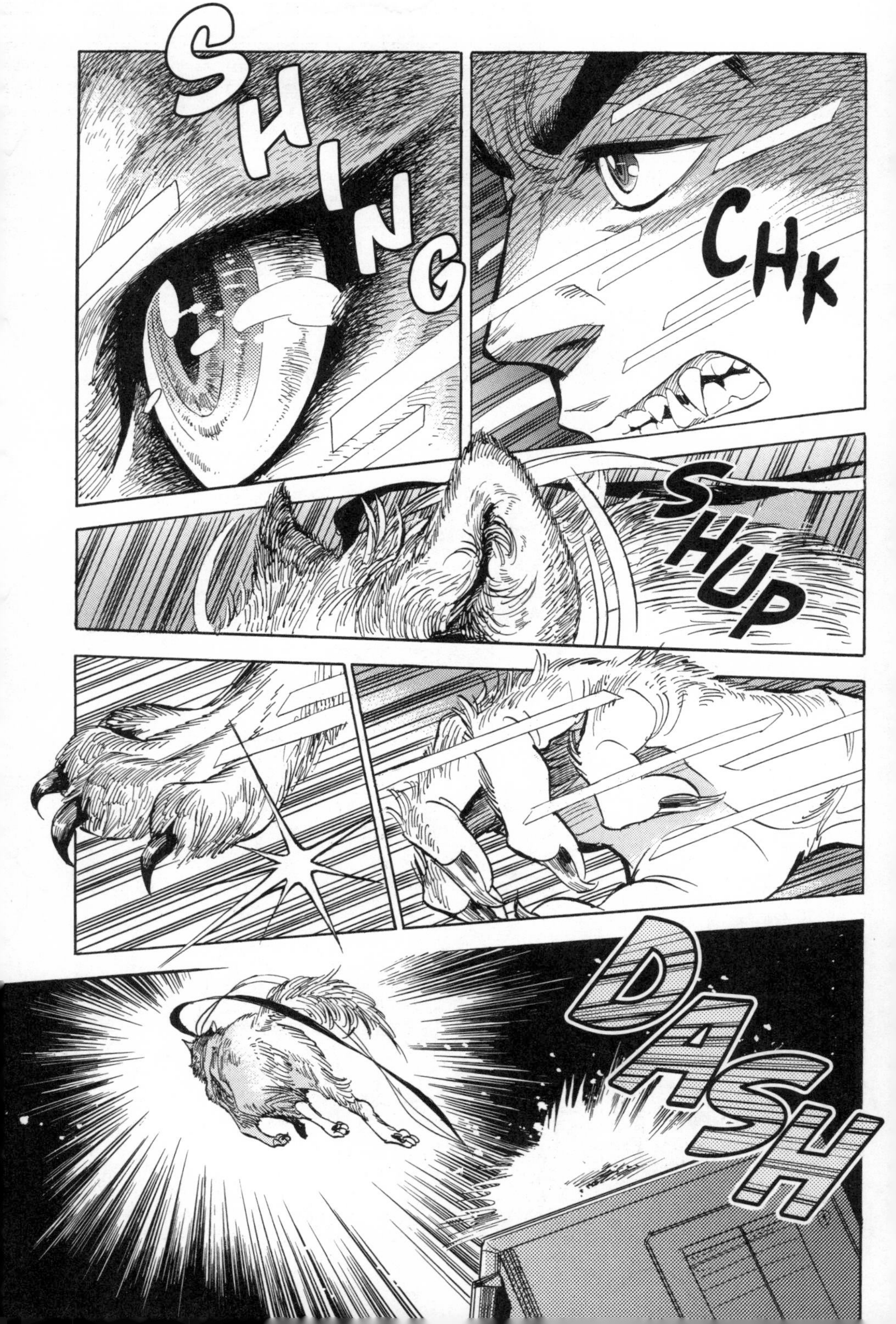
CHK
SHING
SHUP
DASH

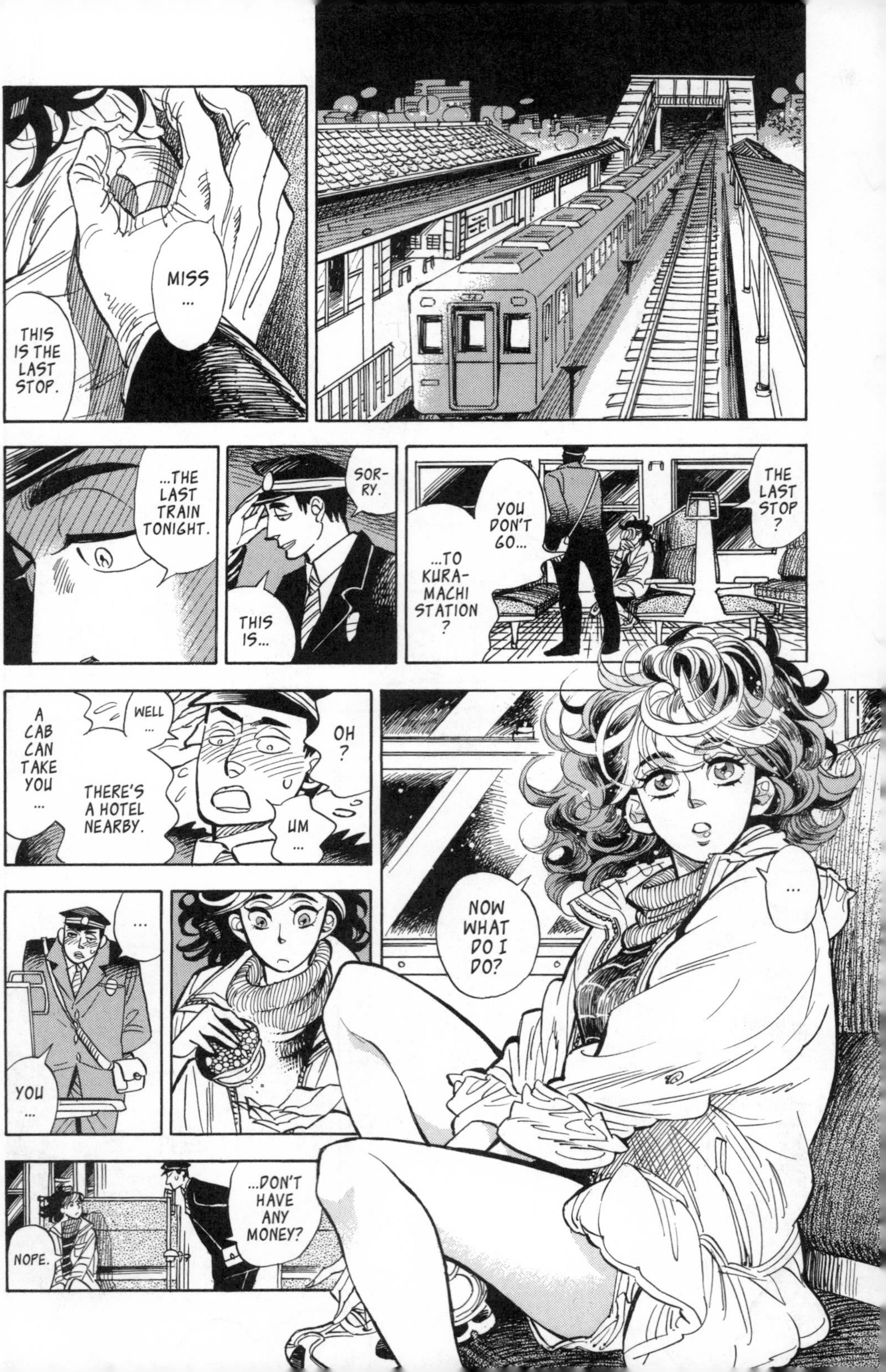
MISS ...
THIS IS THE LAST STOP.
THE LAST STOP?
YOU DON'T GO...
...TO KURA-MACHI STATION?
SOR-RY.
THIS IS...
...THE LAST TRAIN TONIGHT.
...
NOW WHAT DO I DO?
OH?
WELL ...
UM ...
A CAB CAN TAKE YOU ...
THERE'S A HOTEL NEARBY.
...
YOU ...
...DON'T HAVE ANY MONEY?
NOPE.

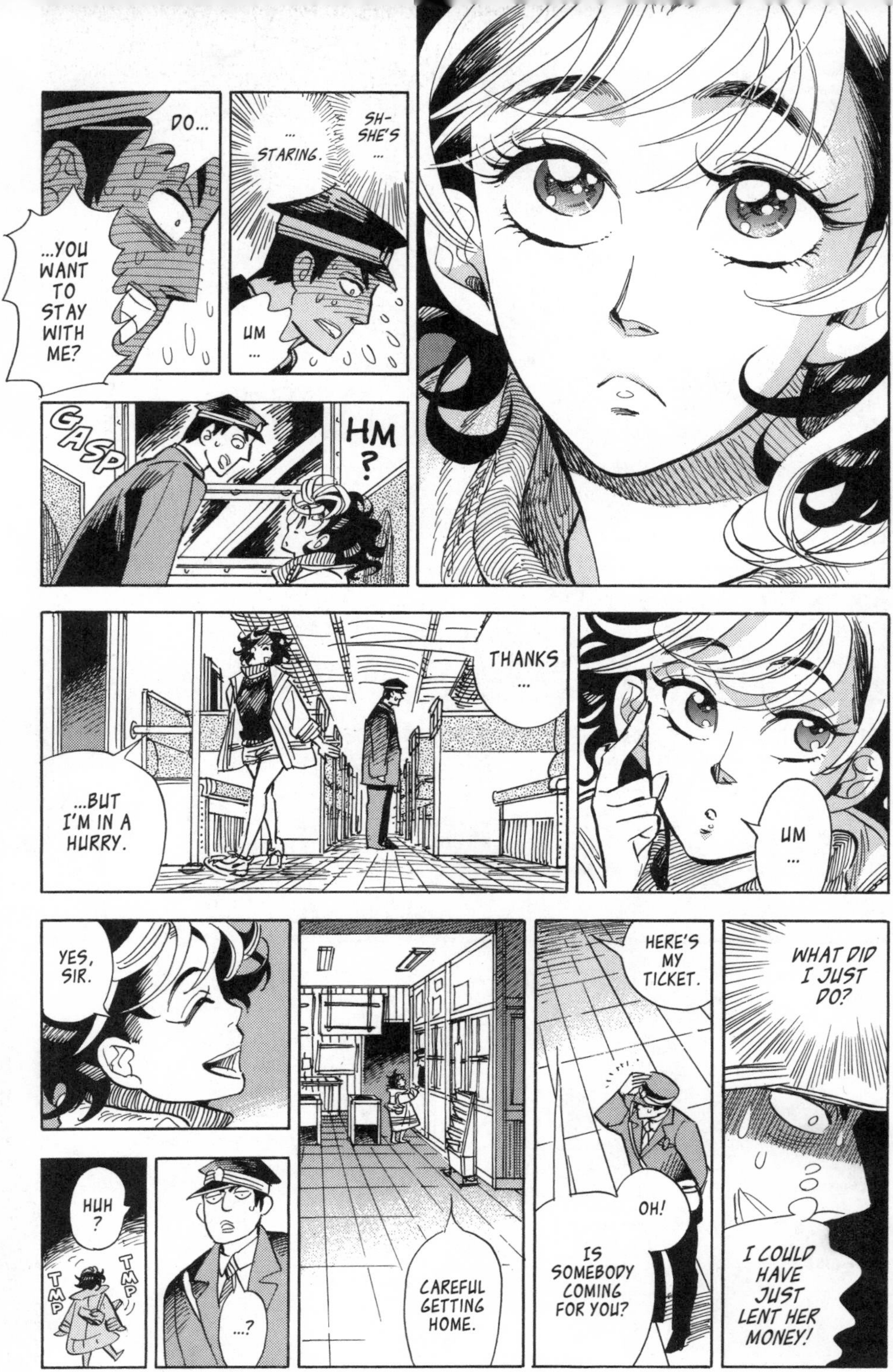
SH-SHE'S ...
... STARING.
UM ...
DO...
...YOU WANT TO STAY WITH ME?
HM ?
GASP
UM ...
THANKS ...
...BUT I'M IN A HURRY.
WHAT DID I JUST DO?
I COULD HAVE JUST LENT HER MONEY!
HERE'S MY TICKET.
OH!
IS SOMEBODY COMING FOR YOU?
CAREFUL GETTING HOME.
YES, SIR.
...?
HUH ?
TMP
TMP

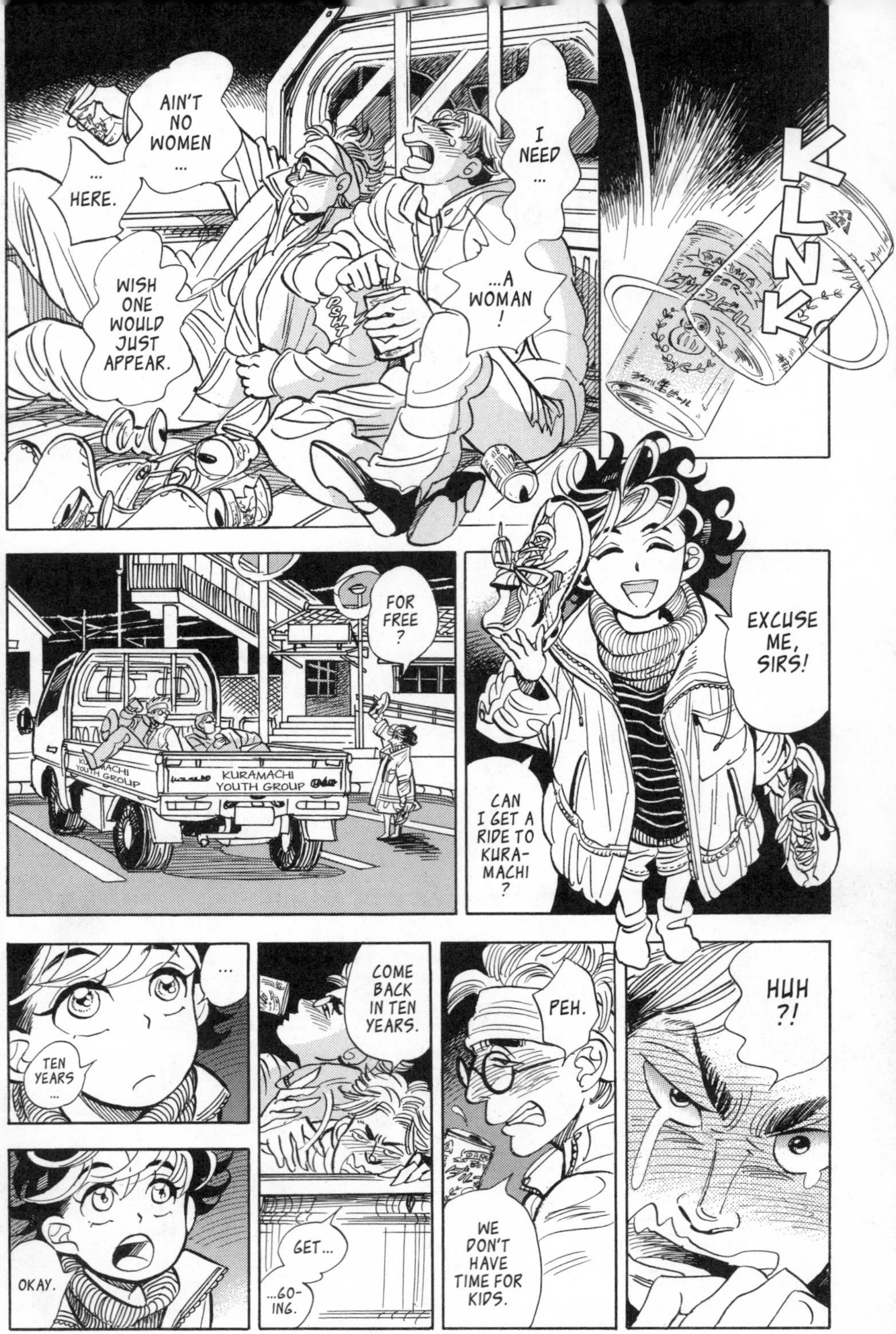

KLNK
I NEED ...
...A WOMAN!
AIN'T NO WOMEN ...
... HERE.
PSHH
WISH ONE WOULD JUST APPEAR.
EXCUSE ME, SIRS!
CAN I GET A RIDE TO KURA-MACHI?
FOR FREE?
KURAMACHI YOUTH GROUP
KURAMACHI YOUTH GROUP
HUH?!
PEH.
WE DON'T HAVE TIME FOR KIDS.
COME BACK IN TEN YEARS.
GET...
...GO-ING.
...
TEN YEARS ...
OKAY.

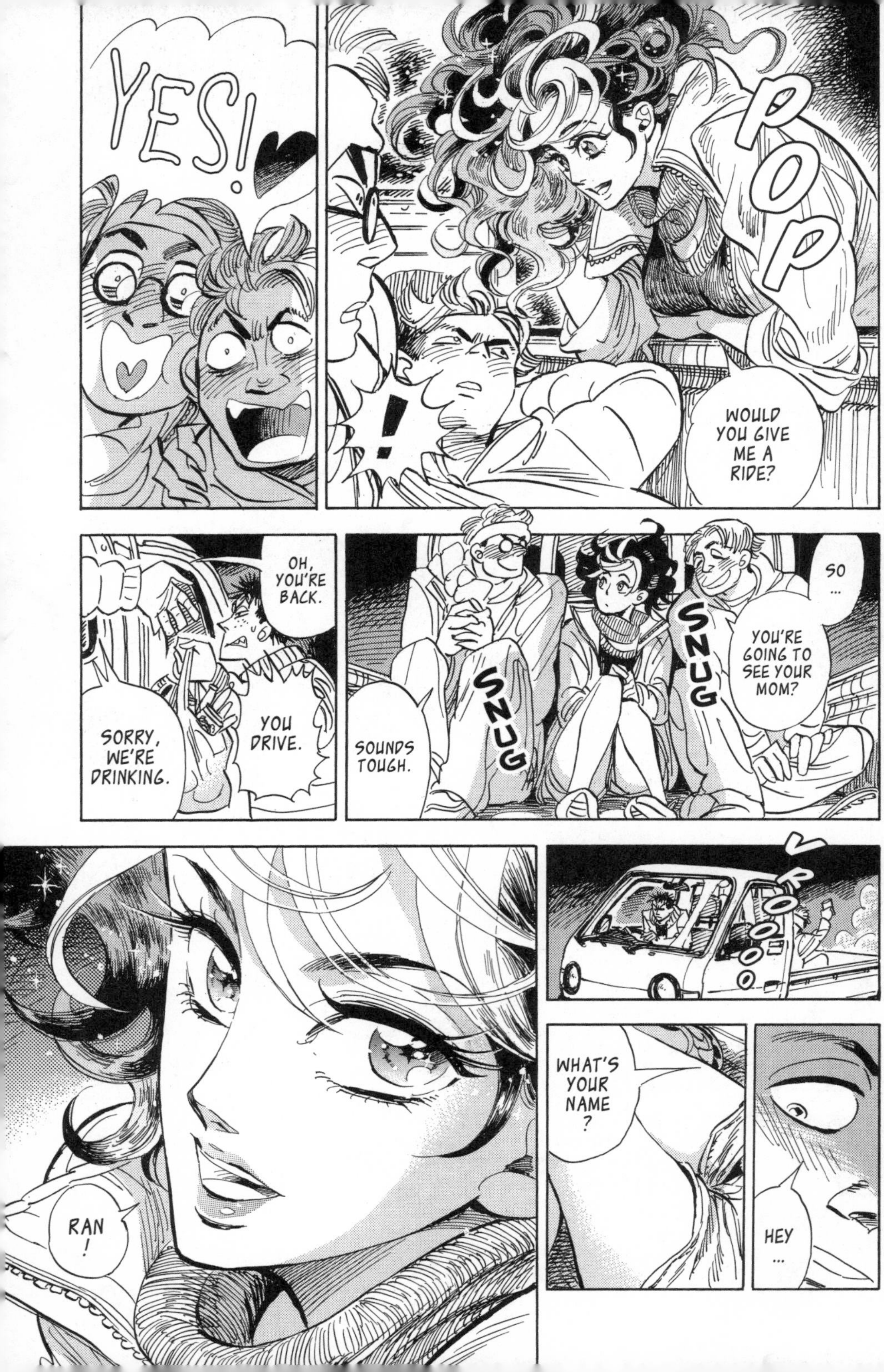
POP
WOULD YOU GIVE ME A RIDE?
!
YES!
SO ...
YOU'RE GOING TO SEE YOUR MOM?
SNUG
SNUG
SOUNDS TOUGH.
OH, YOU'RE BACK.
YOU DRIVE.
SORRY, WE'RE DRINKING.
VROOOOOO
HEY ...
WHAT'S YOUR NAME?
RAN!

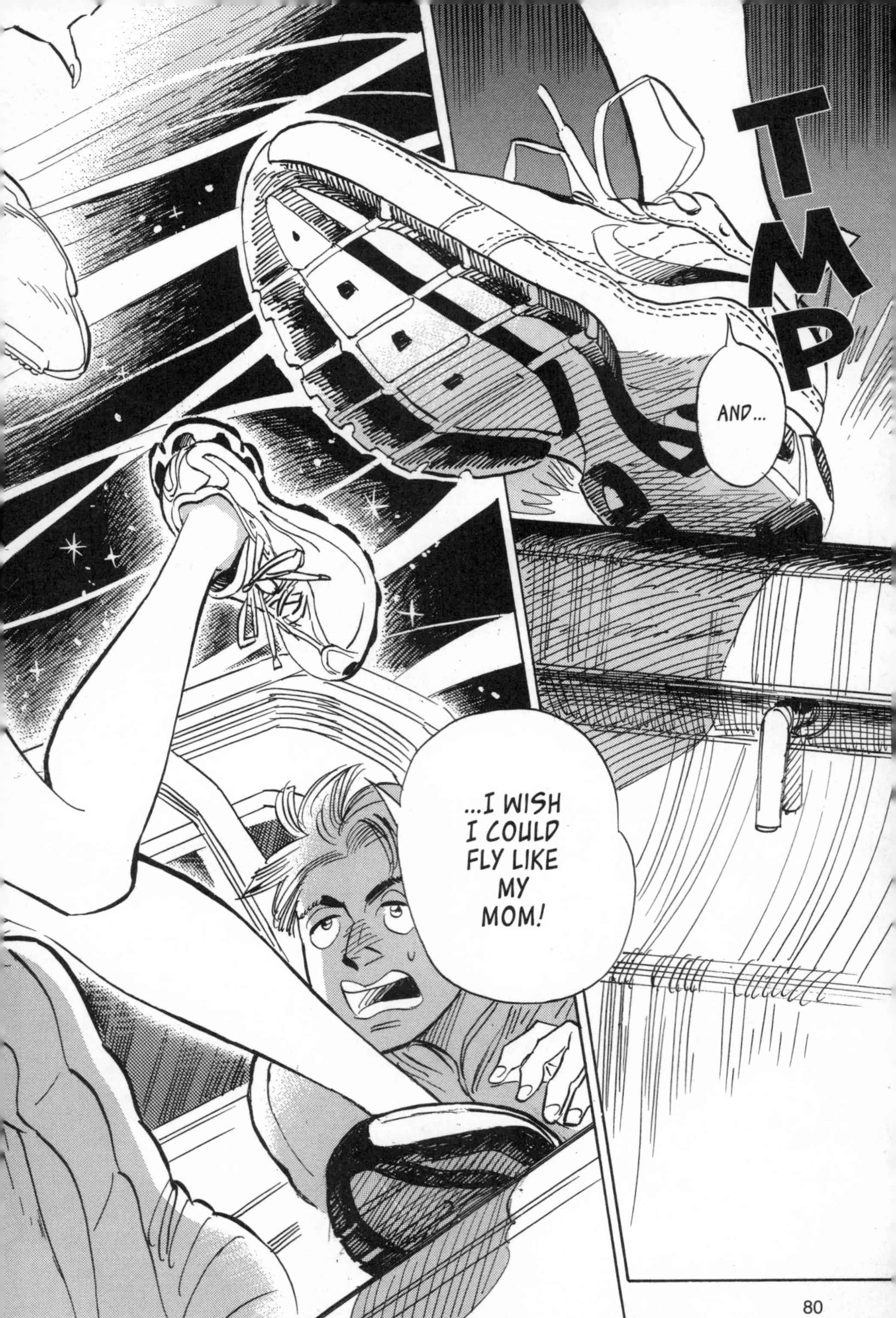
TMP
AND...
...I WISH I COULD FLY LIKE MY MOM!

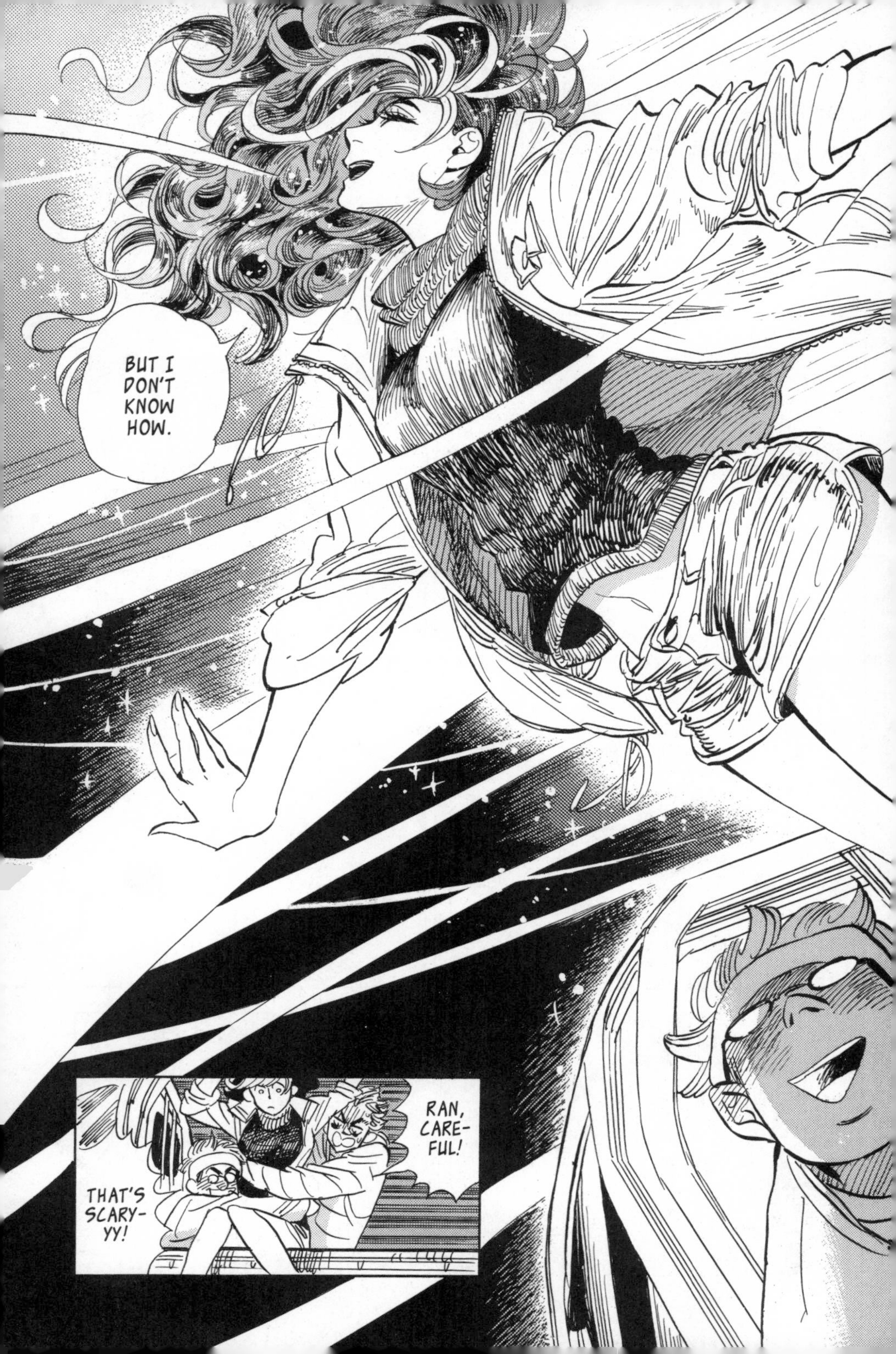
BUT I DON'T KNOW HOW.
RAN, CARE-FUL!
THAT'S SCARY-YY!

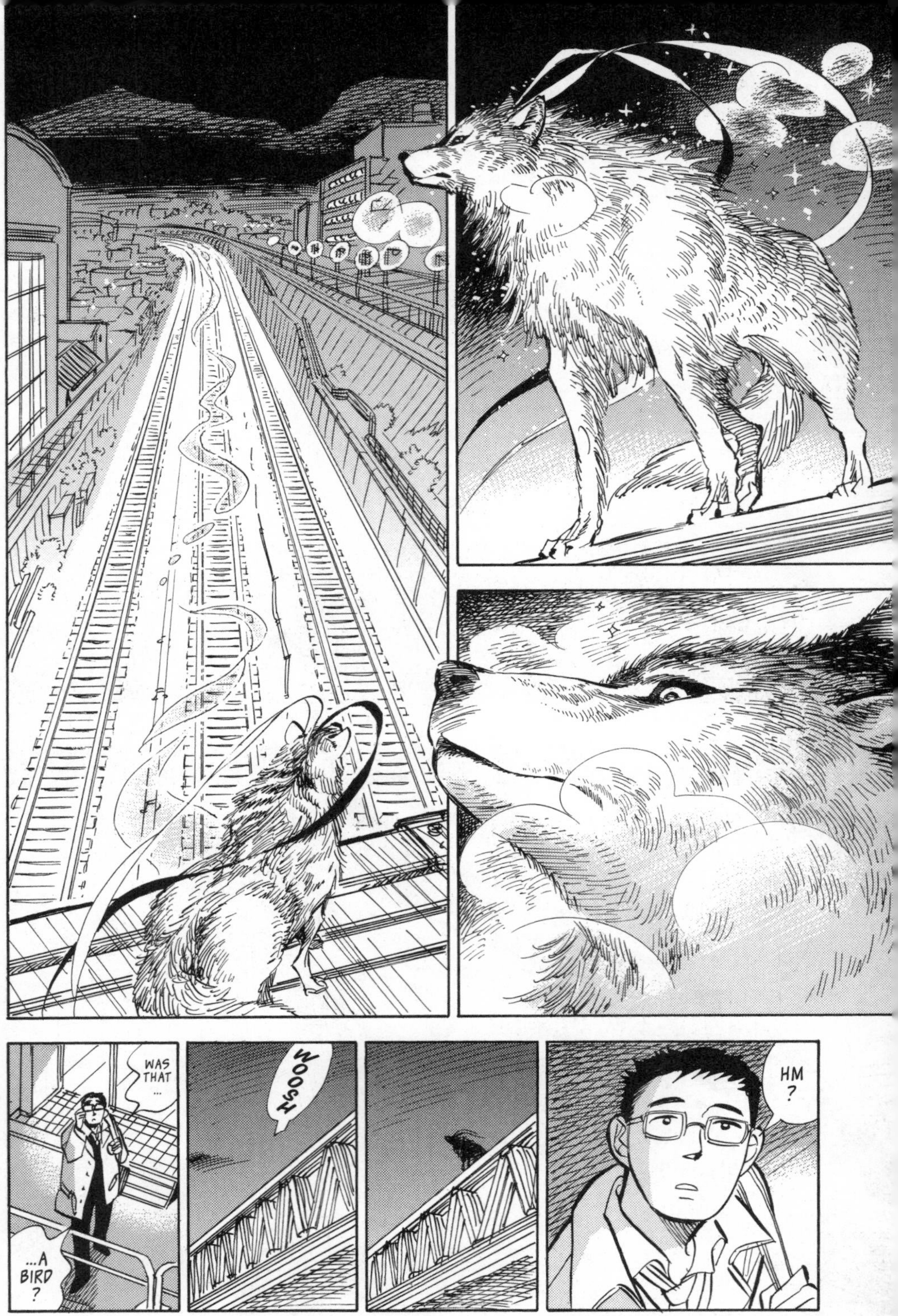
HM ?
WOOSH
WAS THAT ...
...A BIRD ?

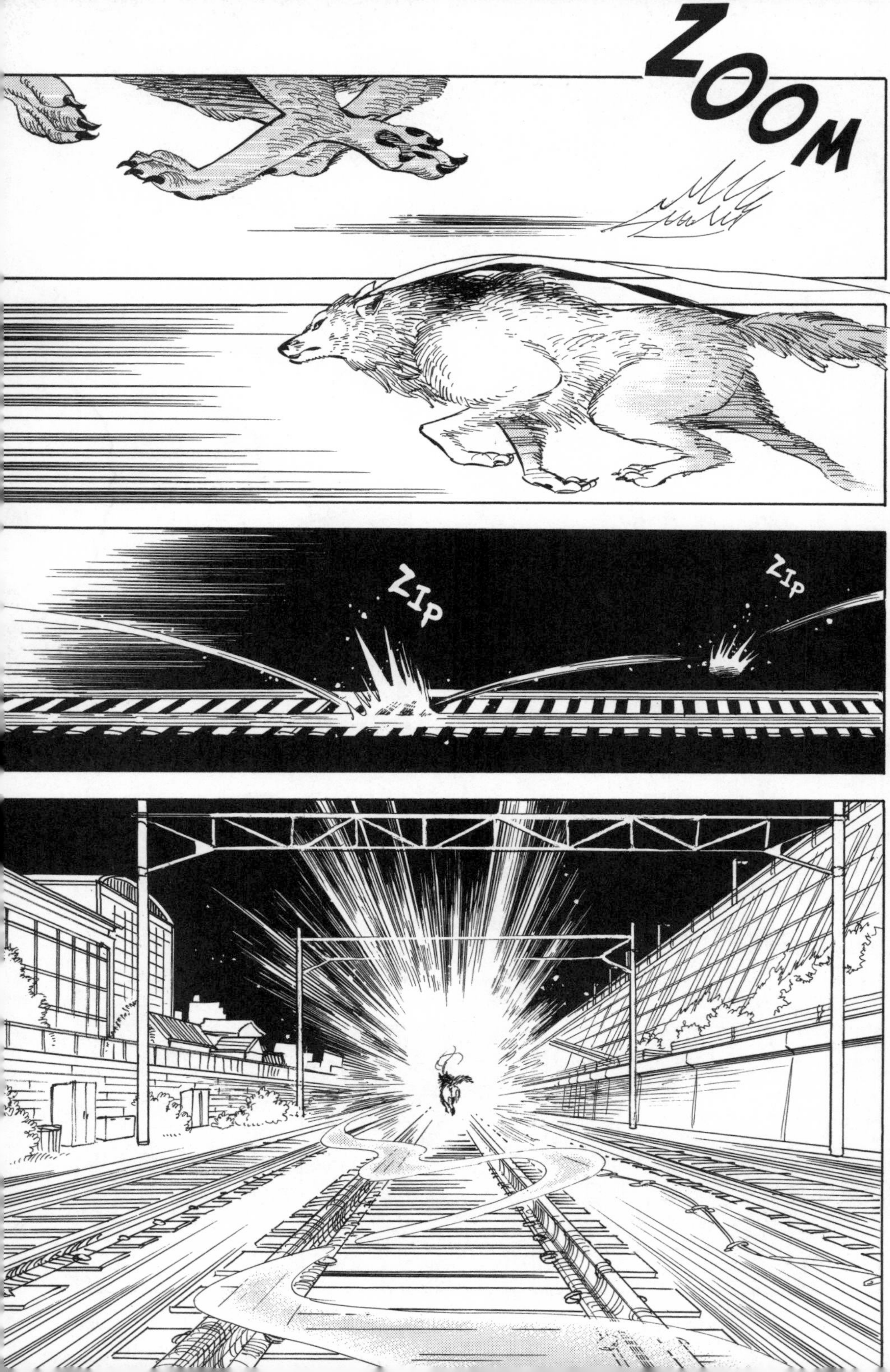
ZOOM
ZIP
ZIP

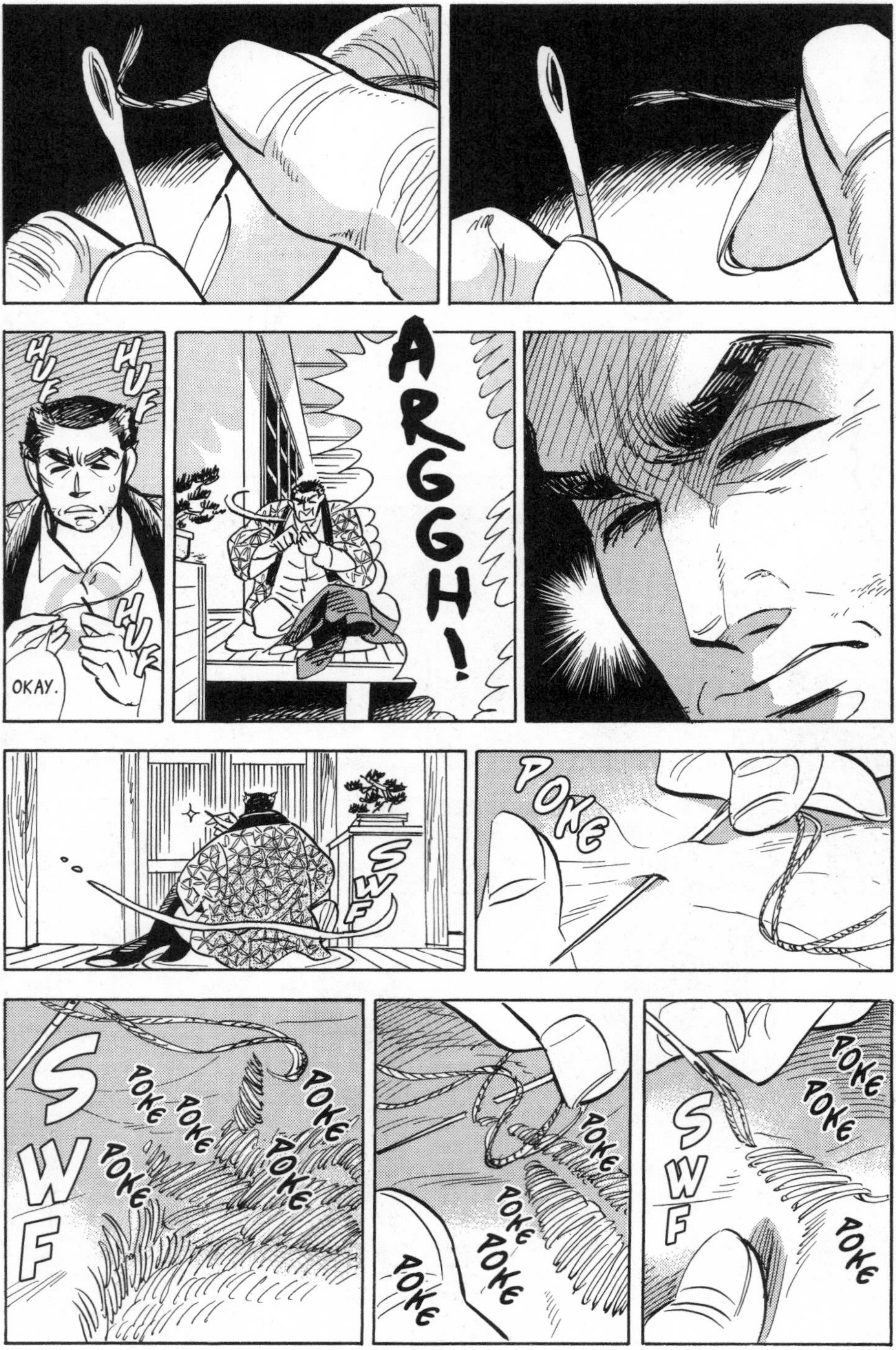
ARGGH!
HUF HUF
HUF HUF
OKAY.
POKE
SWF
POKE POKE
SWF
POKE
POKE
POKE POKE POKE
POKE
SWF
POKE POKE
POKE
POKE POKE
POKE

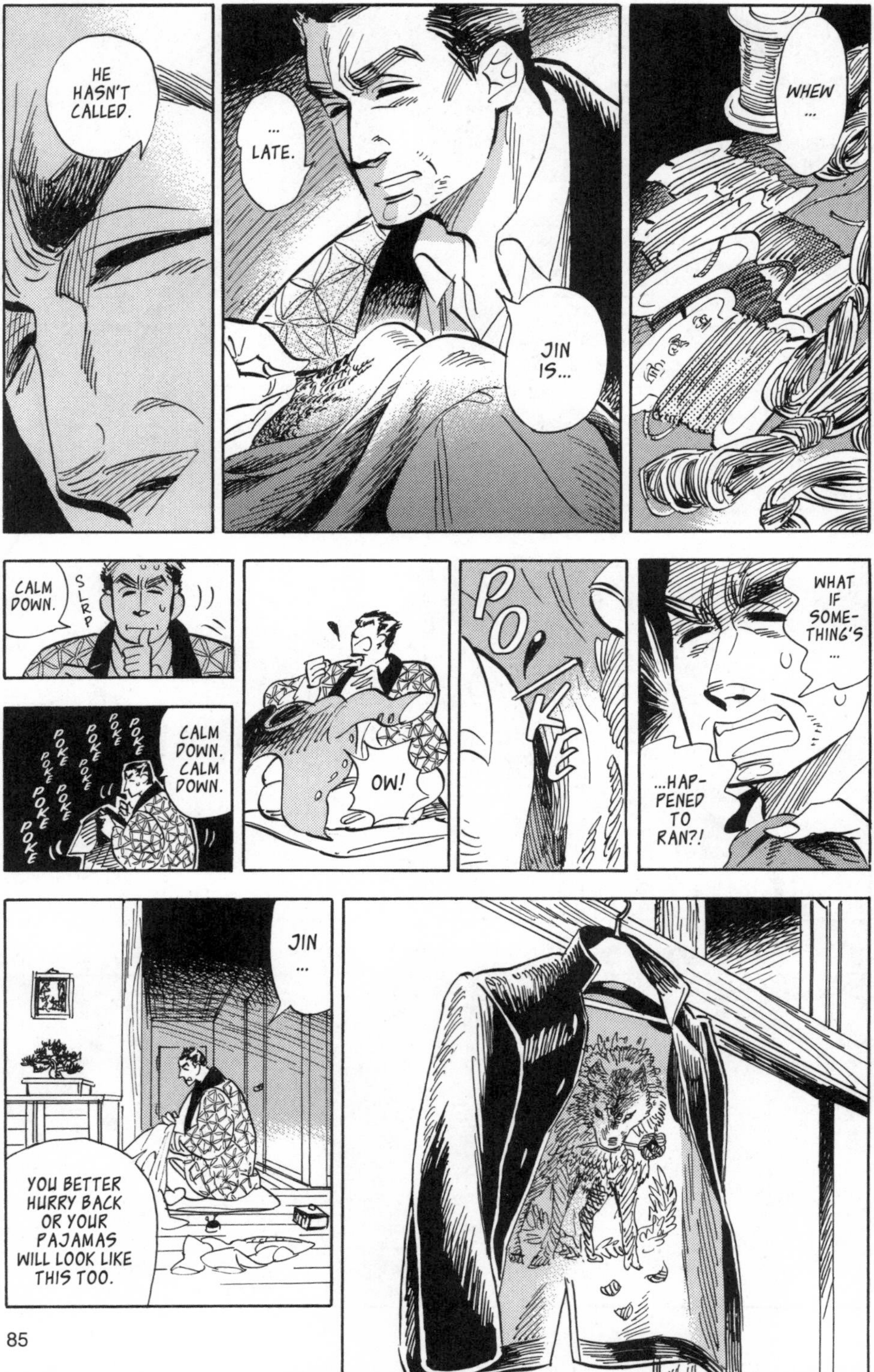
WHEW ...
JIN IS...
... LATE.
HE HASN'T CALLED.
WHAT IF SOMETHING'S ...
...HAPPENED TO RAN?!
POKE
OW!
CALM DOWN.
SLRP
CALM DOWN. CALM DOWN.
POKE POKE POKE POKE POKE POKE POKE POKE POKE
JIN ...
YOU BETTER HURRY BACK OR YOUR PAJAMAS WILL LOOK LIKE THIS TOO.

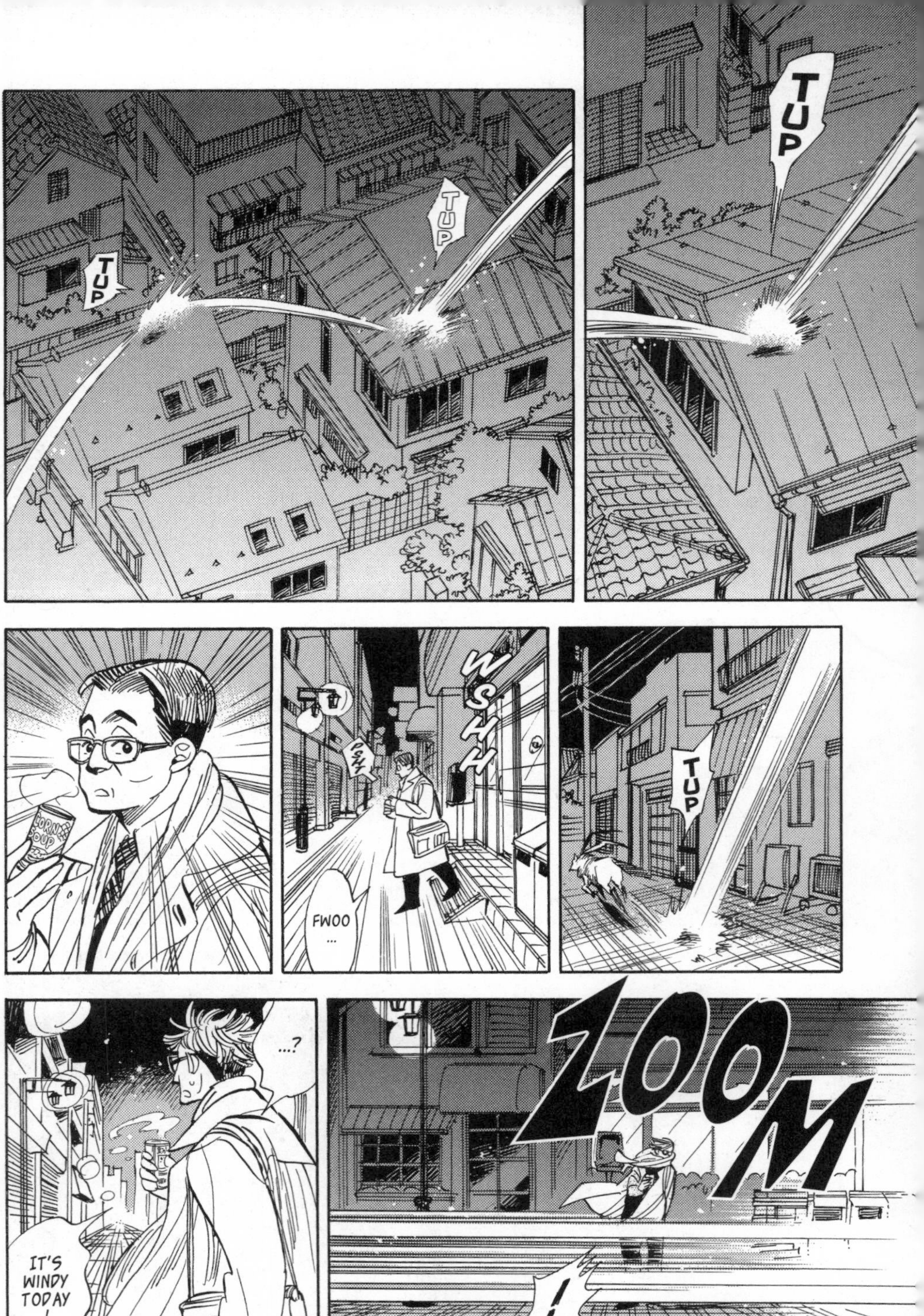
TUP
TUP
TUP
TUP
WSHH
PSHH
FWOO ...
CORN SOUP
ZOOM
!
...?
IT'S WINDY TODAY!

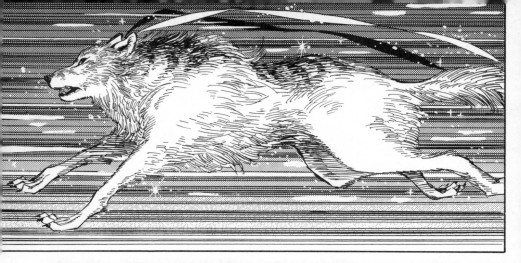

IS IT ABOVE US?

WHAT WAS THAT?

?!

THUD

SO THEN ...

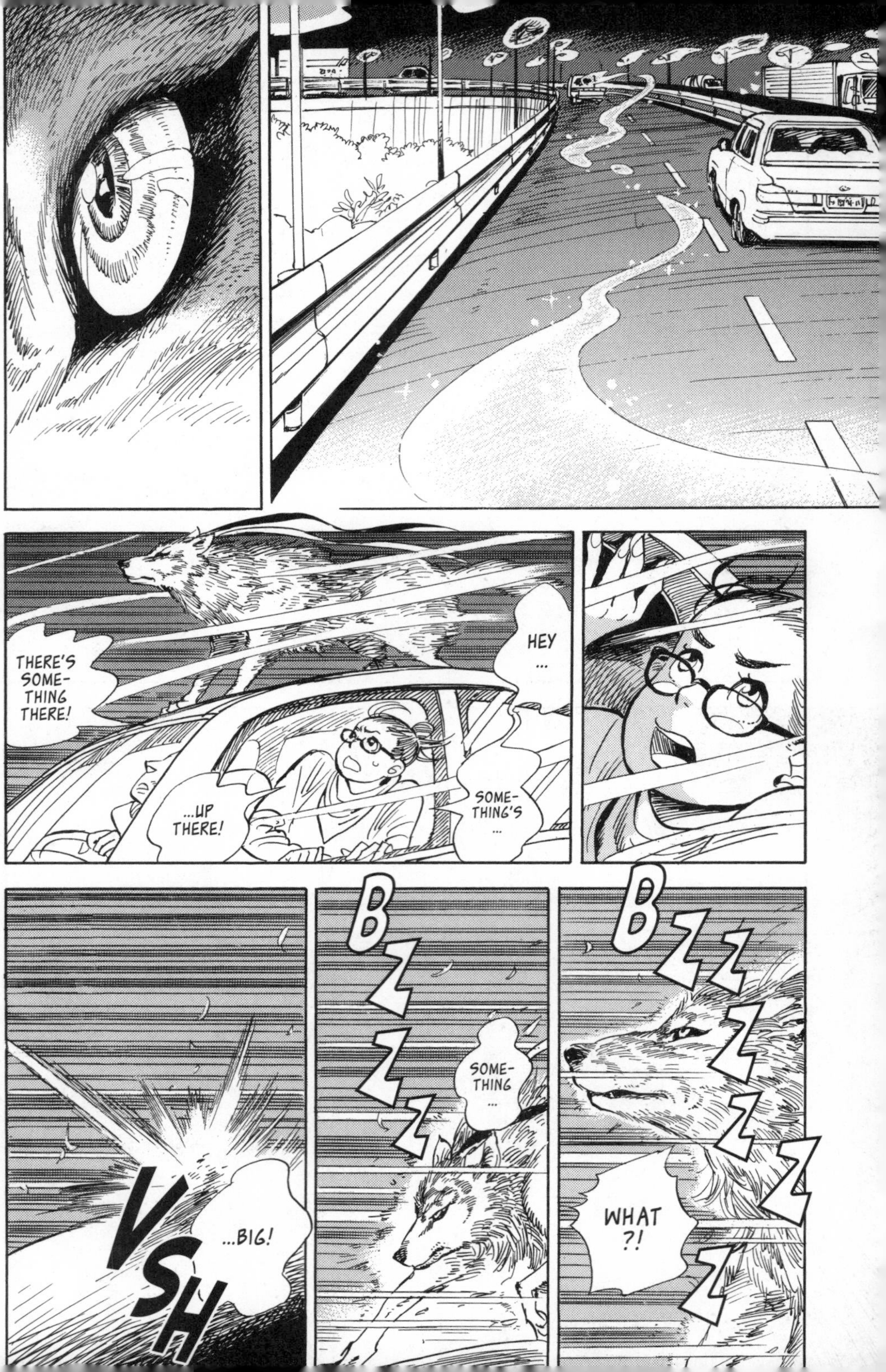
HEY ...
SOME-THING'S ...
...UP THERE!
THERE'S SOME-THING THERE!
BZZZZZZZ
WHAT ?!
BZZZZ
SOME-THING ...
VSH
...BIG!

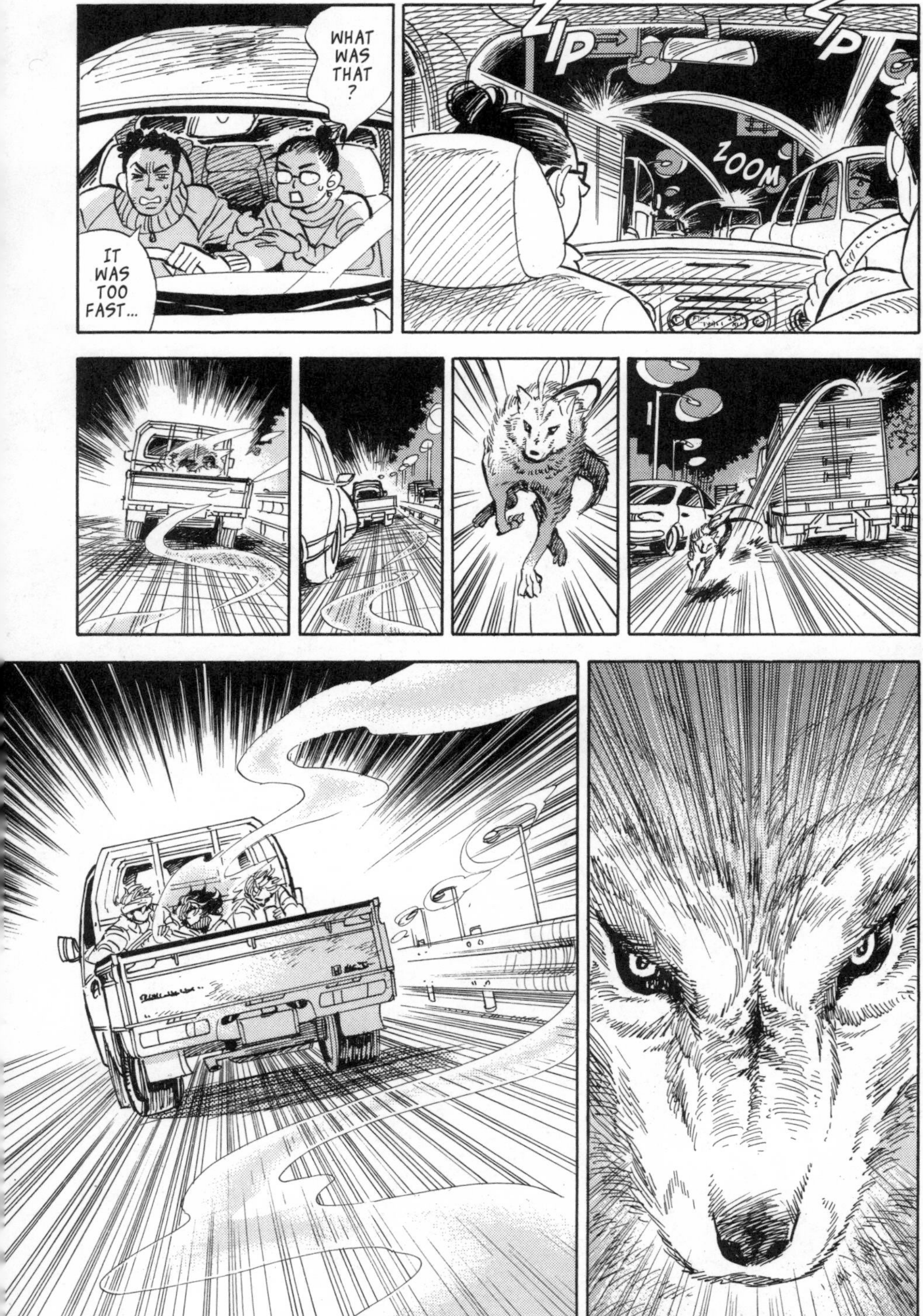
ZIP
ZIP
ZOOM
WHAT WAS THAT?
IT WAS TOO FAST...

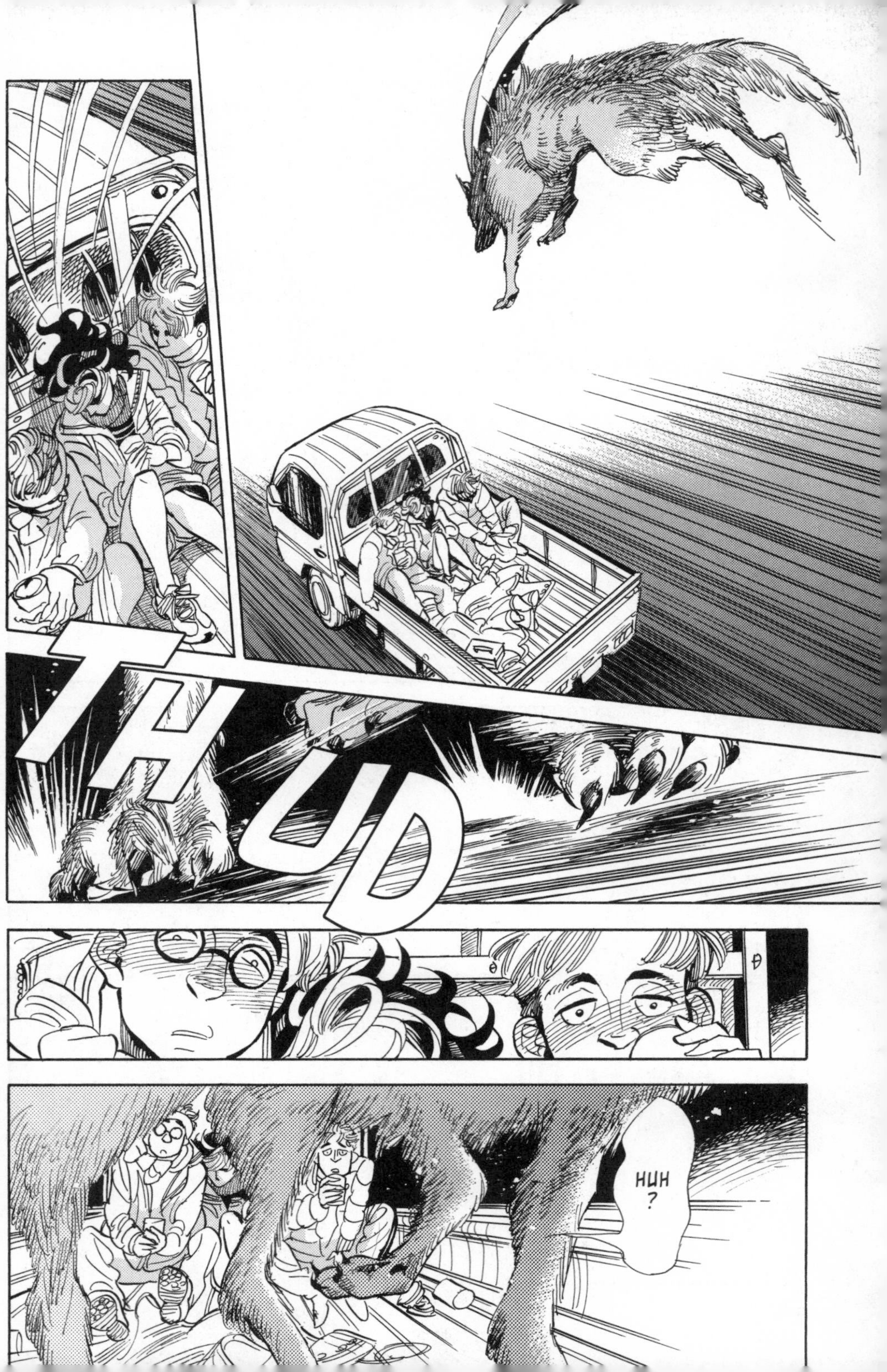
THUD
HUH?

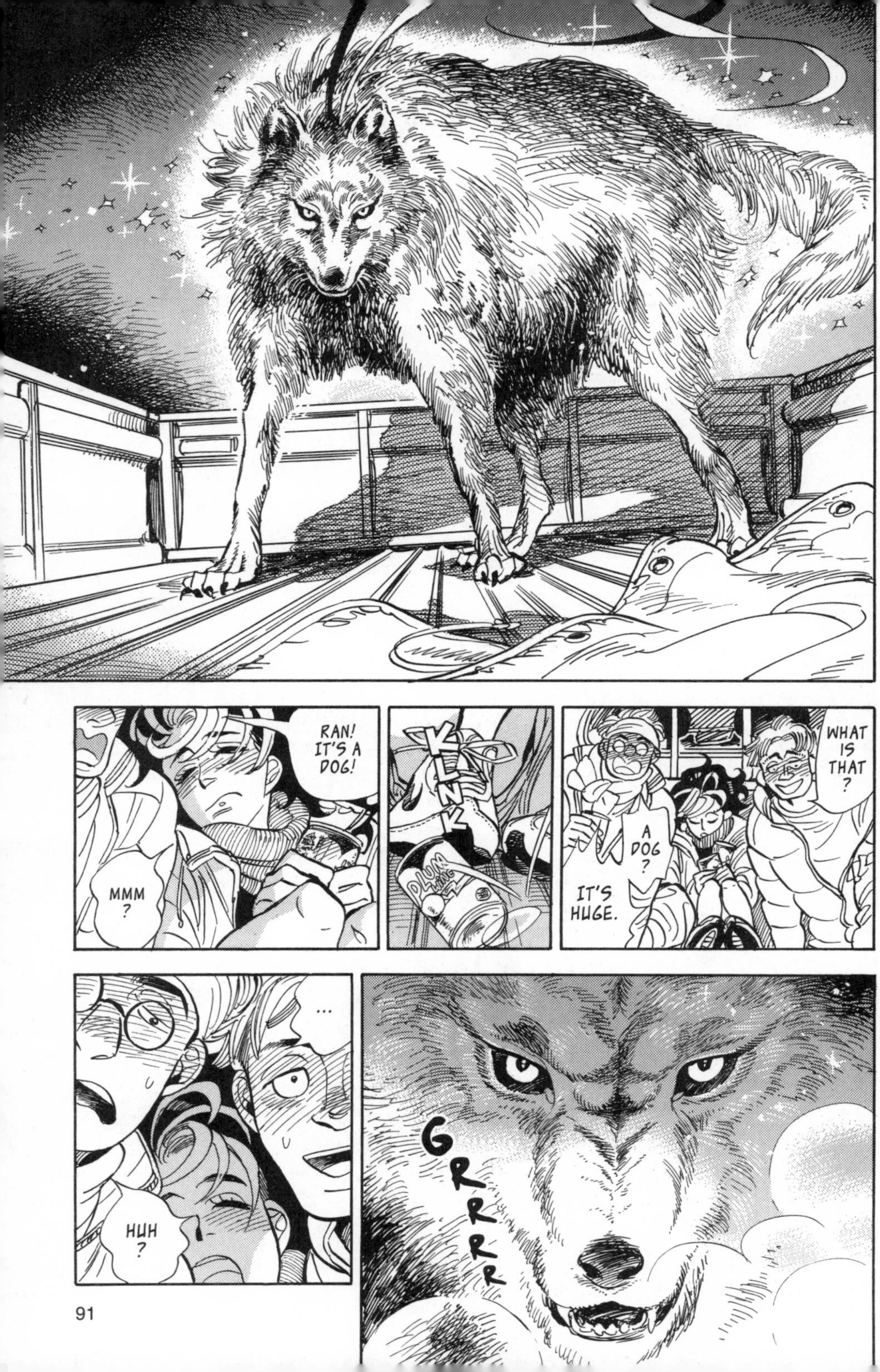
WHAT IS THAT?
A DOG?
IT'S HUGE.
KLNK
PLUM
RAN! IT'S A DOG!
MMM?
GRRRR
...
HUH?

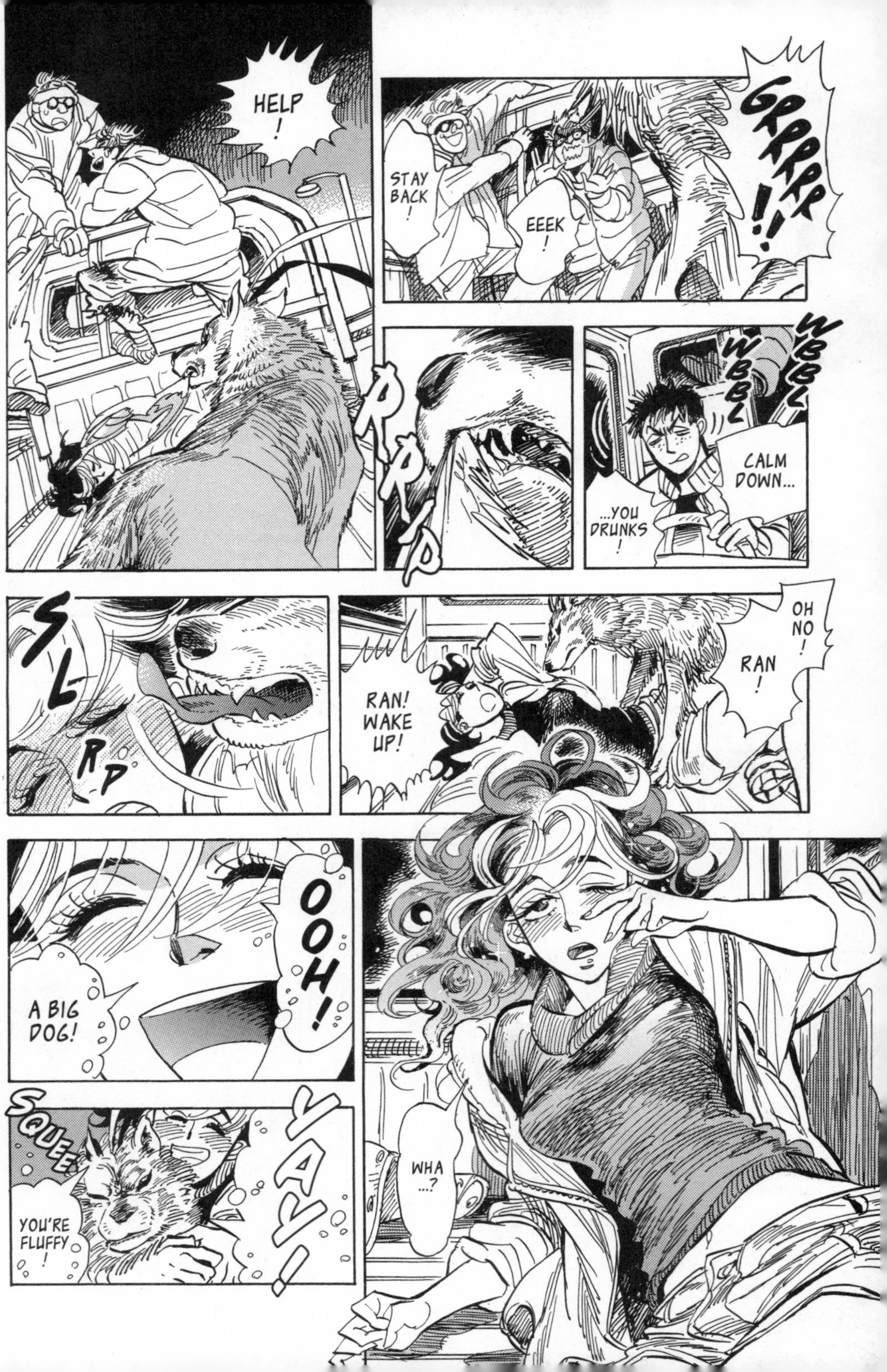
GRRRRR!!
STAY BACK!
EEEK!
WBBL
WBBL
CALM DOWN...
...YOU DRUNKS!
RRIP
HELP!
OH NO!
RAN!
RAN! WAKE UP!
SLRP
WHA...?
OOOH!
A BIG DOG!
YAY!
SQUEEE
YOU'RE FLUFFY!

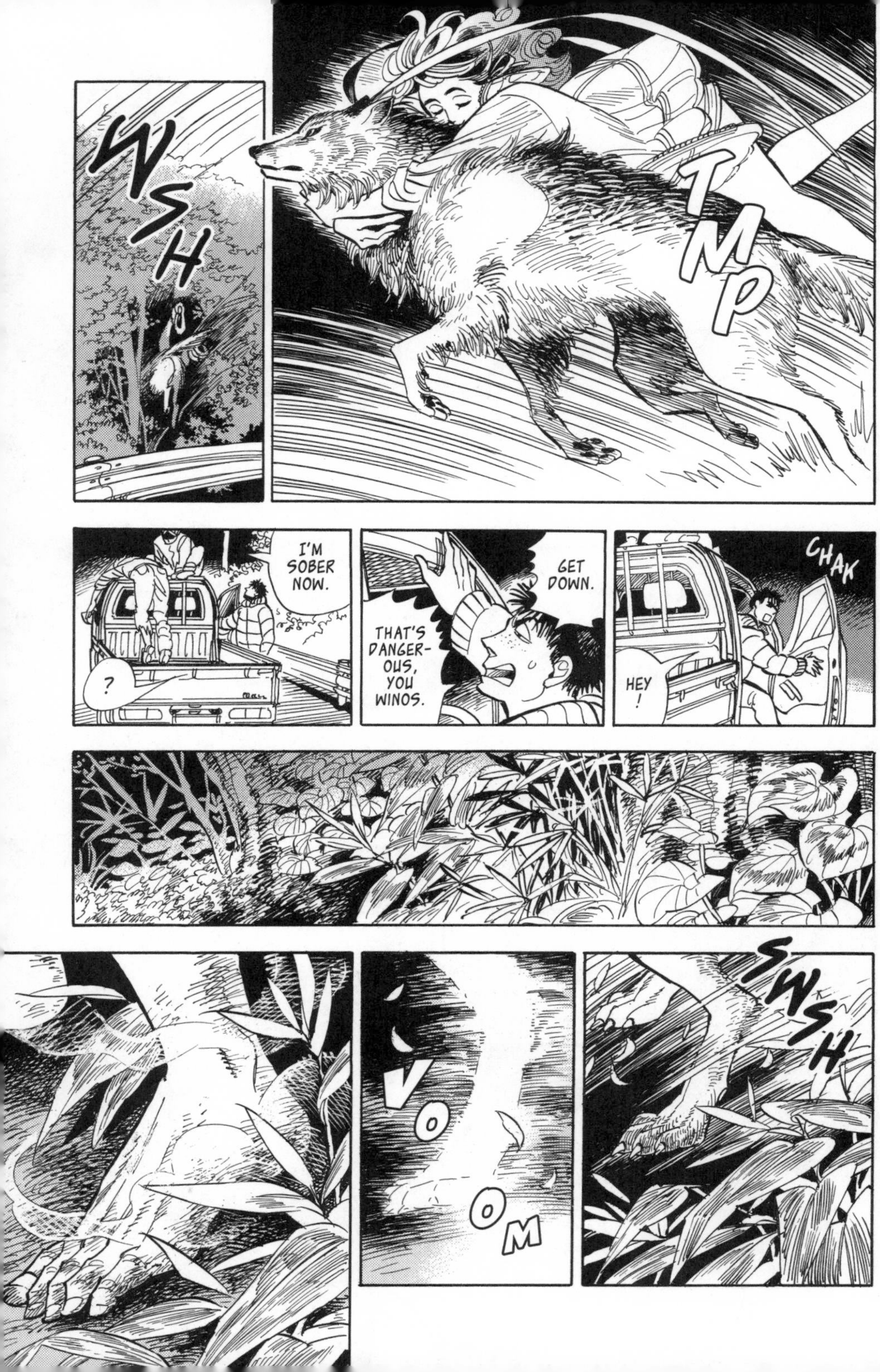
TMP
WSH
CHAK
HEY!
GET DOWN.
THAT'S DANGER-OUS, YOU WINOS.
I'M SOBER NOW.
?
SWSH
VOOM

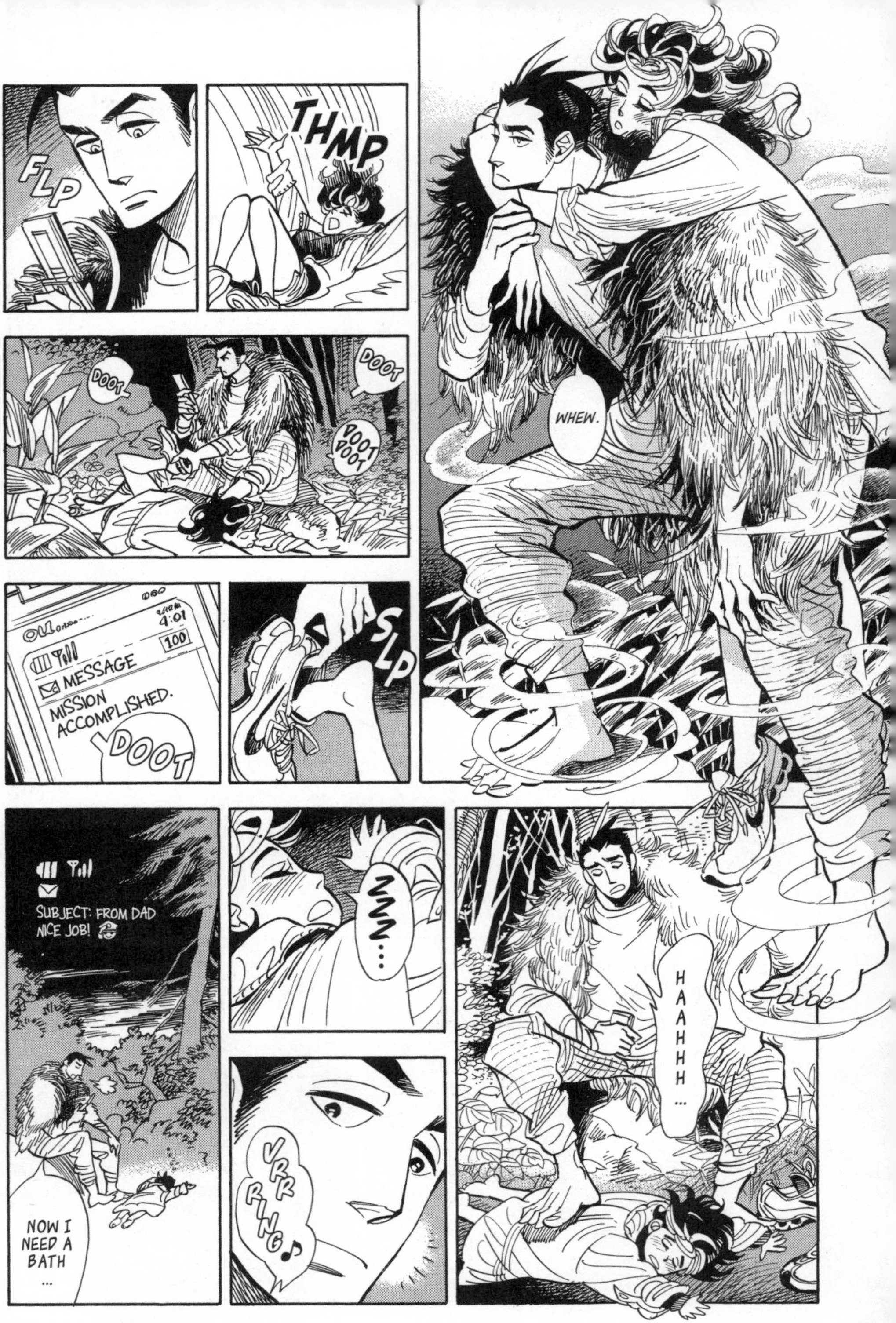
WHEW.
THMP
FLP
DOOT
DOOT
DOOT DOOT
SLP
4:01
100
MESSAGE
MISSION ACCOMPLISHED.
DOOT
HAAAHHH...
ZZZ...
VRR RING♪
SUBJECT: FROM DAD
NICE JOB!
NOW I NEED A BATH ...

Chapter 3 / The End

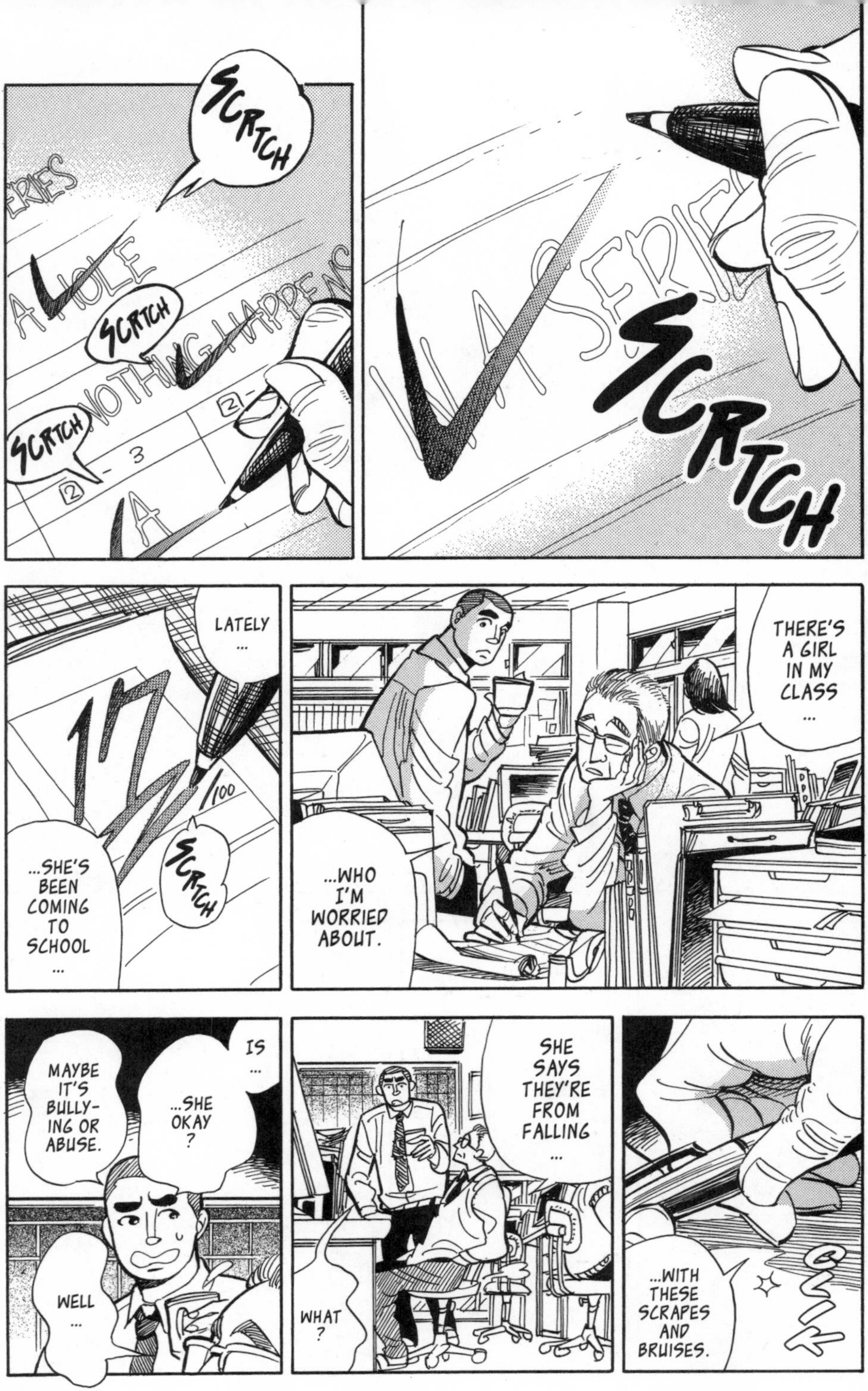
SCRTCH
SCRTCH
SCRTCH
SCRTCH
THERE'S A GIRL IN MY CLASS ...
...WHO I'M WORRIED ABOUT.
LATELY ...
SCRTCH
...SHE'S BEEN COMING TO SCHOOL ...
QUIK
...WITH THESE SCRAPES AND BRUISES.
SHE SAYS THEY'RE FROM FALLING ...
WHAT ?
IS ...
...SHE OKAY ?
MAYBE IT'S BULLY-ING OR ABUSE.
WELL ...

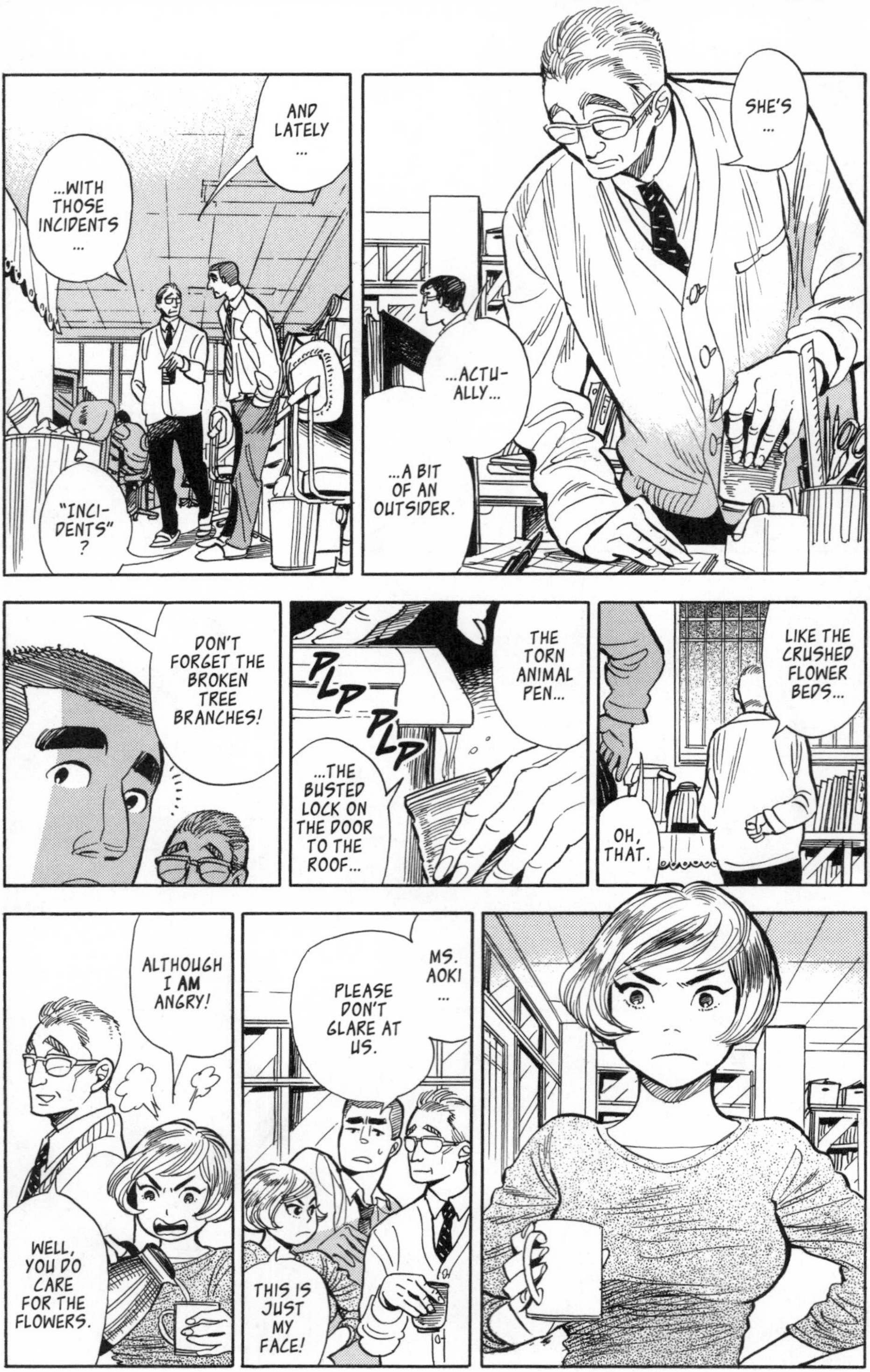
SHE'S ...
...ACTU-ALLY...
...A BIT OF AN OUTSIDER.
AND LATELY ...
...WITH THOSE INCIDENTS ...
"INCI-DENTS"?
LIKE THE CRUSHED FLOWER BEDS...
OH, THAT.
THE TORN ANIMAL PEN...
PLP PLP
...THE BUSTED LOCK ON THE DOOR TO THE ROOF...
DON'T FORGET THE BROKEN TREE BRANCHES!
MS. AOKI ...
PLEASE DON'T GLARE AT US.
THIS IS JUST MY FACE!
ALTHOUGH I AM ANGRY!
WELL, YOU DO CARE FOR THE FLOWERS.

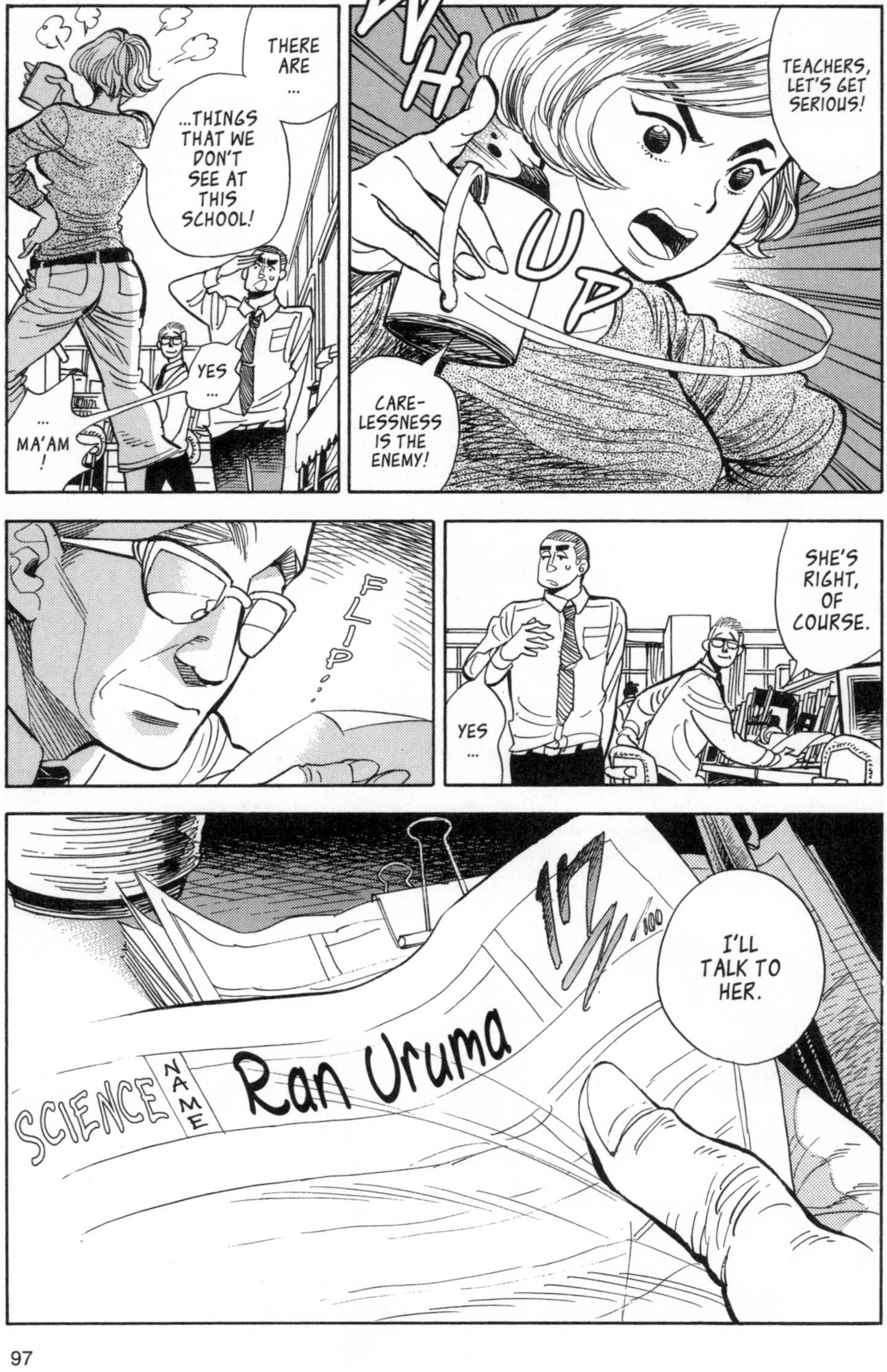
TEACHERS, LET'S GET SERIOUS!
WHUP
CARE-LESSNESS IS THE ENEMY!
THERE ARE ...
...THINGS THAT WE DON'T SEE AT THIS SCHOOL!
YES ...
... MA'AM !
SHE'S RIGHT, OF COURSE.
YES ...
FLIP...
I'LL TALK TO HER.
17/100
SCIENCE
NAME
Ran Uruma

Chapter 4

Floating Laboratory

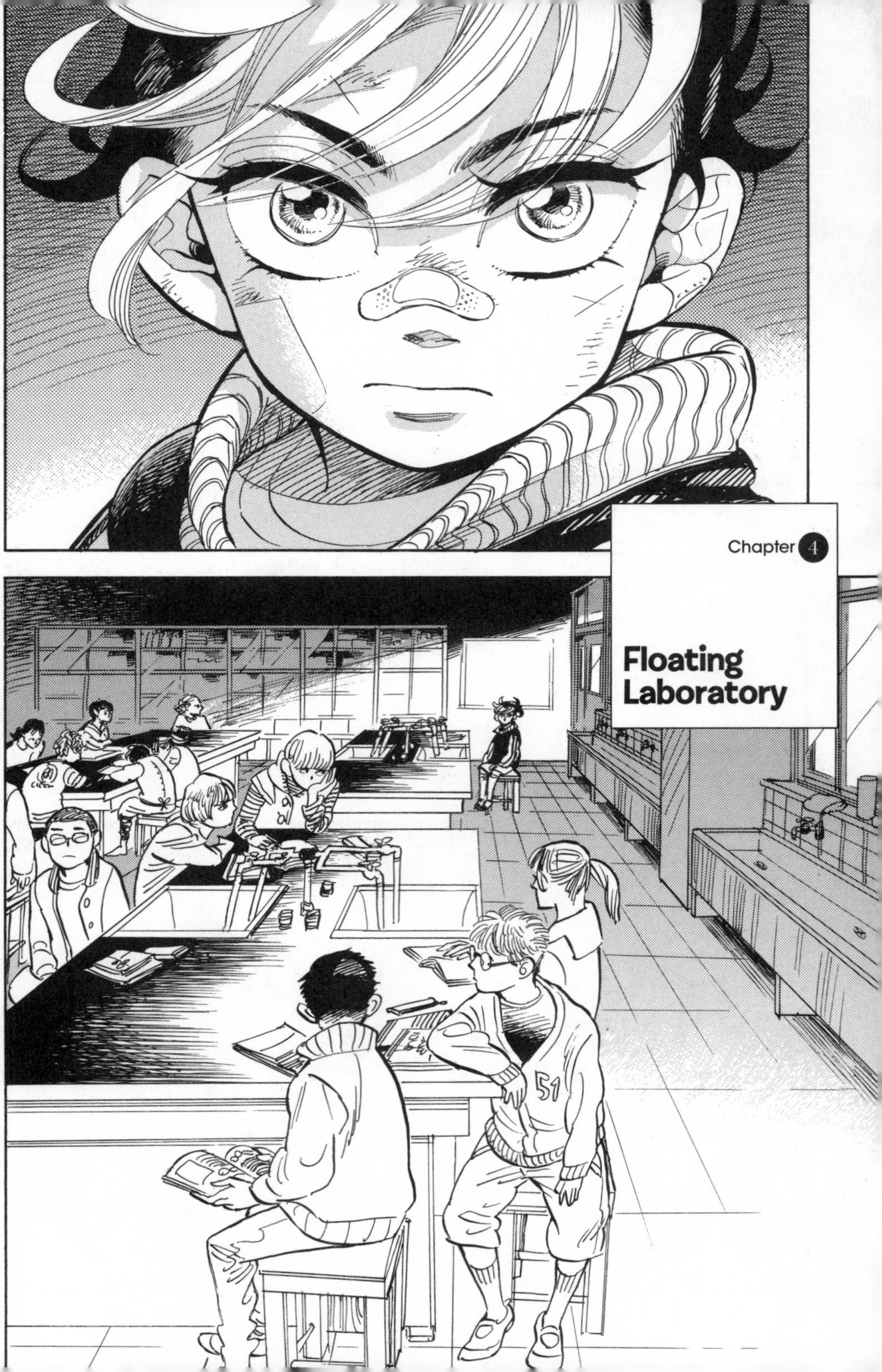

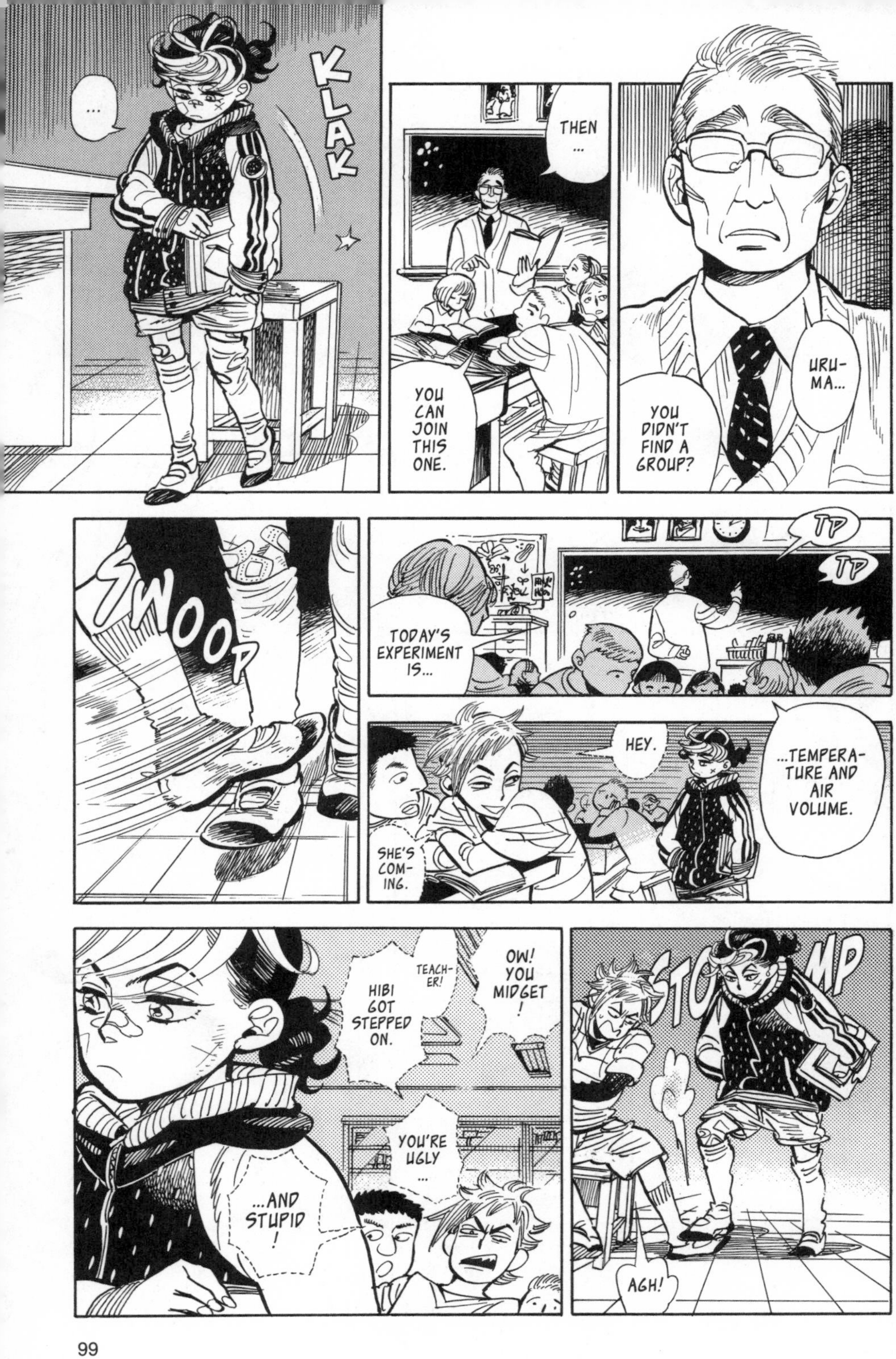
URU-MA...
YOU DIDN'T FIND A GROUP?
THEN ...
YOU CAN JOIN THIS ONE.
...
KLAK
TP
TP
TODAY'S EXPERIMENT IS...
...TEMPERATURE AND AIR VOLUME.
HEY.
SHE'S COMING.
SWOOP
STOMP
AGH!
OW! YOU MIDGET!
TEACHER!
HIBI GOT STEPPED ON.
YOU'RE UGLY...
...AND STUPID!

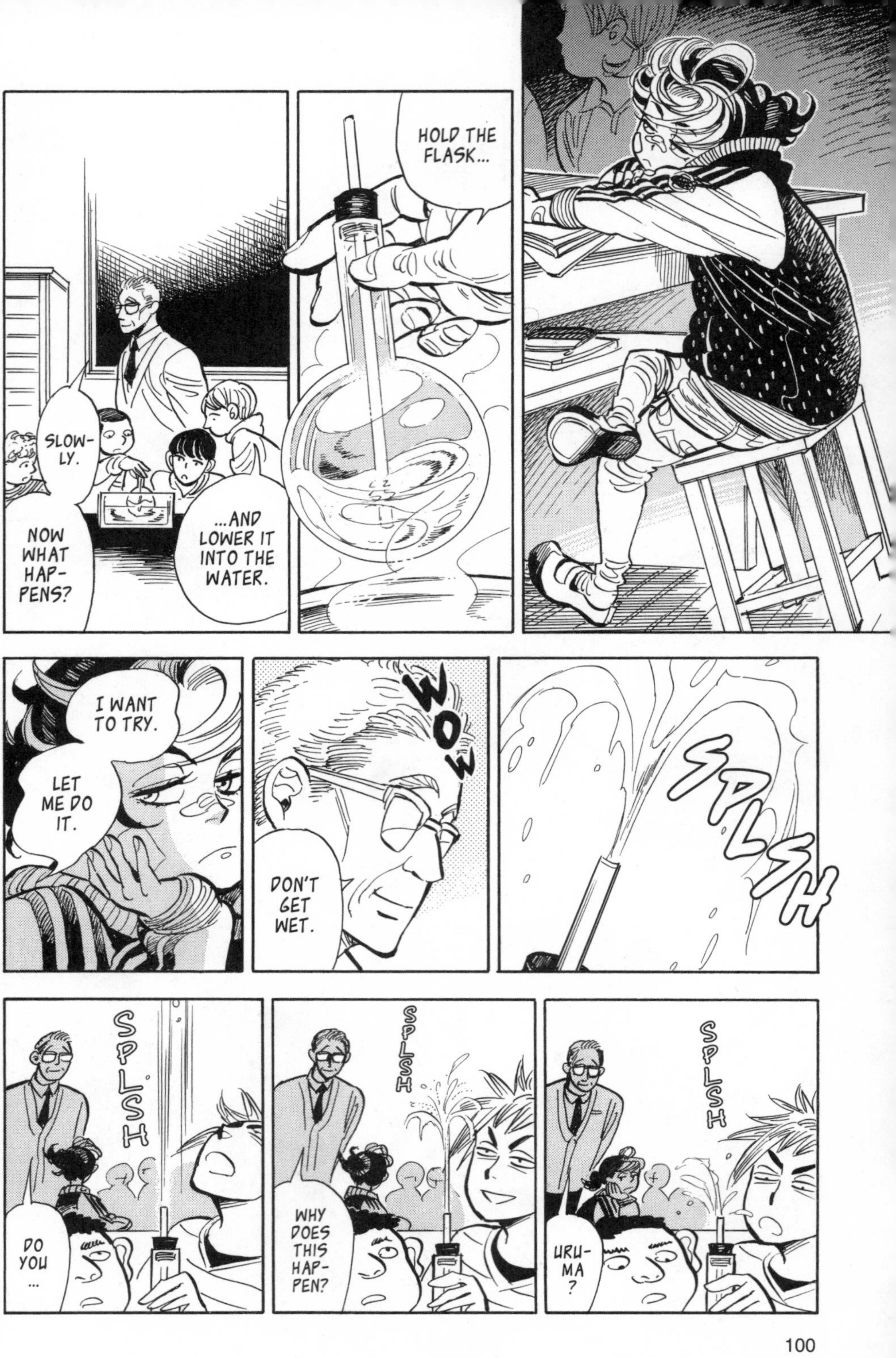
HOLD THE FLASK...
...AND LOWER IT INTO THE WATER.
SLOW-LY.
NOW WHAT HAP-PENS?
SPLSH
WOW
DON'T GET WET.
I WANT TO TRY.
LET ME DO IT.
SPLSH
URU-MA?
SPLSH
WHY DOES THIS HAP-PEN?
SPLSH
DO YOU ...

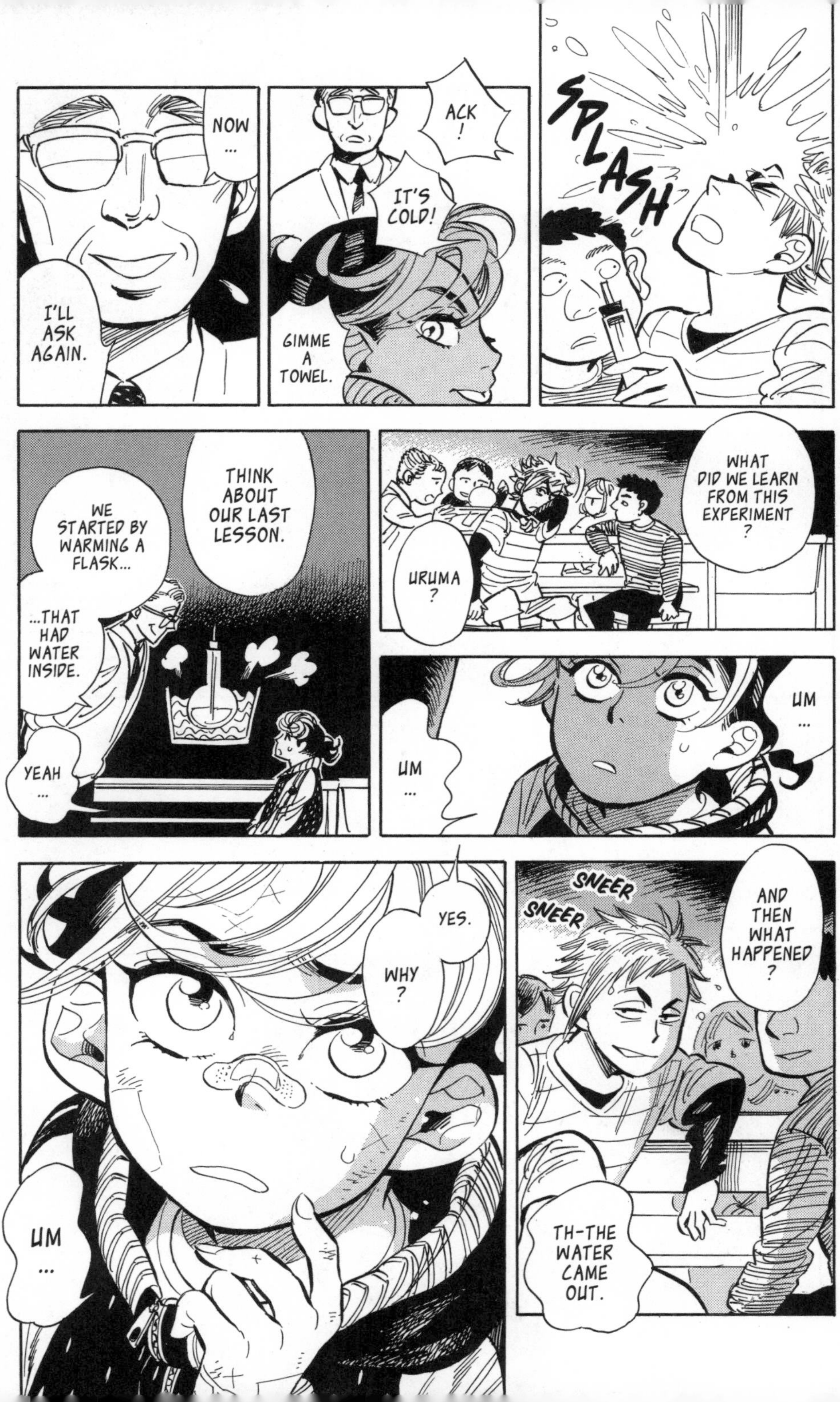
SPLASH
ACK!
IT'S COLD!
GIMME A TOWEL.
NOW...
I'LL ASK AGAIN.
WHAT DID WE LEARN FROM THIS EXPERIMENT?
URUMA?
UM...
UM...
THINK ABOUT OUR LAST LESSON.
WE STARTED BY WARMING A FLASK...
...THAT HAD WATER INSIDE.
YEAH...
SNEER
SNEER
AND THEN WHAT HAPPENED?
TH-THE WATER CAME OUT.
YES.
WHY?
UM...

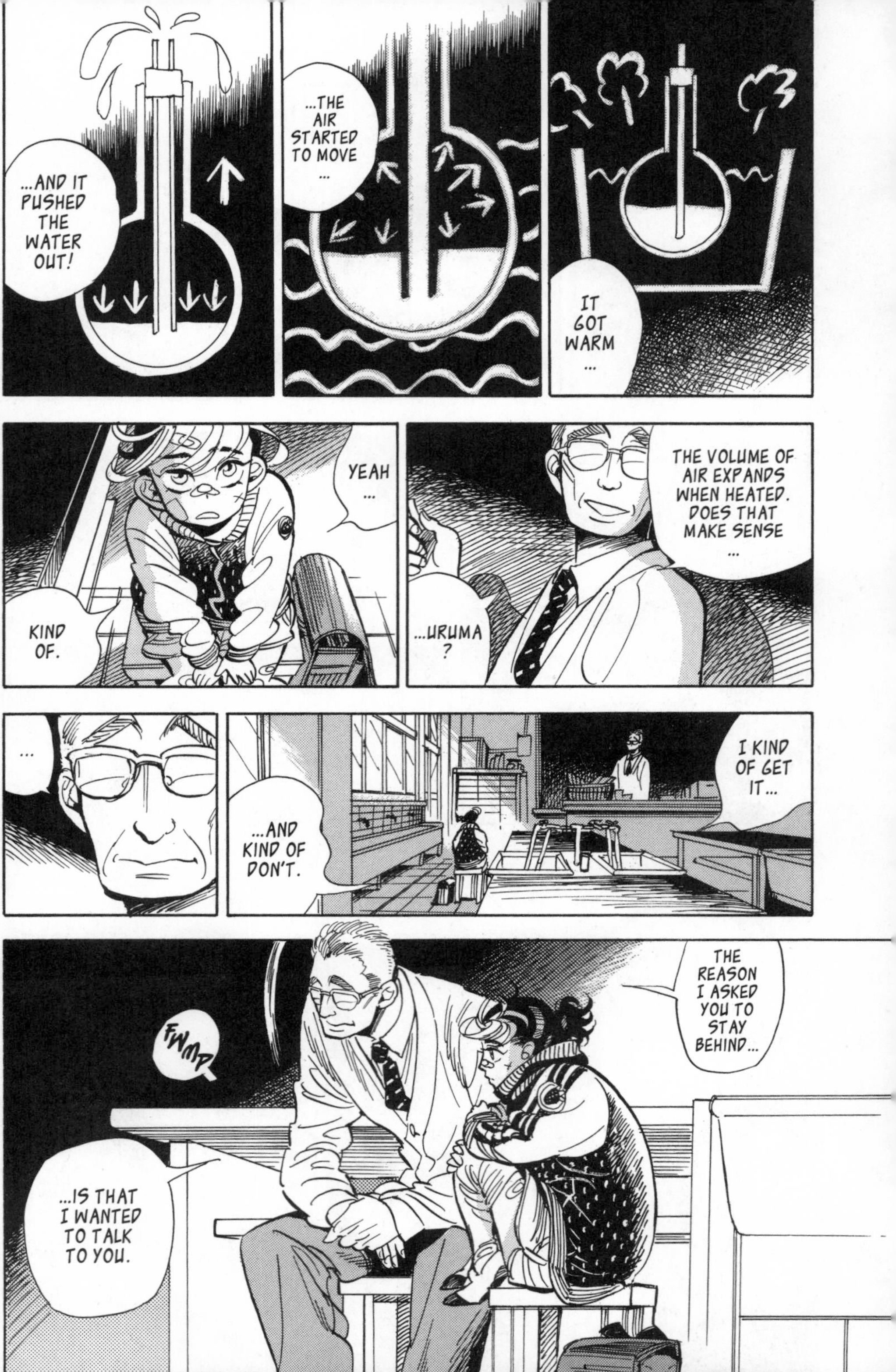
IT GOT WARM ...
...THE AIR STARTED TO MOVE ...
...AND IT PUSHED THE WATER OUT!
THE VOLUME OF AIR EXPANDS WHEN HEATED. DOES THAT MAKE SENSE ...
...URUMA ?
YEAH ...
KIND OF.
I KIND OF GET IT...
...AND KIND OF DON'T.
...
THE REASON I ASKED YOU TO STAY BEHIND...
FWMP
...IS THAT I WANTED TO TALK TO YOU.

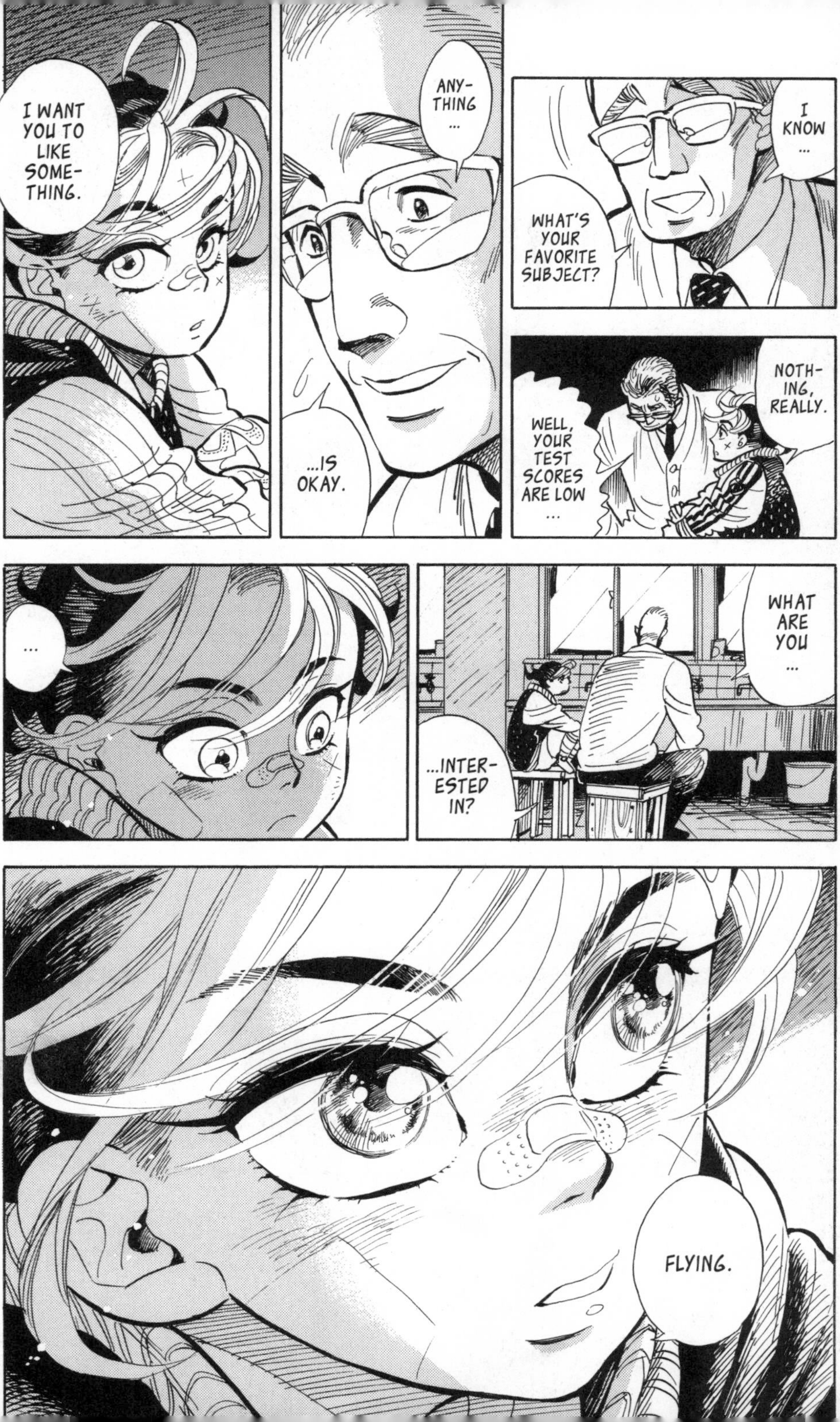
I KNOW ...
WHAT'S YOUR FAVORITE SUBJECT?
NOTHING, REALLY.
WELL, YOUR TEST SCORES ARE LOW ...
ANYTHING ...
...IS OKAY.
I WANT YOU TO LIKE SOMETHING.
WHAT ARE YOU ...
...INTERESTED IN?
...
FLYING.

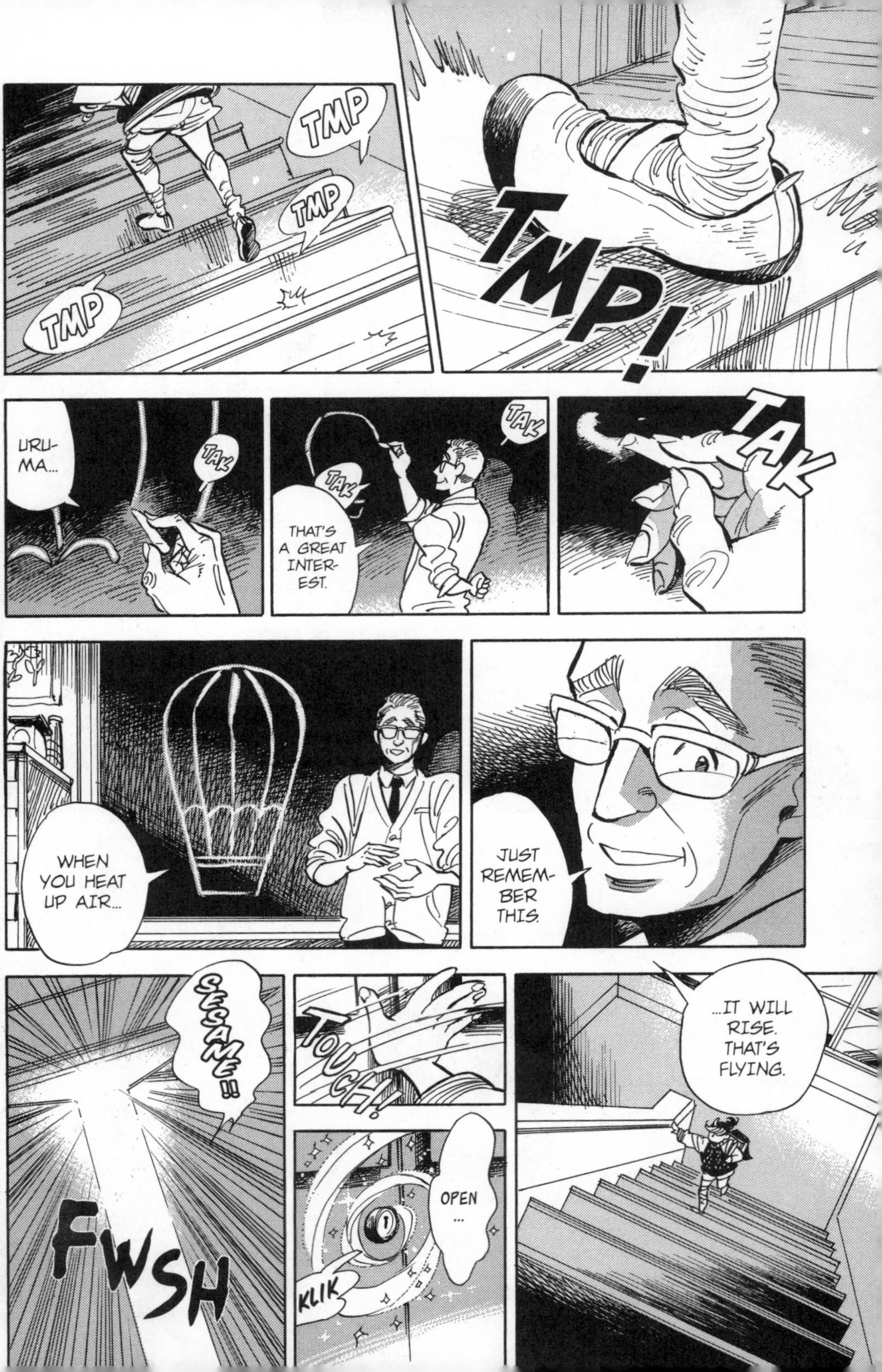
TMP!
TMP
TMP
TMP
TAK
TAK
TAK
THAT'S A GREAT INTER-EST.
TAK
URU-MA...
JUST REMEM-BER THIS.
WHEN YOU HEAT UP AIR...
...IT WILL RISE. THAT'S FLYING.
TOUCH!
OPEN ...
KLIK
SESAME!!
FWSH

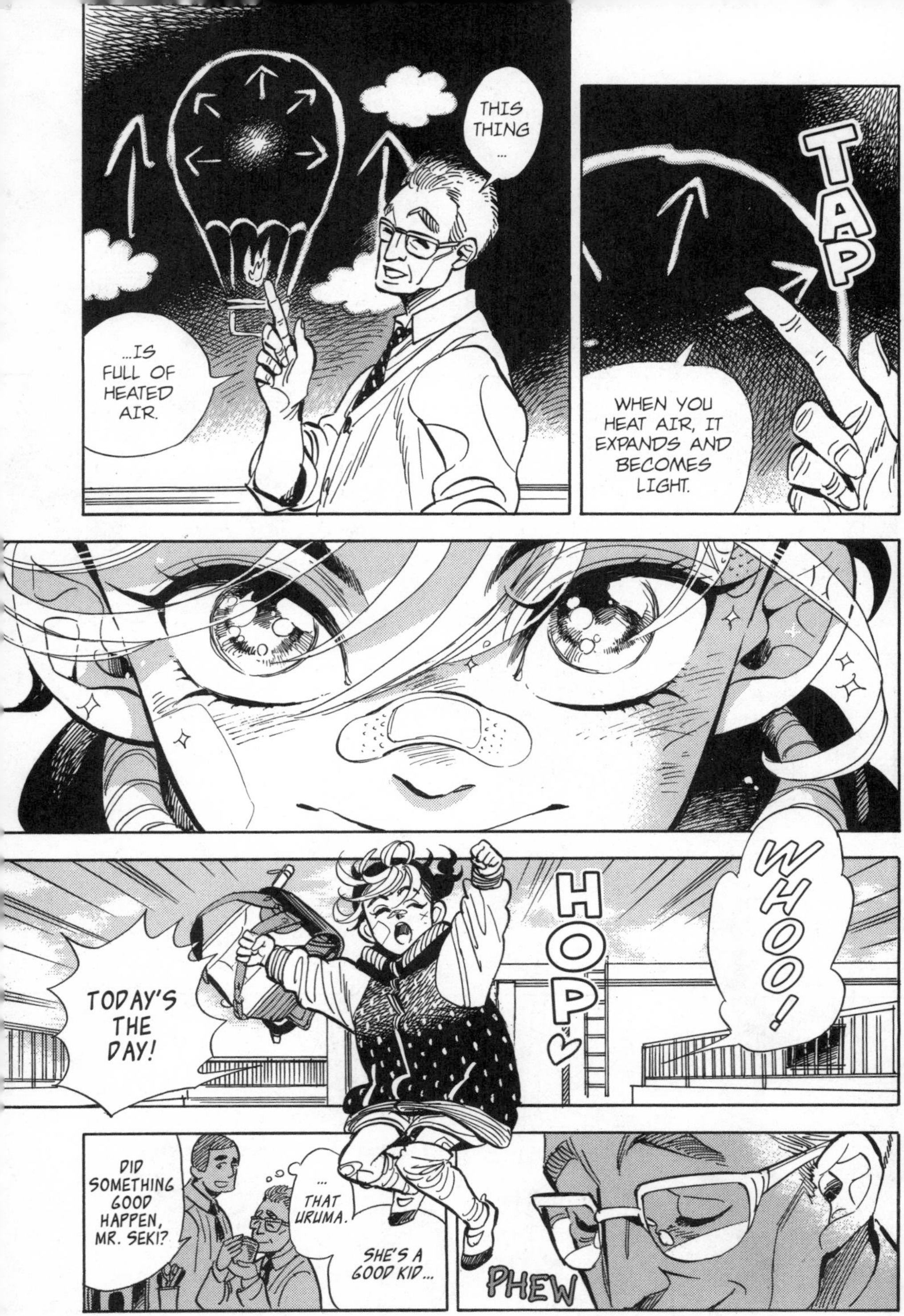
TAP
WHEN YOU HEAT AIR, IT EXPANDS AND BECOMES LIGHT.
THIS THING ...
...IS FULL OF HEATED AIR.
WHOO!
HOP
TODAY'S THE DAY!
PHEW
... THAT URUMA.
SHE'S A GOOD KID...
DID SOMETHING GOOD HAPPEN, MR. SEKI?

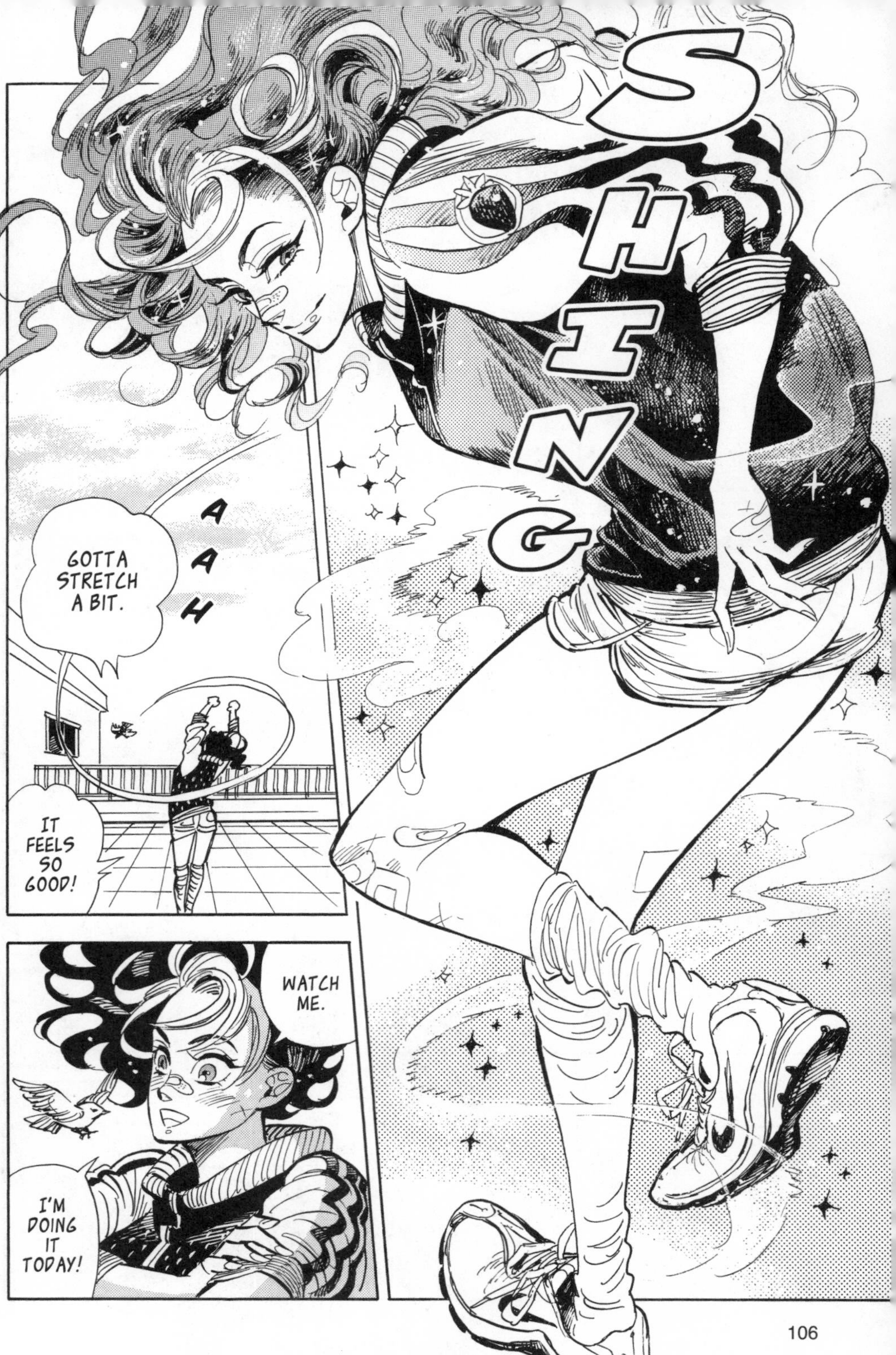
SHING
AAH
GOTTA STRETCH A BIT.
IT FEELS SO GOOD!
WATCH ME.
I'M DOING IT TODAY!

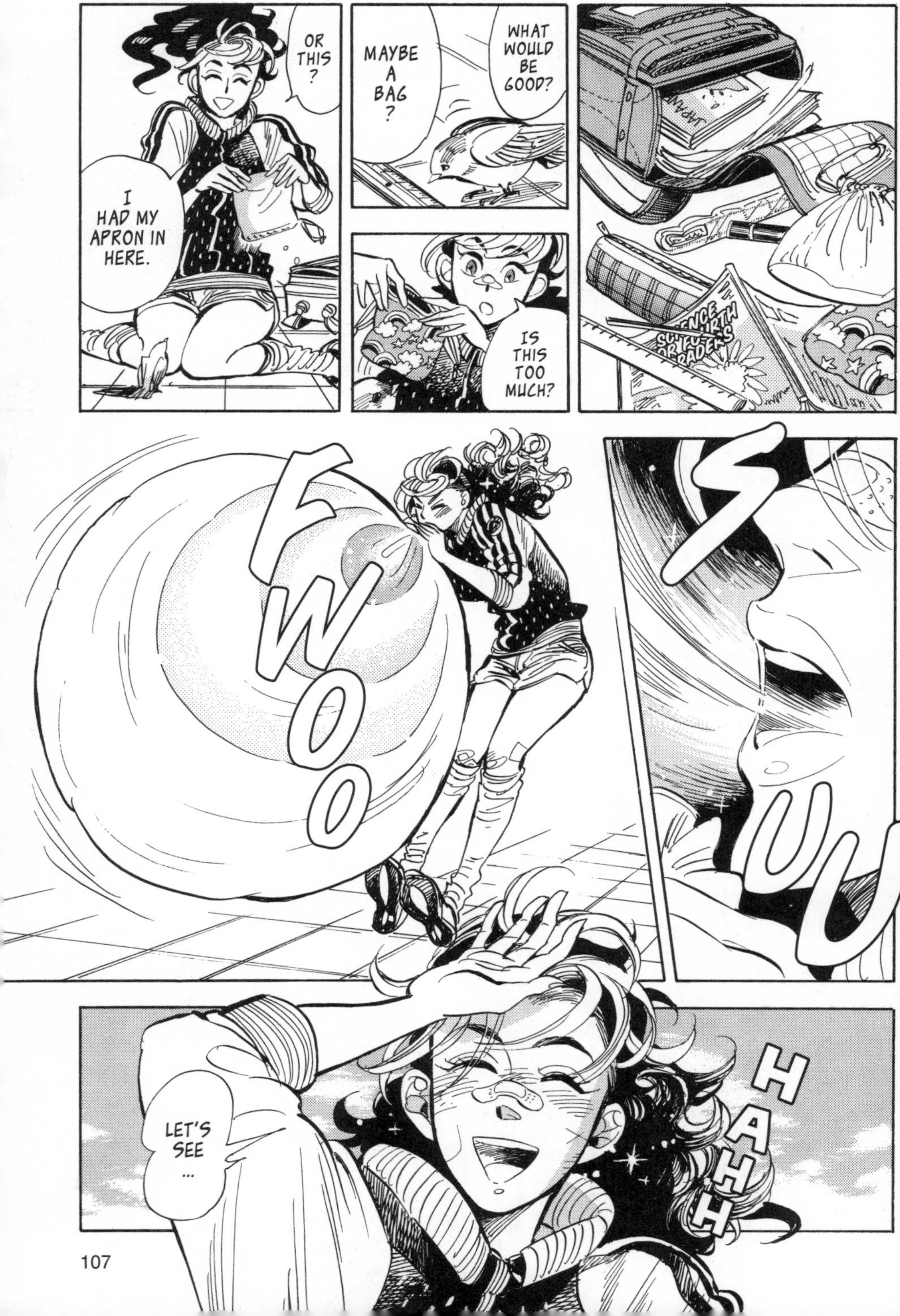

WHAT WOULD BE GOOD?
MAYBE A BAG?
IS THIS TOO MUCH?
OR THIS?
I HAD MY APRON IN HERE.
SUU
WOO
HAHHH
LET'S SEE ...

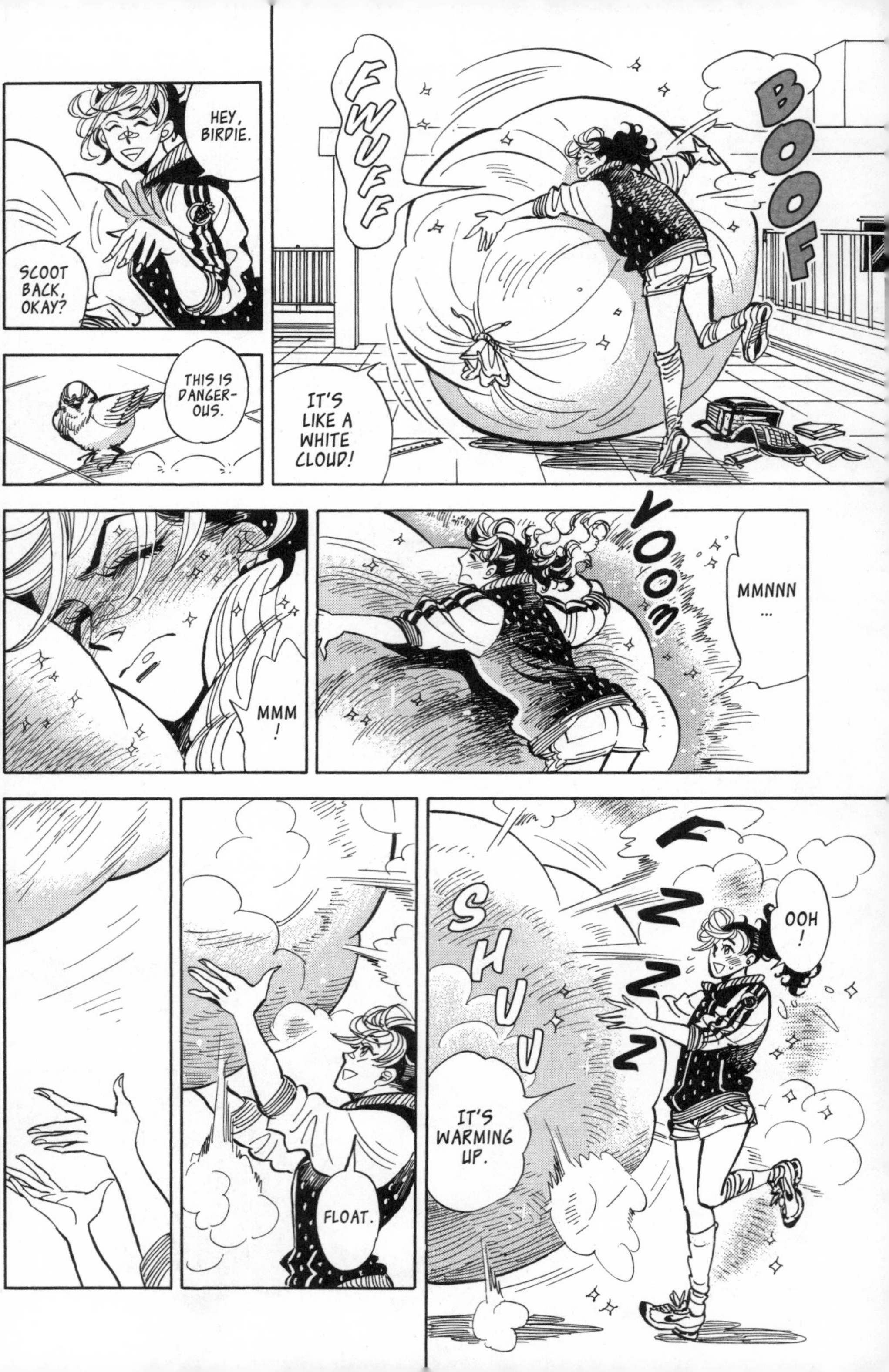
BOOF
FWUFF
IT'S LIKE A WHITE CLOUD!
HEY, BIRDIE.
SCOOT BACK, OKAY?
THIS IS DANGER-OUS.
VOOM
MMNNN...
MMM!
OOH!
FZZZZ
SHUUU
IT'S WARMING UP.
FLOAT.

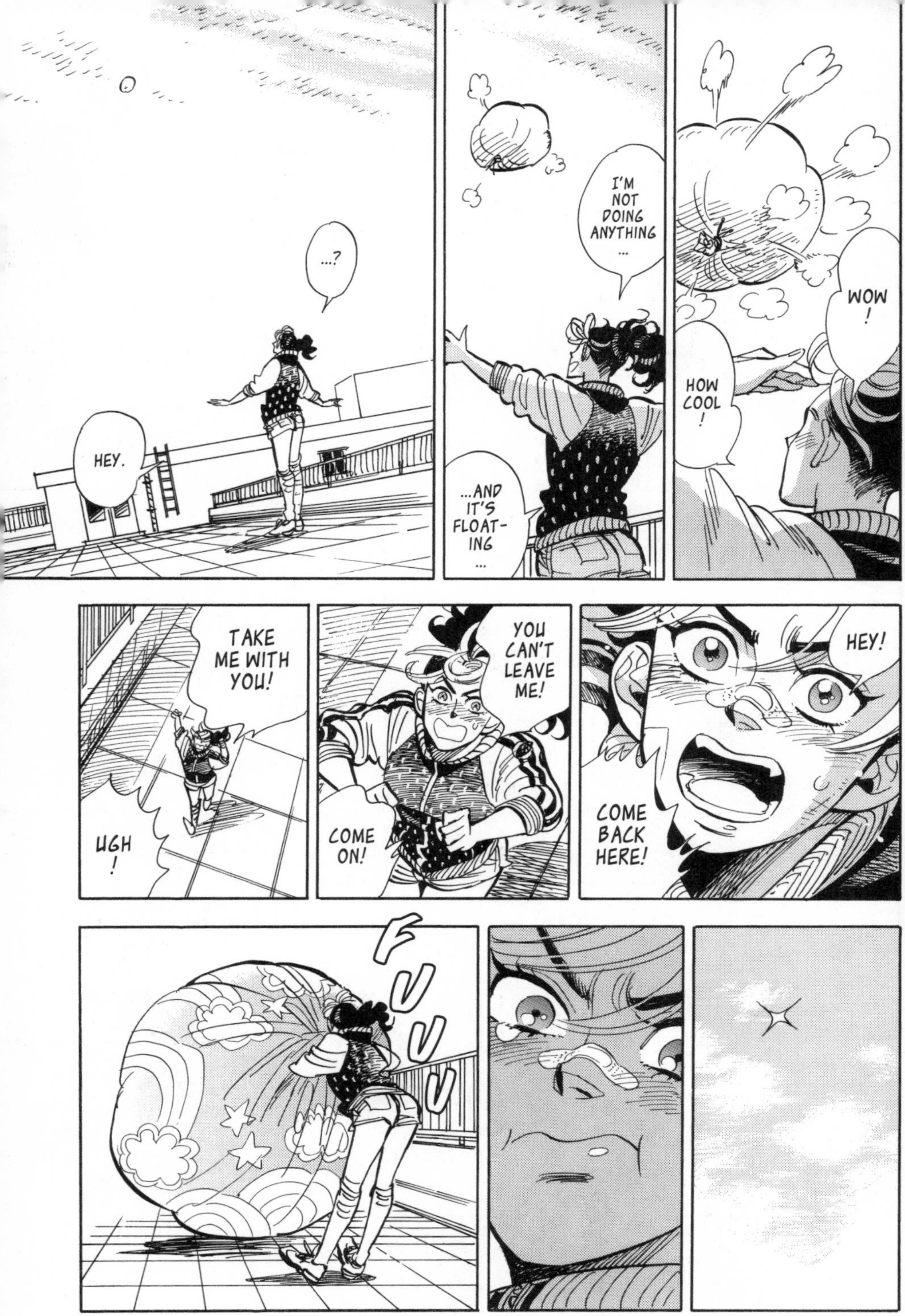
WOW!
HOW COOL!
I'M NOT DOING ANYTHING...
...AND IT'S FLOATING...
...?
HEY.
HEY!
COME BACK HERE!
YOU CAN'T LEAVE ME!
COME ON!
TAKE ME WITH YOU!
UGH!
FUUUU

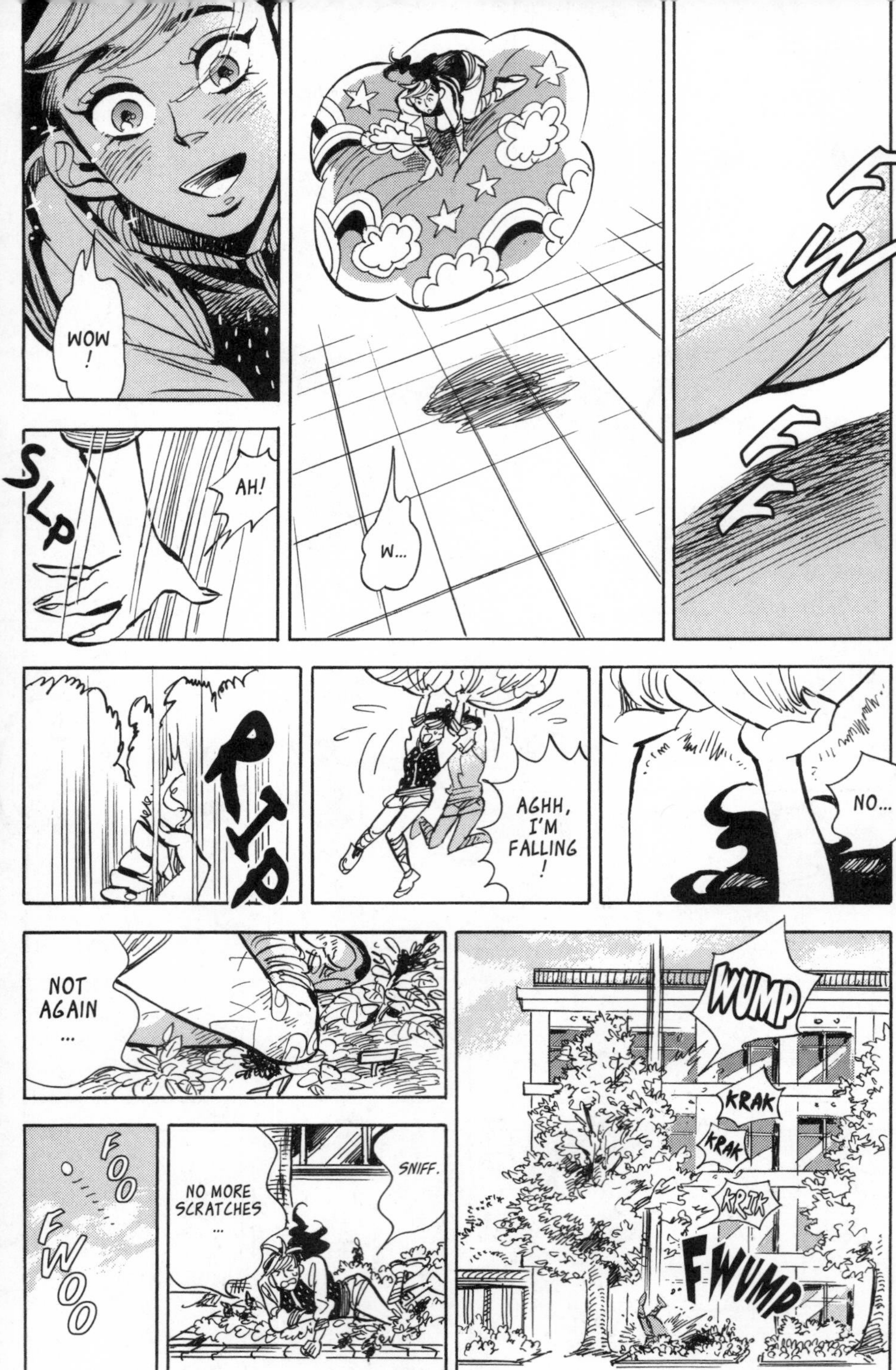
W...
WOW!
SLP
AH!
NO...
AGHH, I'M FALLING!
RIP
WUMP
KRAK
KRAK
KRIK
FWUMP
NOT AGAIN ...
SNIFF.
NO MORE SCRATCHES ...
FOO
FWOO

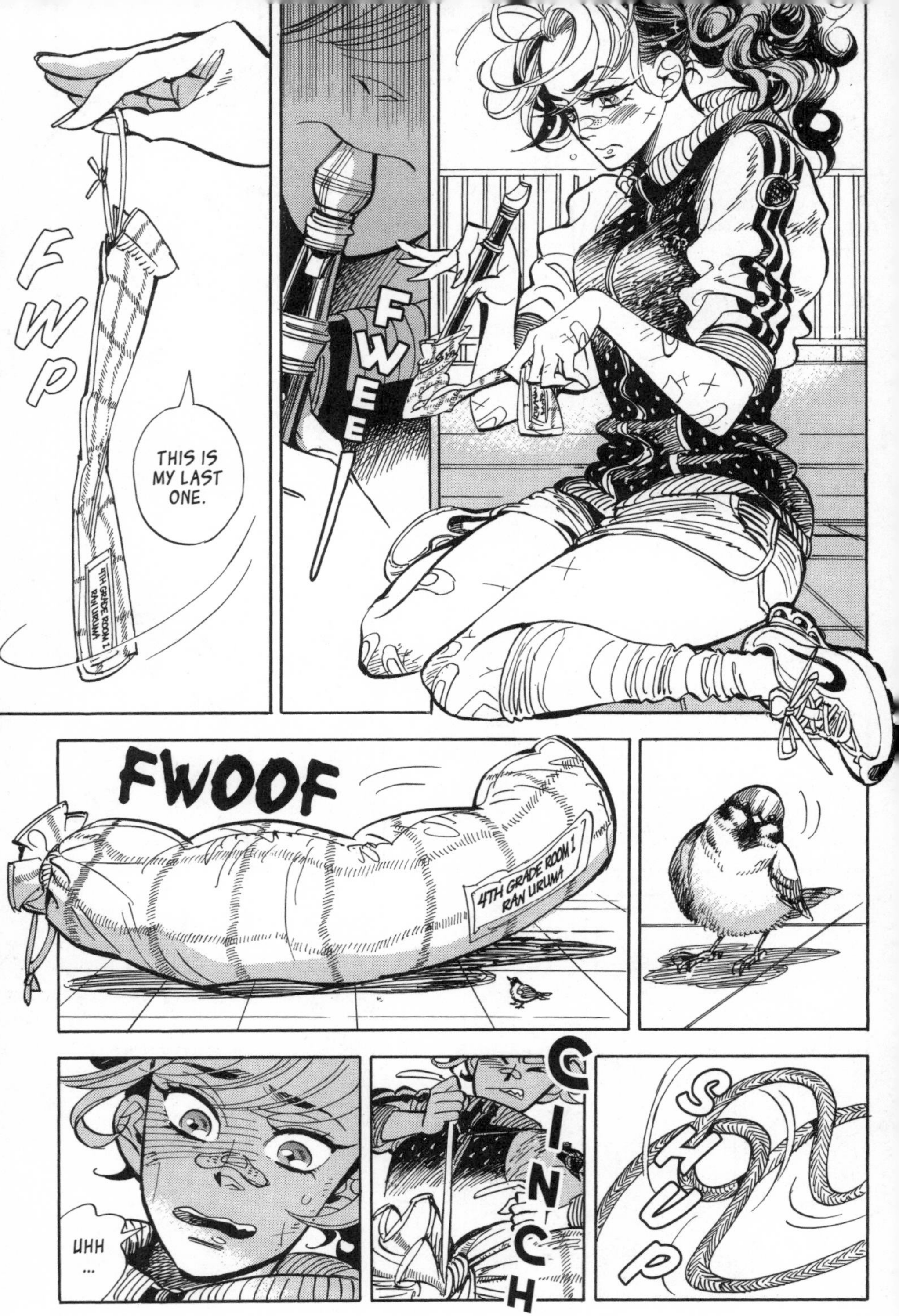
FWEE
FWP
THIS IS MY LAST ONE.
FWOOF
4TH GRADE ROOM 1
RAN URUMA
SHUP
CINCH
UHH...

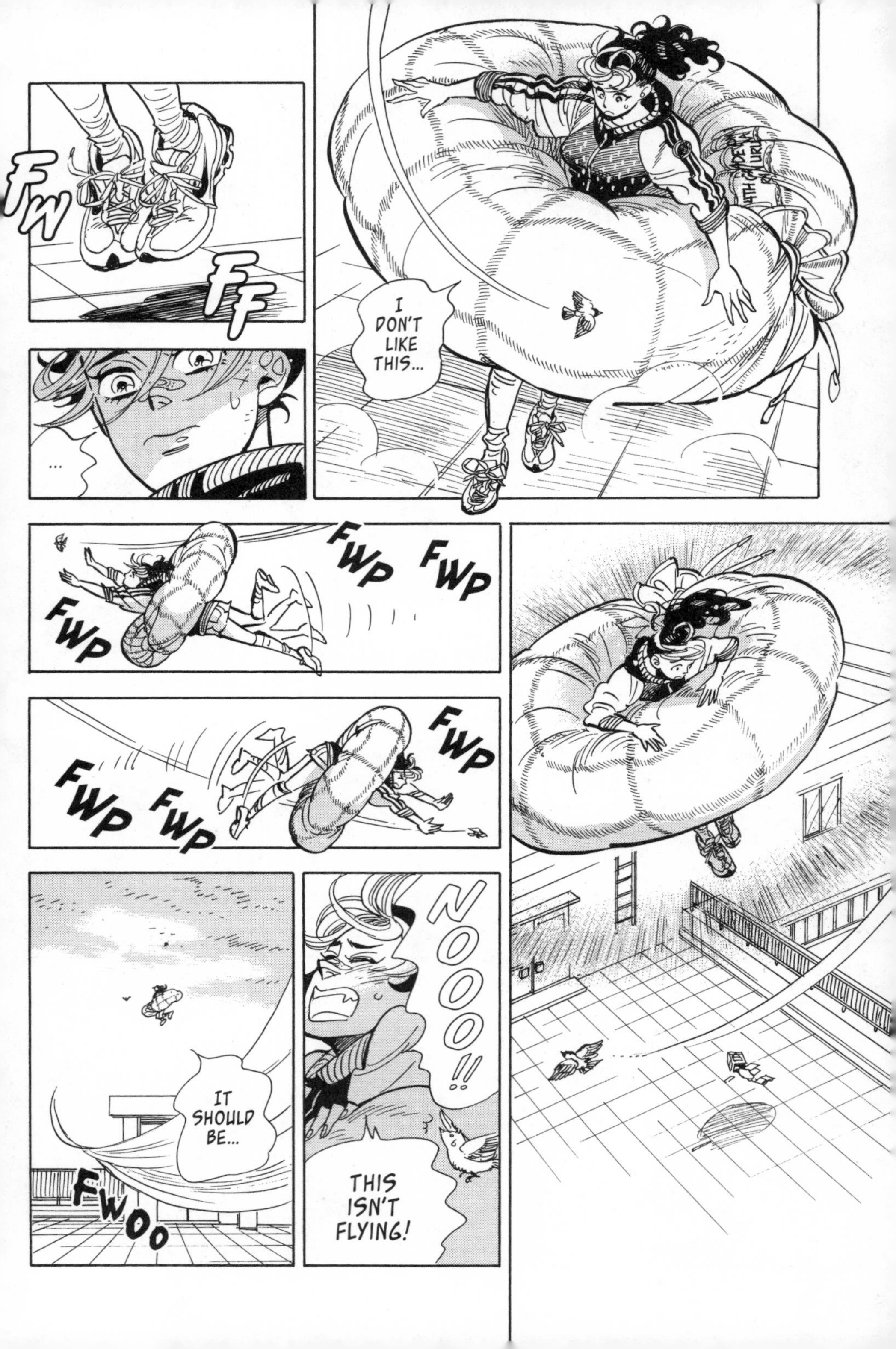

I DON'T LIKE THIS...
FW
FF
...
FWP
FWP
FWP
FWP
FWP
FWP
NOOOO!!
THIS ISN'T FLYING!
IT SHOULD BE...
FWOO

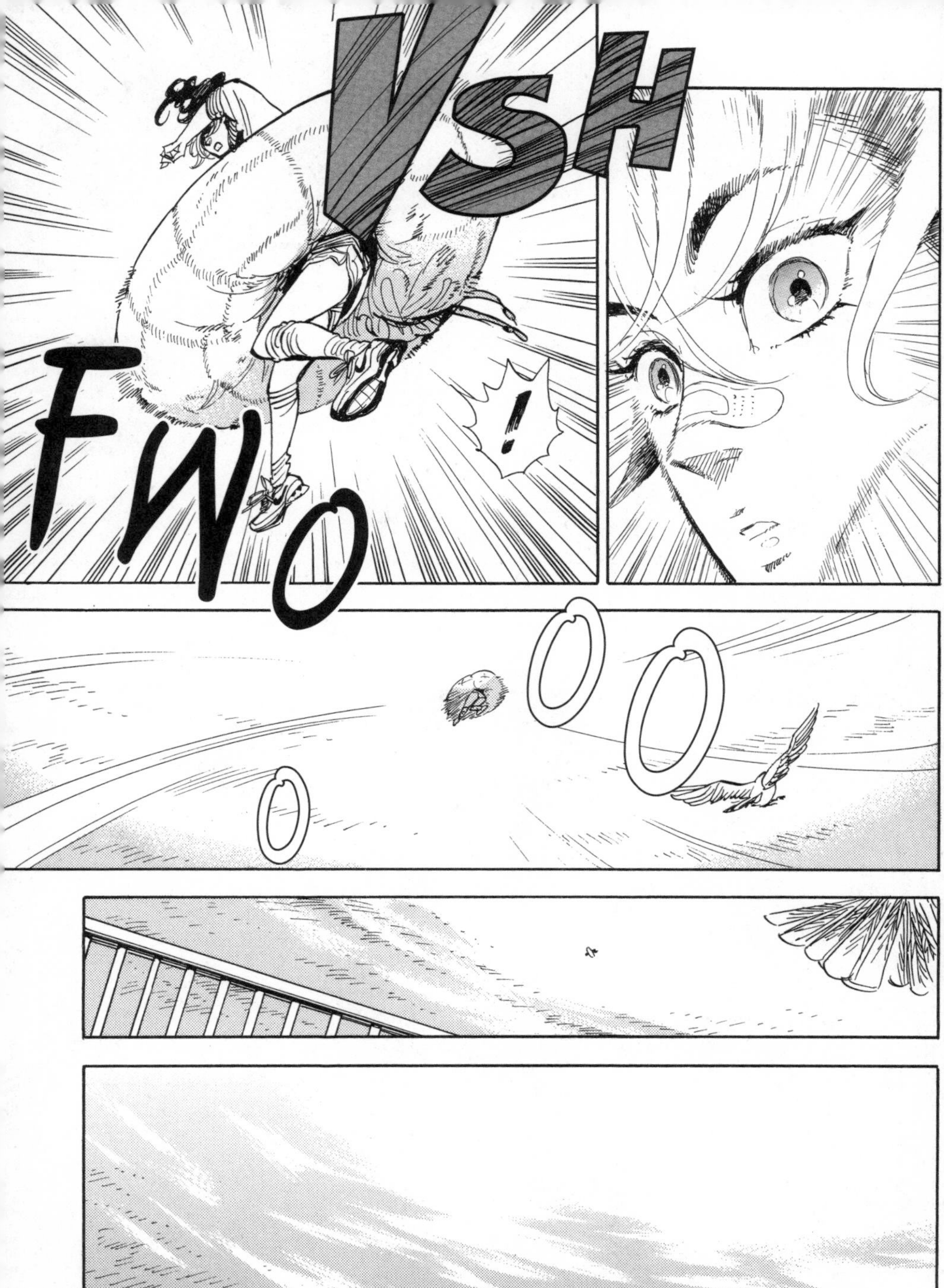
VSH
!
FWO
OOO

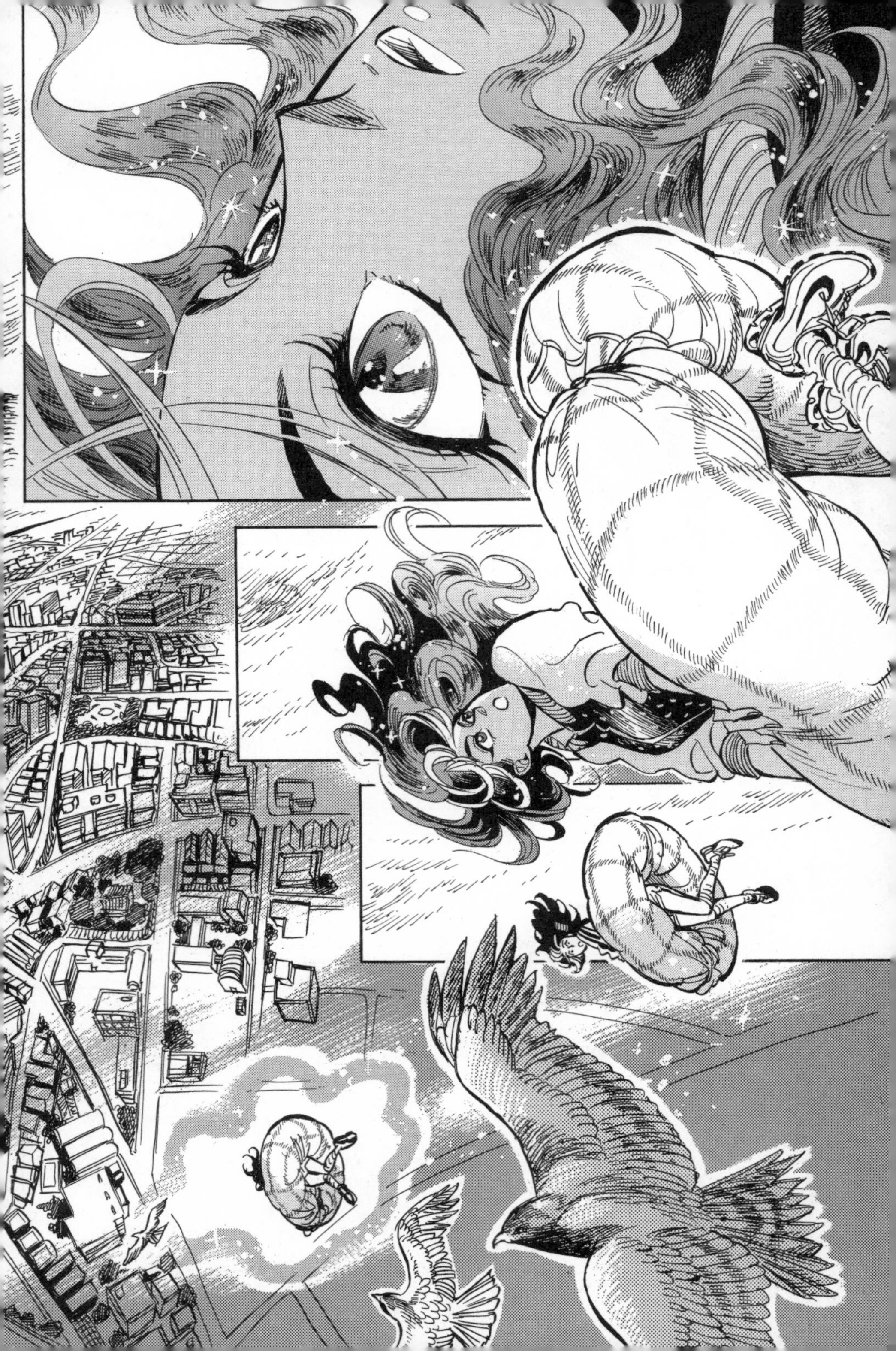

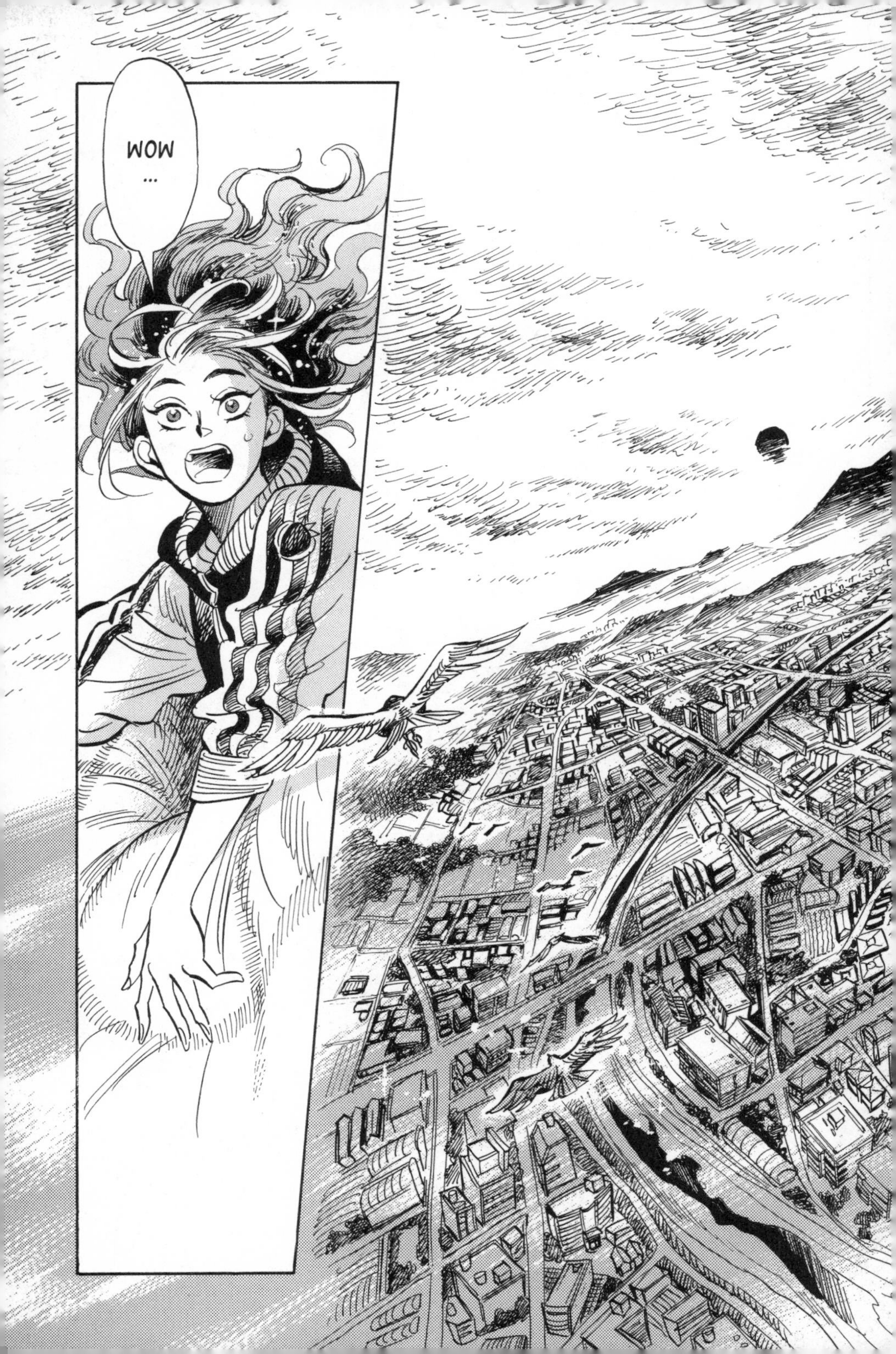
WOW ...

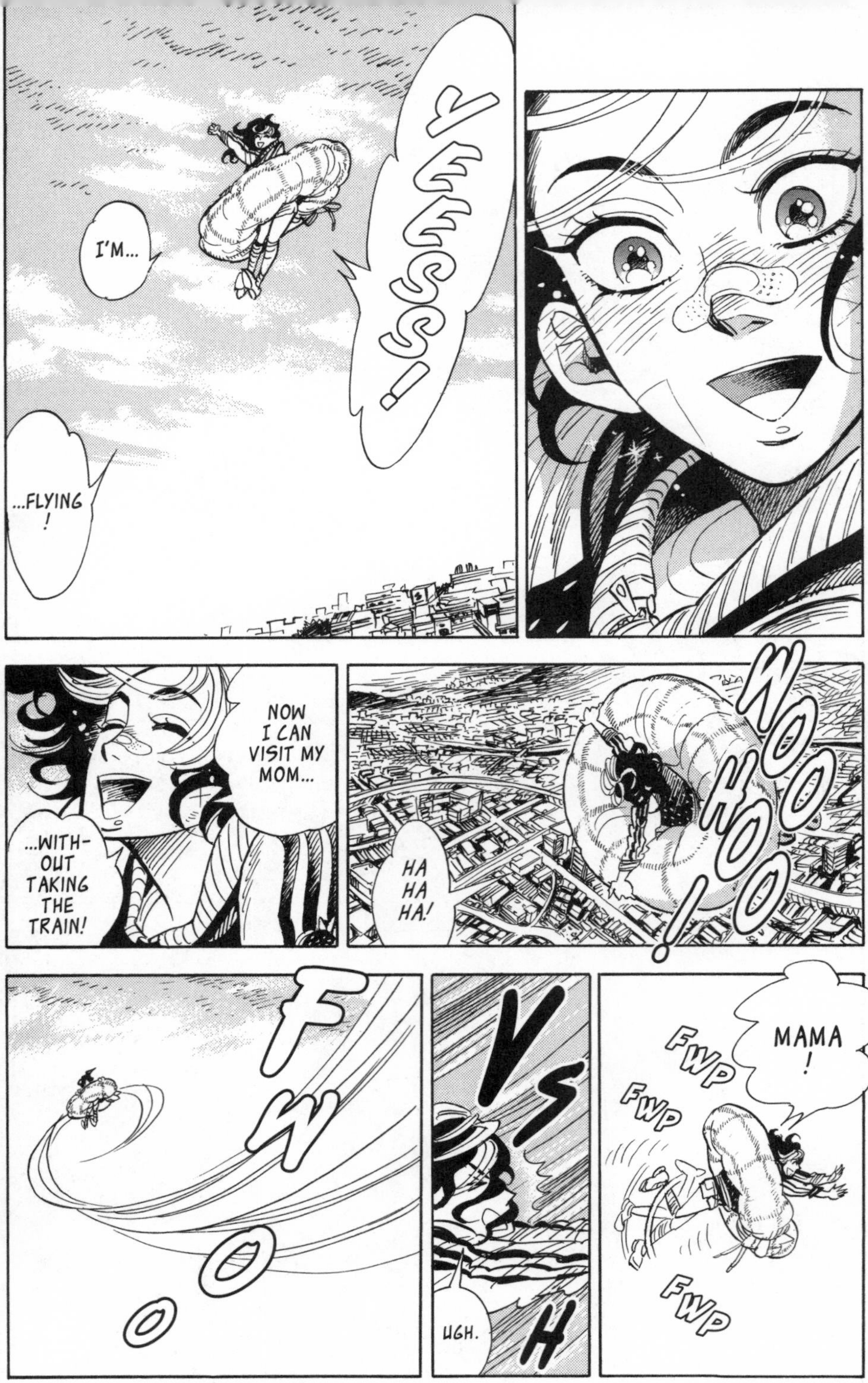
YEESS!
I'M...
...FLYING!
WOOHOOO!
HA HA HA!
NOW I CAN VISIT MY MOM...
...WITH-OUT TAKING THE TRAIN!
MAMA!
FWP
FWP
FWP
VSH
UGH.
FWOOO

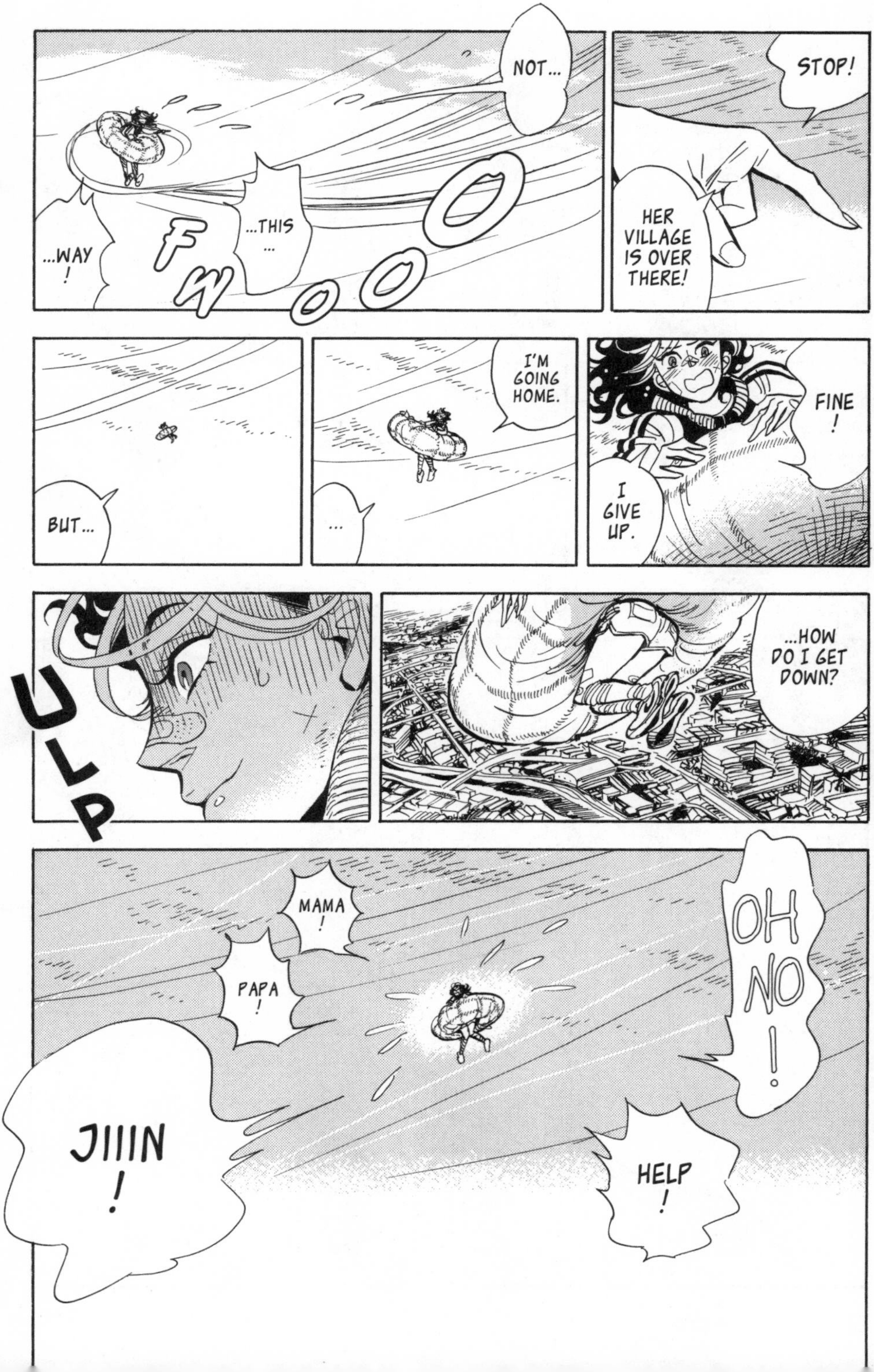
STOP!
HER VILLAGE IS OVER THERE!
NOT...
FWOOOO
...THIS...
...WAY!
FINE!
I GIVE UP.
I'M GOING HOME.
...
BUT...
...HOW DO I GET DOWN?
ULP
OH NO!
MAMA!
PAPA!
HELP!
JIIIN!

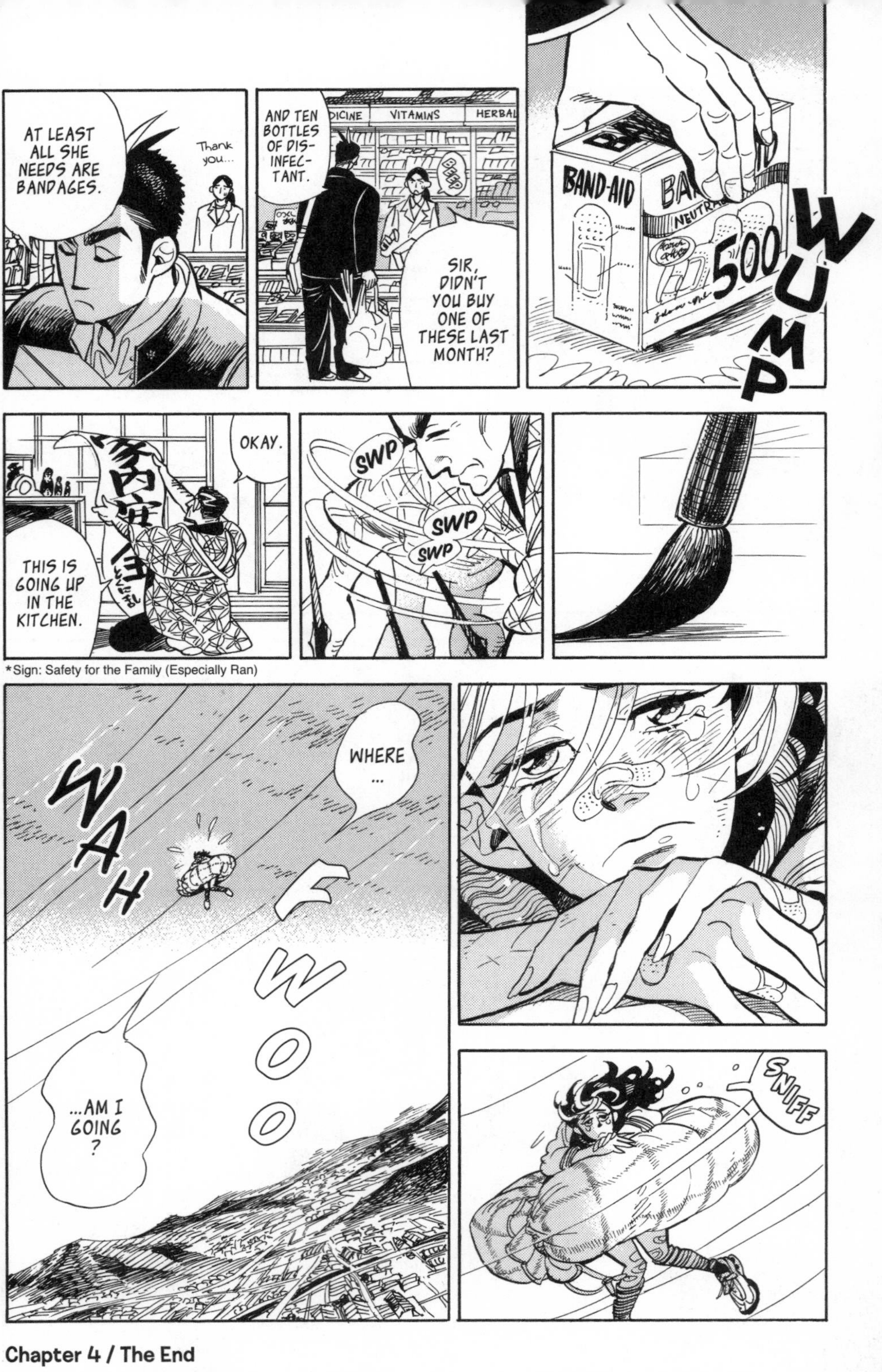
BAND-AID
500
WUMP
VITAMINS
AND TEN BOTTLES OF DIS-INFECTANT.
BEEP
SIR, DIDN'T YOU BUY ONE OF THESE LAST MONTH?
AT LEAST ALL SHE NEEDS ARE BANDAGES.
Thank you...
SWP
SWP
SWP
OKAY.
THIS IS GOING UP IN THE KITCHEN.
SNIFF
WHERE ...
WAH
WOOO
...AM I GOING?

*Sign: Safety for the Family (Especially Ran)

Chapter 4 / The End

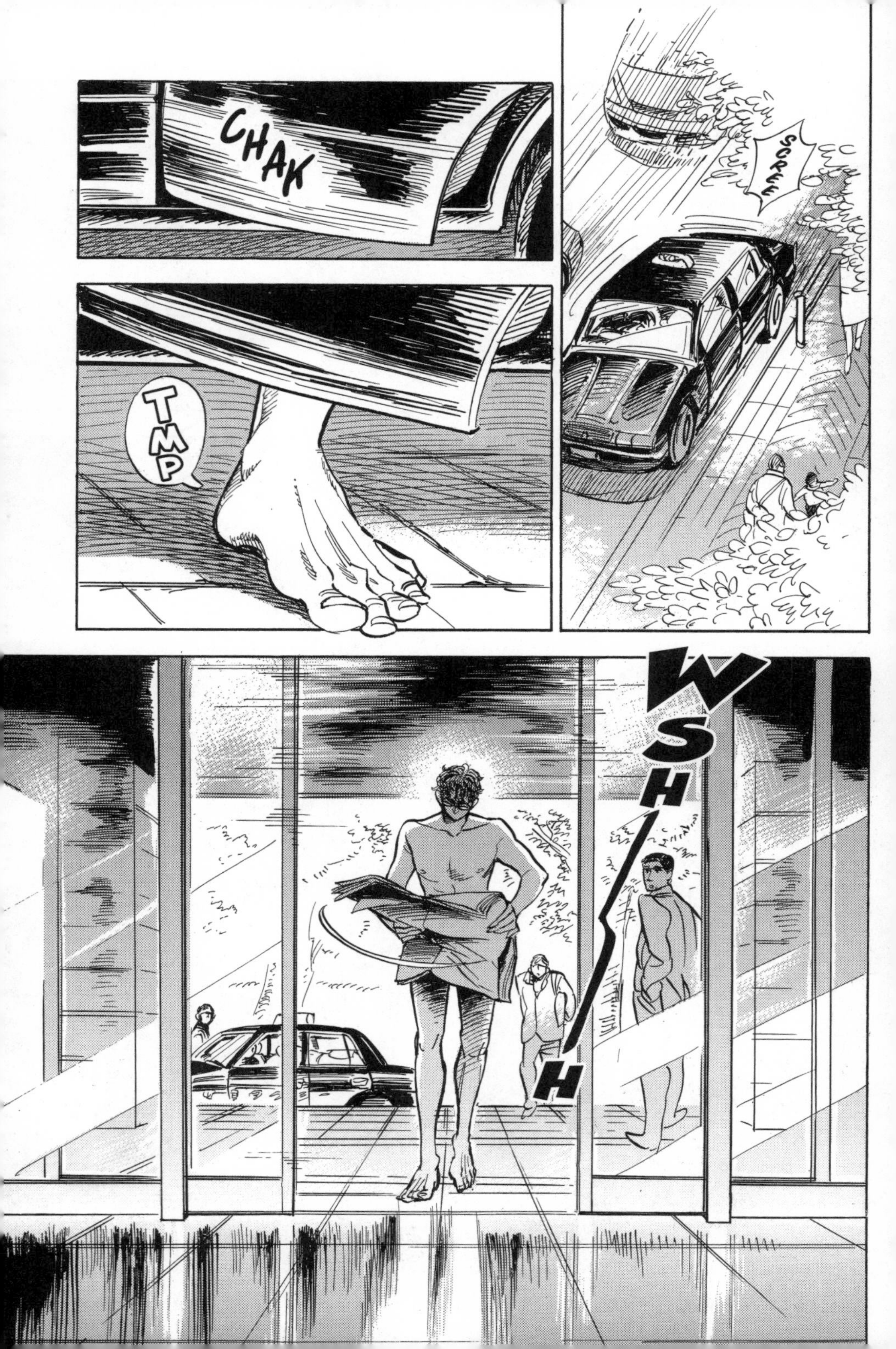
SCREE
CHAK
TMP
WSHHH

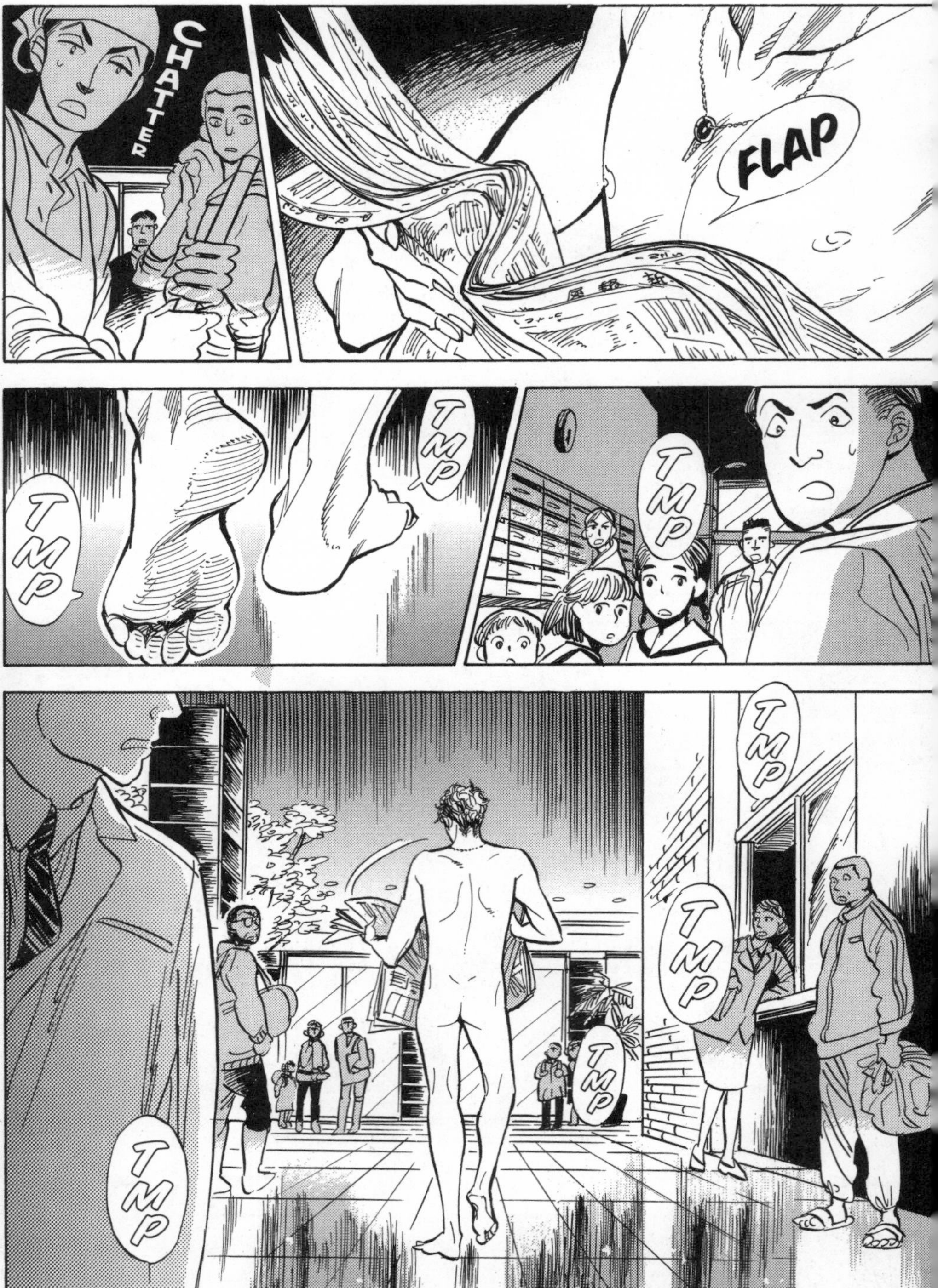
FLAP
CHATTER
TMP
TMP
TMP
TMP
TMP
TMP
TMP
TMP

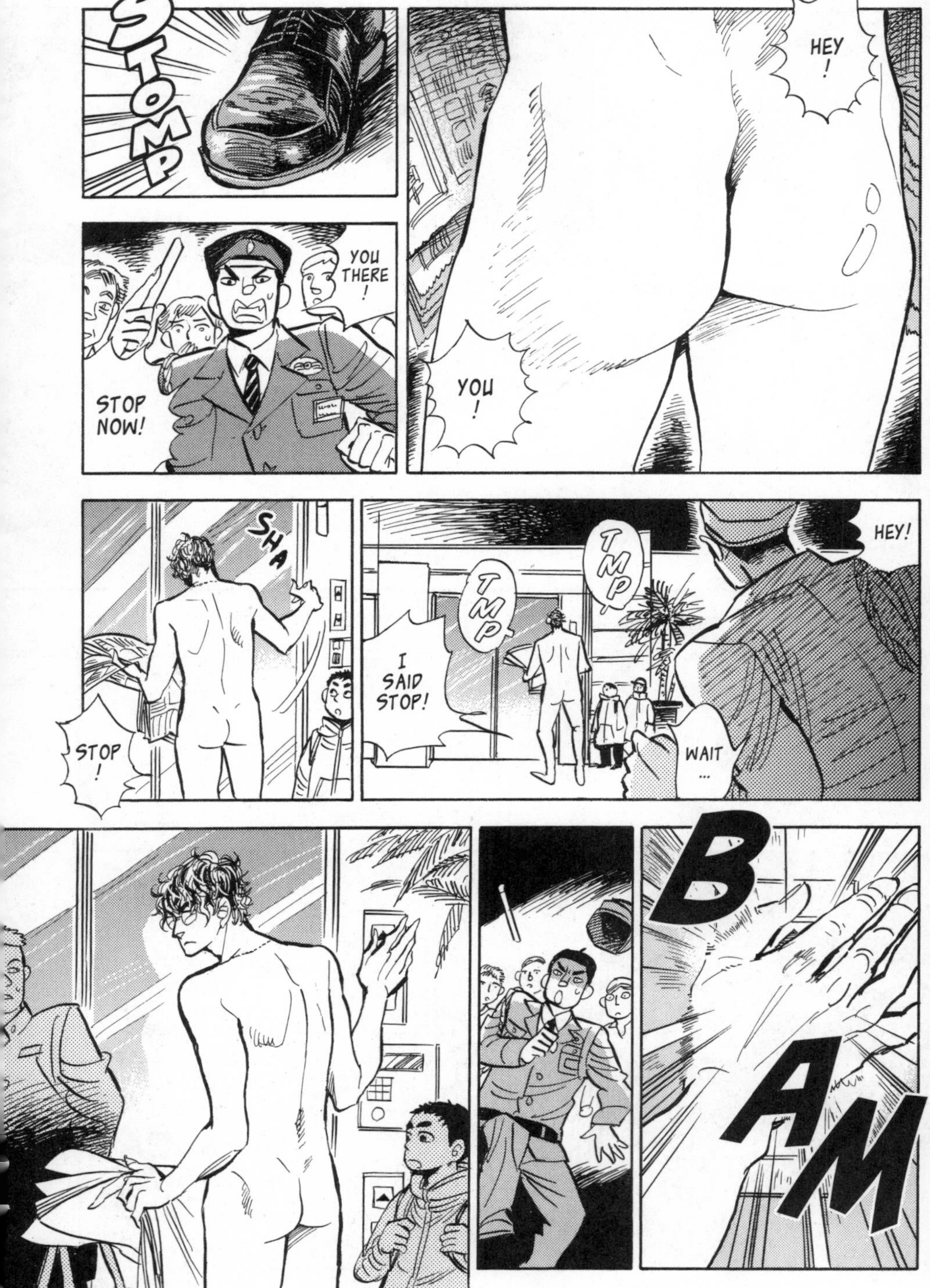
HEY!
YOU!
STOMP
YOU THERE!
STOP NOW!
HEY!
TMP
TMP
I SAID STOP!
WAIT...
SHA
STOP!
BAM

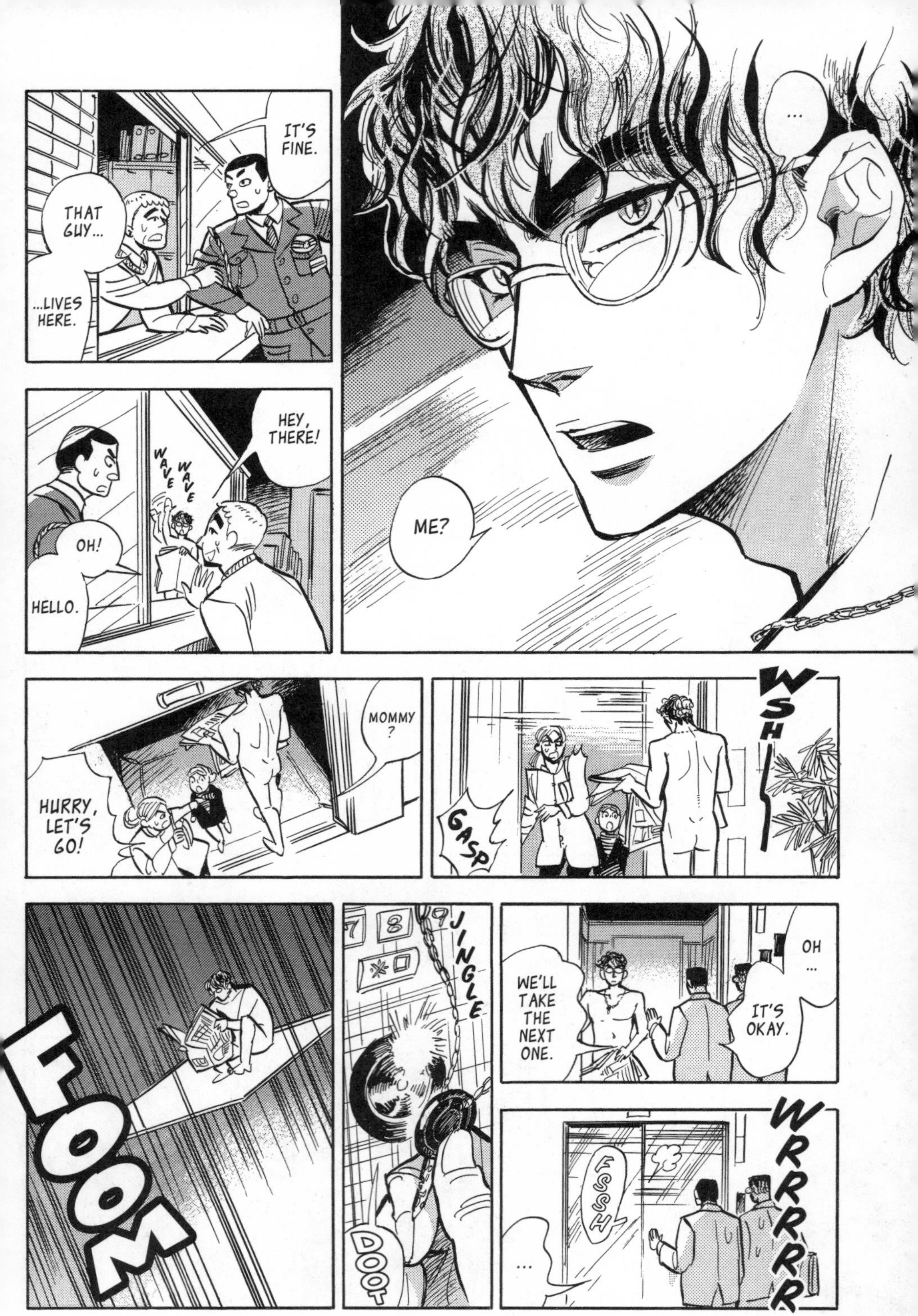
...
ME?
IT'S FINE.
THAT GUY...
...LIVES HERE.
HEY, THERE!
WAVE WAVE
OH!
HELLO.
WSH
GASP
MOMMY?
HURRY, LET'S GO!
OH ...
IT'S OKAY.
WE'LL TAKE THE NEXT ONE.
WRRRRR
FSSH
...
JINGLE
DOOT
FOOM

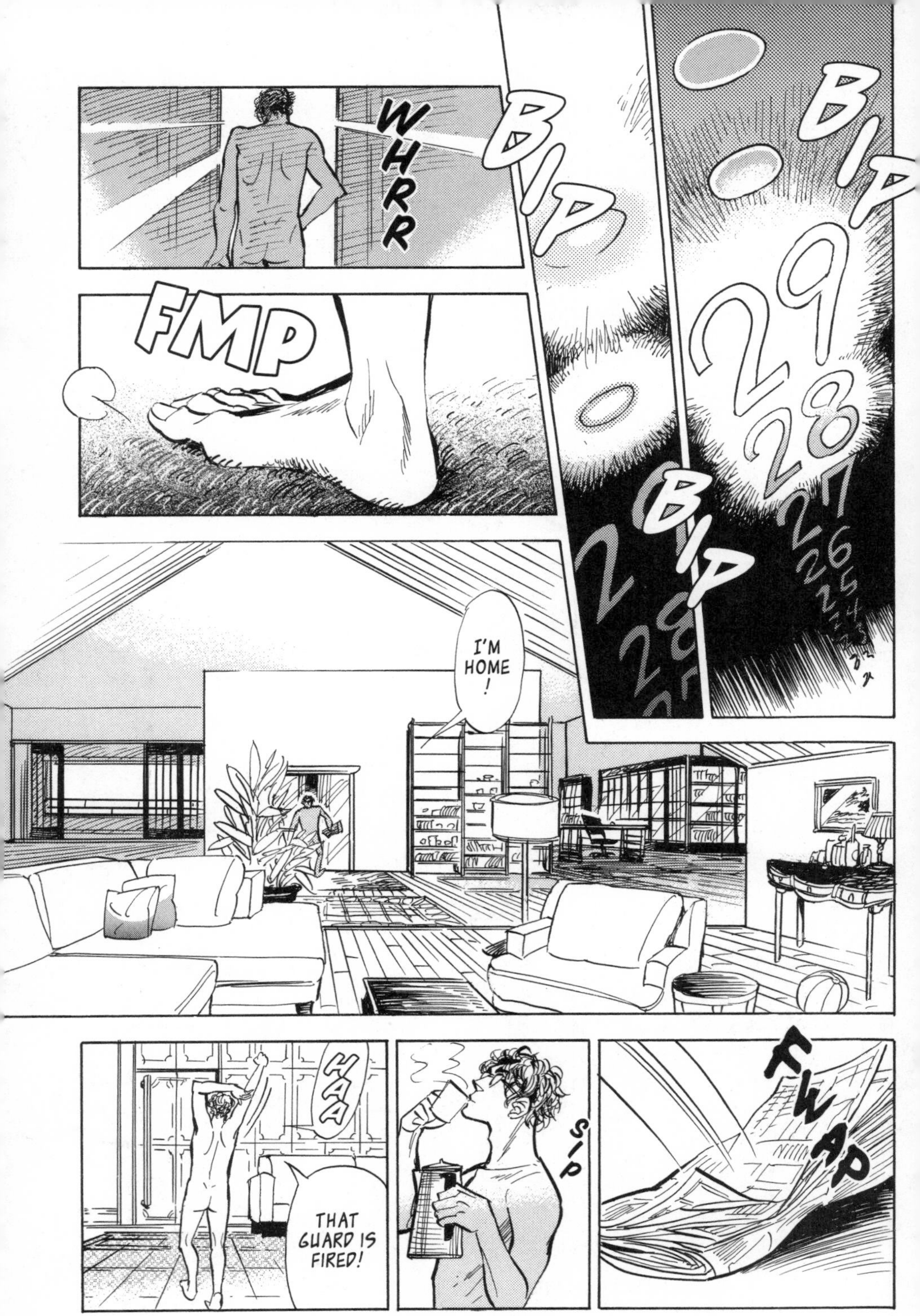
BIP
29
28
27
26
BIP
BIP
WHRR
FMP
I'M HOME!
FWAP
SIP
HAA
THAT GUARD IS FIRED!

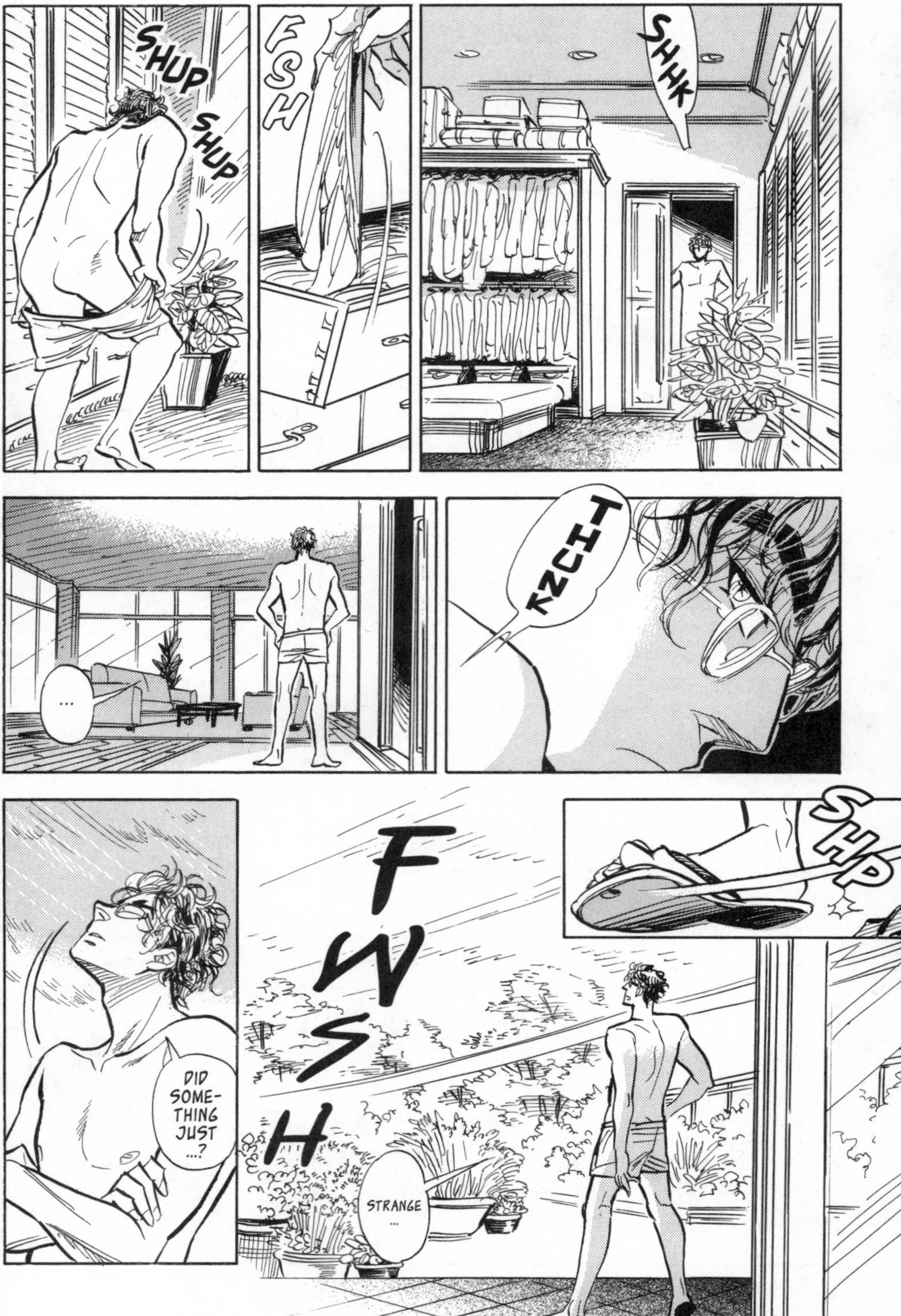
SHHK
FSH
SHUP SHUP
THUNK
...
SHP
FWSH
STRANGE ...
DID SOMETHING JUST ...?

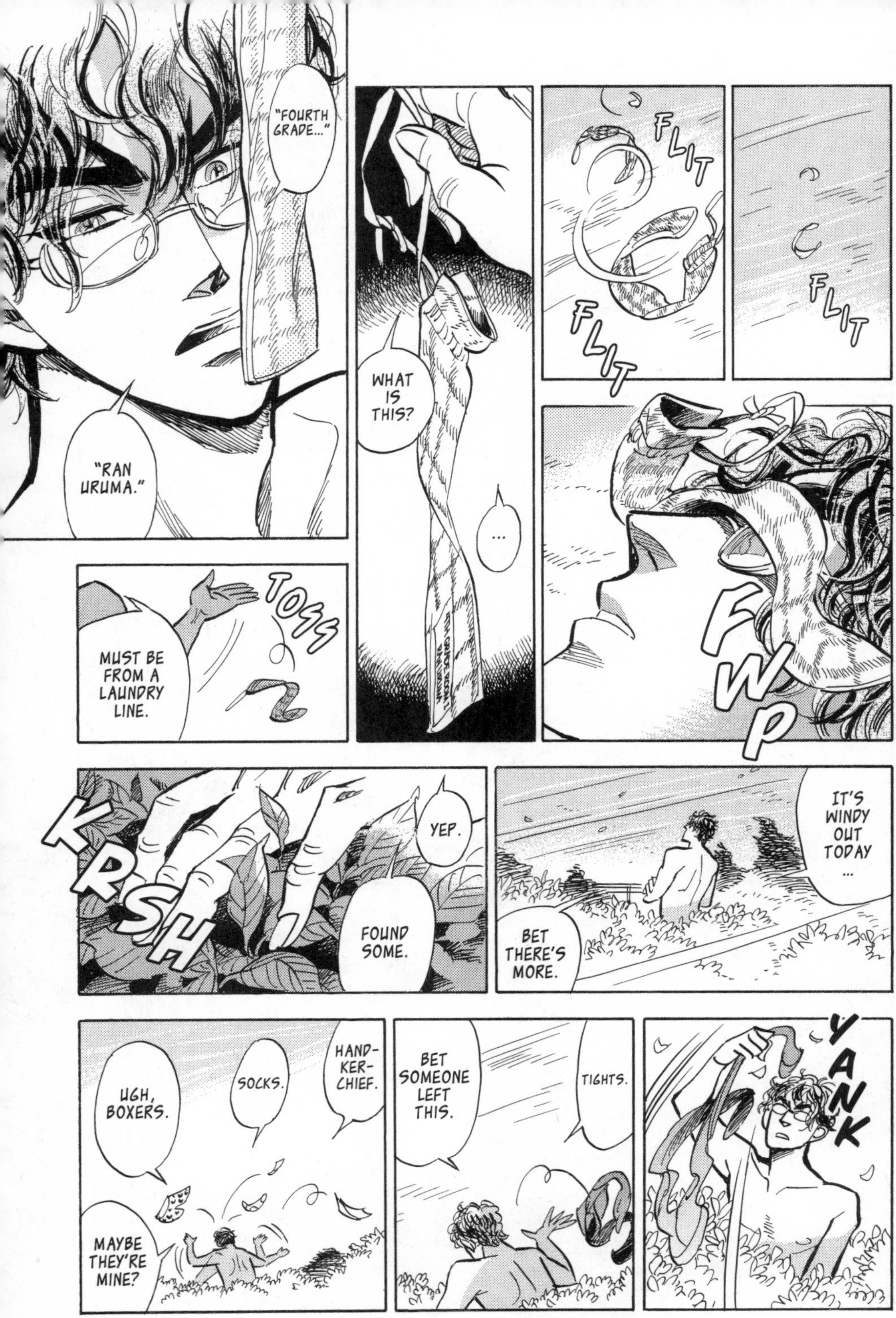
FLIT
FLIT
FLIT
FWP
WHAT IS THIS?
...
"FOURTH GRADE..."
"RAN URUMA."
TOSS
MUST BE FROM A LAUNDRY LINE.
IT'S WINDY OUT TODAY ...
BET THERE'S MORE.
YEP.
FOUND SOME.
KRSH
YANK
TIGHTS.
BET SOMEONE LEFT THIS.
HAND-KER-CHIEF.
SOCKS.
UGH, BOXERS.
MAYBE THEY'RE MINE?

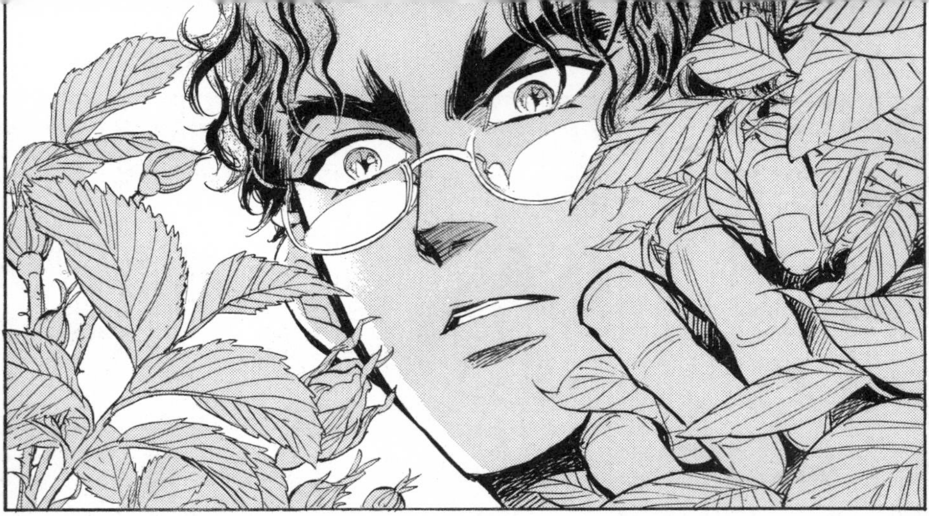

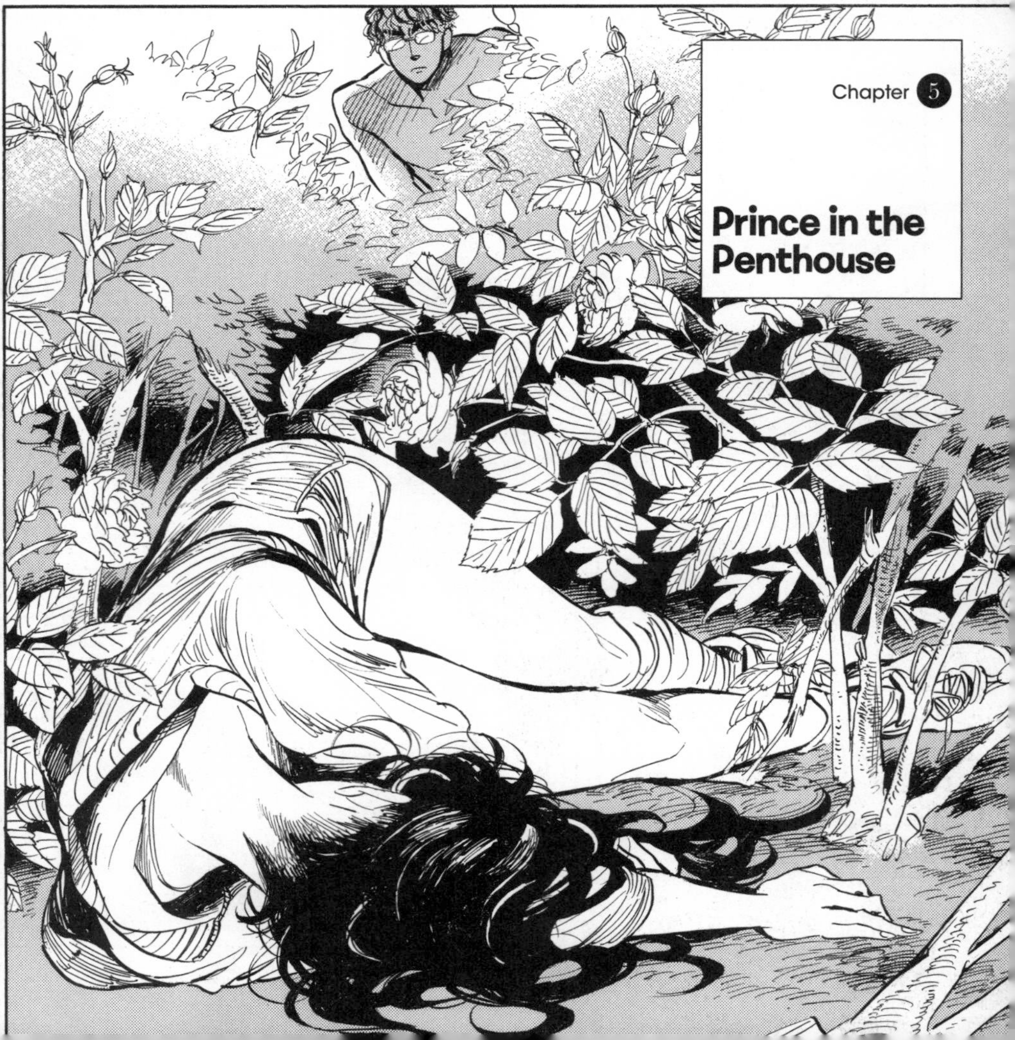

Chapter 5

Prince in the Penthouse

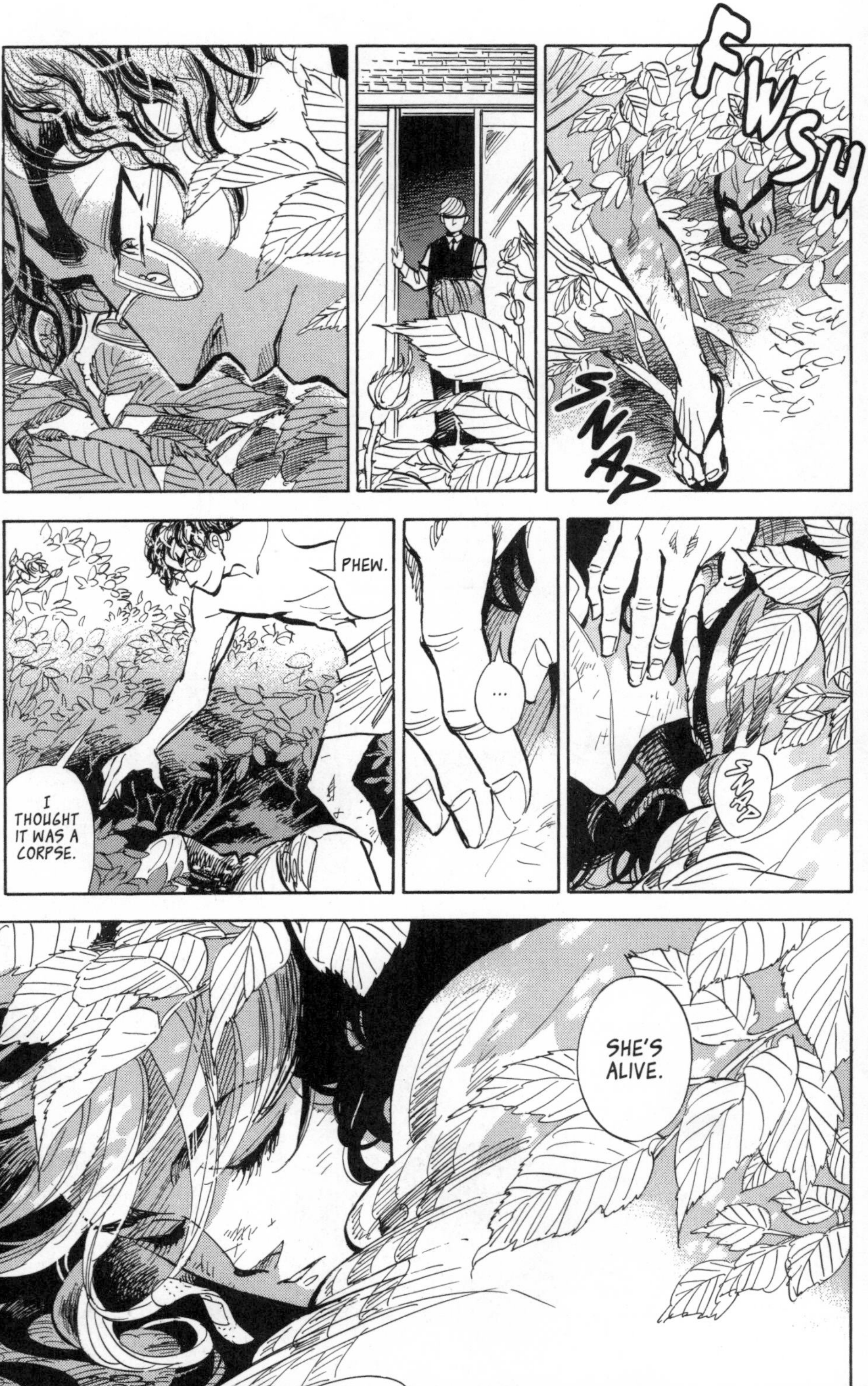
FWSH
SNAP
SNAP
...
PHEW.
I THOUGHT IT WAS A CORPSE.
SHE'S ALIVE.

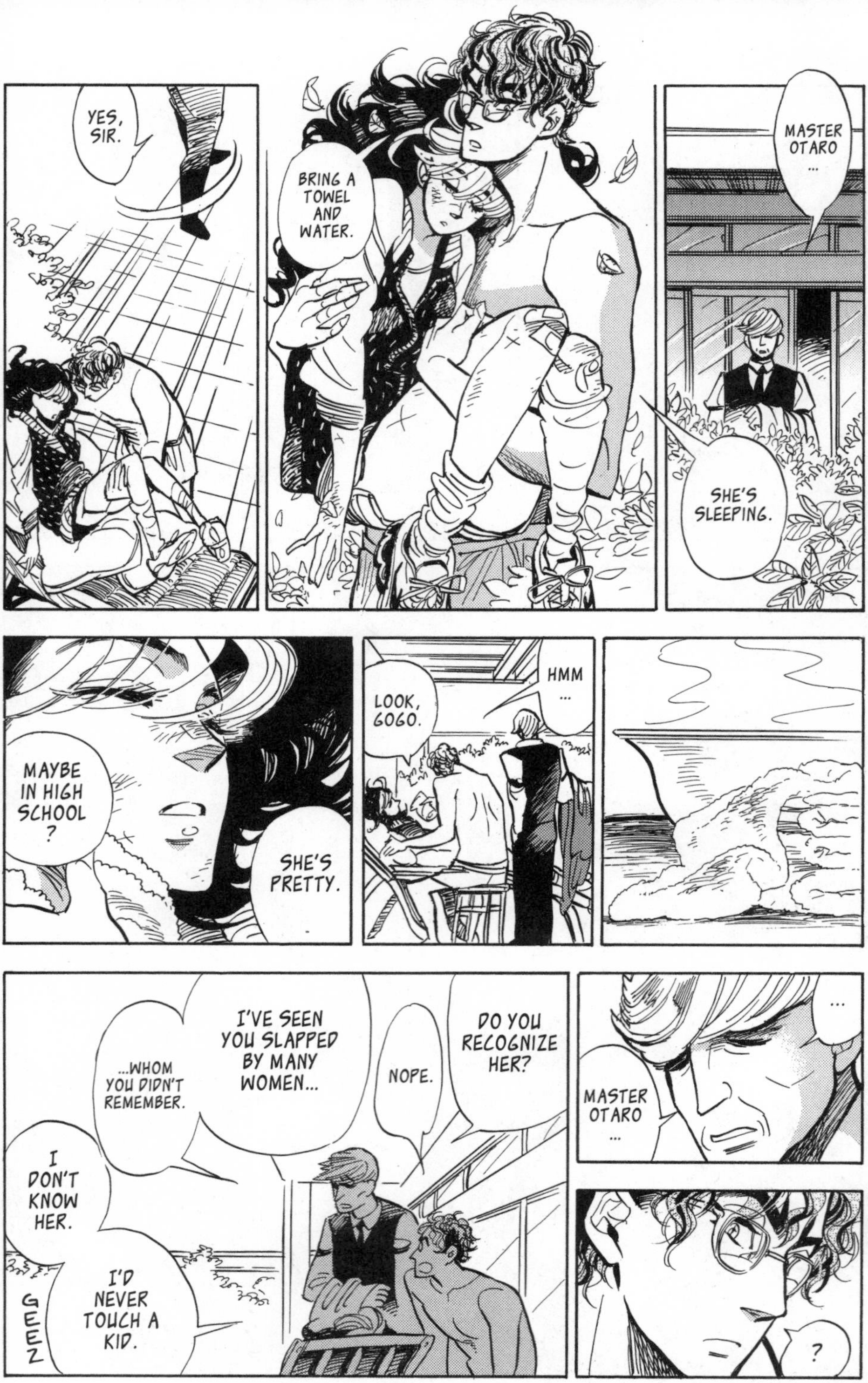
MASTER OTARO ...
SHE'S SLEEPING.
BRING A TOWEL AND WATER.
YES, SIR.
HMM ...
LOOK, GOGO.
SHE'S PRETTY.
MAYBE IN HIGH SCHOOL ?
...
MASTER OTARO ...
?
DO YOU RECOGNIZE HER?
NOPE.
I'VE SEEN YOU SLAPPED BY MANY WOMEN...
...WHOM YOU DIDN'T REMEMBER.
I DON'T KNOW HER.
I'D NEVER TOUCH A KID.
GEEZ

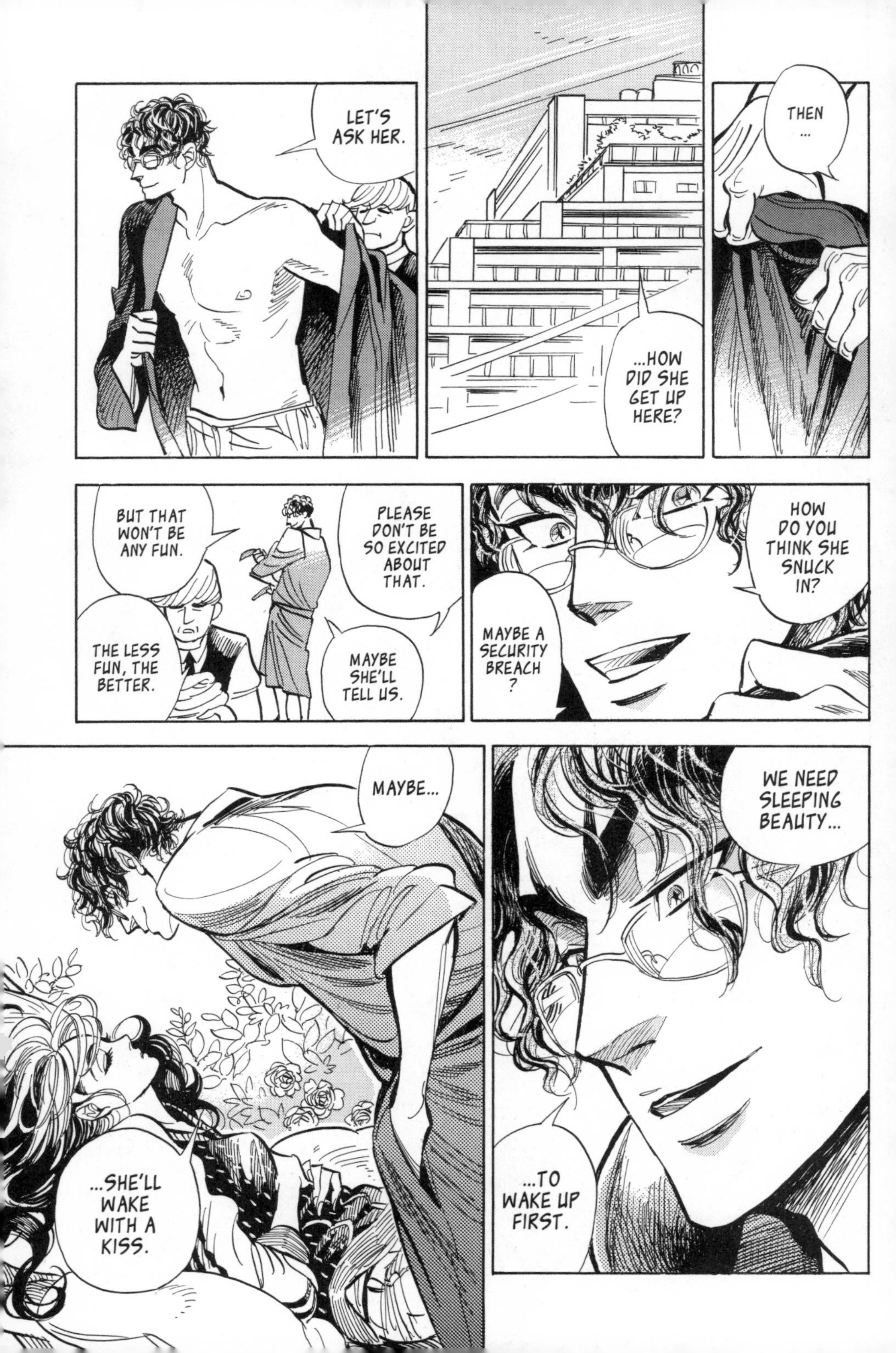
THEN ...
...HOW DID SHE GET UP HERE?
LET'S ASK HER.
HOW DO YOU THINK SHE SNUCK IN?
MAYBE A SECURITY BREACH?
PLEASE DON'T BE SO EXCITED ABOUT THAT.
BUT THAT WON'T BE ANY FUN.
MAYBE SHE'LL TELL US.
THE LESS FUN, THE BETTER.
WE NEED SLEEPING BEAUTY...
...TO WAKE UP FIRST.
MAYBE...
...SHE'LL WAKE WITH A KISS.

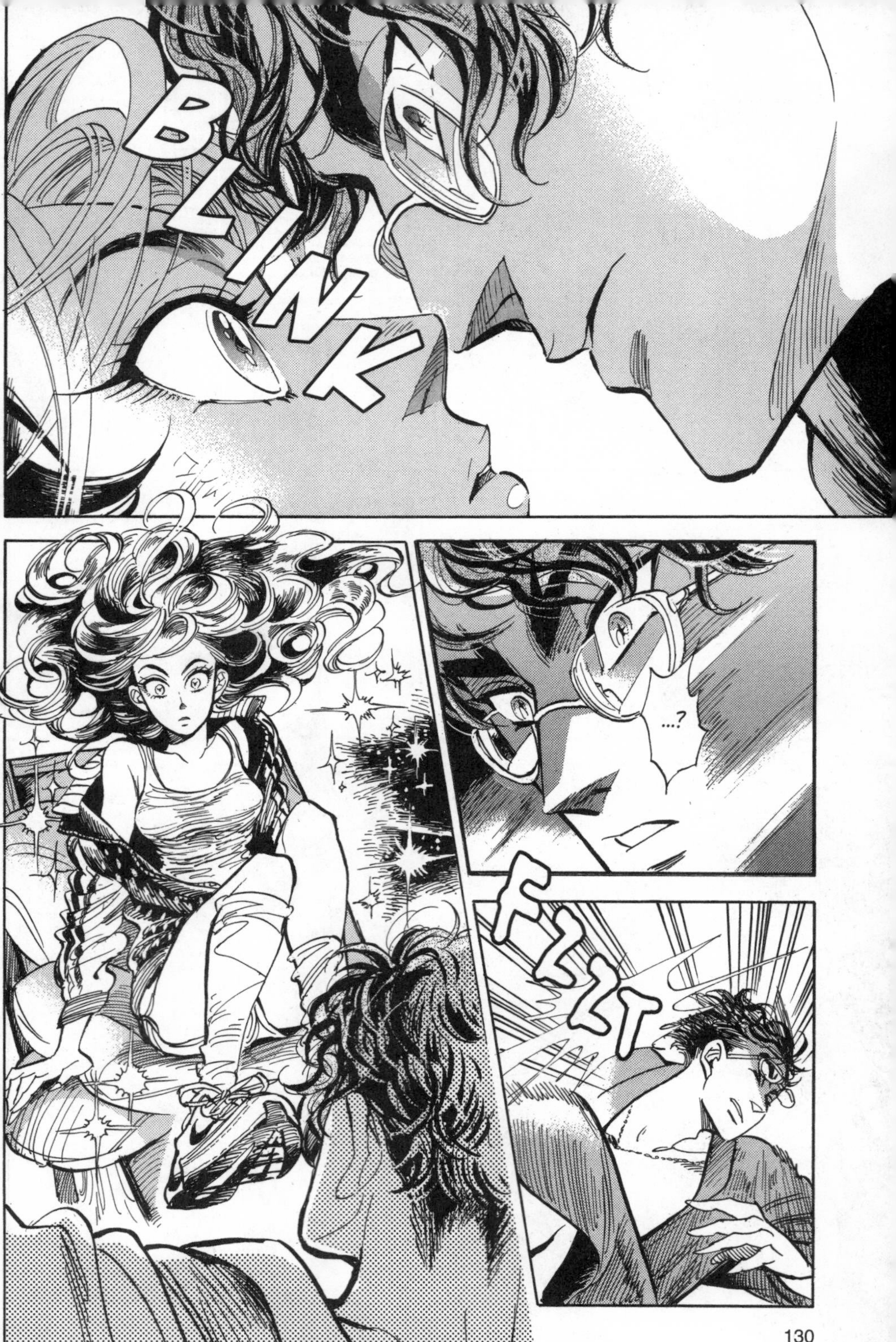
BLINK
...?
FLIT

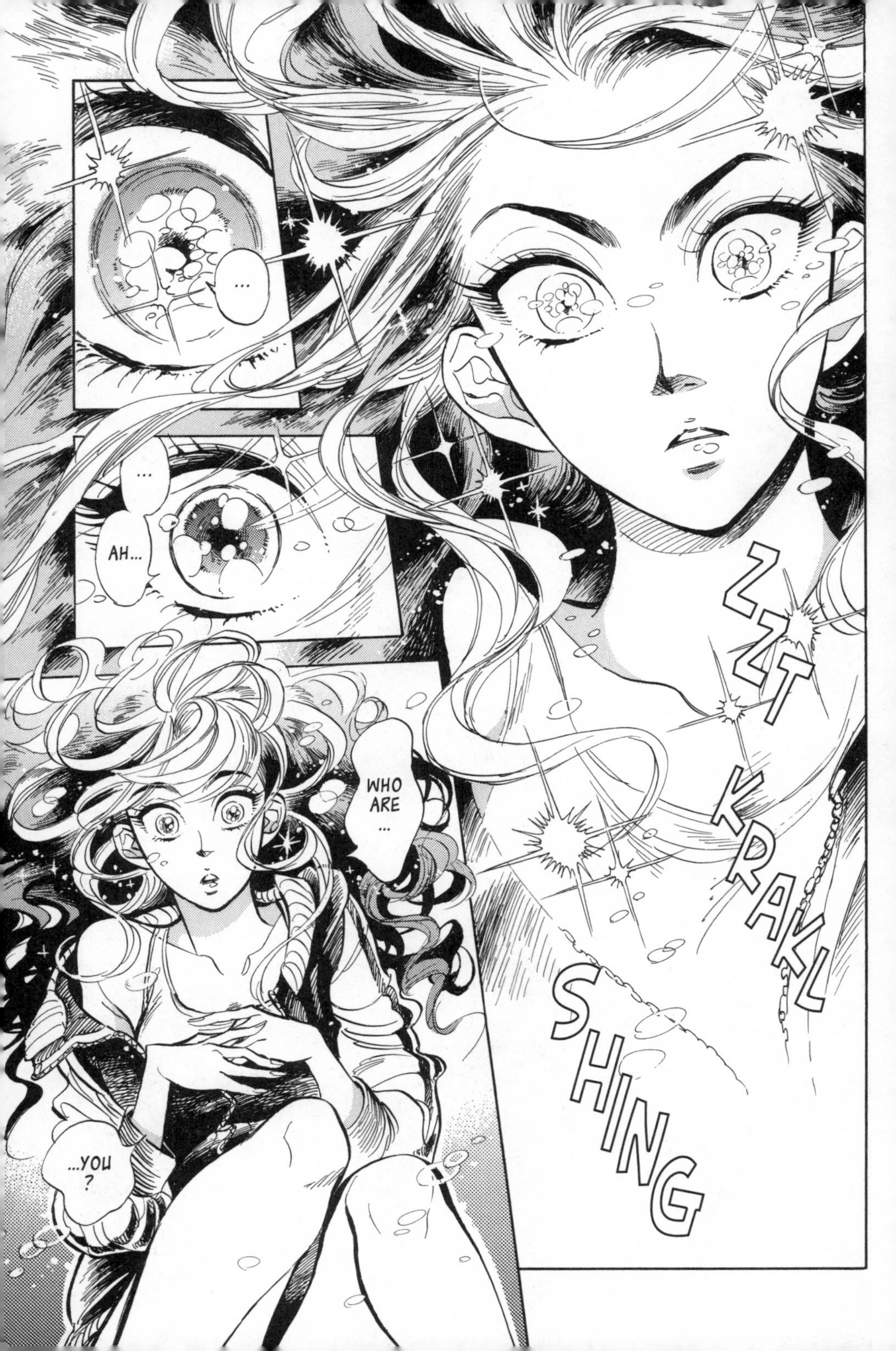
ZZT
KRAKL
SHING
...
...
AH...
WHO ARE ...
...YOU ?

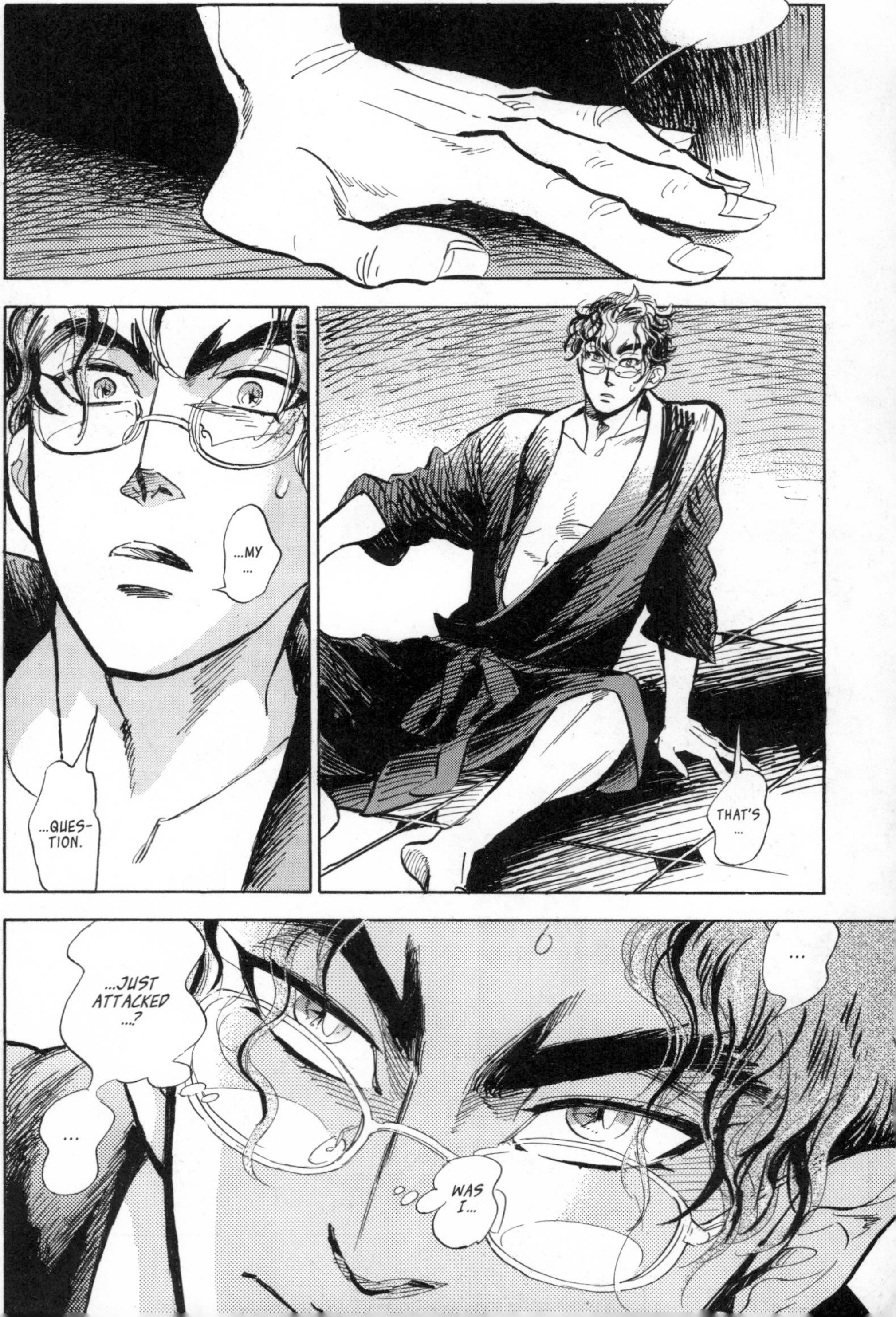
THAT'S ...
...MY ...
...QUES-TION.
...
WAS I...
...JUST ATTACKED ...?
...

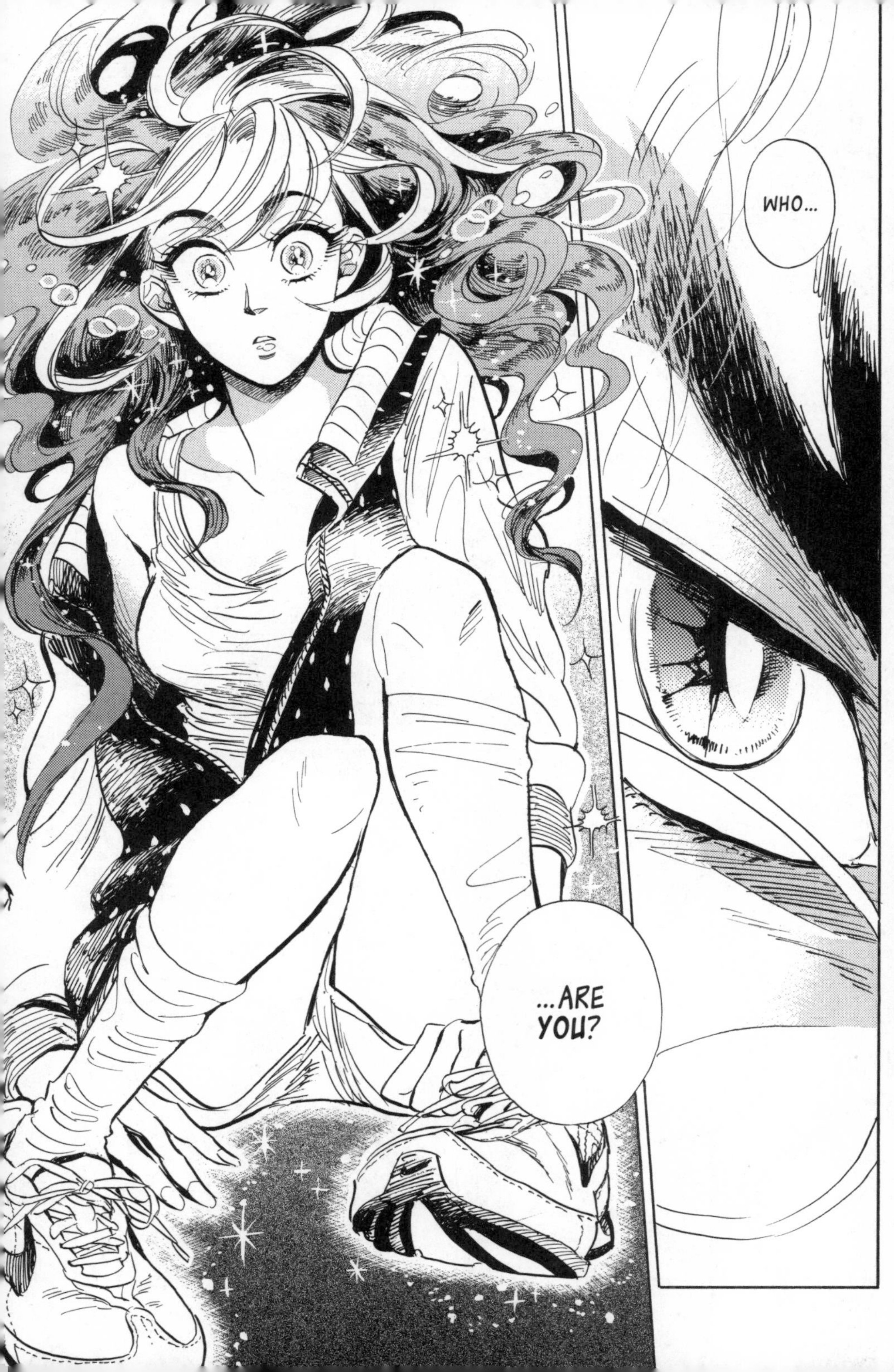
WHO...
...ARE YOU?

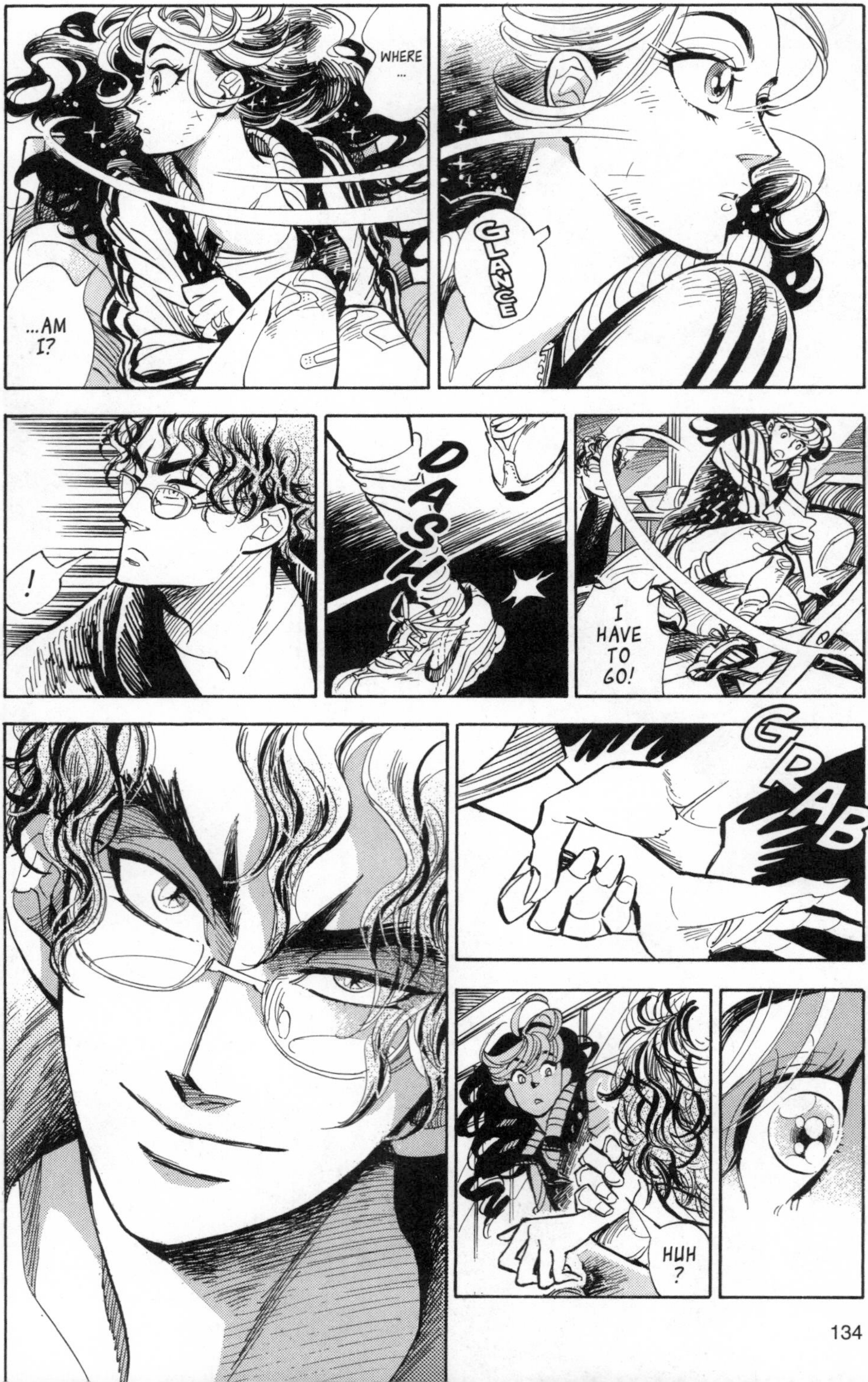
GLANCE
WHERE ...
...AM I?
I HAVE TO GO!
DASH
!
GRAB
HUH ?

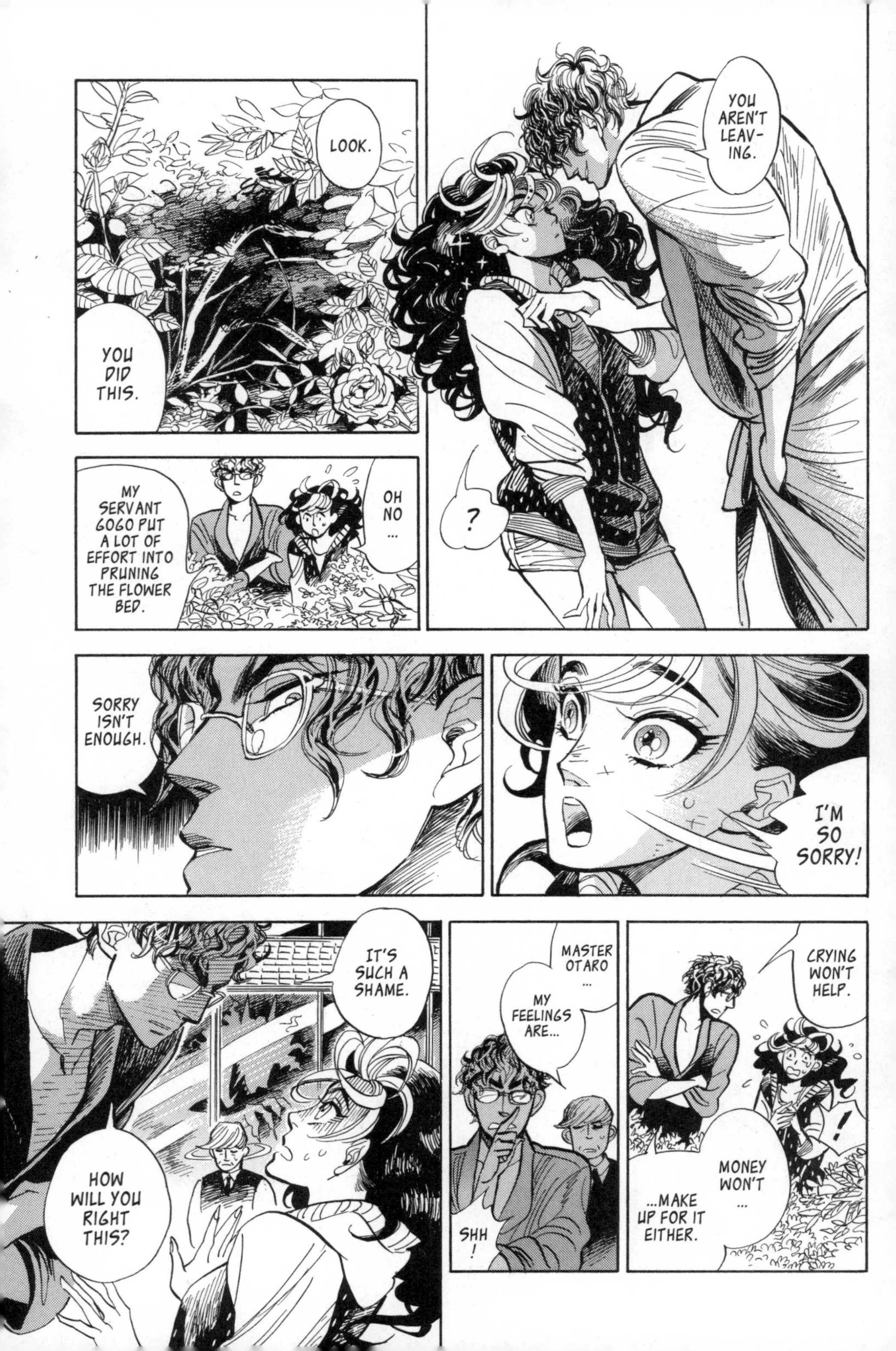

YOU AREN'T LEAV-ING.
?
LOOK.
YOU DID THIS.
OH NO ...
MY SERVANT GOGO PUT A LOT OF EFFORT INTO PRUNING THE FLOWER BED.
I'M SO SORRY!
SORRY ISN'T ENOUGH.
CRYING WON'T HELP.
!
MONEY WON'T ...
...MAKE UP FOR IT EITHER.
MASTER OTARO ...
MY FEELINGS ARE...
SHH!
IT'S SUCH A SHAME.
HOW WILL YOU RIGHT THIS?

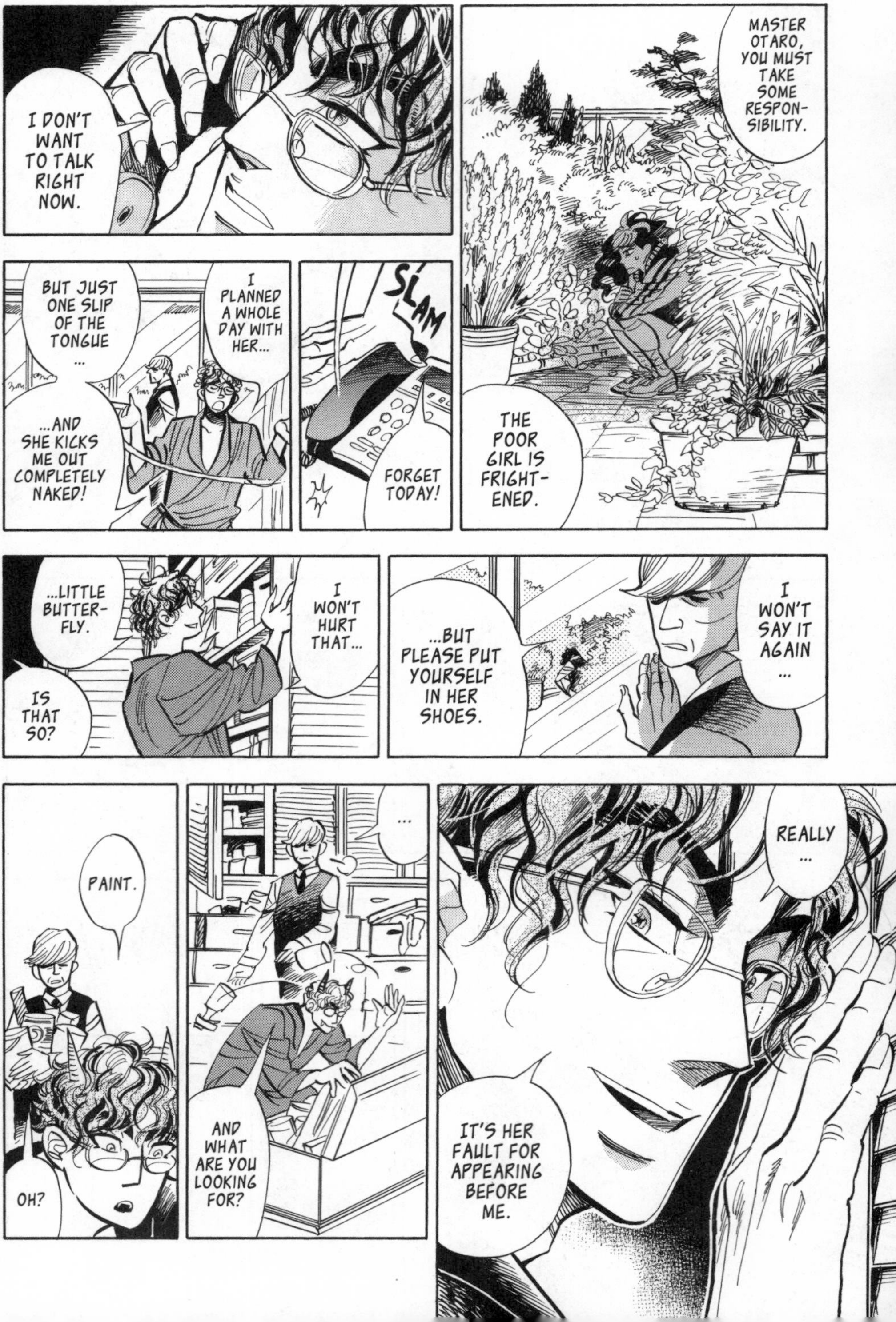
MASTER OTARO, YOU MUST TAKE SOME RESPON-SIBILITY.
THE POOR GIRL IS FRIGHT-ENED.
I DON'T WANT TO TALK RIGHT NOW.
SLAM
FORGET TODAY!
I PLANNED A WHOLE DAY WITH HER...
BUT JUST ONE SLIP OF THE TONGUE ...
...AND SHE KICKS ME OUT COMPLETELY NAKED!
I WON'T SAY IT AGAIN ...
...BUT PLEASE PUT YOURSELF IN HER SHOES.
I WON'T HURT THAT...
...LITTLE BUTTER-FLY.
IS THAT SO?
REALLY ...
IT'S HER FAULT FOR APPEARING BEFORE ME.
...
AND WHAT ARE YOU LOOKING FOR?
PAINT.
OH?

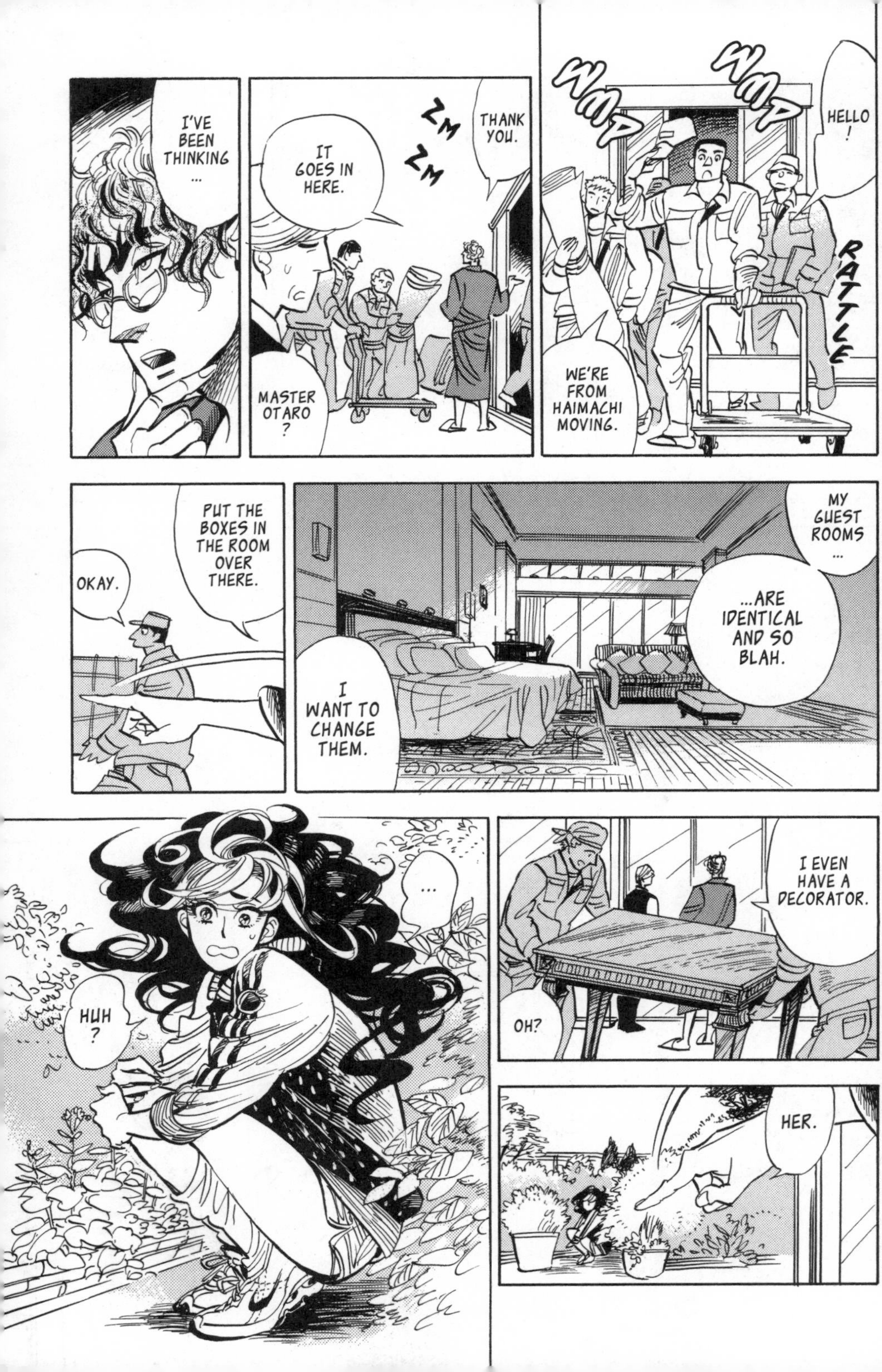
WMP
WMP
HELLO!
RATTLE
WE'RE FROM HAIMACHI MOVING.
THANK YOU.
ZM
ZM
IT GOES IN HERE.
MASTER OTARO?
I'VE BEEN THINKING...
MY GUEST ROOMS...
...ARE IDENTICAL AND SO BLAH.
I WANT TO CHANGE THEM.
PUT THE BOXES IN THE ROOM OVER THERE.
OKAY.
I EVEN HAVE A DECORATOR.
OH?
HER.
...
HUH?

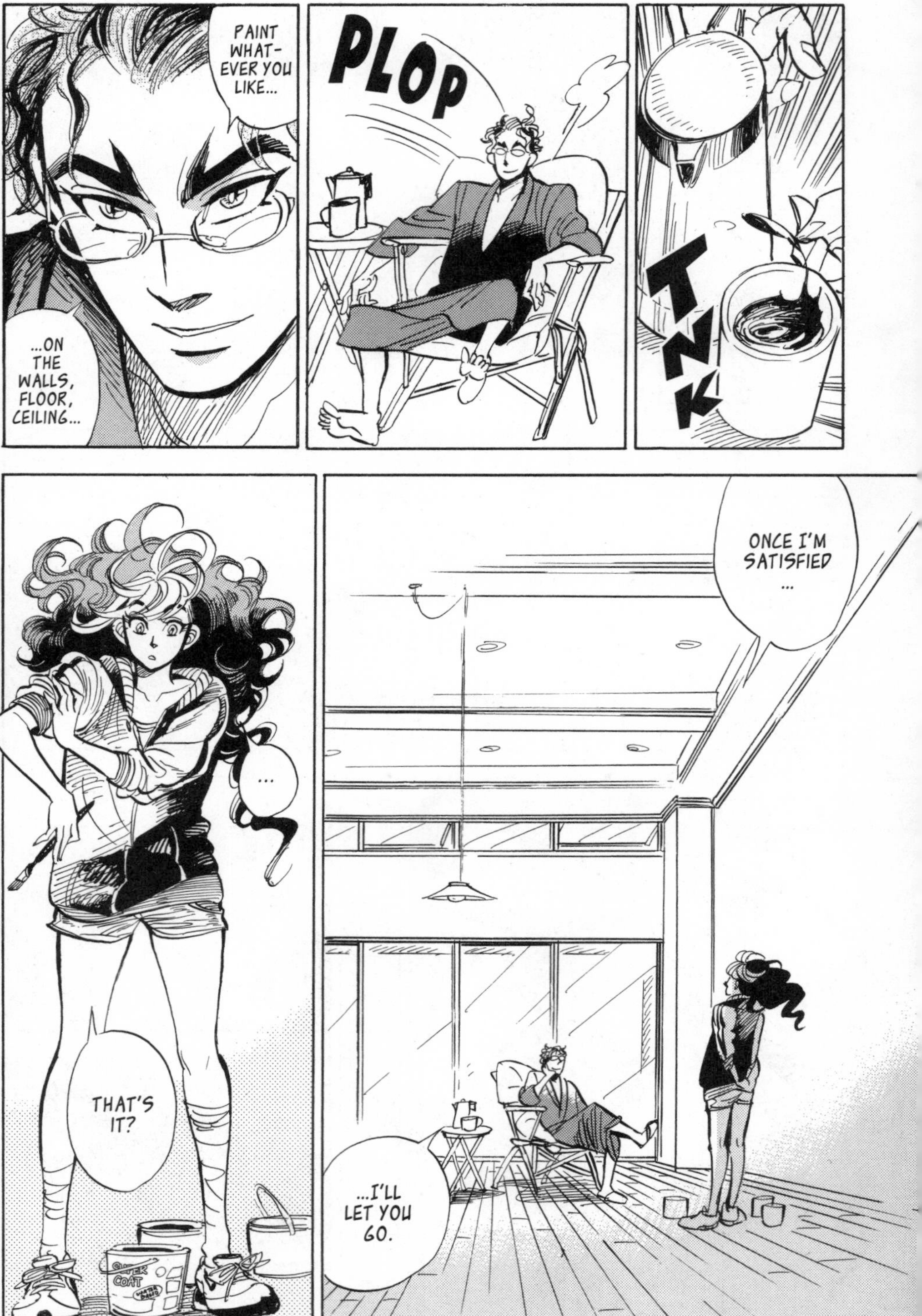
TNK
PLOP
PAINT WHAT-EVER YOU LIKE...
...ON THE WALLS, FLOOR, CEILING...
ONCE I'M SATISFIED ...
...I'LL LET YOU GO.
...
THAT'S IT?

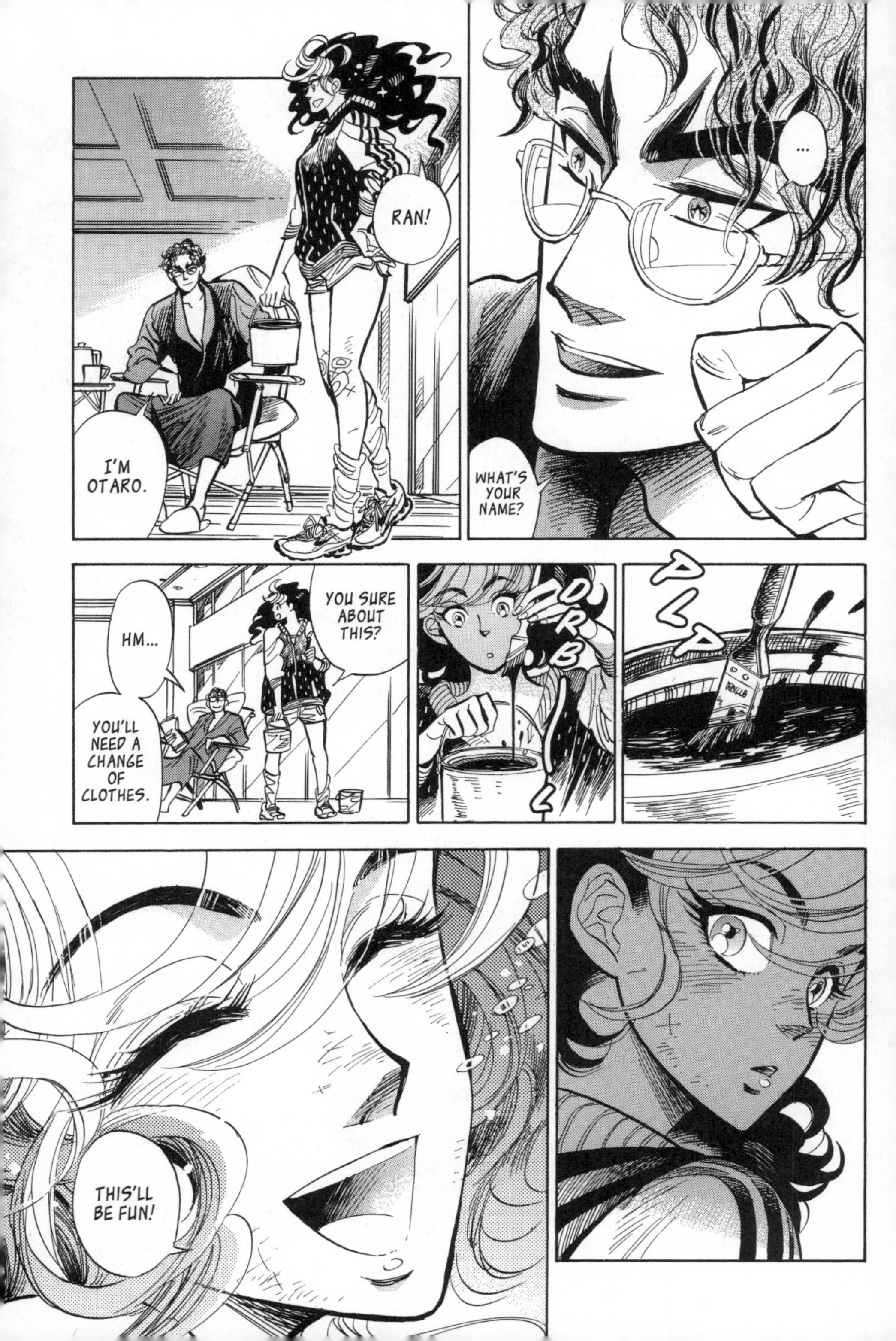
...
WHAT'S YOUR NAME?
RAN!
I'M OTARO.
PLP
ORB
L
YOU SURE ABOUT THIS?
HM...
YOU'LL NEED A CHANGE OF CLOTHES.
THIS'LL BE FUN!

MFF MFF

THIS IS HUGE.

...IT'S SMALLER THAN JIN'S.

BUT...

FWF

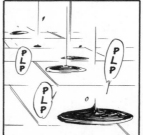

...

ONLY BLACK PAINT?

PLP PLP PLP

WRL

SWP

♪

HERE GOES.

ONLY BLACK.

FWP

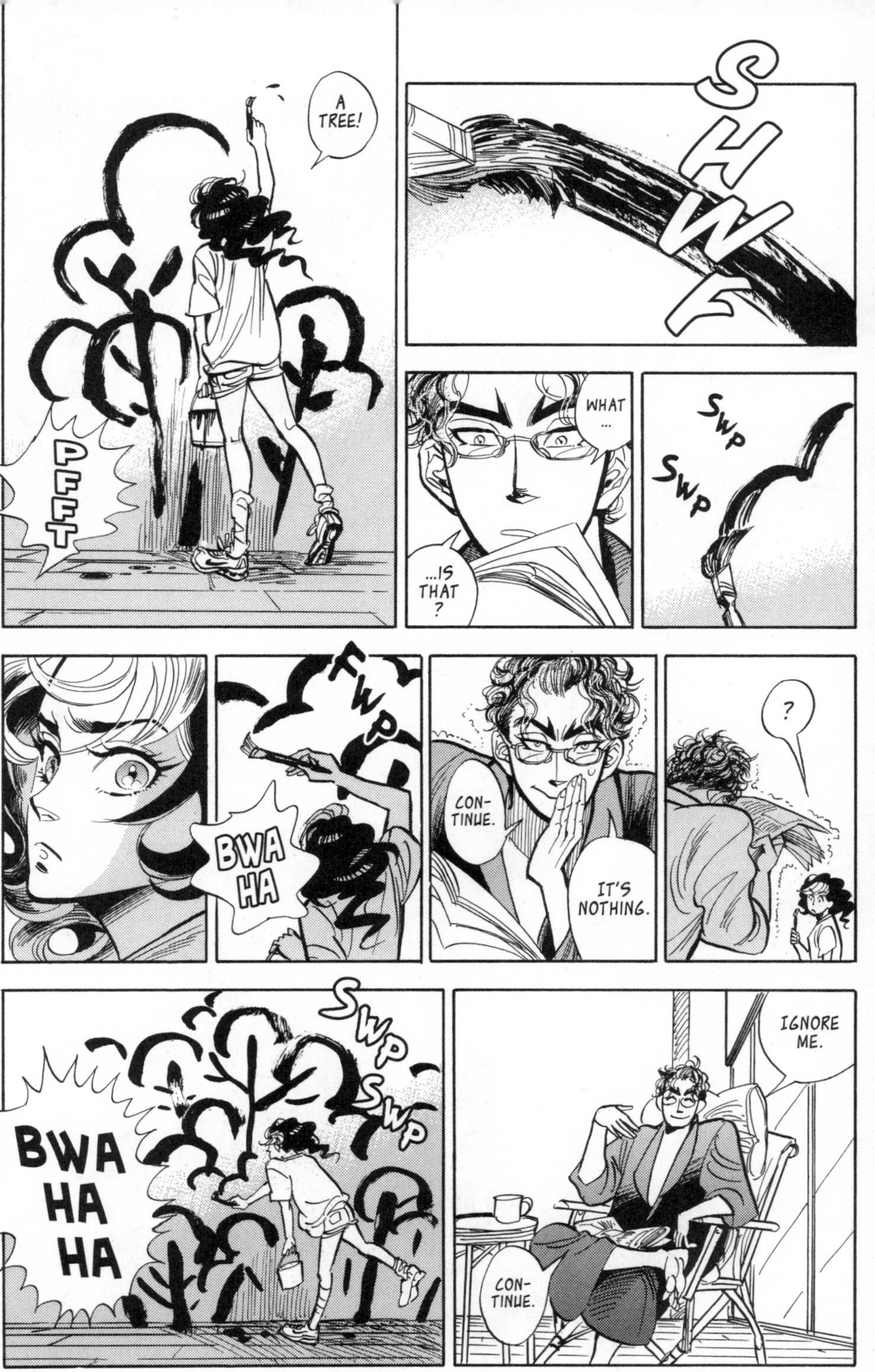
SHWY
SWP
SWP
WHAT ...
...IS THAT ?
A TREE!
PFFT
?
IT'S NOTHING.
CON-TINUE.
FWP
BWA HA
IGNORE ME.
CON-TINUE.
SWP
SWP
BWA HA HA HA

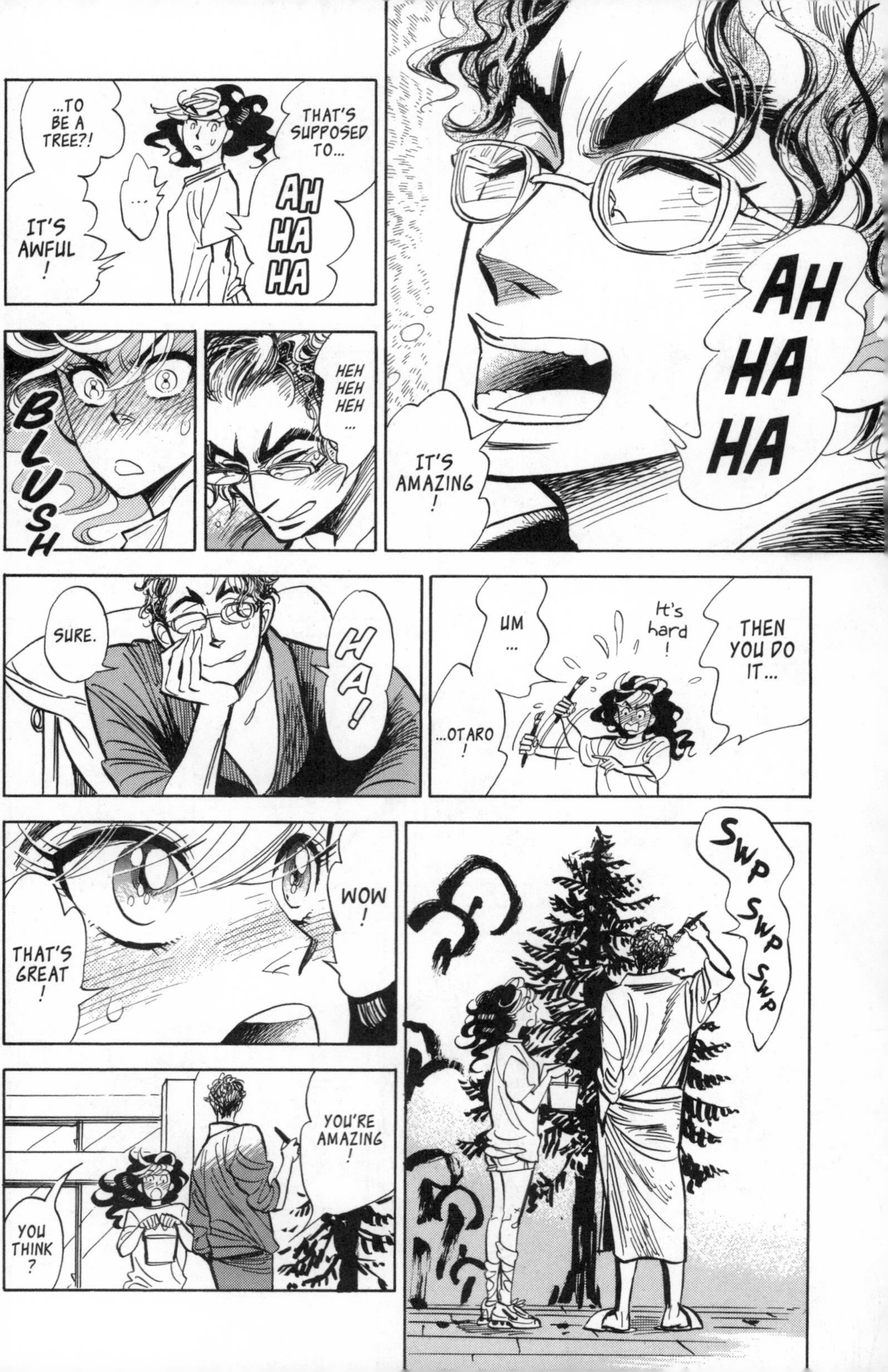
AH HA HA HA
IT'S AMAZING!
THAT'S SUPPOSED TO...
AH HA HA
...
...TO BE A TREE?!
IT'S AWFUL!
HEH HEH HEH...
BLUSH
THEN YOU DO IT...
It's hard!
UM...
...OTARO!
HA!
SURE.
SWP SWP SWP
WOW!
THAT'S GREAT!
YOU'RE AMAZING!
YOU THINK?

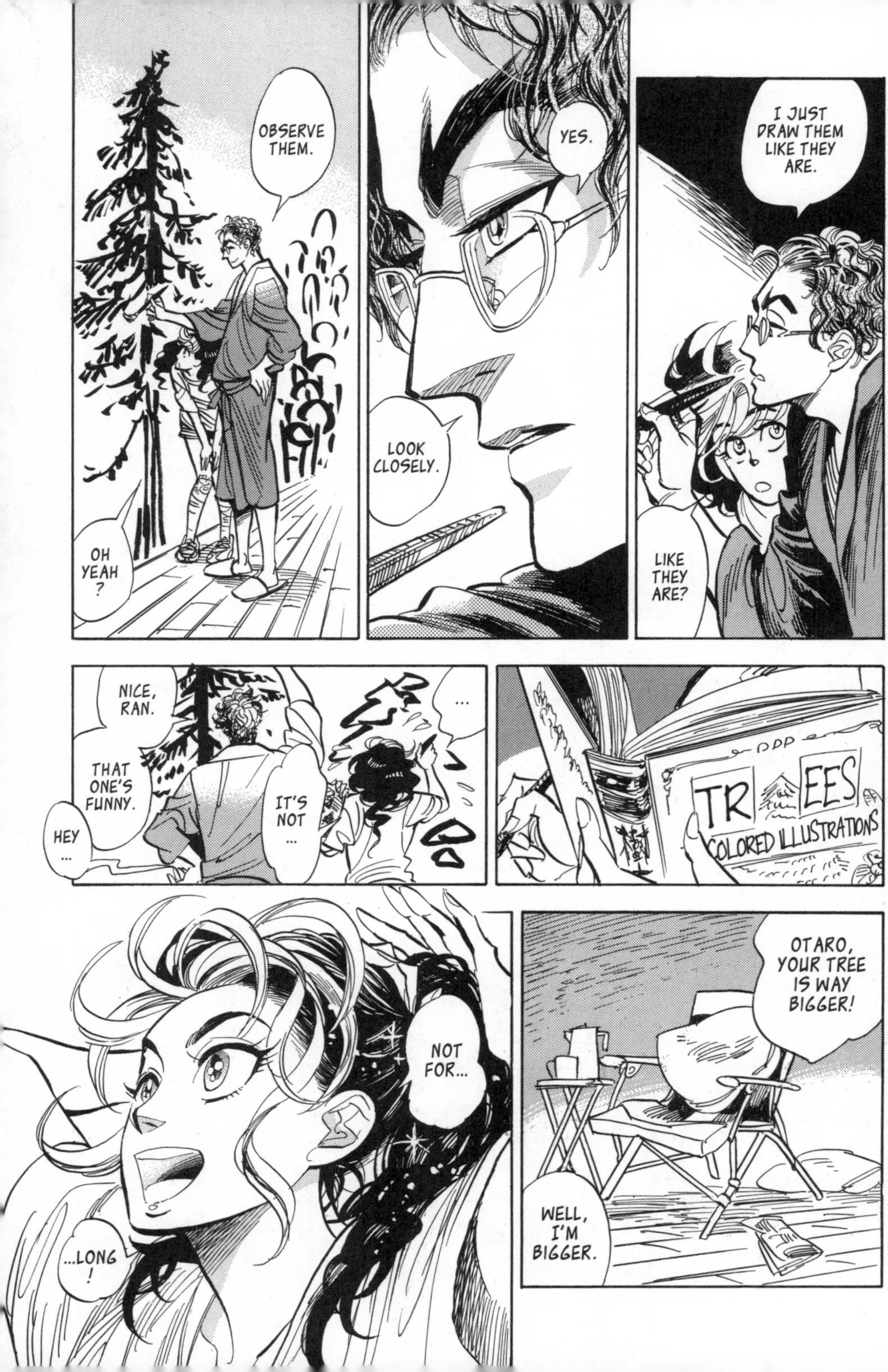
I JUST DRAW THEM LIKE THEY ARE.
LIKE THEY ARE?
YES.
LOOK CLOSELY.
OBSERVE THEM.
OH YEAH?
TREES
COLORED ILLUSTRATIONS
...
IT'S NOT ...
NICE, RAN.
THAT ONE'S FUNNY.
HEY ...
OTARO, YOUR TREE IS WAY BIGGER!
WELL, I'M BIGGER.
NOT FOR...
...LONG!

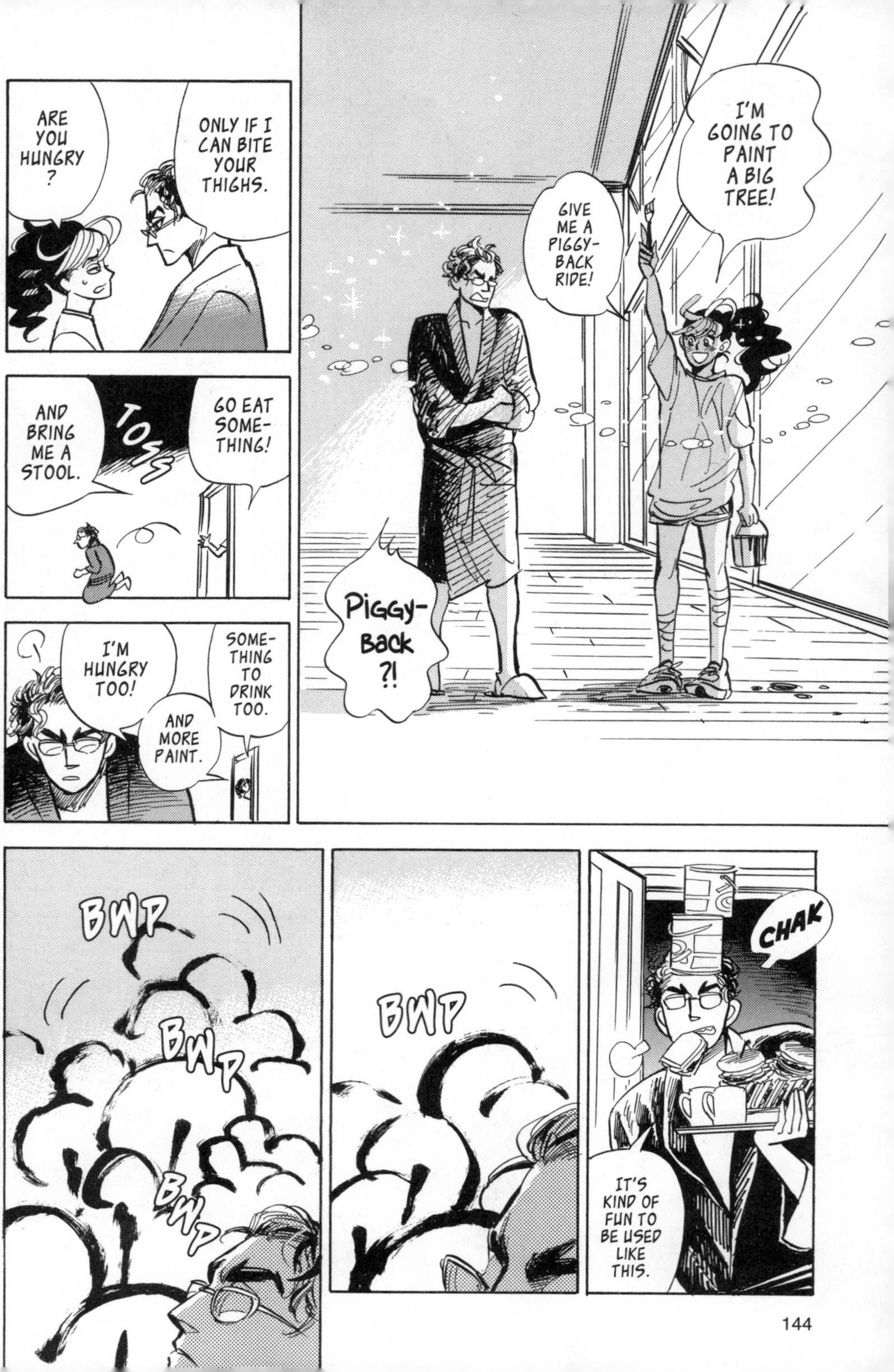
I'M GOING TO PAINT A BIG TREE!
GIVE ME A PIGGY-BACK RIDE!
Piggy-back?!
ONLY IF I CAN BITE YOUR THIGHS.
ARE YOU HUNGRY?
GO EAT SOME-THING!
TOSS
AND BRING ME A STOOL.
SOME-THING TO DRINK TOO.
I'M HUNGRY TOO!
AND MORE PAINT.
CHAK
IT'S KIND OF FUN TO BE USED LIKE THIS.
BWP
BWP
BWP
BWP

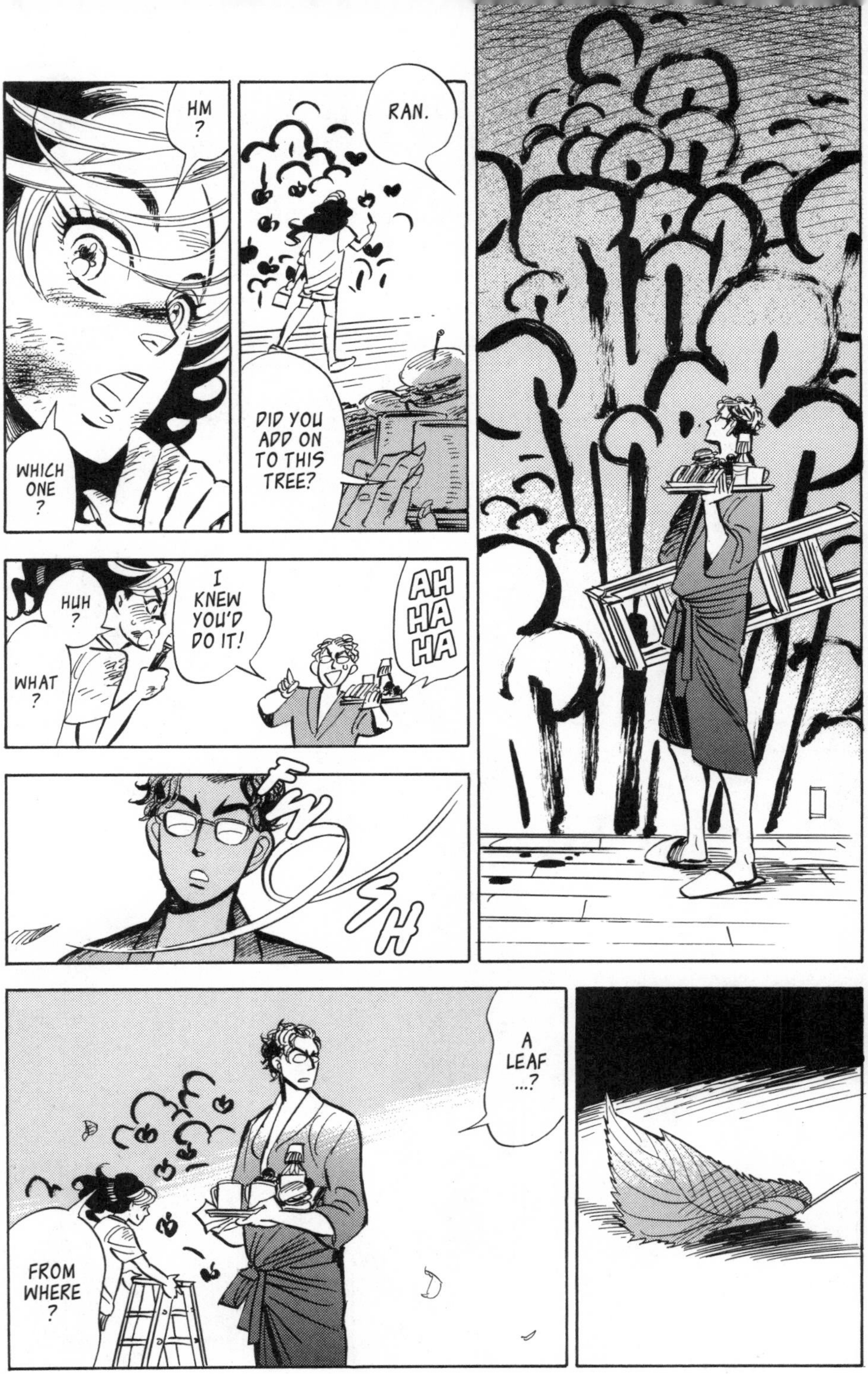
RAN.
DID YOU ADD ON TO THIS TREE?
HM?
WHICH ONE?
AH HA HA
I KNEW YOU'D DO IT!
HUH?
WHAT?
FWOOSH
A LEAF ...?
FROM WHERE?

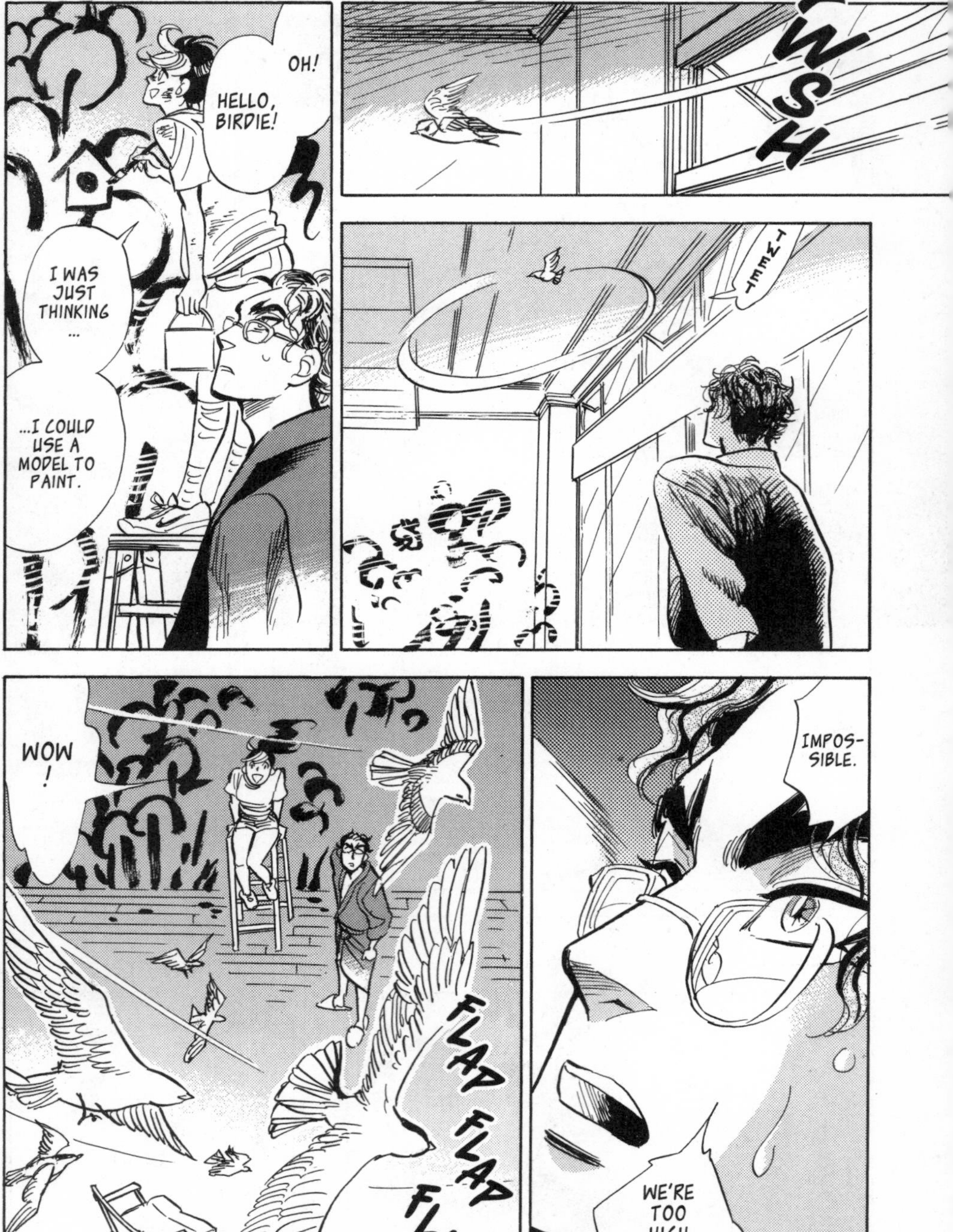
FWSH
TWEET
OH!
HELLO, BIRDIE!
I WAS JUST THINKING ...
...I COULD USE A MODEL TO PAINT.
IMPOS-SIBLE.
WE'RE TOO HIGH UP FOR BIRDS!
WOW!
FLAP FLAP FLAP

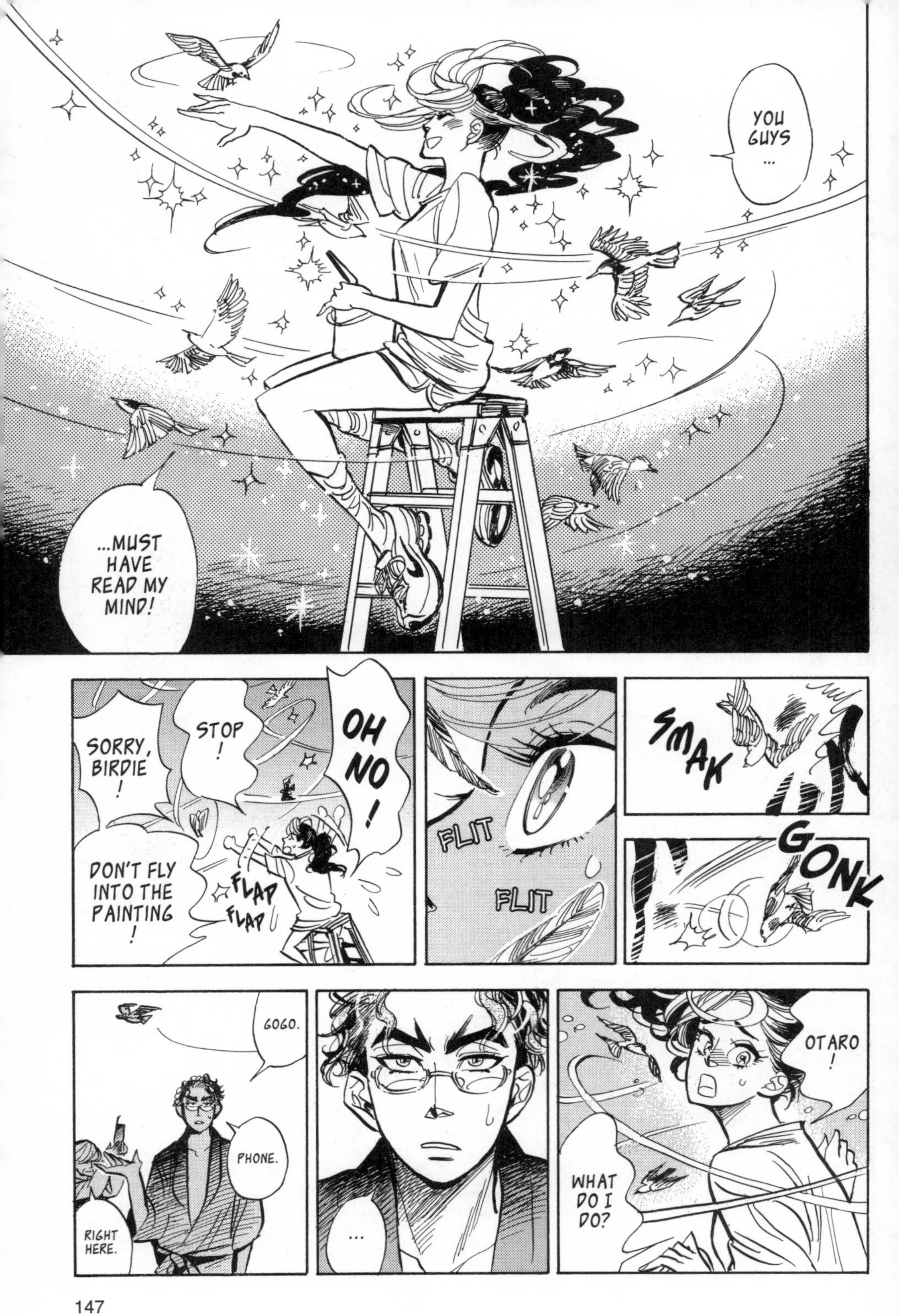
YOU GUYS ...
...MUST HAVE READ MY MIND!
SMAK
GONK
FLIT
FLIT
OH NO!
STOP!
SORRY, BIRDIE!
DON'T FLY INTO THE PAINTING!
FLAP FLAP
OTARO!
WHAT DO I DO?
...
GOGO.
PHONE.
RIGHT HERE.

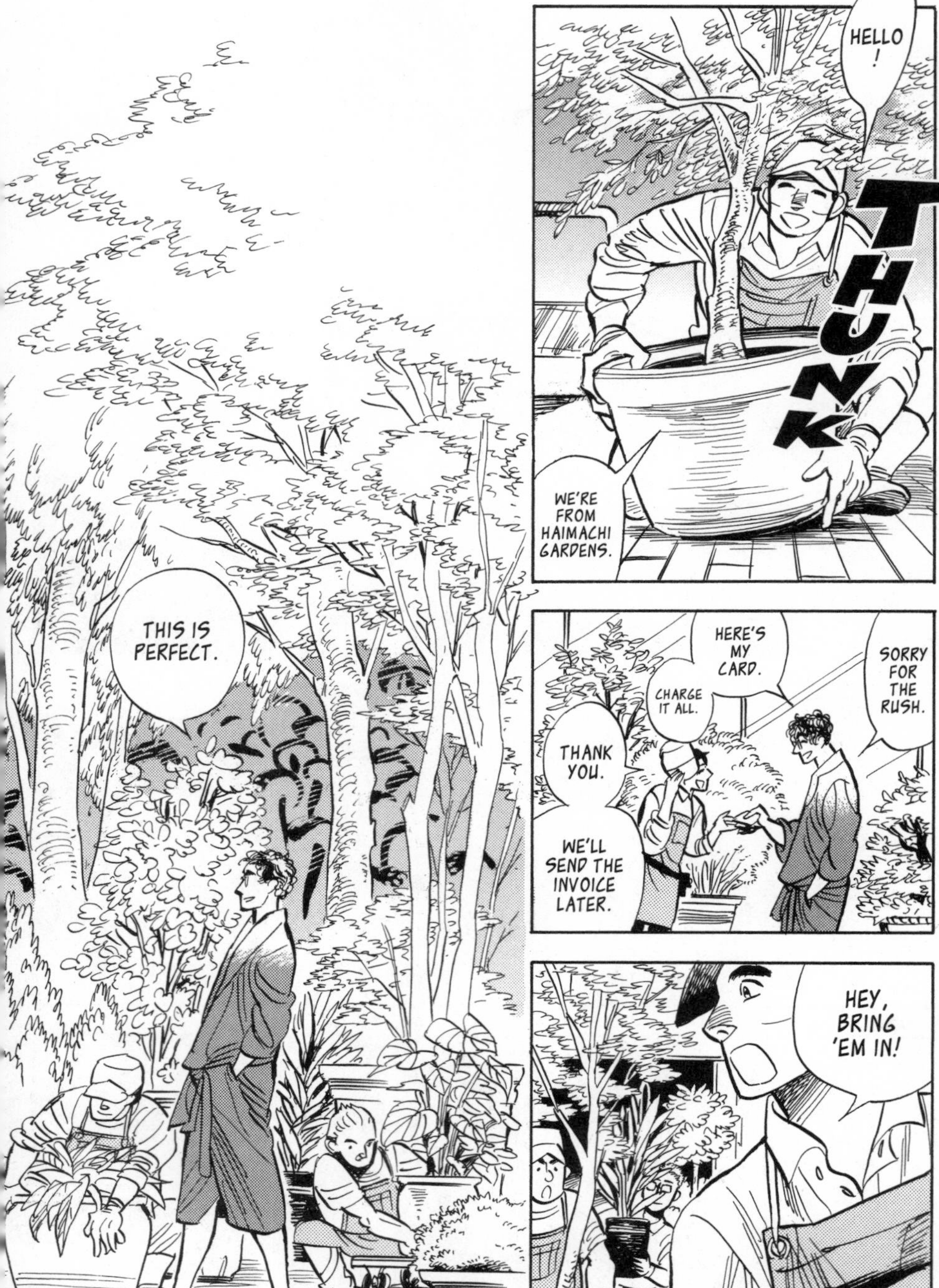
HELLO!
THUNK
WE'RE FROM HAIMACHI GARDENS.
SORRY FOR THE RUSH.
HERE'S MY CARD.
CHARGE IT ALL.
THANK YOU.
WE'LL SEND THE INVOICE LATER.
HEY, BRING 'EM IN!
THIS IS PERFECT.

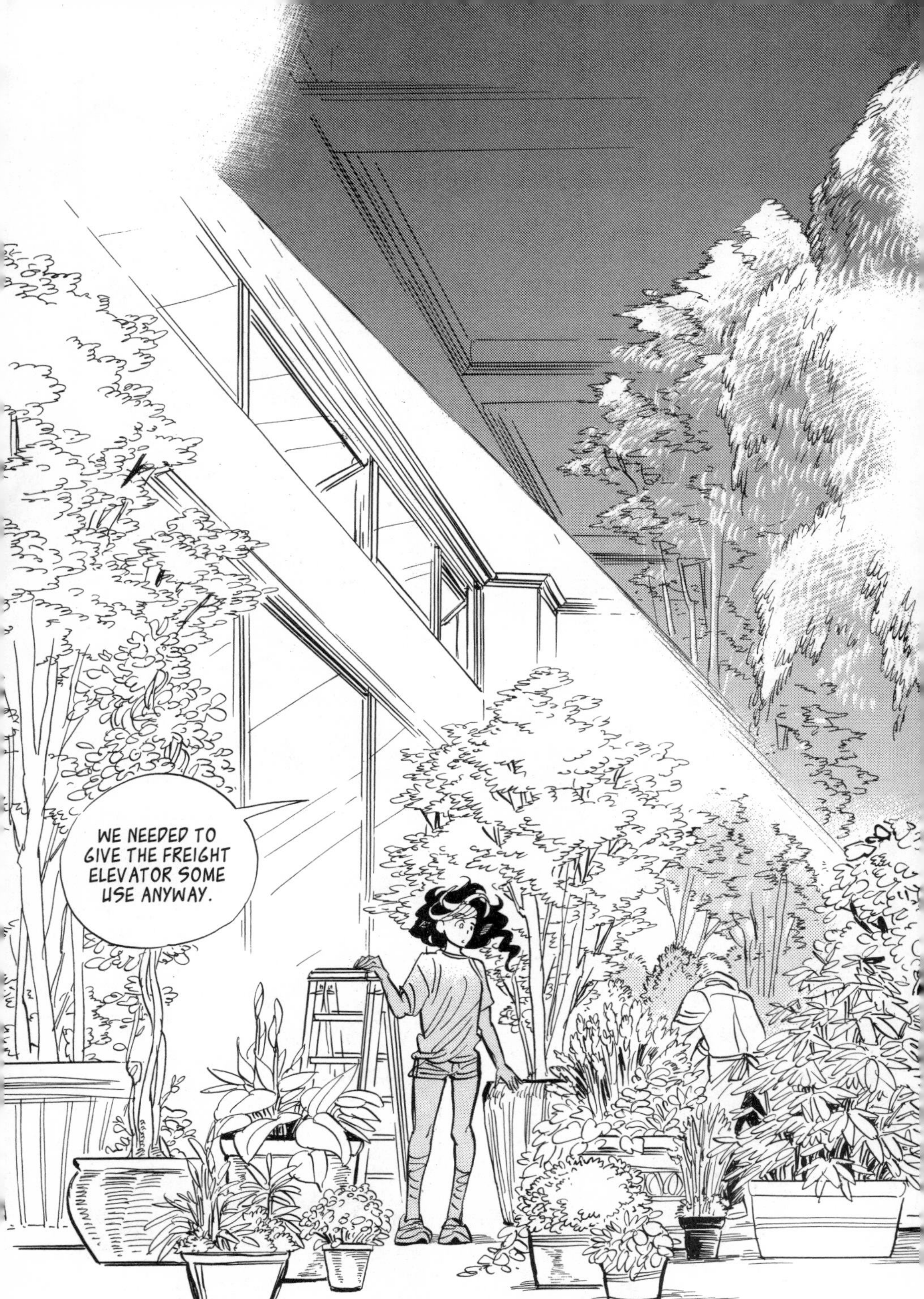
WE NEEDED TO GIVE THE FREIGHT ELEVATOR SOME USE ANYWAY.

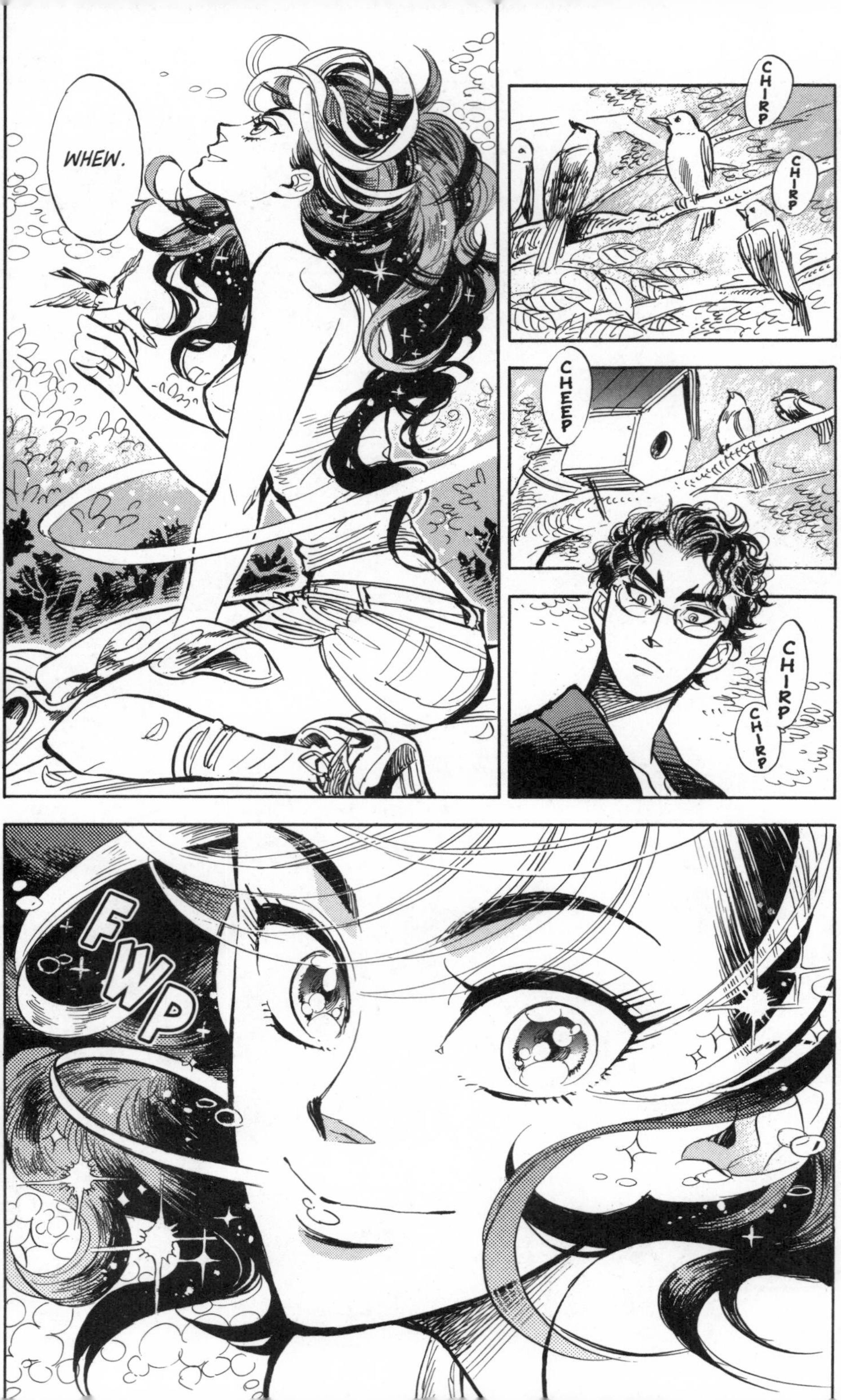
CHIRP
CHIRP
CHEEP
CHIRP
CHIRP
WHEW.
FWP

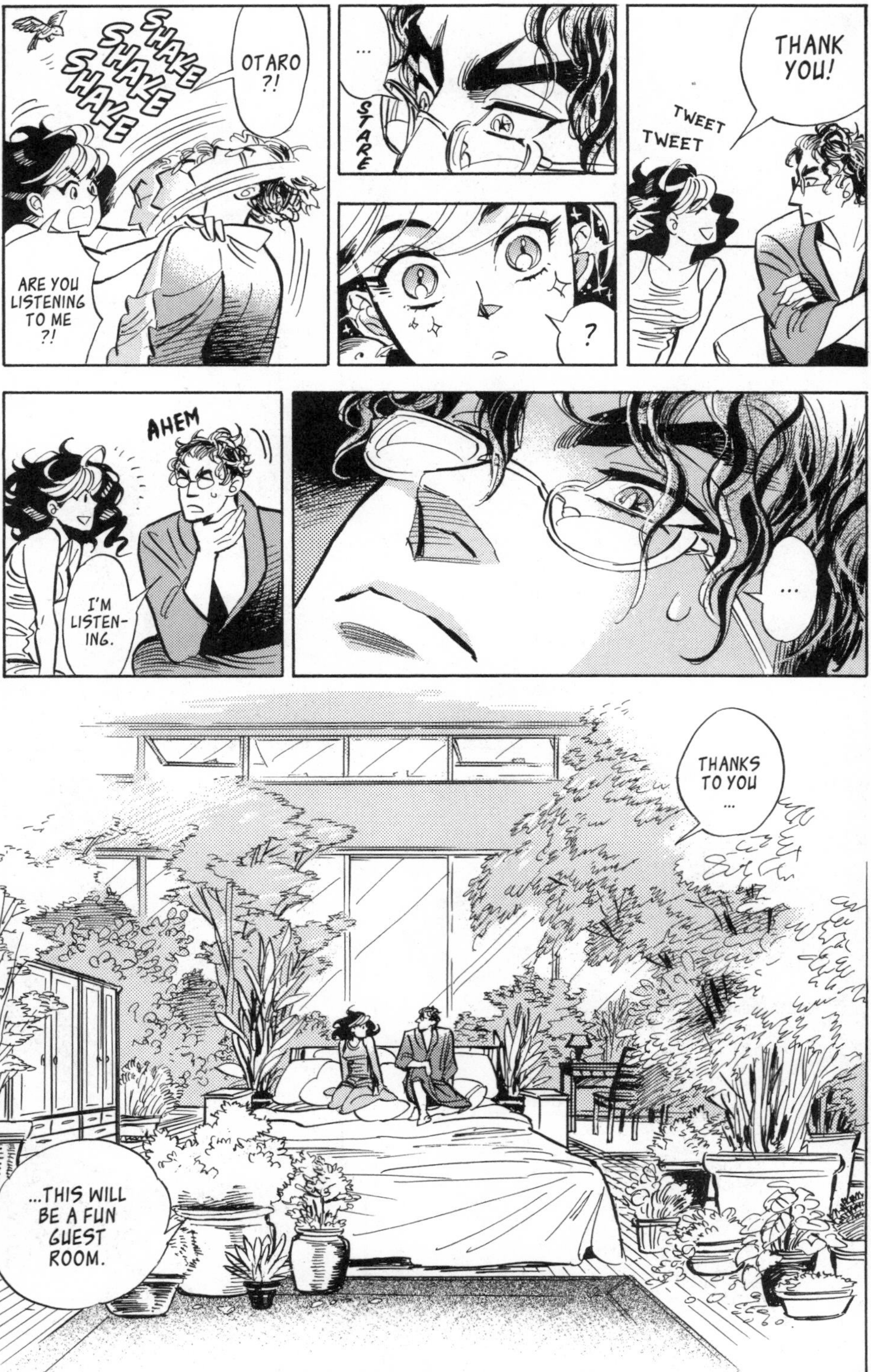
THANK YOU!
TWEET TWEET
...
STARE
?
SHAKE SHAKE SHAKE
OTARO ?!
ARE YOU LISTENING TO ME ?!
...
AHEM
I'M LISTEN-ING.
THANKS TO YOU ...
...THIS WILL BE A FUN GUEST ROOM.

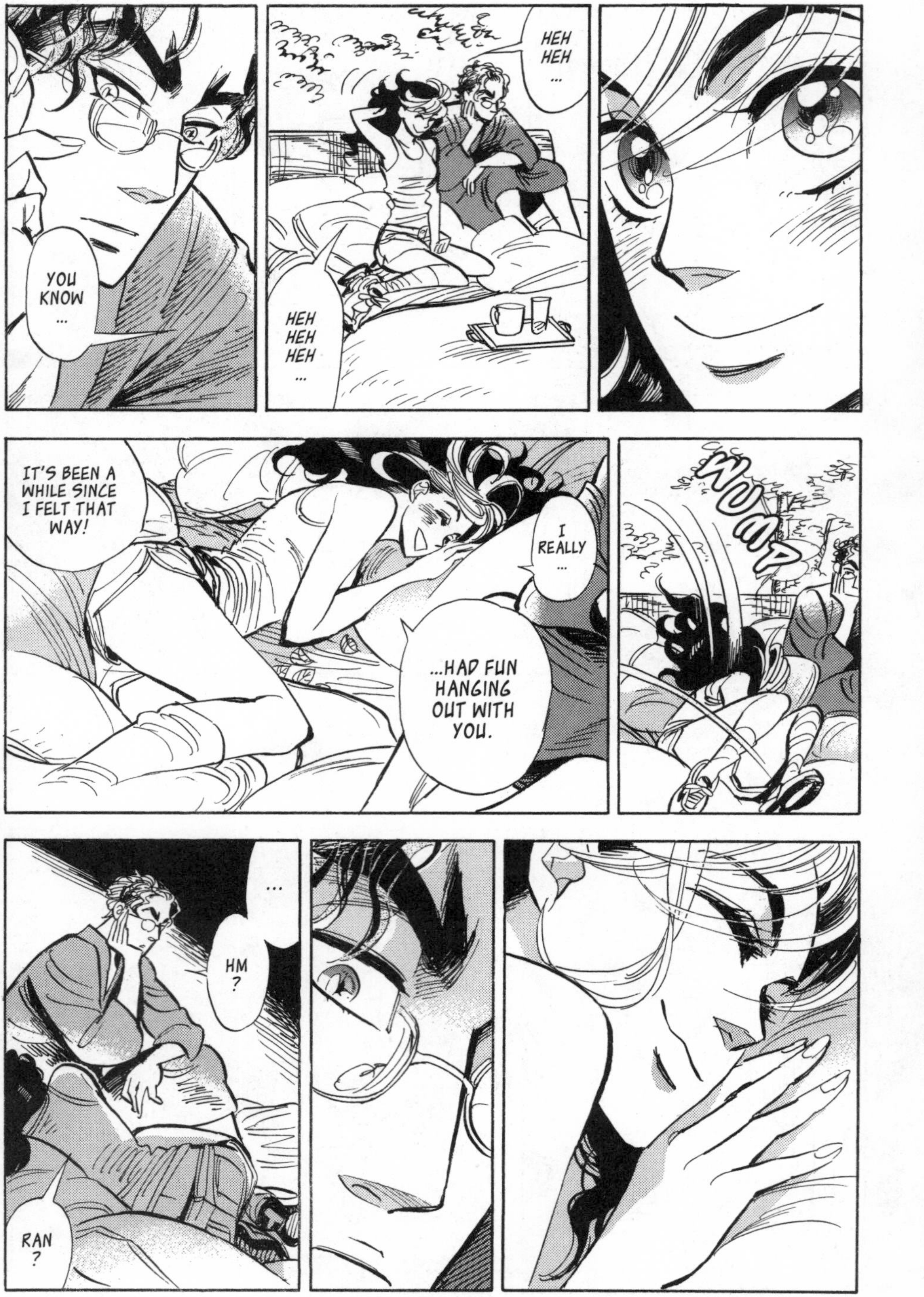
HEH HEH ...
HEH HEH HEH ...
YOU KNOW ...
WUMP
I REALLY ...
...HAD FUN HANGING OUT WITH YOU.
IT'S BEEN A WHILE SINCE I FELT THAT WAY!
...
HM ?
RAN ?

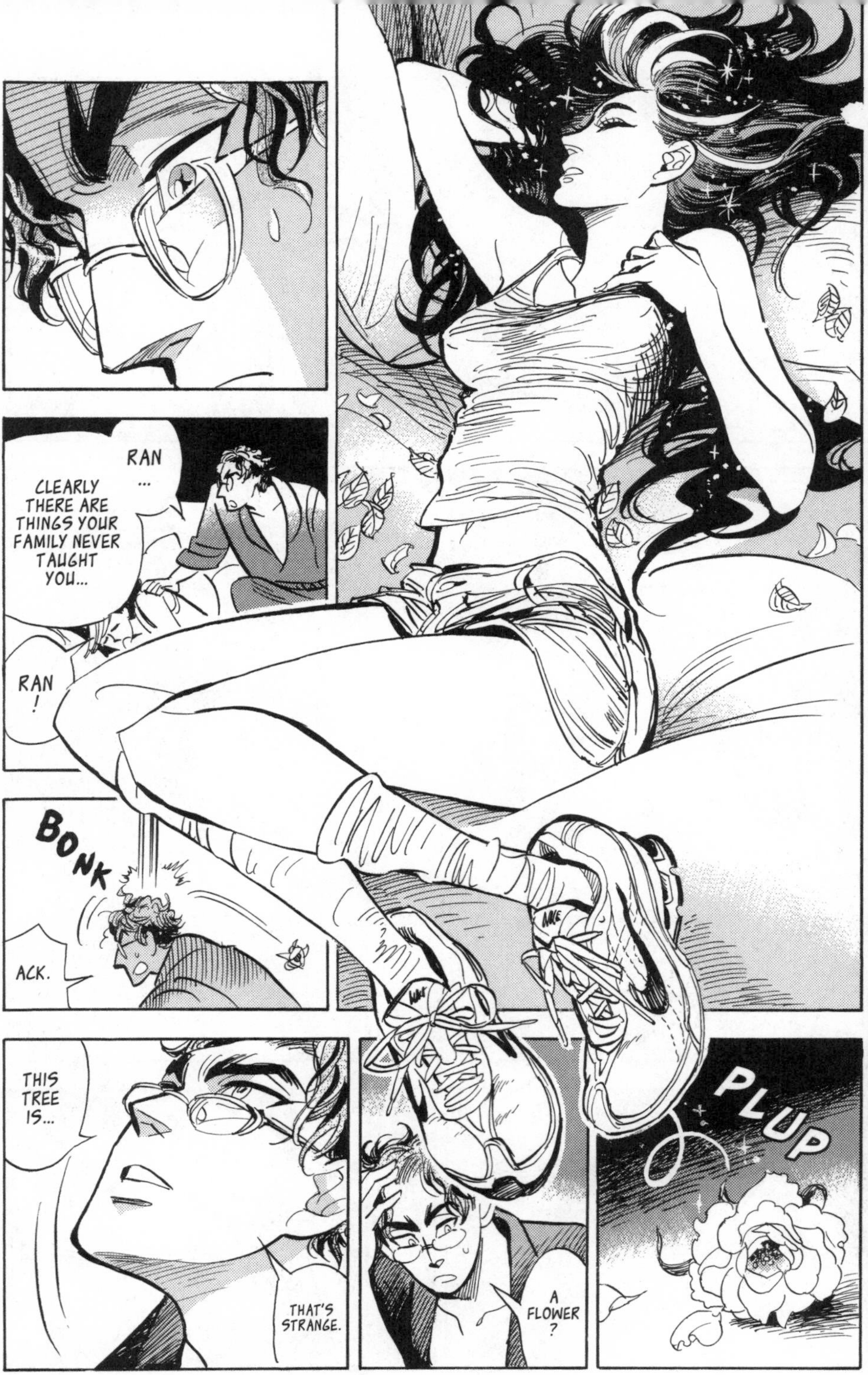
RAN ...
CLEARLY THERE ARE THINGS YOUR FAMILY NEVER TAUGHT YOU...
RAN !
BONK
ACK.
PLUP
A FLOWER ?
THIS TREE IS...
THAT'S STRANGE.

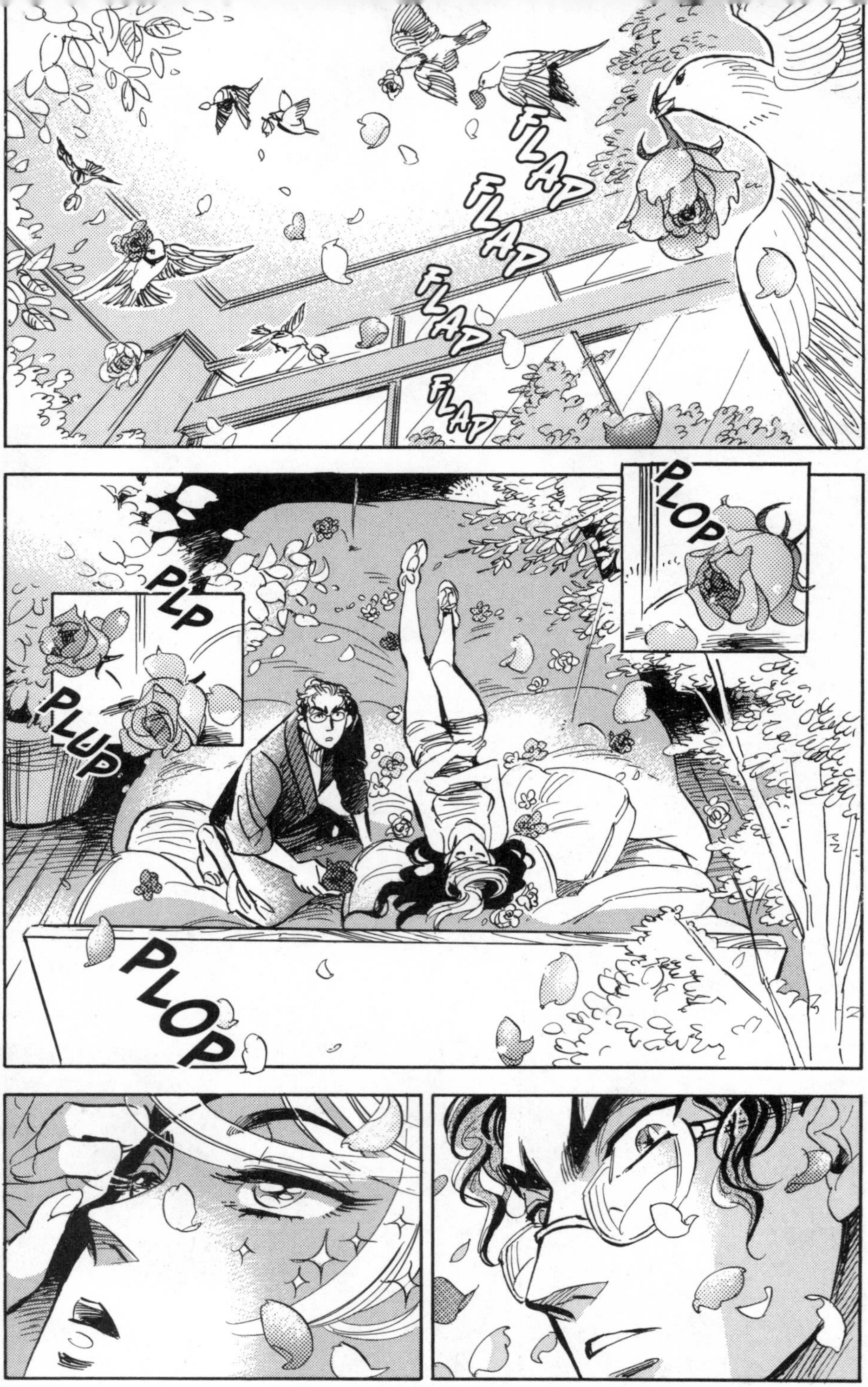
FLAP
FLAP
FLAP
FLAP
FLAP
PLOP
PLP
PLUP
PLOP

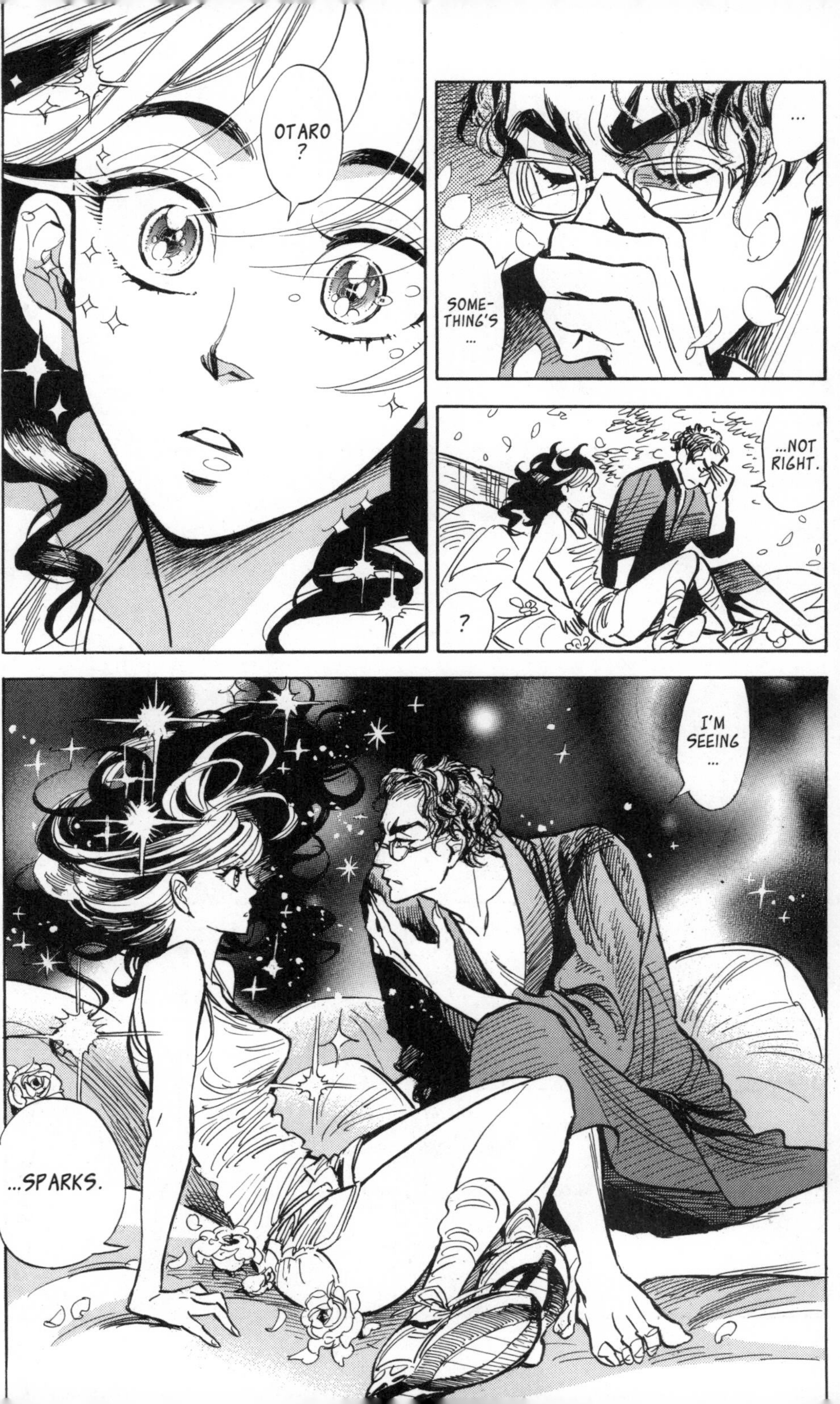
...
SOME-THING'S ...
...NOT RIGHT.
?
OTARO ?
I'M SEEING ...
...SPARKS.

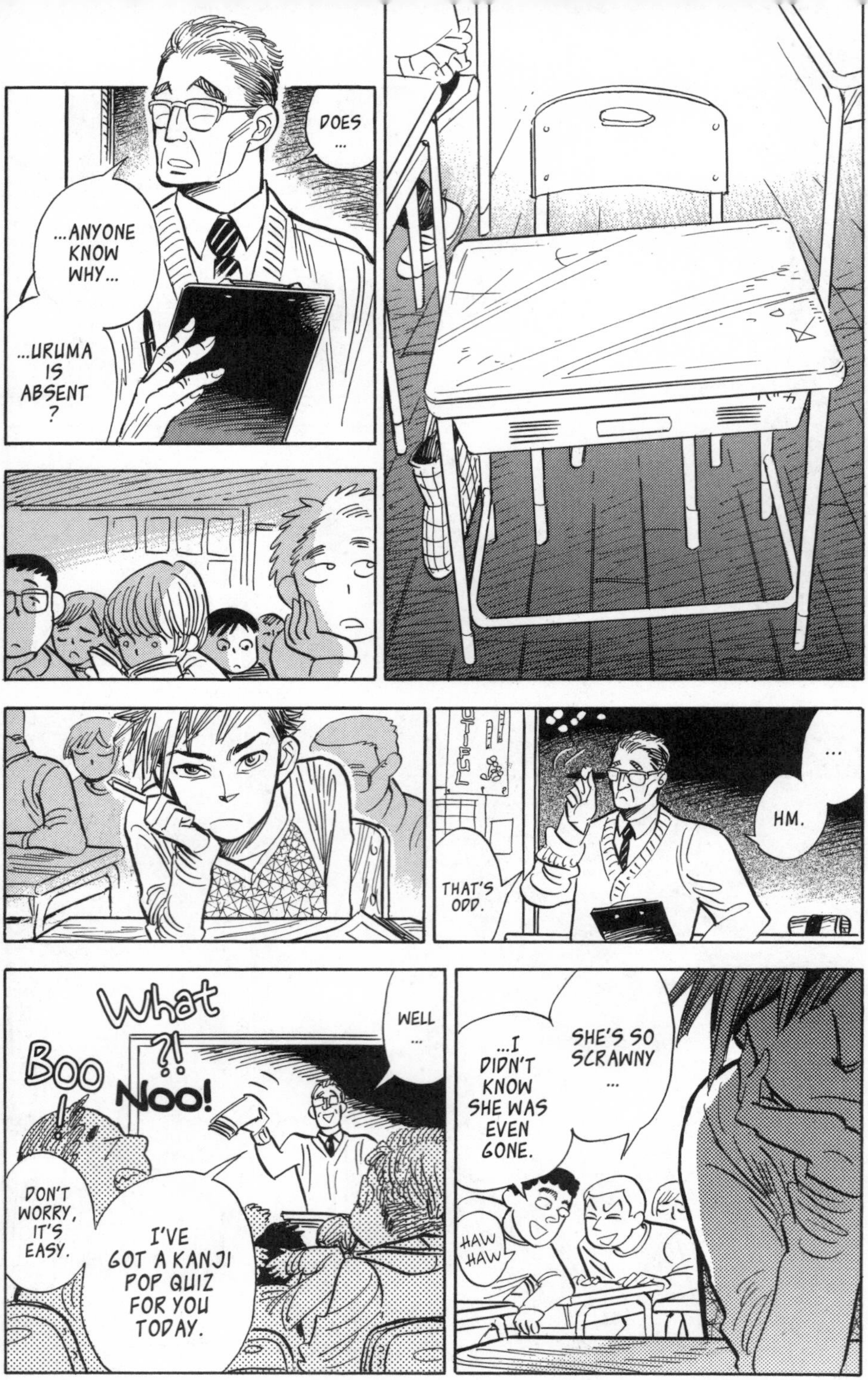
DOES ...
...ANYONE KNOW WHY...
...URUMA IS ABSENT ?
...
HM.
THAT'S ODD.
SHE'S SO SCRAWNY ...
...I DIDN'T KNOW SHE WAS EVEN GONE.
HAW HAW
WELL ...
I'VE GOT A KANJI POP QUIZ FOR YOU TODAY.
What ?!
Noo!
DON'T WORRY, IT'S EASY.
Boo !

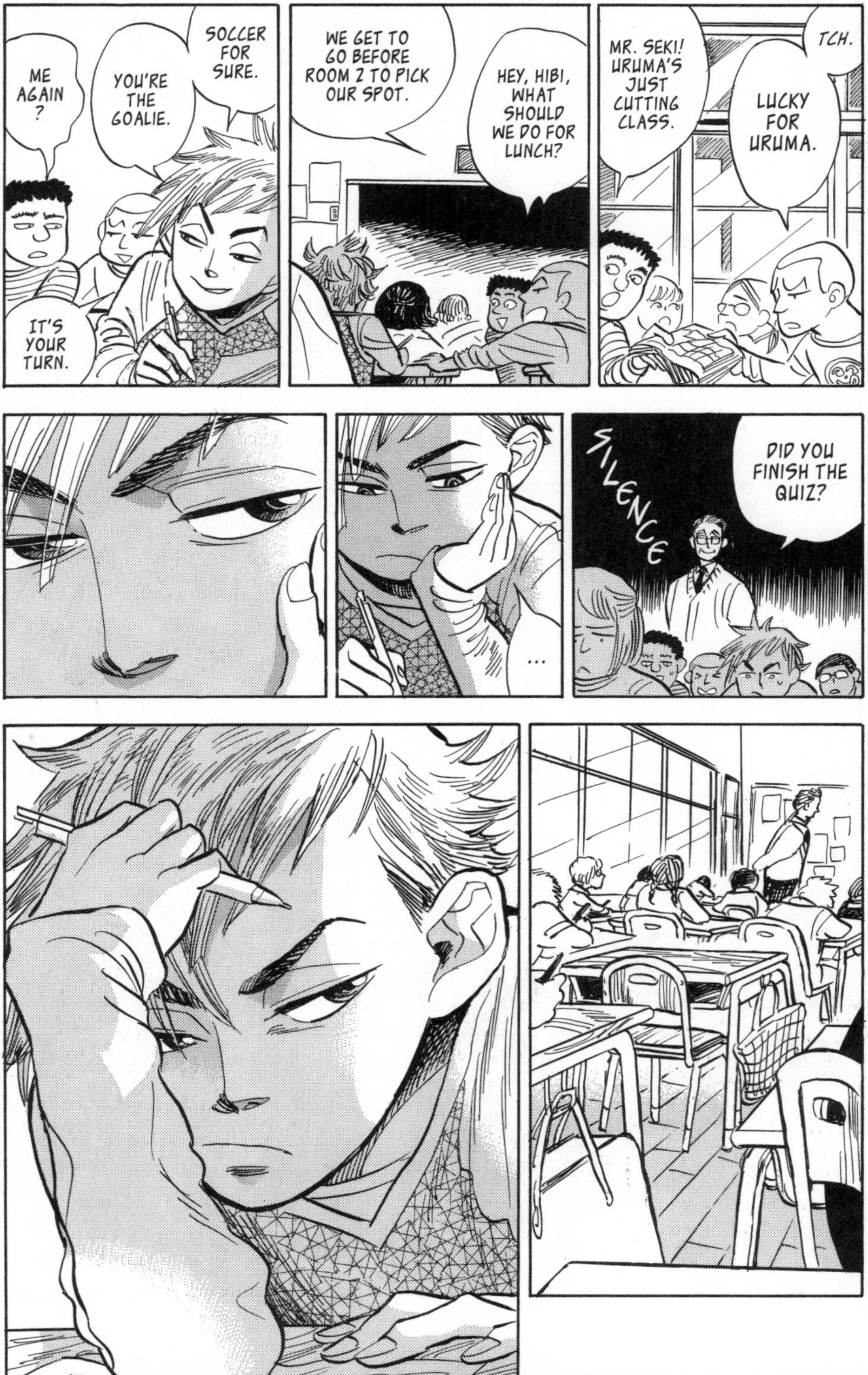
TCH.
LUCKY FOR URUMA.
MR. SEKI! URUMA'S JUST CUTTING CLASS.
HEY, HIBI, WHAT SHOULD WE DO FOR LUNCH?
WE GET TO GO BEFORE ROOM 2 TO PICK OUR SPOT.
SOCCER FOR SURE.
YOU'RE THE GOALIE.
ME AGAIN?
IT'S YOUR TURN.
DID YOU FINISH THE QUIZ?
SILENCE
...

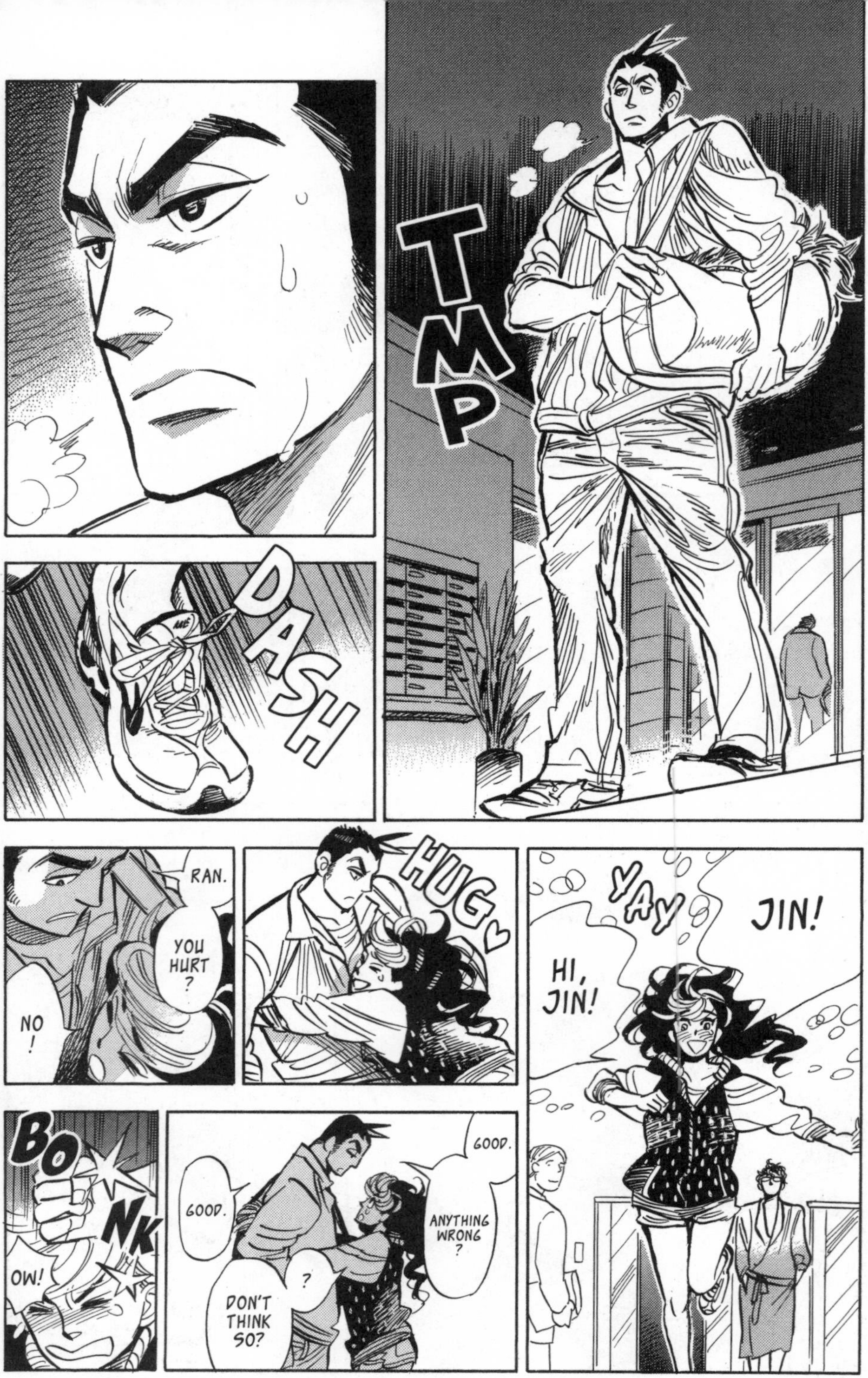
TMP
DASH
JIN!
YAY
HI, JIN!
HUG
RAN.
YOU HURT?
NO!
GOOD.
ANYTHING WRONG?
GOOD.
?
DON'T THINK SO?
BONK
OW!

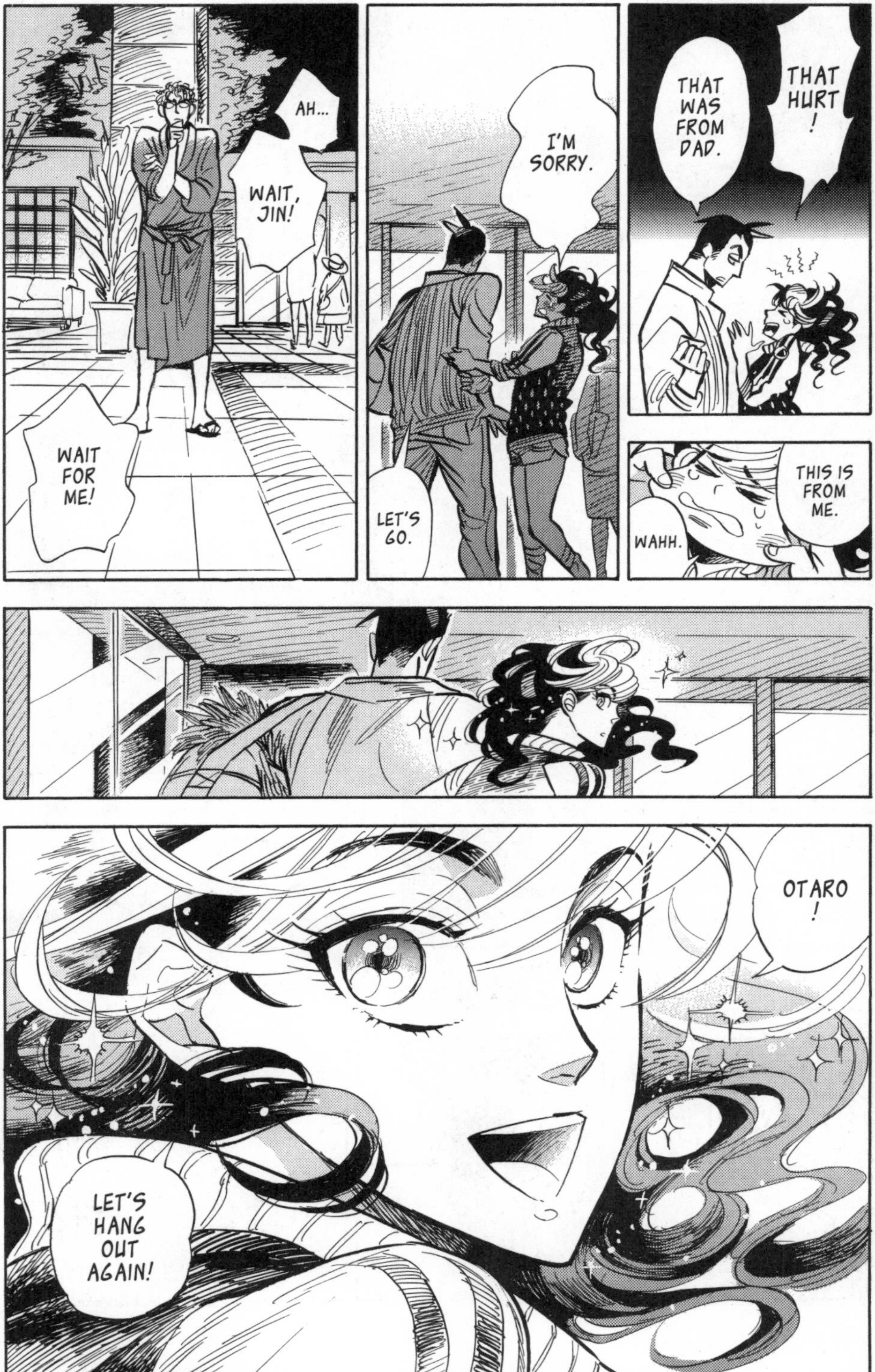
THAT HURT!
THAT WAS FROM DAD.
THIS IS FROM ME.
WAHH.
I'M SORRY.
LET'S GO.
AH...
WAIT, JIN!
WAIT FOR ME!
OTARO!
LET'S HANG OUT AGAIN!

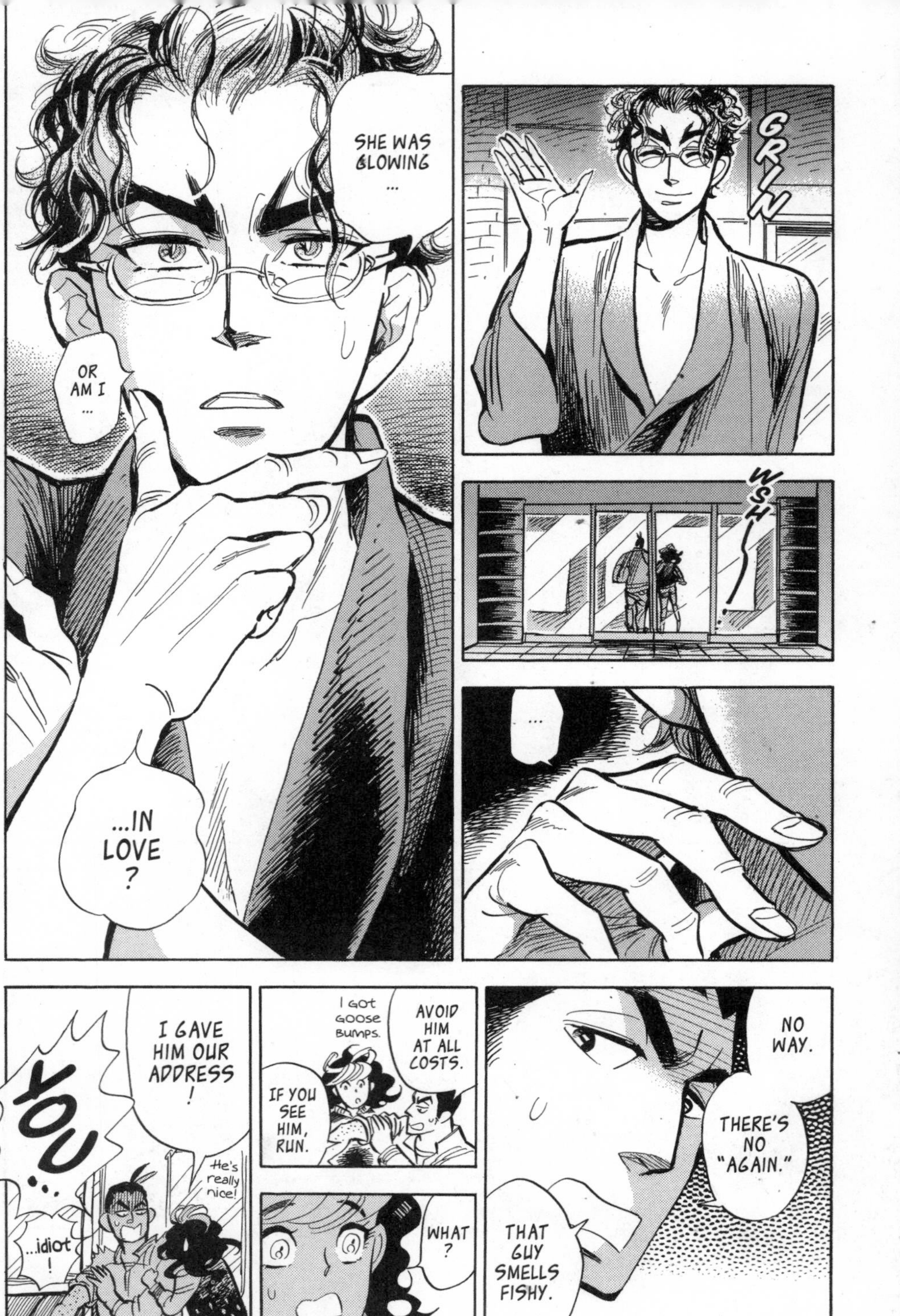
GRIN
WSH
...
SHE WAS GLOWING ...
OR AM I ...
...IN LOVE ?
NO WAY.
THERE'S NO "AGAIN."
THAT GUY SMELLS FISHY.
AVOID HIM AT ALL COSTS.
I GOT GOOSE BUMPS.
IF YOU SEE HIM, RUN.
WHAT ?
I GAVE HIM OUR ADDRESS !
YOU...
He's really nice!
...idiot !

Chapter 5 / The End

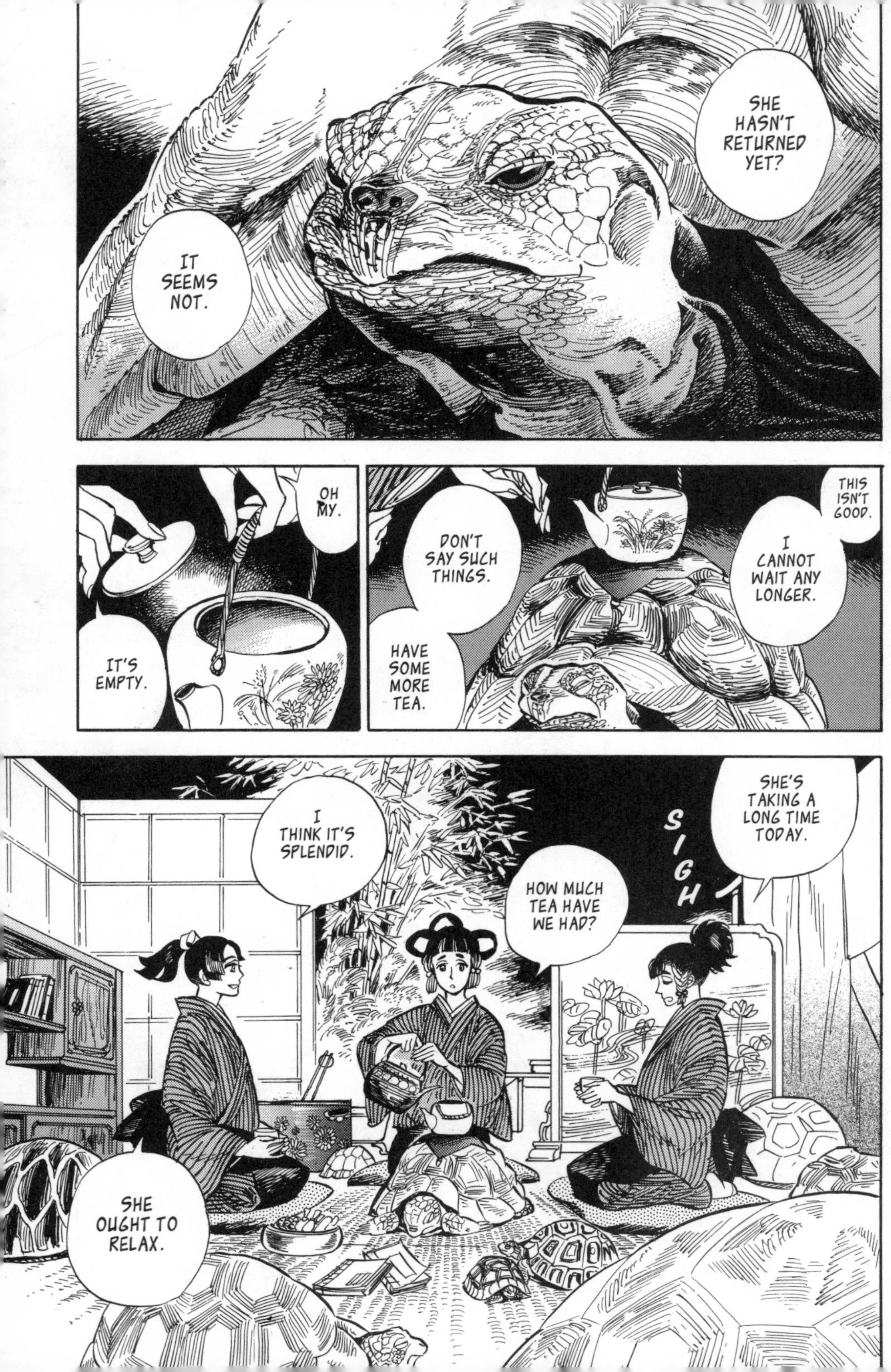
SHE HASN'T RETURNED YET?
IT SEEMS NOT.
THIS ISN'T GOOD.
I CANNOT WAIT ANY LONGER.
DON'T SAY SUCH THINGS.
HAVE SOME MORE TEA.
OH MY.
IT'S EMPTY.
SHE'S TAKING A LONG TIME TODAY.
SIGH
HOW MUCH TEA HAVE WE HAD?
I THINK IT'S SPLENDID.
SHE OUGHT TO RELAX.

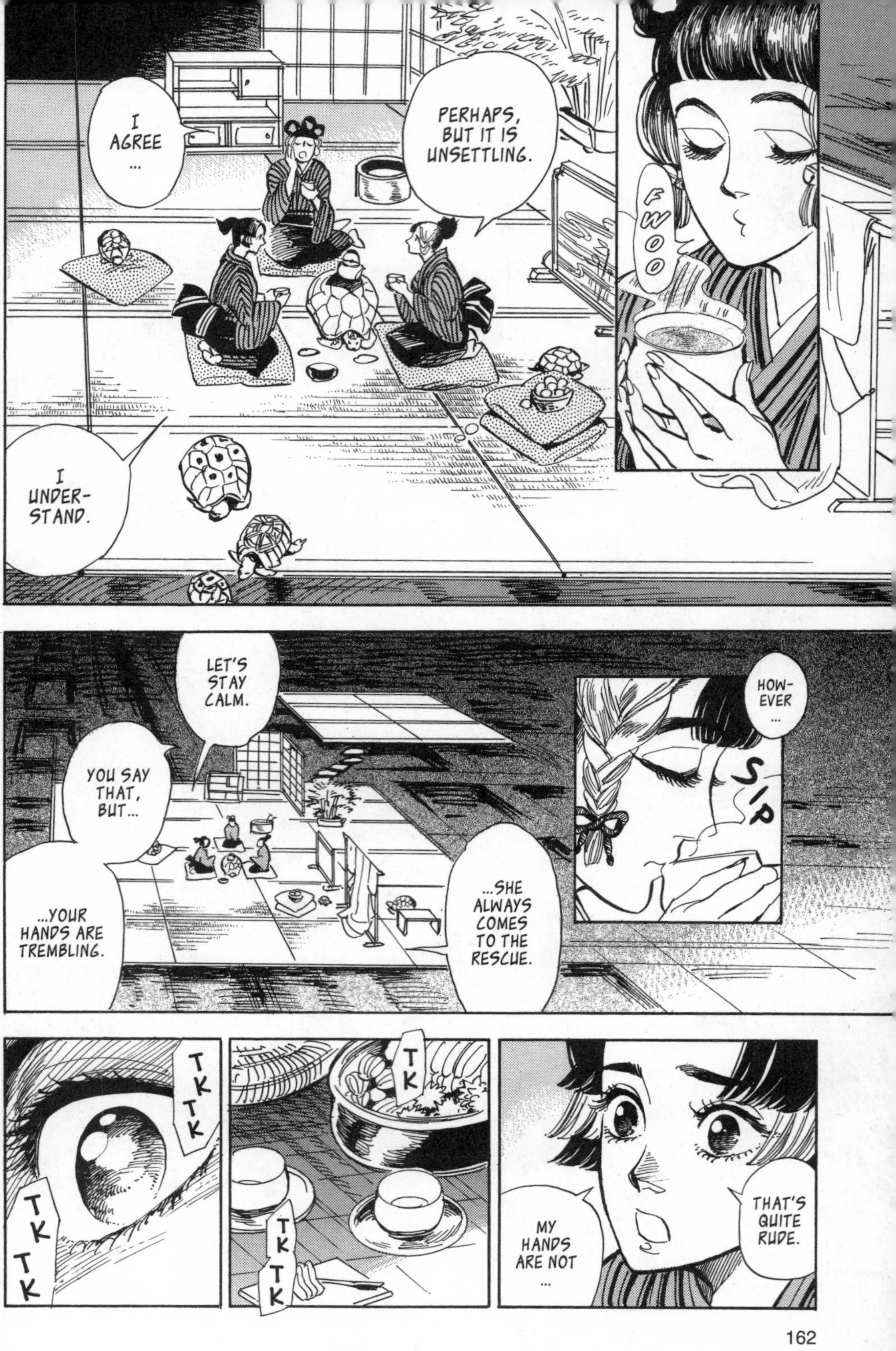
FWOO
PERHAPS, BUT IT IS UNSETTLING.
I AGREE ...
I UNDER-STAND.
HOW-EVER ...
SIP
...SHE ALWAYS COMES TO THE RESCUE.
LET'S STAY CALM.
YOU SAY THAT, BUT...
...YOUR HANDS ARE TREMBLING.
THAT'S QUITE RUDE.
MY HANDS ARE NOT ...
TK
TK TK TK
TK TK TK
TK TK TK

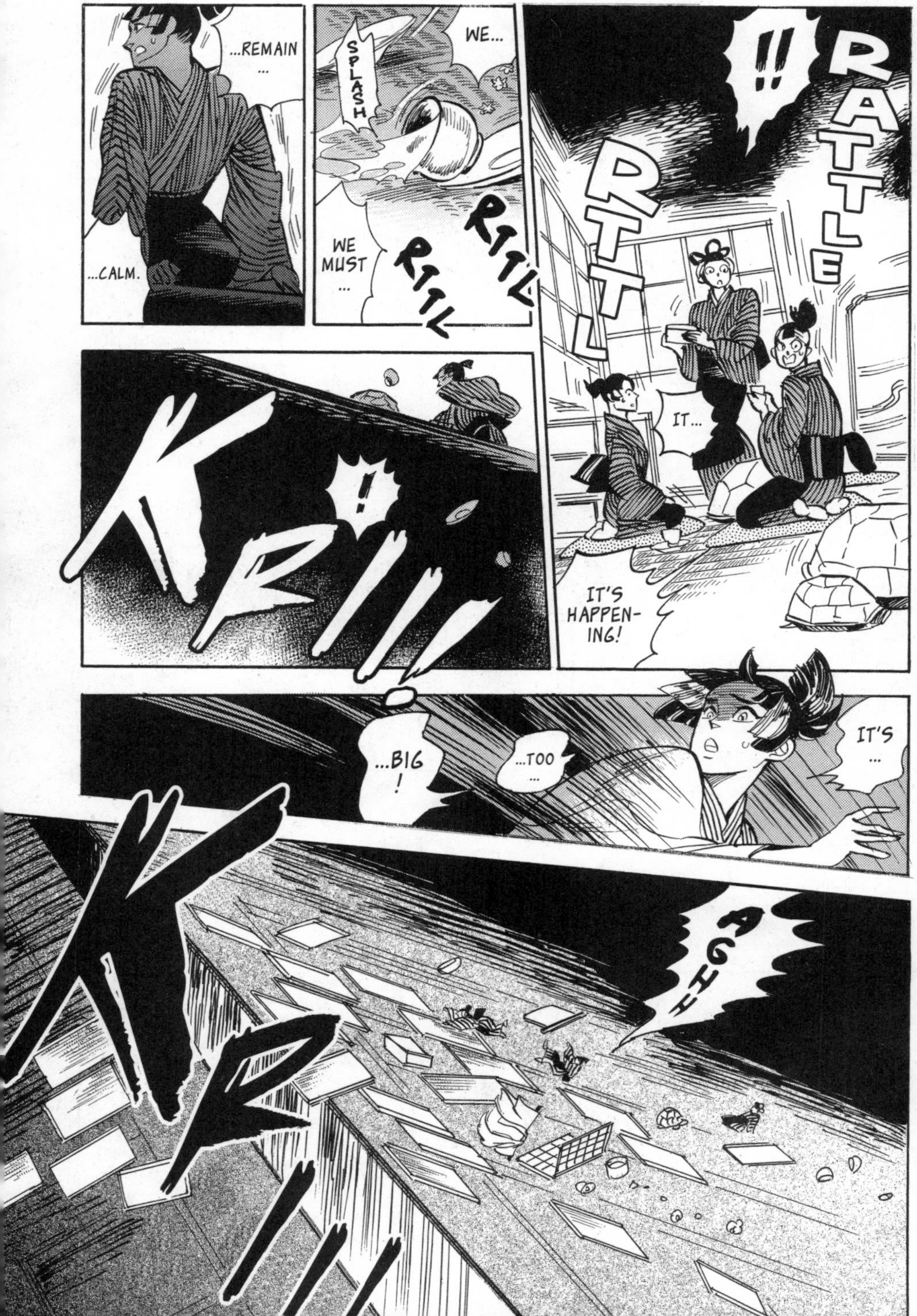
!!
RATTLE
RATTL
IT...
IT'S HAPPEN-ING!
WE...
SPLASH
WE MUST...
RTTL
RTTL
...REMAIN...
...CALM.
KRII
!
IT'S...
...TOO...
...BIG!
AGHH

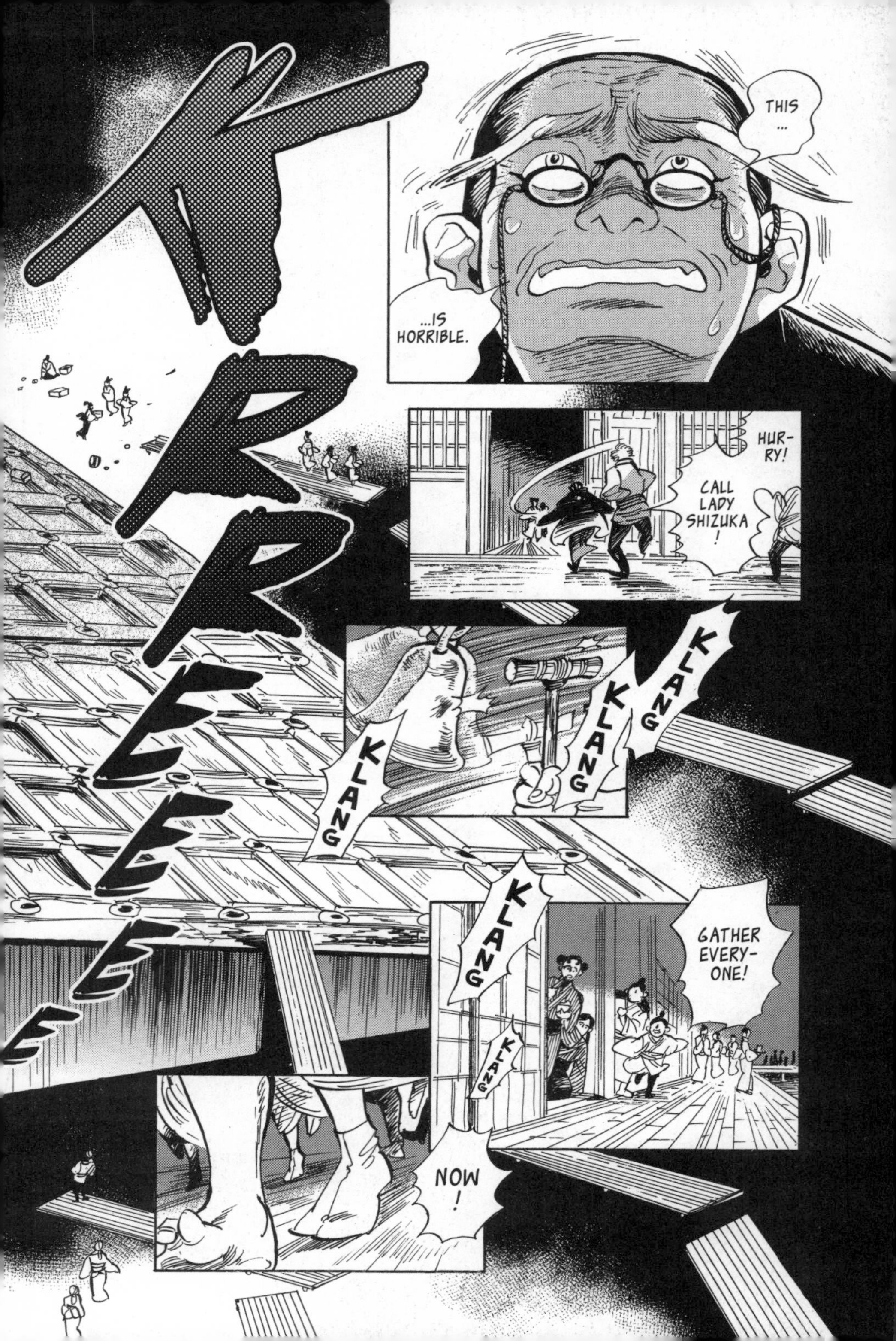
THIS ...
...IS HORRIBLE.
KRREEEE
HURRY!
CALL LADY SHIZUKA!
KLANG
KLANG
KLANG
GATHER EVERY-ONE!
KLANG
KLANG
NOW!

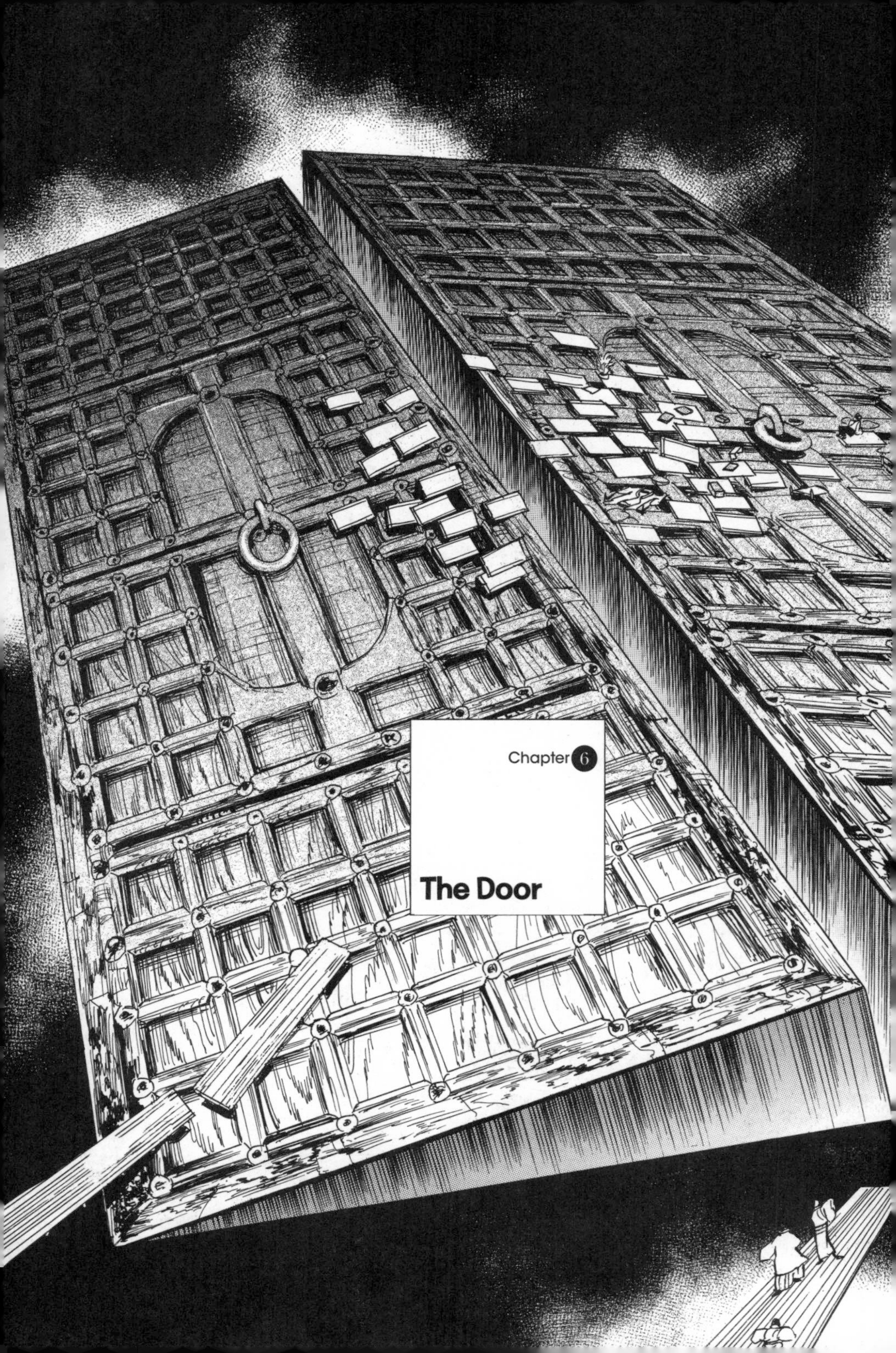
Chapter 6
The Door

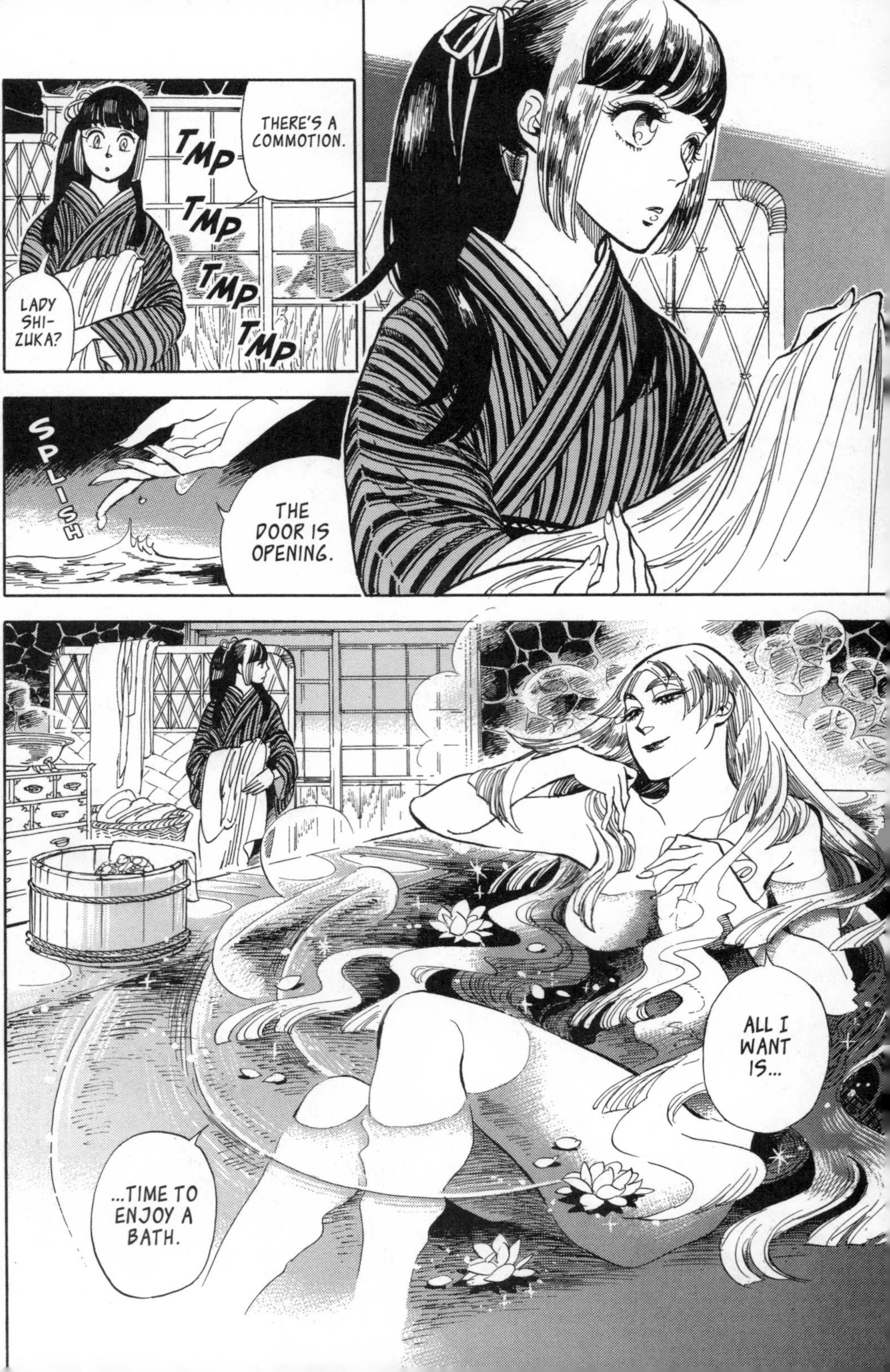
THERE'S A COMMOTION.
TMP TMP TMP TMP
LADY SHI-ZUKA?
THE DOOR IS OPENING.
SPLISH
ALL I WANT IS...
...TIME TO ENJOY A BATH.

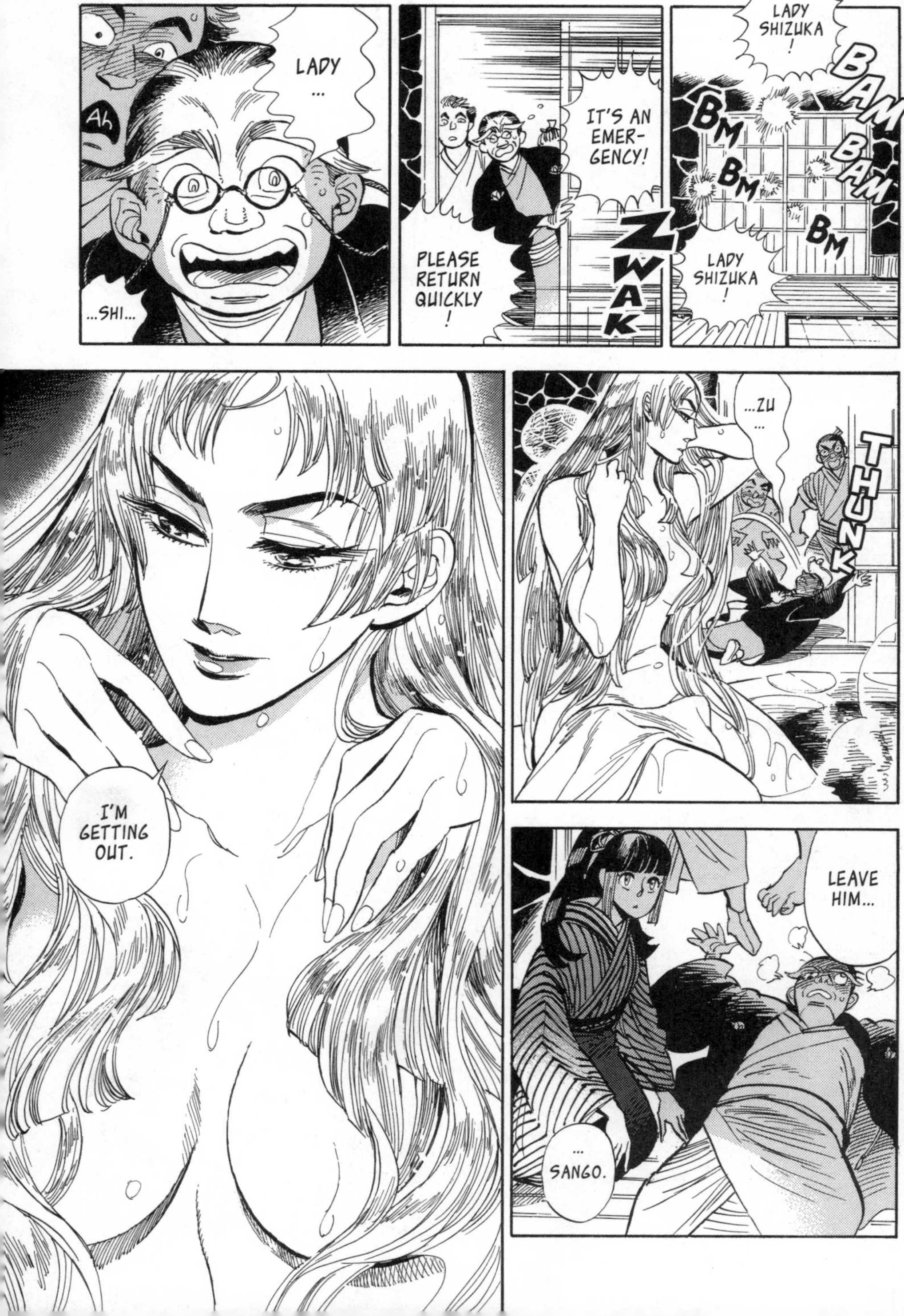
LADY SHIZUKA!
BAM BAM
BM BM BM BM
LADY SHIZUKA!
IT'S AN EMERGENCY!
PLEASE RETURN QUICKLY!
ZWAK
LADY...
Ah
...SHI...
...ZU...
THUNK
LEAVE HIM...
...SANGO.
I'M GETTING OUT.

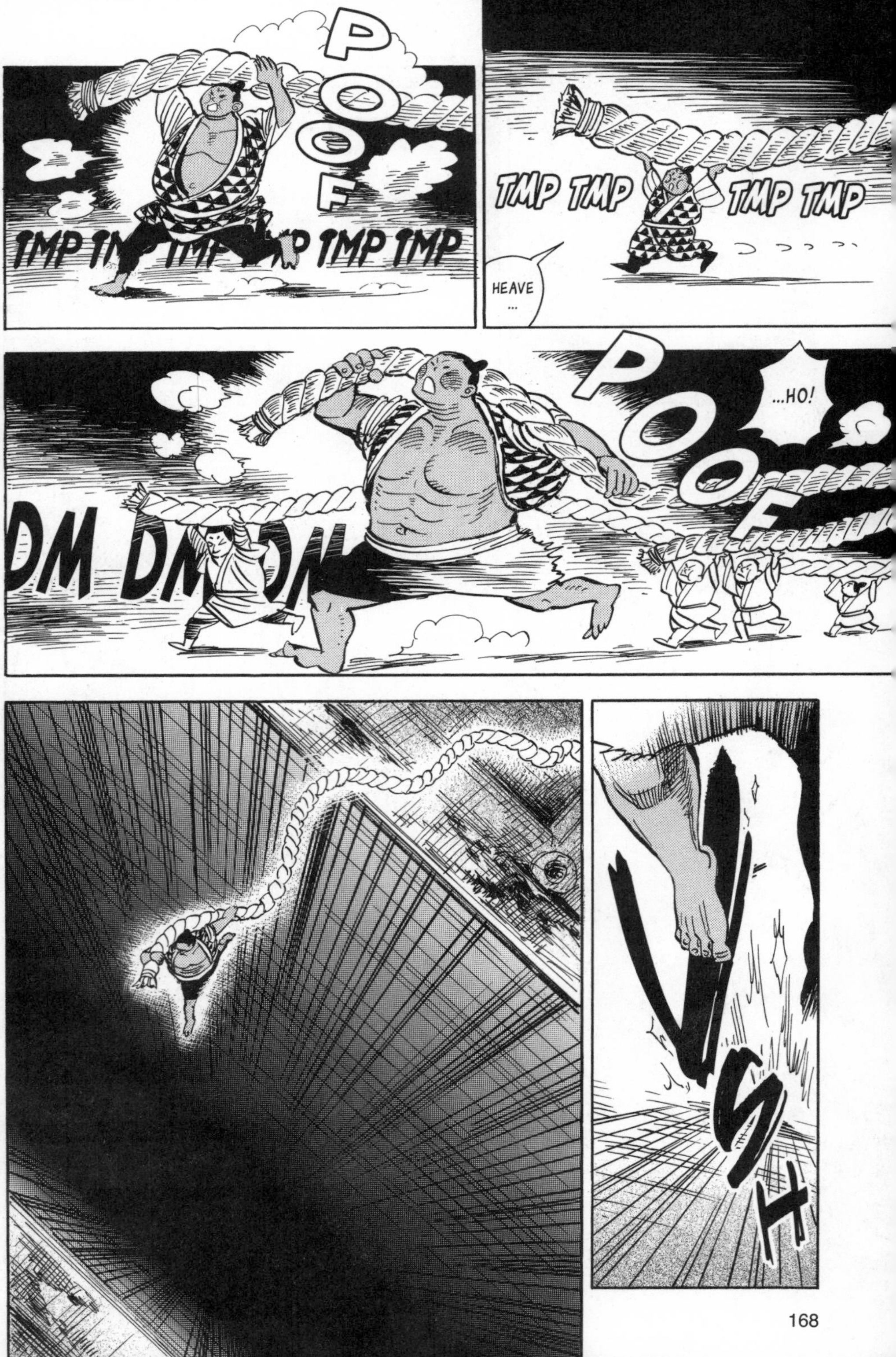

TMP TMP
HEAVE...
TMP TMP
POOF
TMP TMP TMP
...HO!
POOF
DM DM DM
VSH

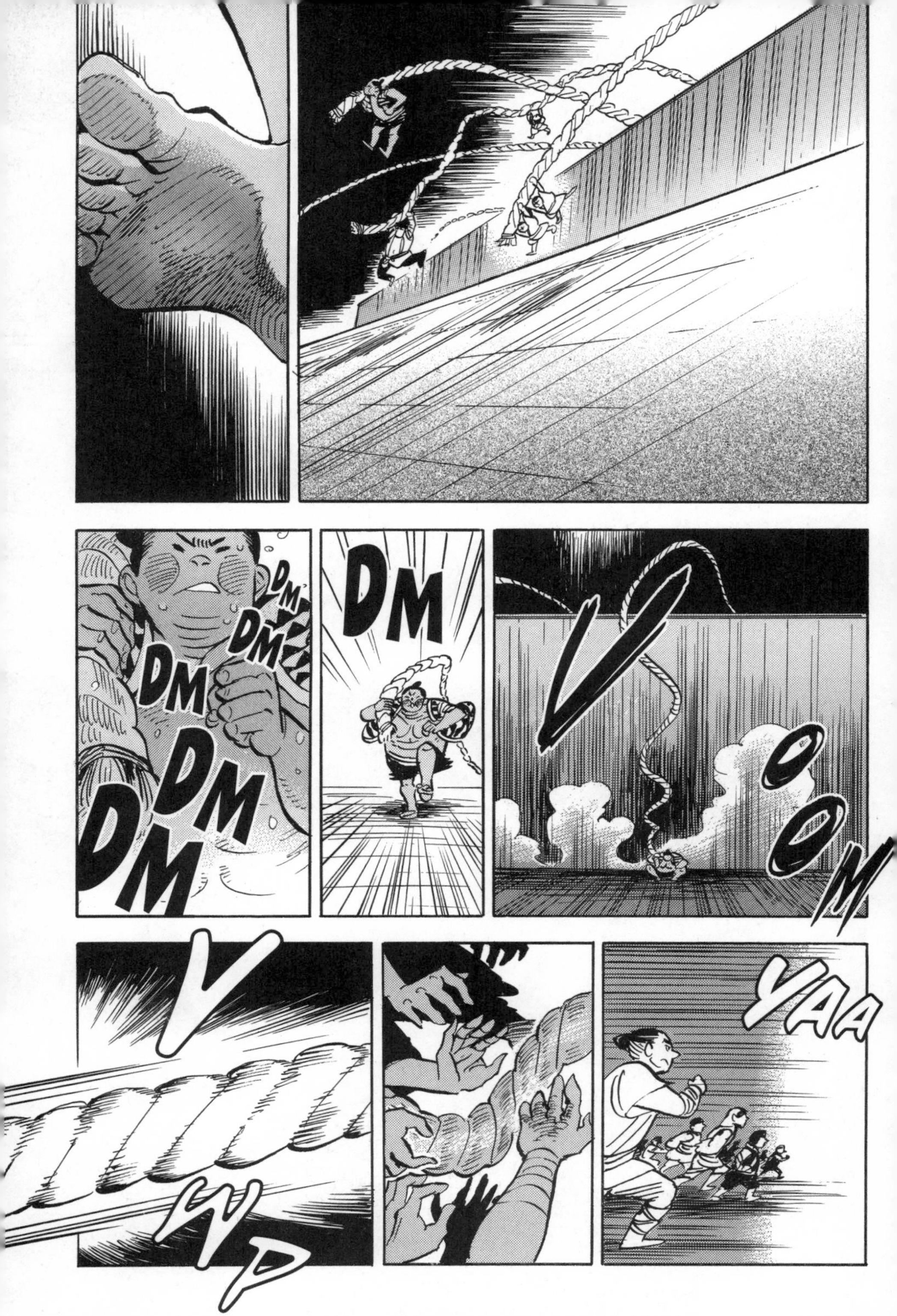

VOOOM
DM
DM
DM
DM
DM
DM
DM
YAA
V
WP

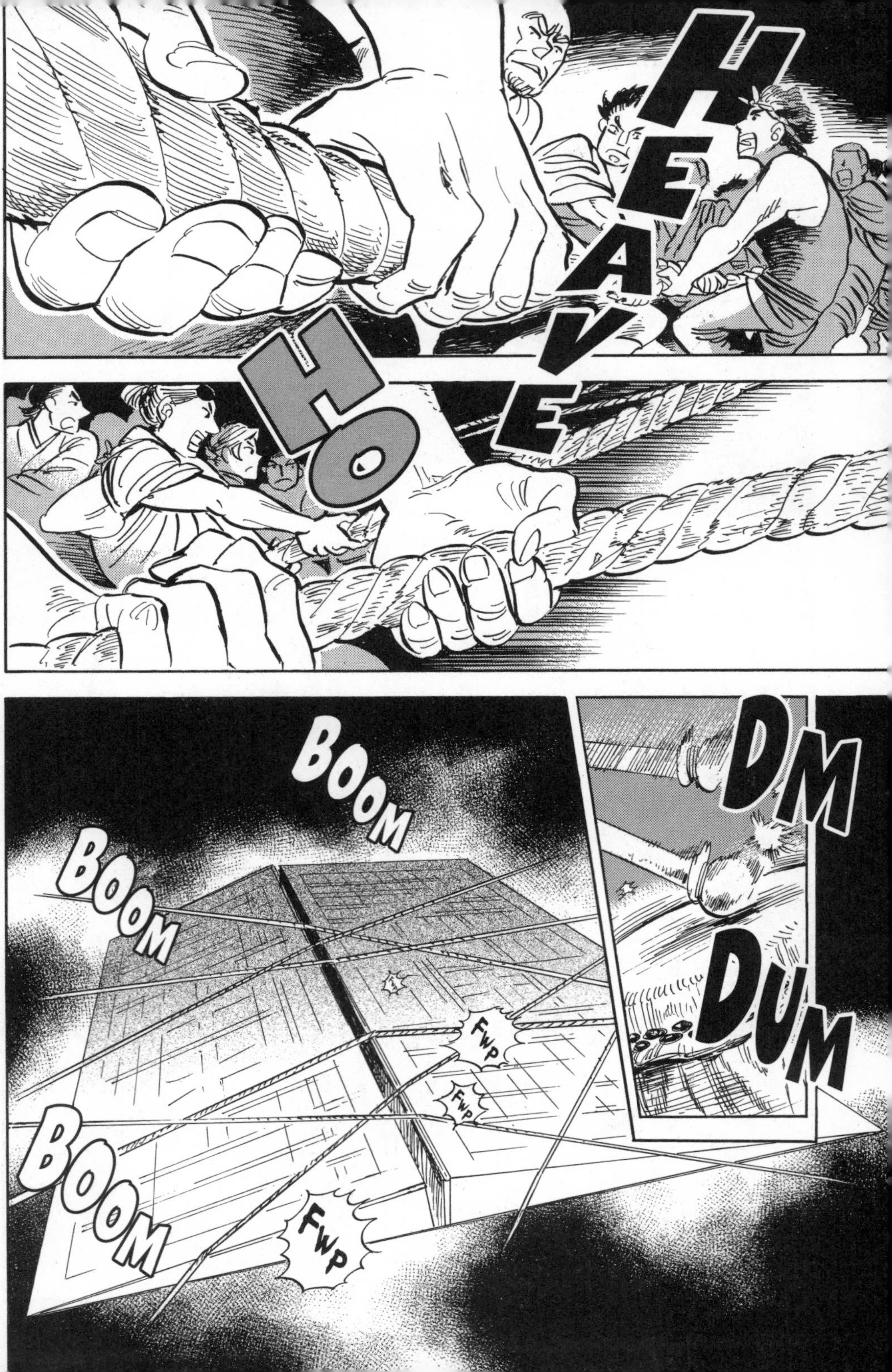
HEAVE
HO
DM
DUM
BOOM
BOOM
BOOM
FWP
FWP
FWP

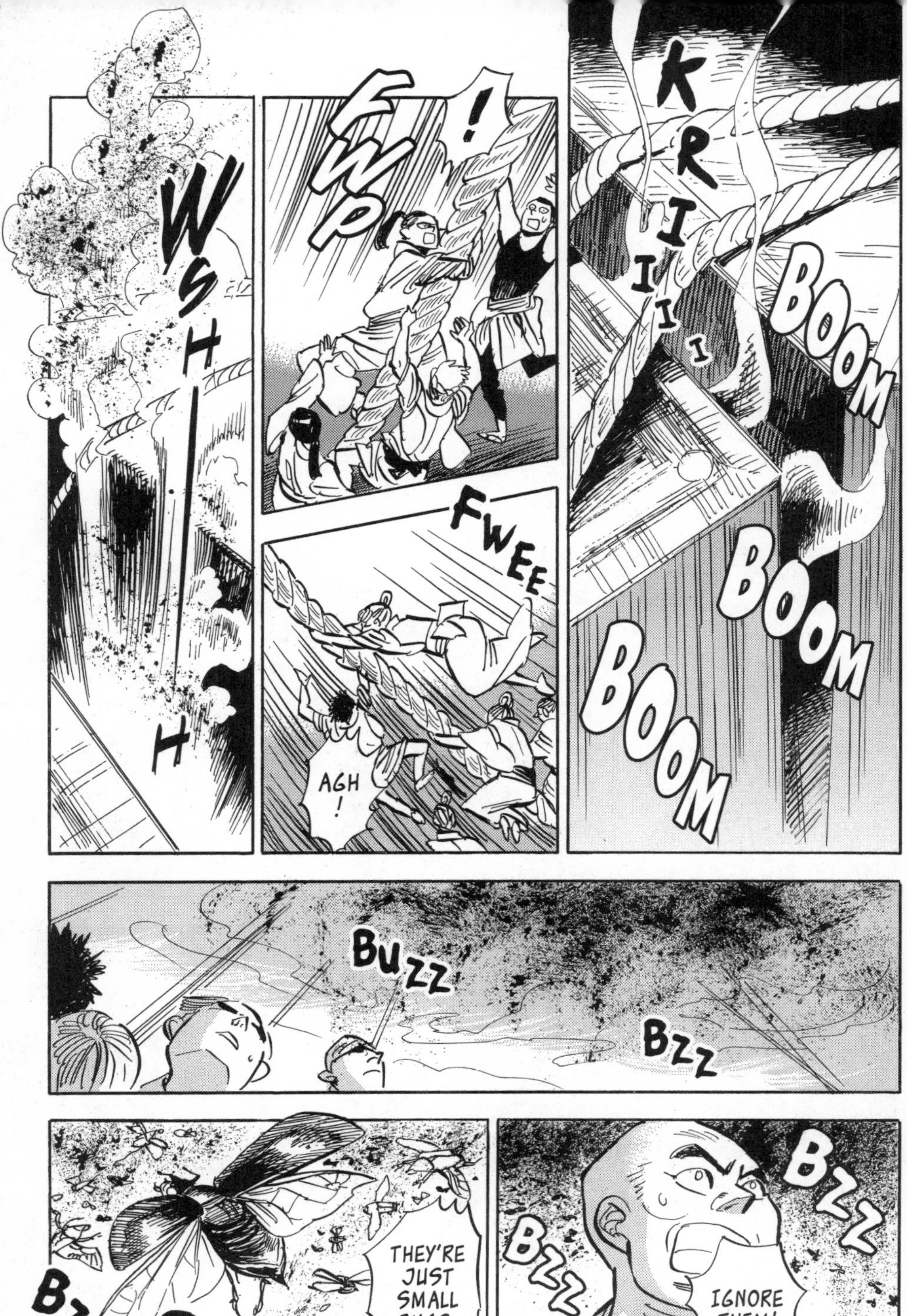
KRIIIII
BOOM
BOOM
BOOM
FWP
!
FWEE
AGH!
WSHH
Buzz
Bzz
Bzz
Bzz
IGNORE THEM!
THEY'RE JUST SMALL BUGS.
Bzz
Bzz

VOM
VOOOM
ZP
ZP
ZP
ZP
BOOOM
BOOOM
BOOOM
ZP
ZP
ZP

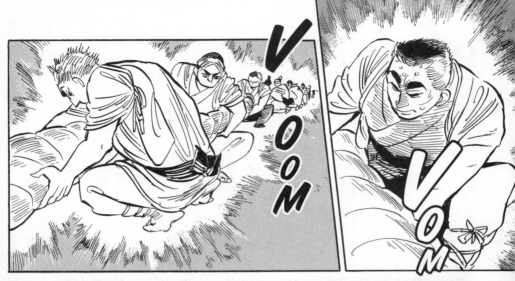

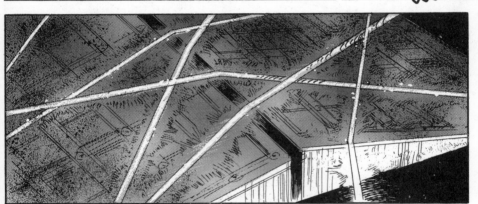

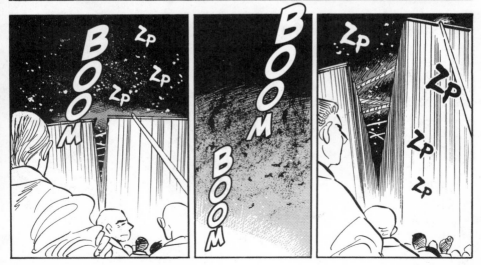

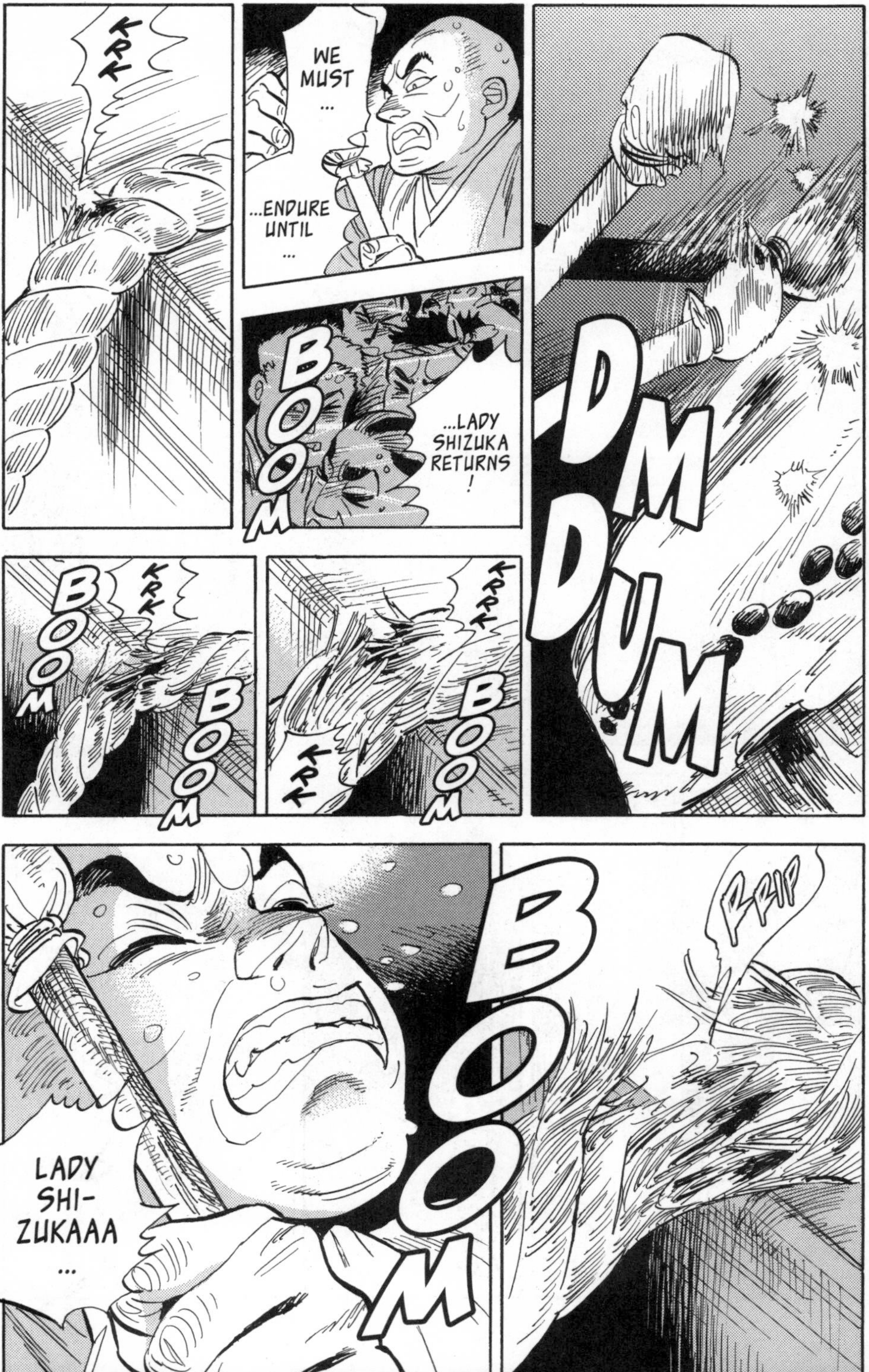
DMDUM
WE MUST...
...ENDURE UNTIL...
BOOOM
...LADY SHIZUKA RETURNS!
KRK
KRRK
BOOOM
KRK
KRK
BOOOM
BOOOM
RRIP
BOOOM
LADY SHI-ZUKAAA...

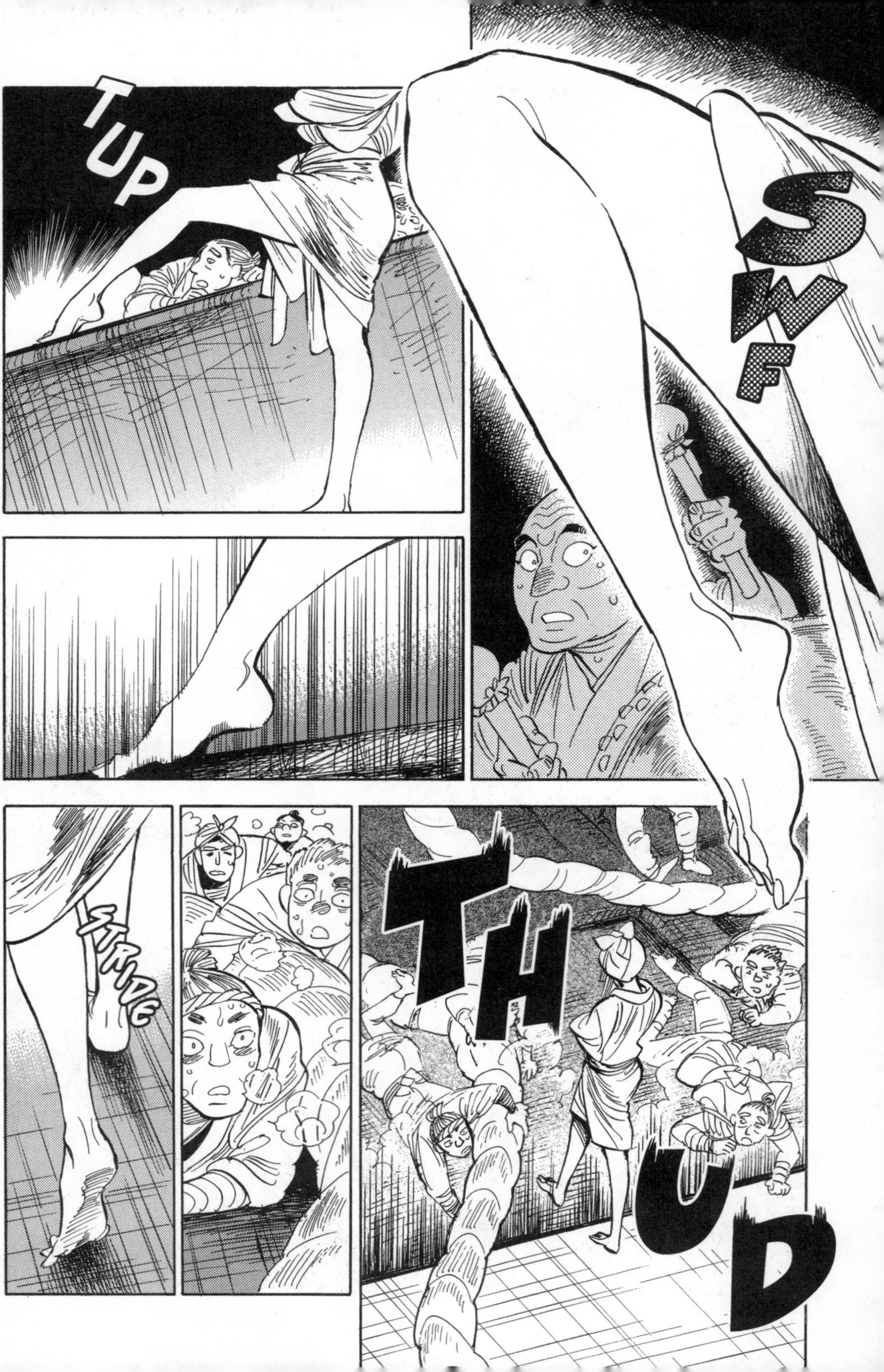
SWF
TUP
THUD
STRIDE

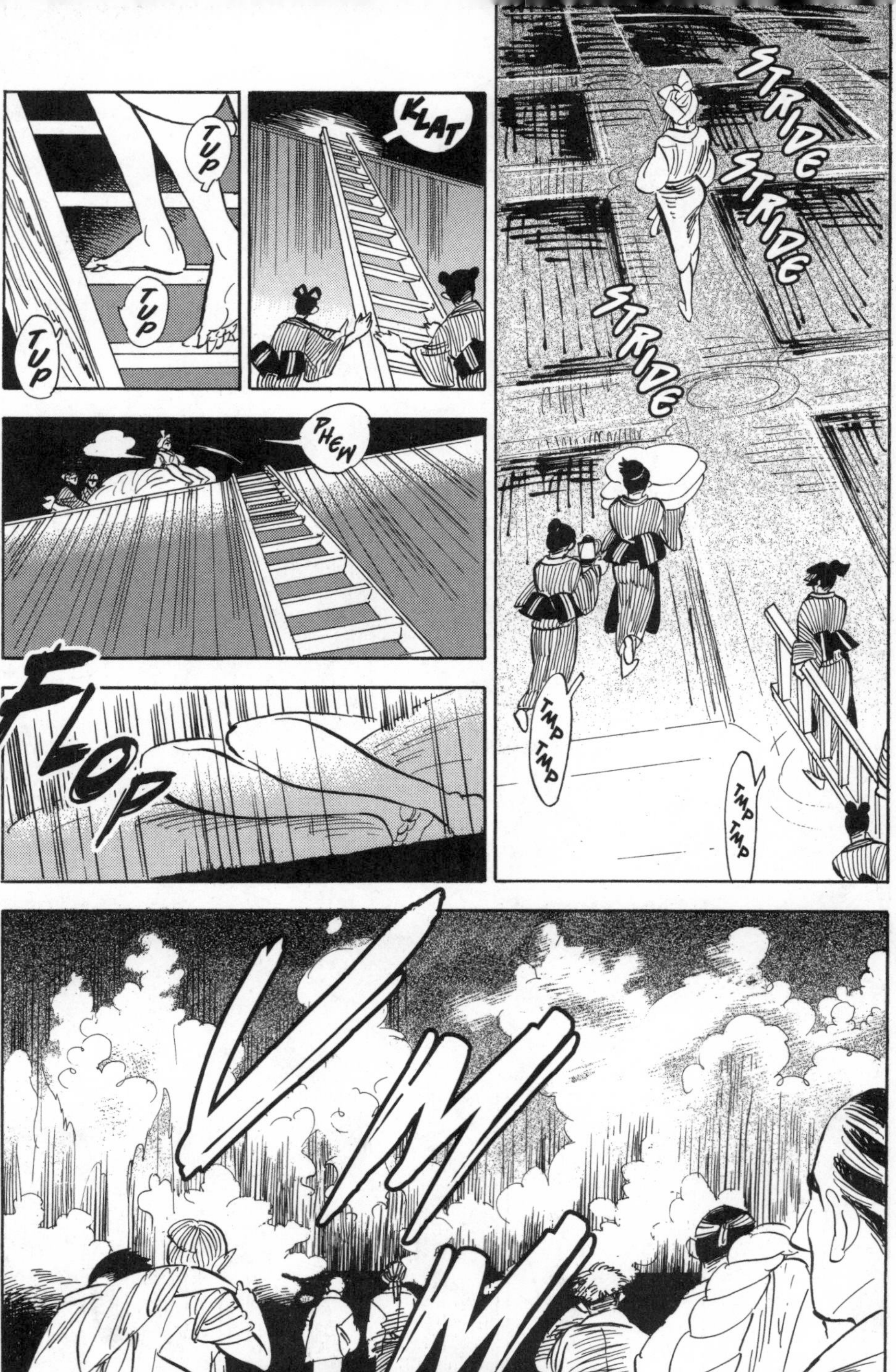
STRIDE
STRIDE
STRIDE
STRIDE
TMP TMP
TMP TMP
KLAT
TUP
TUP
TUP
PHEW
FLOP
VMM

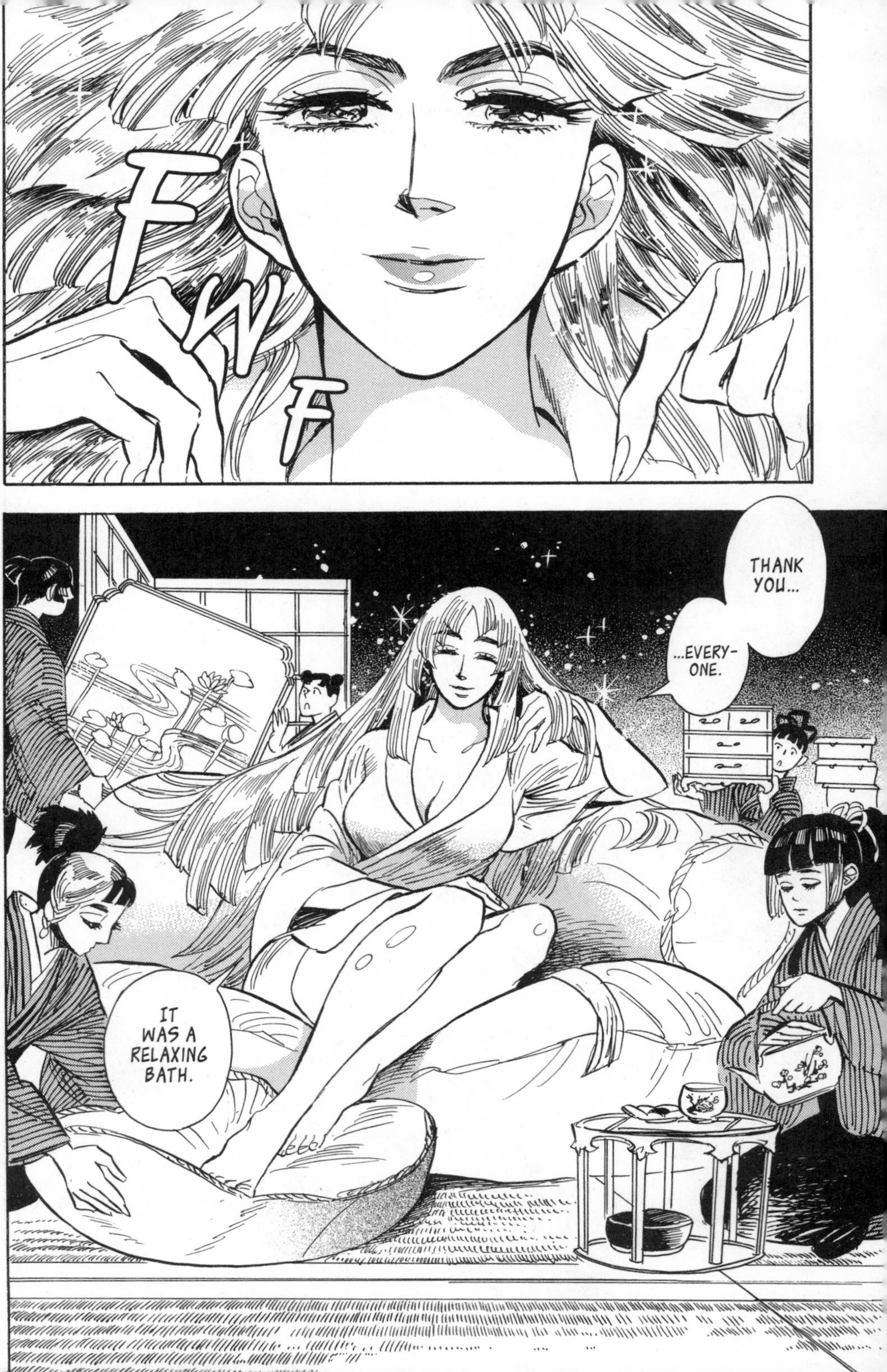
FWF
THANK YOU...
...EVERY-ONE.
IT WAS A RELAXING BATH.

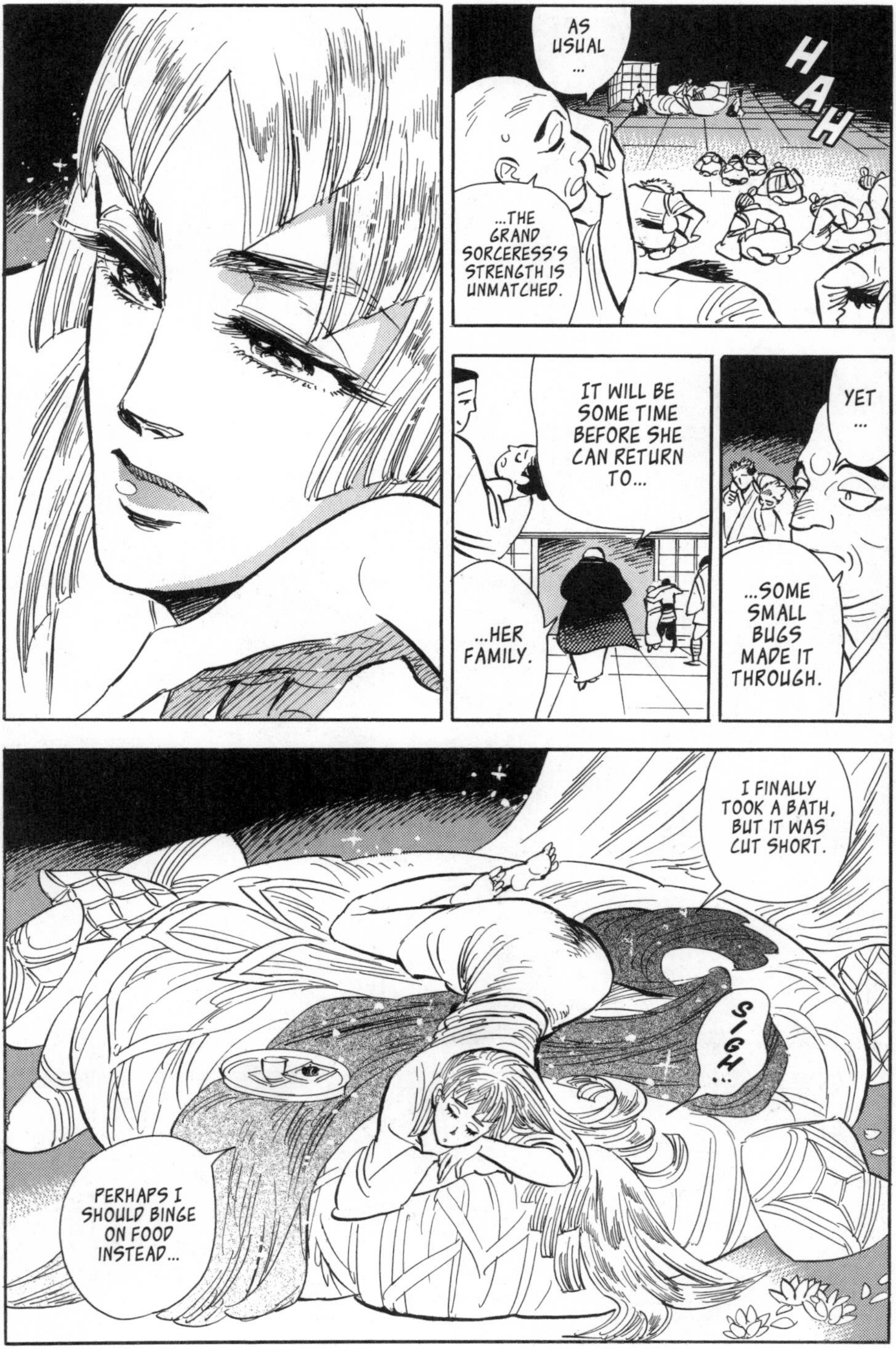
AS USUAL ...
HAH
...THE GRAND SORCERESS'S STRENGTH IS UNMATCHED.
YET ...
...SOME SMALL BUGS MADE IT THROUGH.
IT WILL BE SOME TIME BEFORE SHE CAN RETURN TO...
...HER FAMILY.
I FINALLY TOOK A BATH, BUT IT WAS CUT SHORT.
SIGH ...
PERHAPS I SHOULD BINGE ON FOOD INSTEAD...

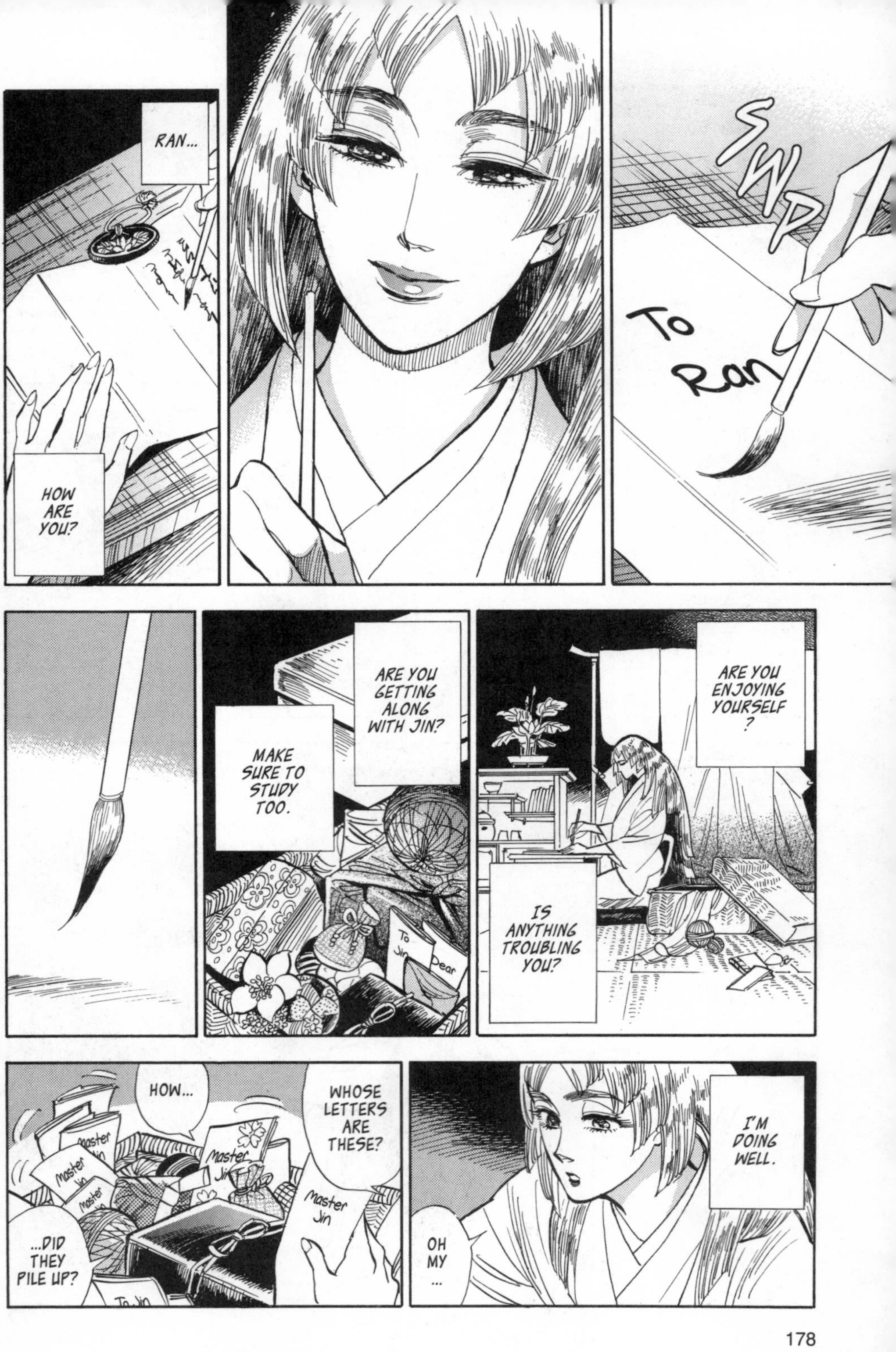
SWP
To Ran
RAN...
HOW ARE YOU?
ARE YOU ENJOYING YOURSELF?
IS ANYTHING TROUBLING YOU?
ARE YOU GETTING ALONG WITH JIN?
MAKE SURE TO STUDY TOO.
To Jin
Dear
I'M DOING WELL.
OH MY...
WHOSE LETTERS ARE THESE?
Master Jin
HOW...
Master Jin
Master Jin
...DID THEY PILE UP?
To Jin

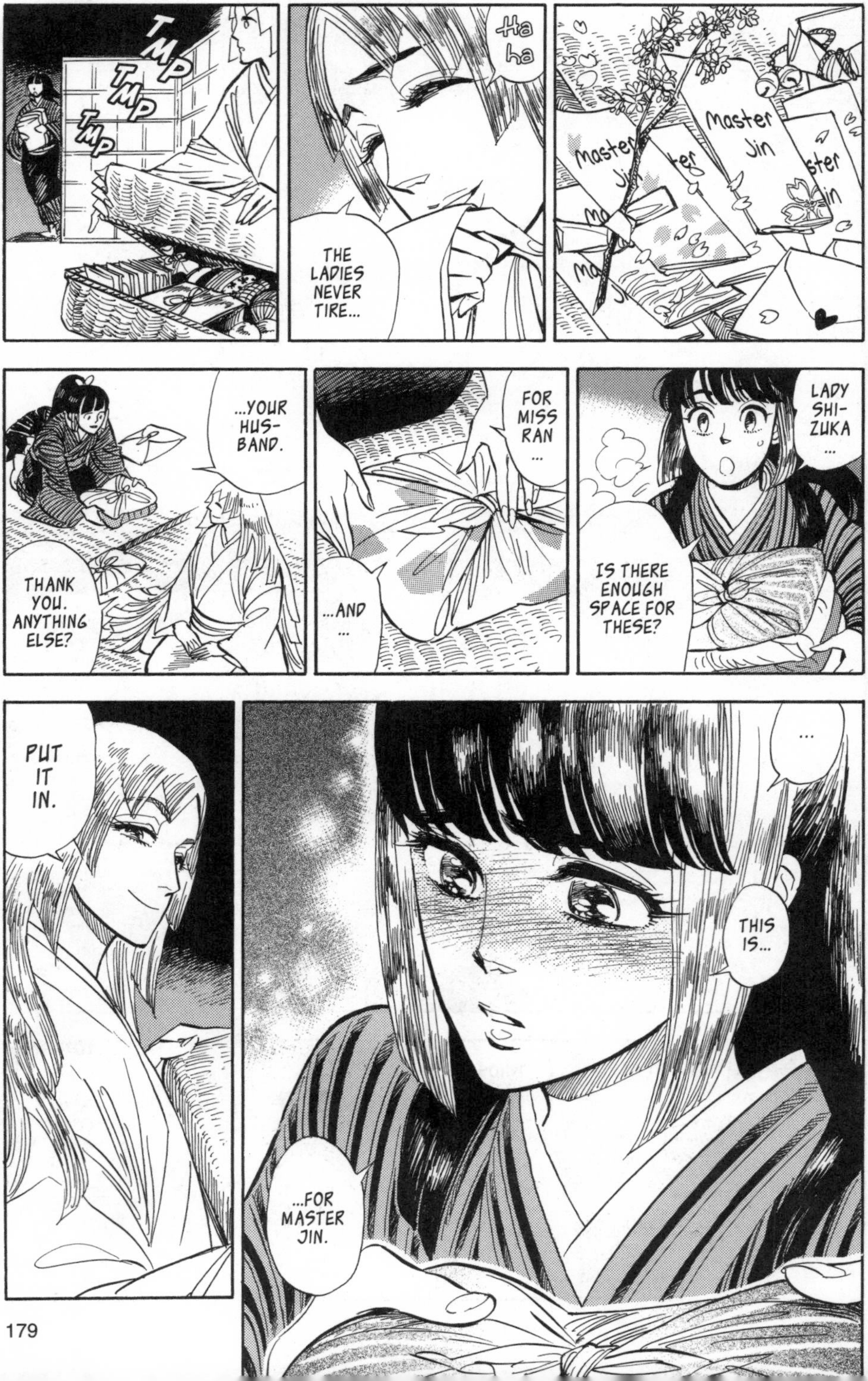
Master Jin
Master Jin
Master Jin
Ha ha
THE LADIES NEVER TIRE...
TMP TMP TMP
LADY SHI-ZUKA...
IS THERE ENOUGH SPACE FOR THESE?
FOR MISS RAN...
...AND...
...YOUR HUS-BAND.
THANK YOU. ANYTHING ELSE?
...
THIS IS...
...FOR MASTER JIN.
PUT IT IN.

FWP
FWP

...A BIRD.

FLY AWAY TO...

LISTEN CAREFULLY.

YOU ARE NOW...

...HAIMACHI...

NUMBER 9-1, IN THE TENTH DISTRICT.

WHERE AGAIN?

UM...

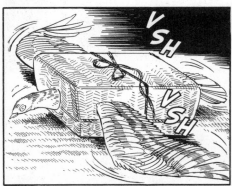

VSH
VSH

SHWP

FWOOO

DON'T TAKE ANY DETOURS!

FLAP

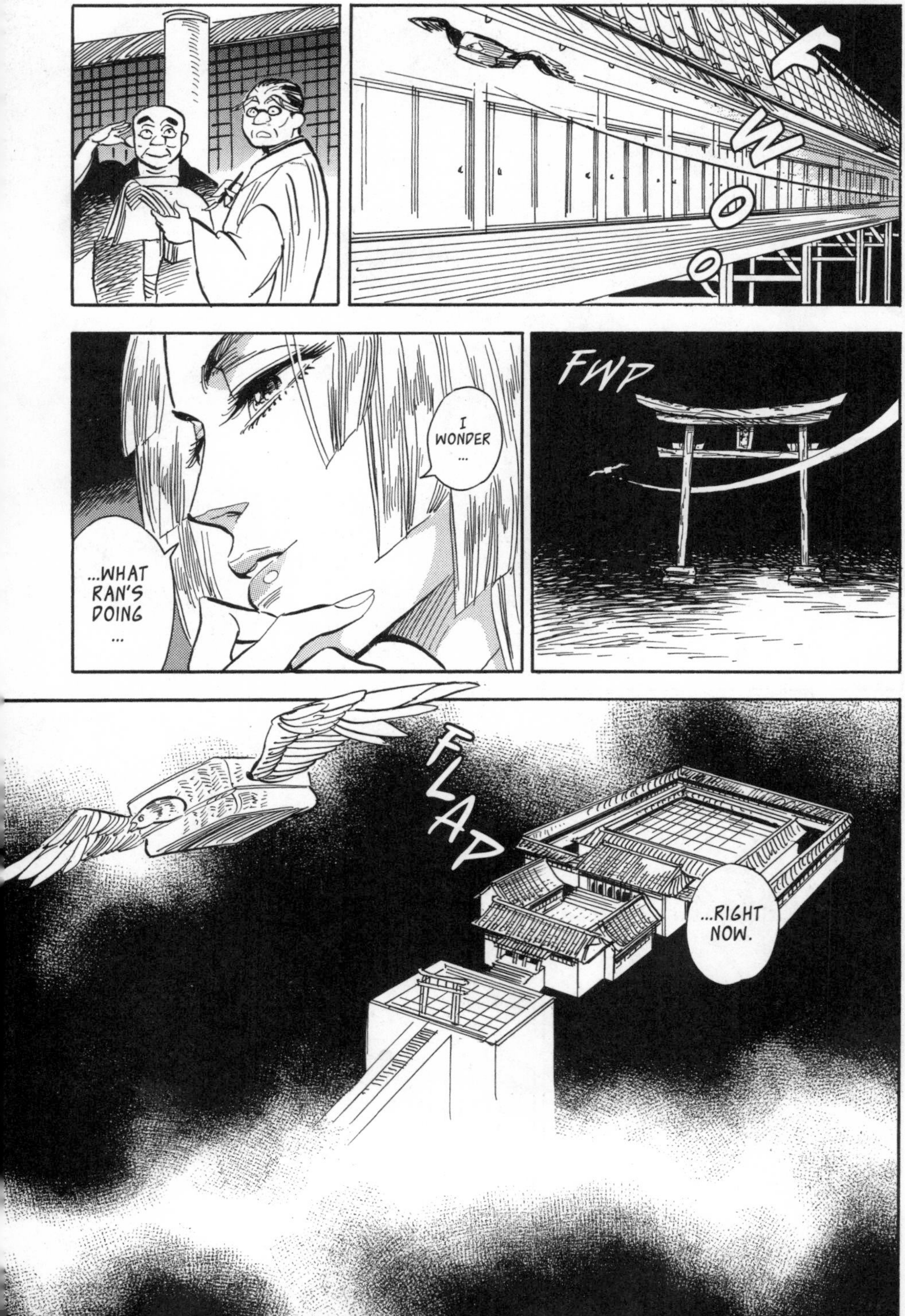
FWOO
FWP
I WONDER ...
...WHAT RAN'S DOING ...
FLAP
...RIGHT NOW.

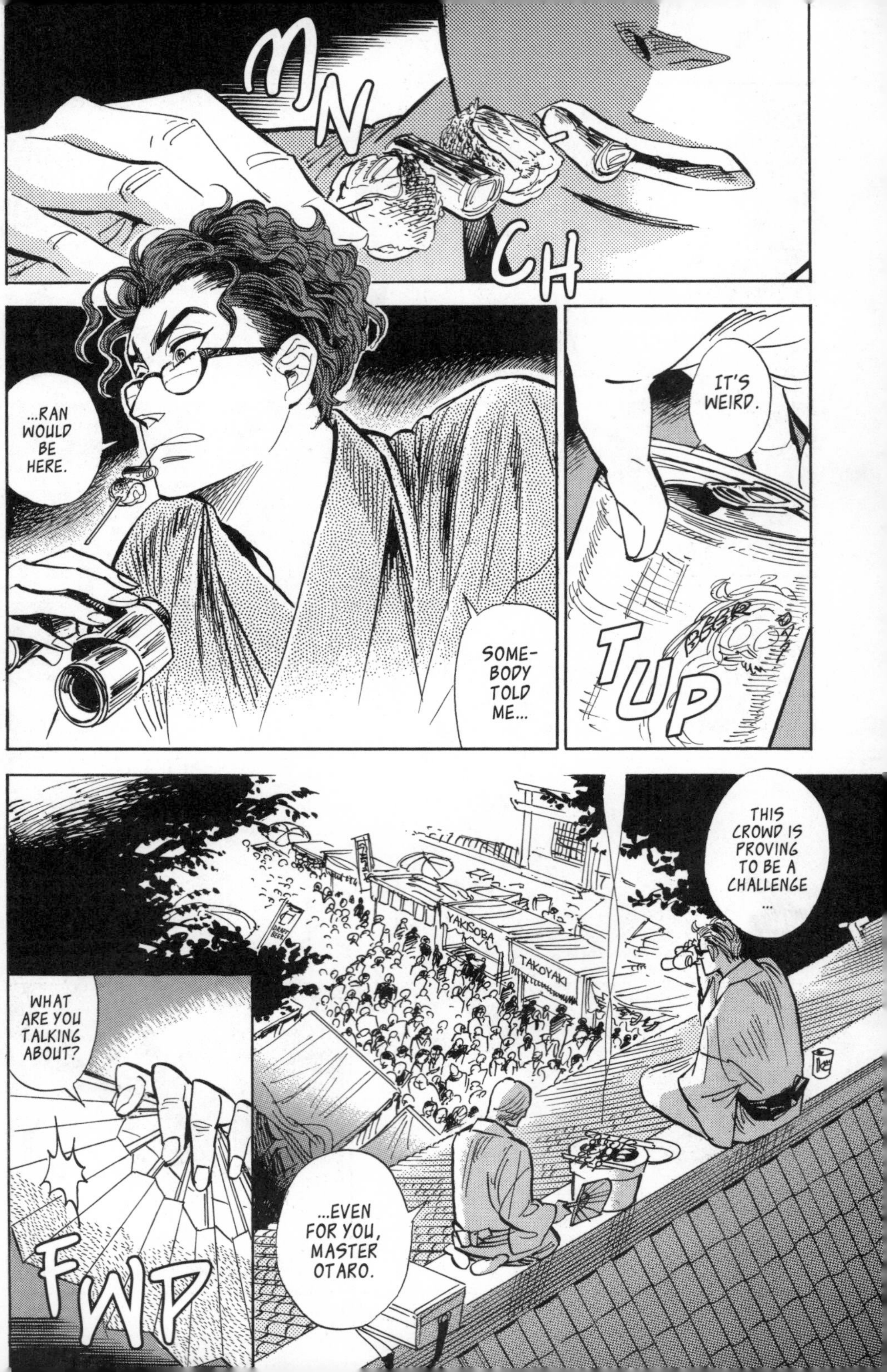
MN
CH
IT'S WEIRD.
TUP
SOME-BODY TOLD ME...
...RAN WOULD BE HERE.
THIS CROWD IS PROVING TO BE A CHALLENGE ...
YAKISOBA
TAKOYAKI
...EVEN FOR YOU, MASTER OTARO.
WHAT ARE YOU TALKING ABOUT?
FWP

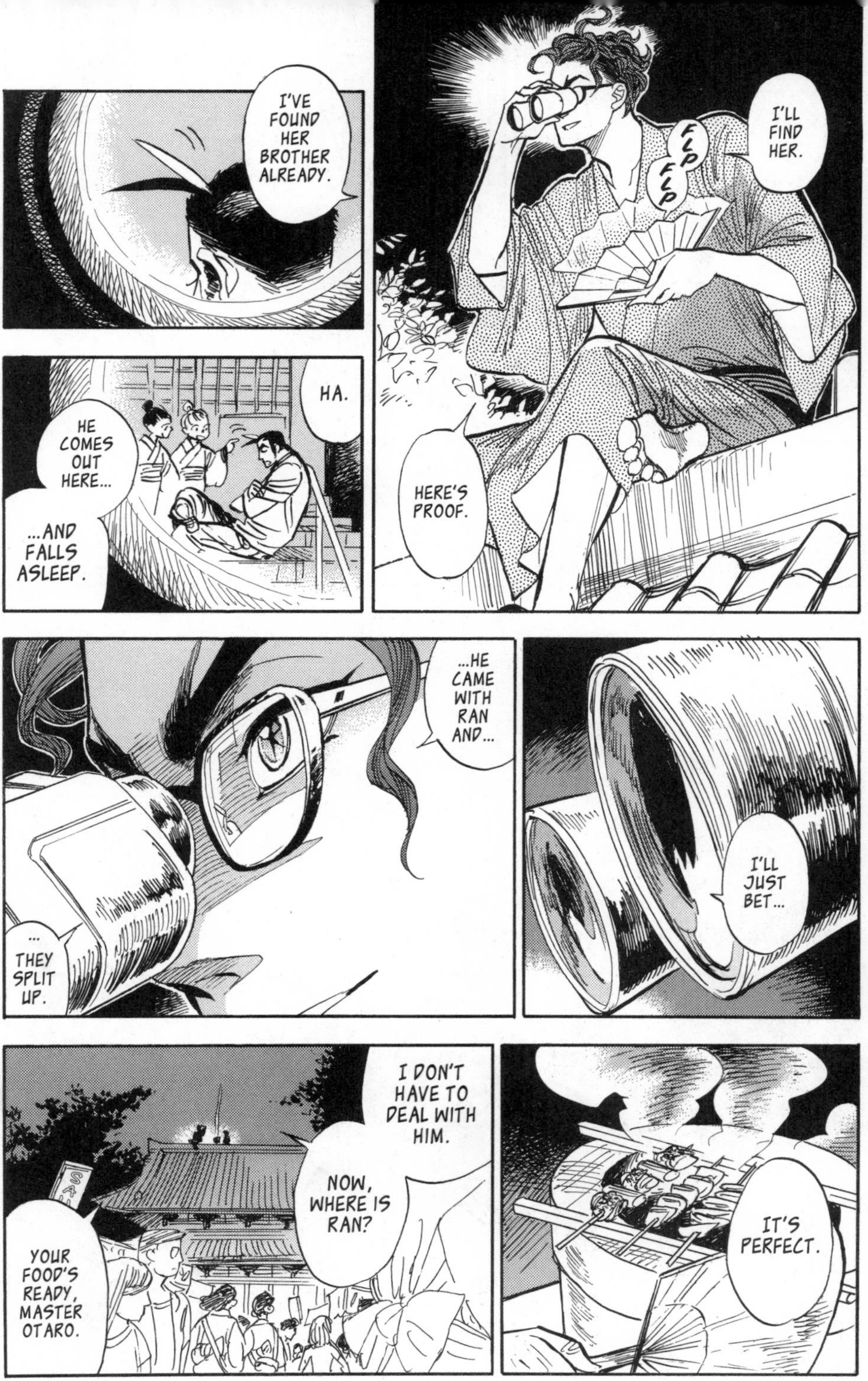
I'LL FIND HER.
FLP FLP FLP
HERE'S PROOF.
I'VE FOUND HER BROTHER ALREADY.
HA.
HE COMES OUT HERE...
...AND FALLS ASLEEP.
I'LL JUST BET...
...HE CAME WITH RAN AND...
... THEY SPLIT UP.
IT'S PERFECT.
I DON'T HAVE TO DEAL WITH HIM.
NOW, WHERE IS RAN?
YOUR FOOD'S READY, MASTER OTARO.

EX-
CUSE
...

UM
...

...ME
THROUGH
!

LET
...

SMUSH

TOSS

JIIIN!

JIN!

SHOOP

...MY
...

...SHOE
!

YANK

YANK

GIVE
ME
BACK
...

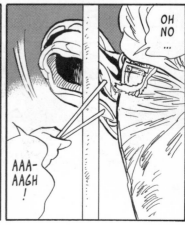

OH
NO
...

AAA-
AAGH
!

184

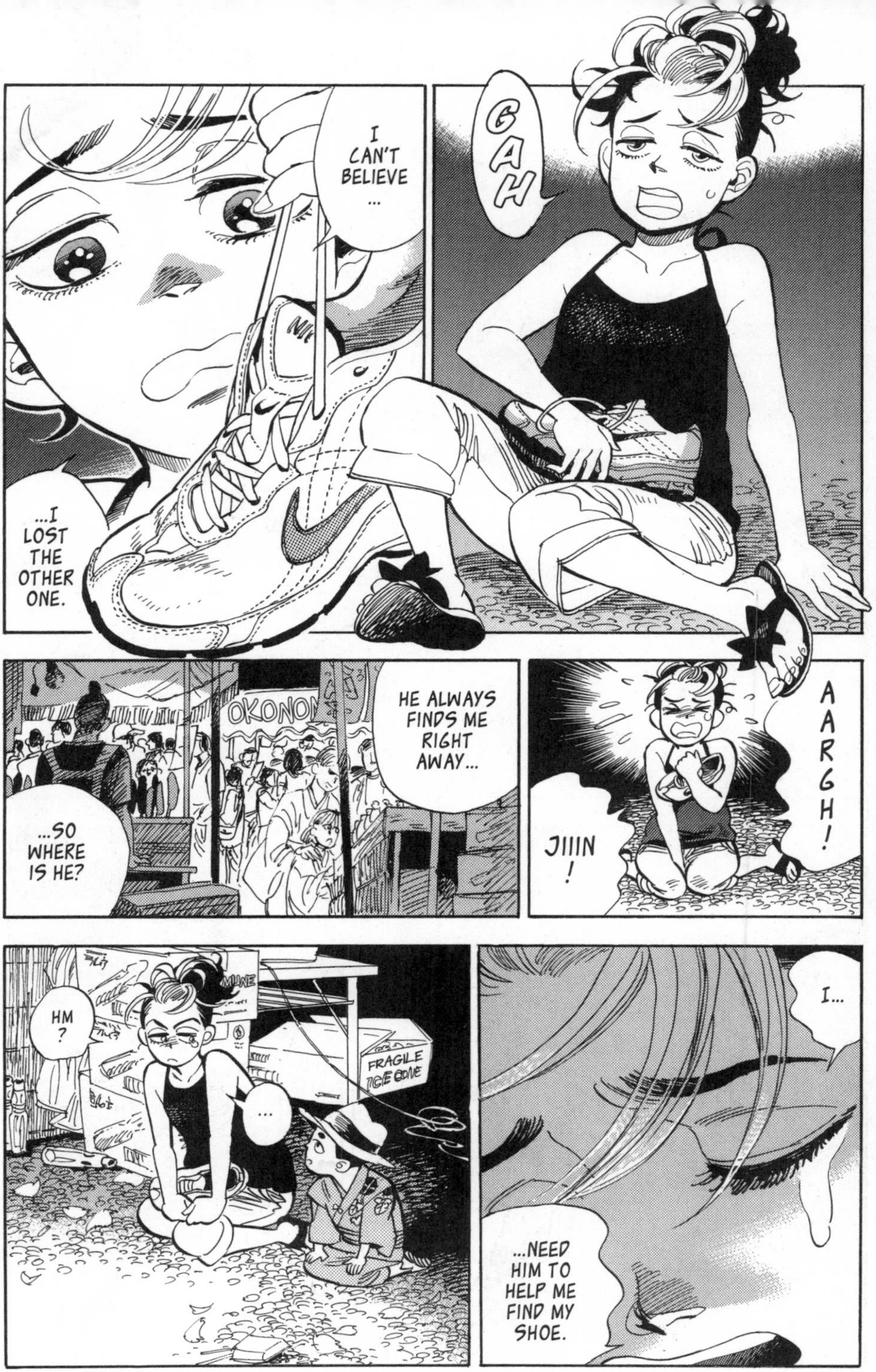
GAH
I CAN'T BELIEVE ...
...I LOST THE OTHER ONE.
AARGH!
JIIIN!
HE ALWAYS FINDS ME RIGHT AWAY...
...SO WHERE IS HE?
OKONOM
I...
...NEED HIM TO HELP ME FIND MY SHOE.
HM?
...
FRAGILE

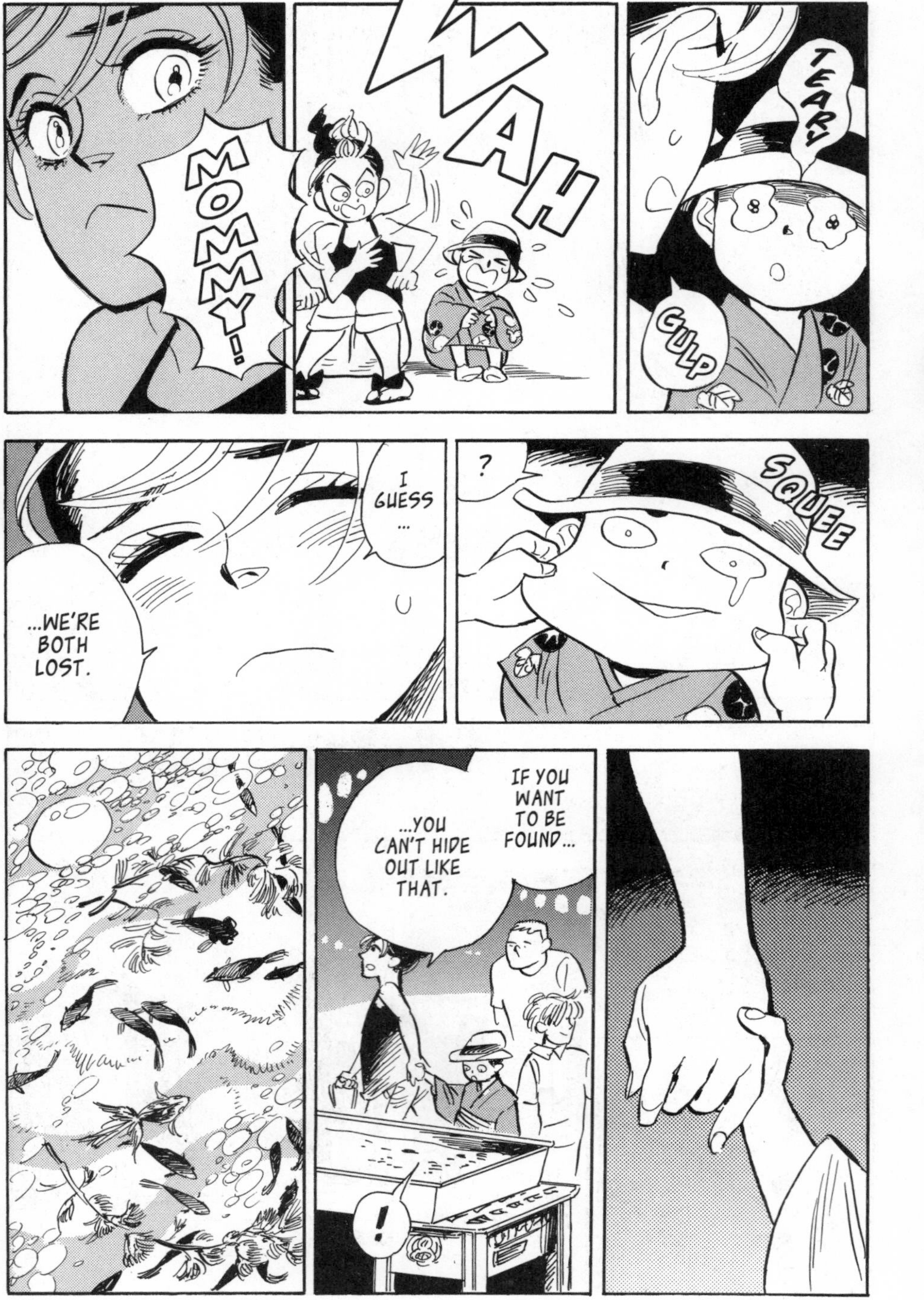
TEARY
GULP
WAH
MOMMY!
?
SQUEE
I GUESS...
...WE'RE BOTH LOST.
IF YOU WANT TO BE FOUND...
...YOU CAN'T HIDE OUT LIKE THAT.
!

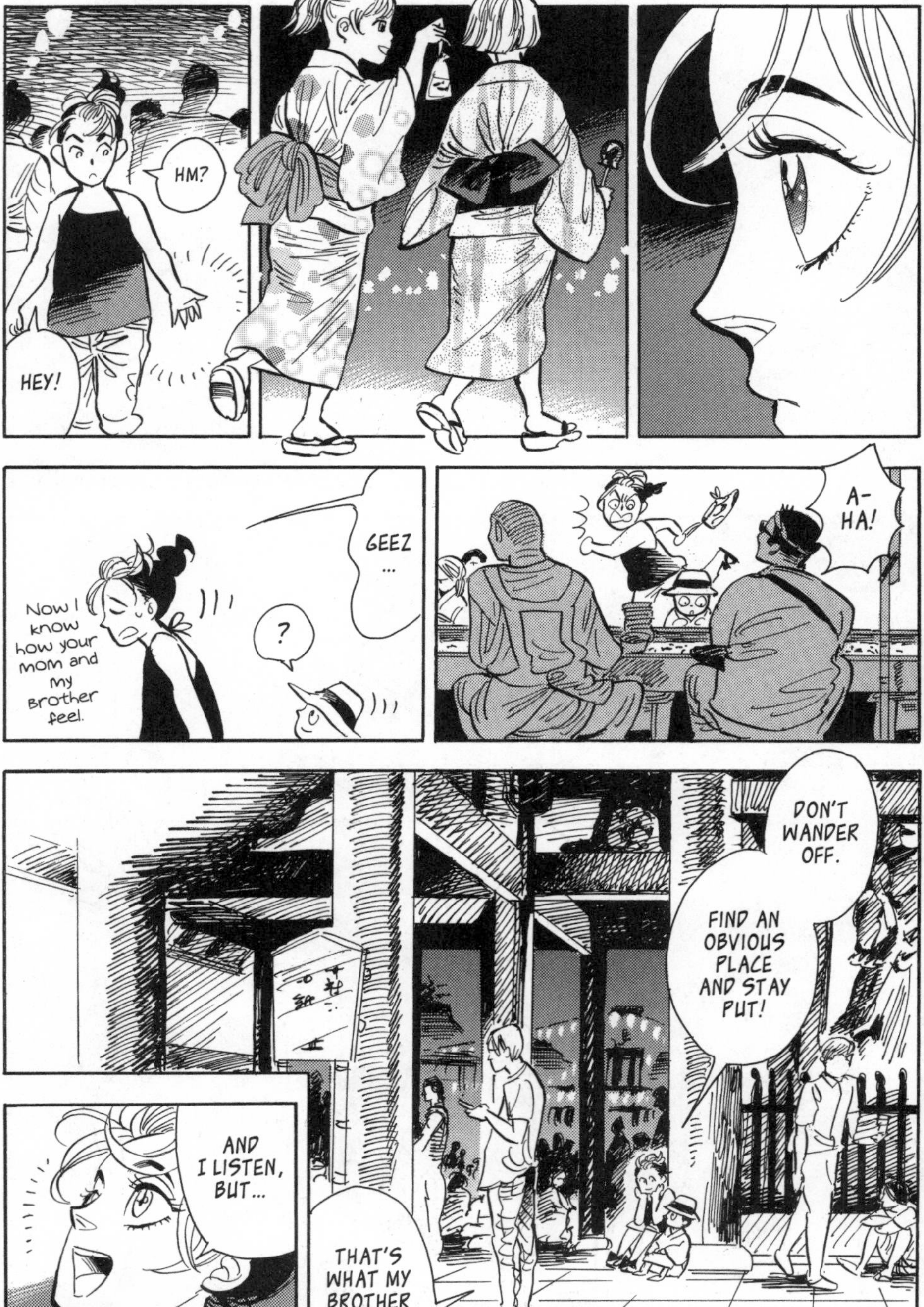
HM?
HEY!
A-HA!
GEEZ ...
Now I know how your mom and my brother feel.
?
DON'T WANDER OFF.
FIND AN OBVIOUS PLACE AND STAY PUT!
THAT'S WHAT MY BROTHER SAYS.
AND I LISTEN, BUT...

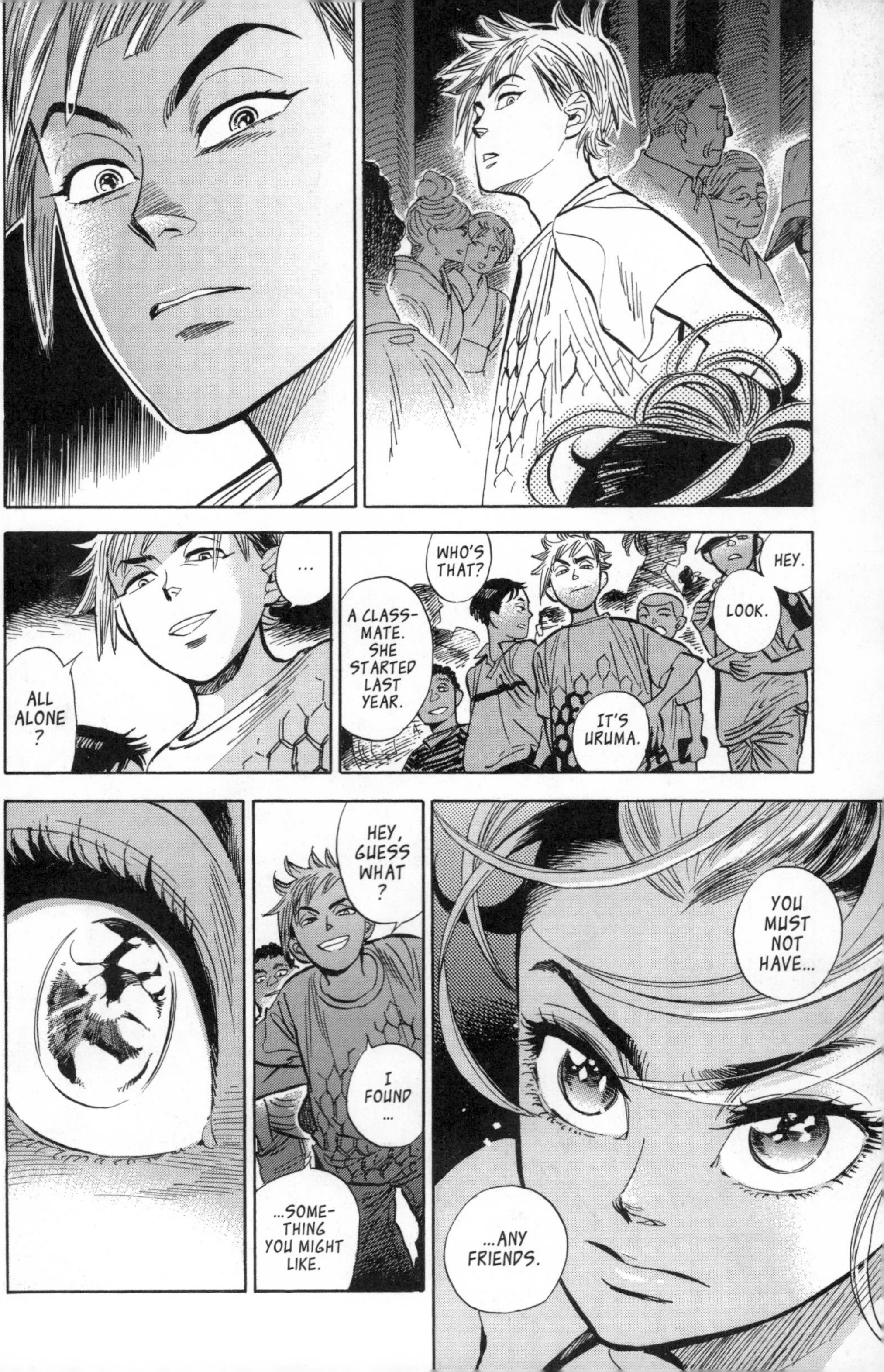
HEY.
LOOK.
WHO'S THAT?
A CLASS-MATE. SHE STARTED LAST YEAR.
IT'S URUMA.
...
ALL ALONE?
YOU MUST NOT HAVE...
...ANY FRIENDS.
HEY, GUESS WHAT?
I FOUND...
...SOME-THING YOU MIGHT LIKE.

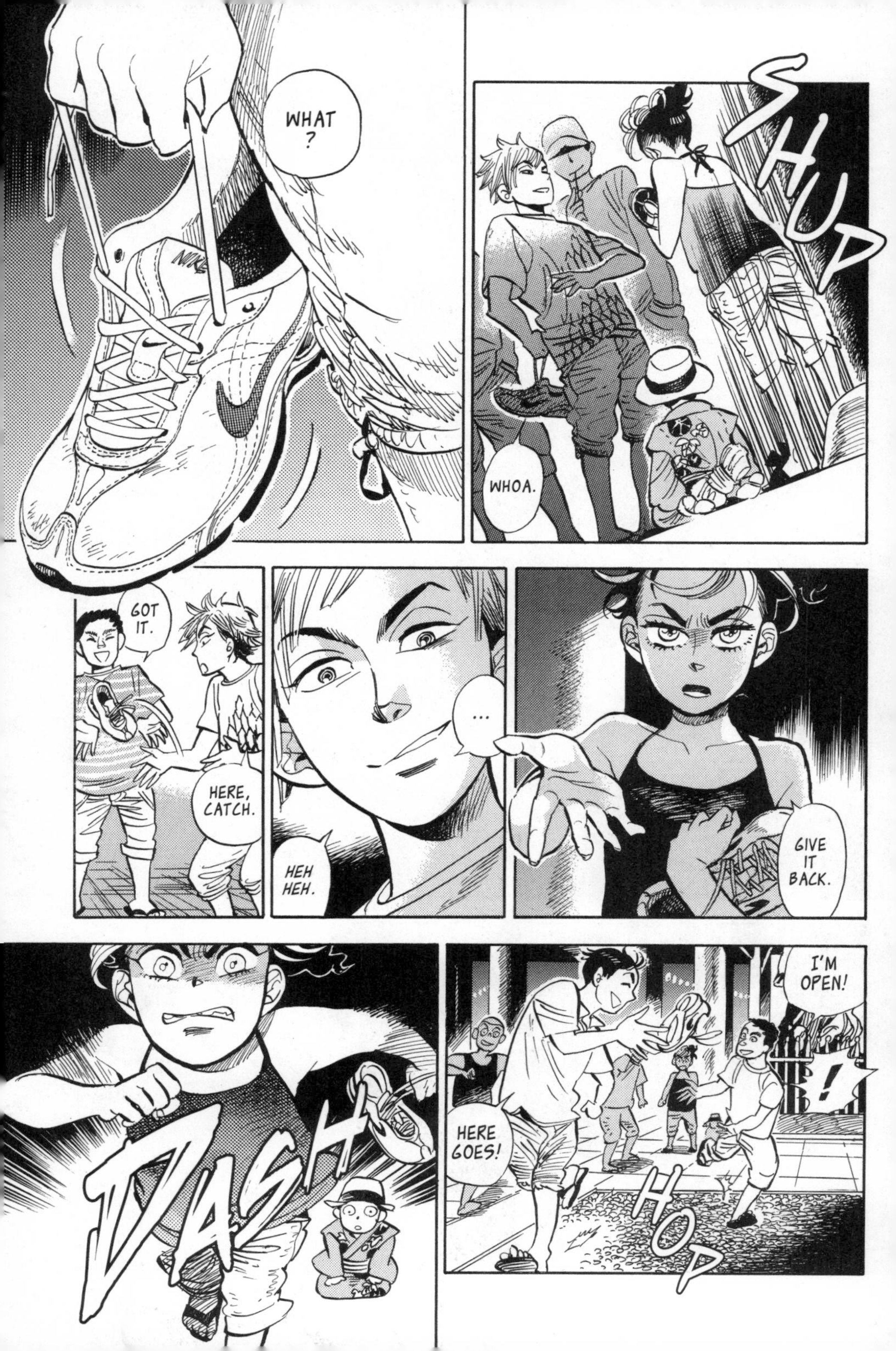
SHUP
WHOA.
WHAT ?
GIVE IT BACK.
...
HEH HEH.
GOT IT.
HERE, CATCH.
I'M OPEN!
!
HERE GOES!
HOP
DASH

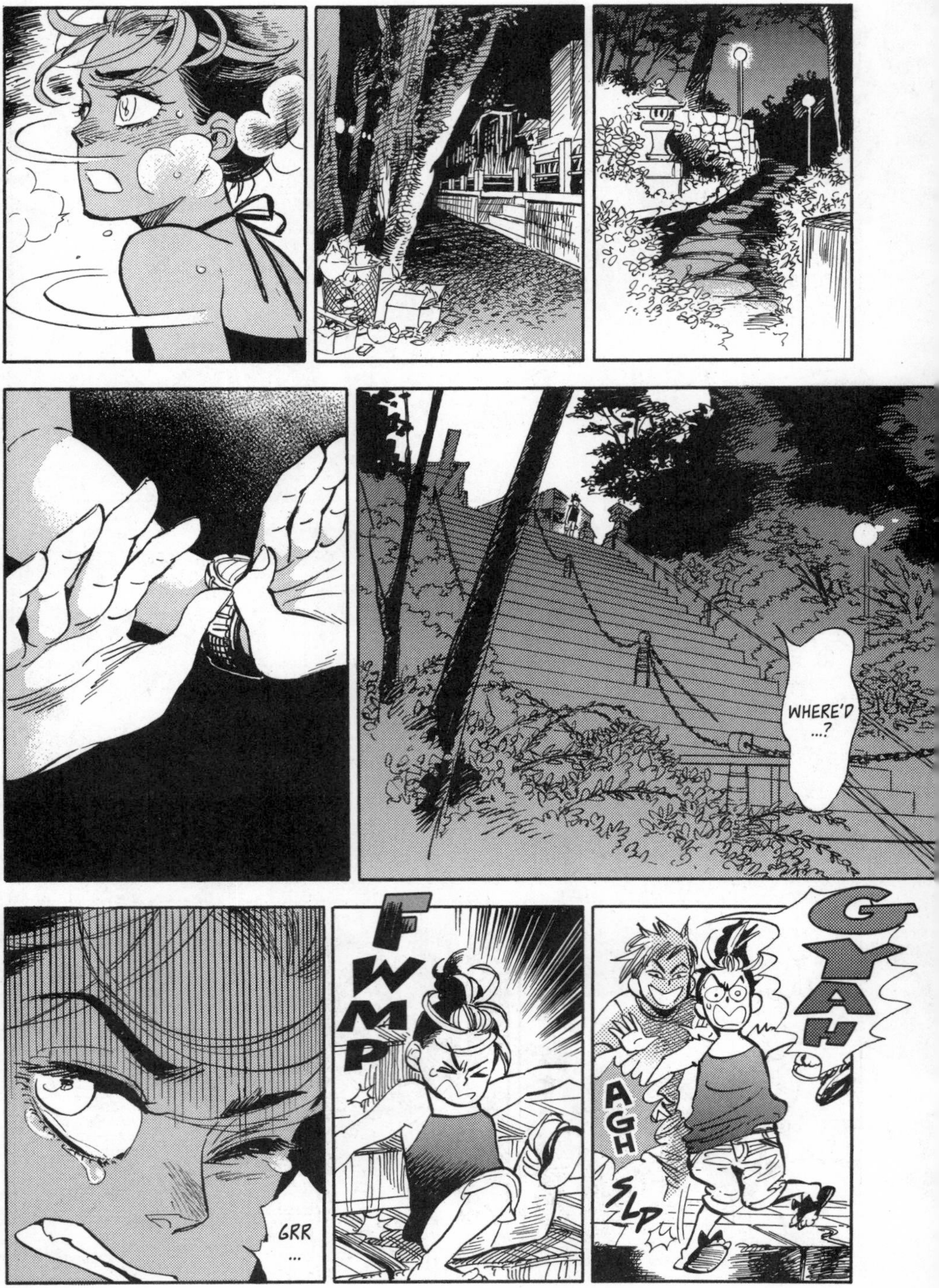
WHERE'D ...?
GYAH
AGH
SLP
FWMP
GRR ...

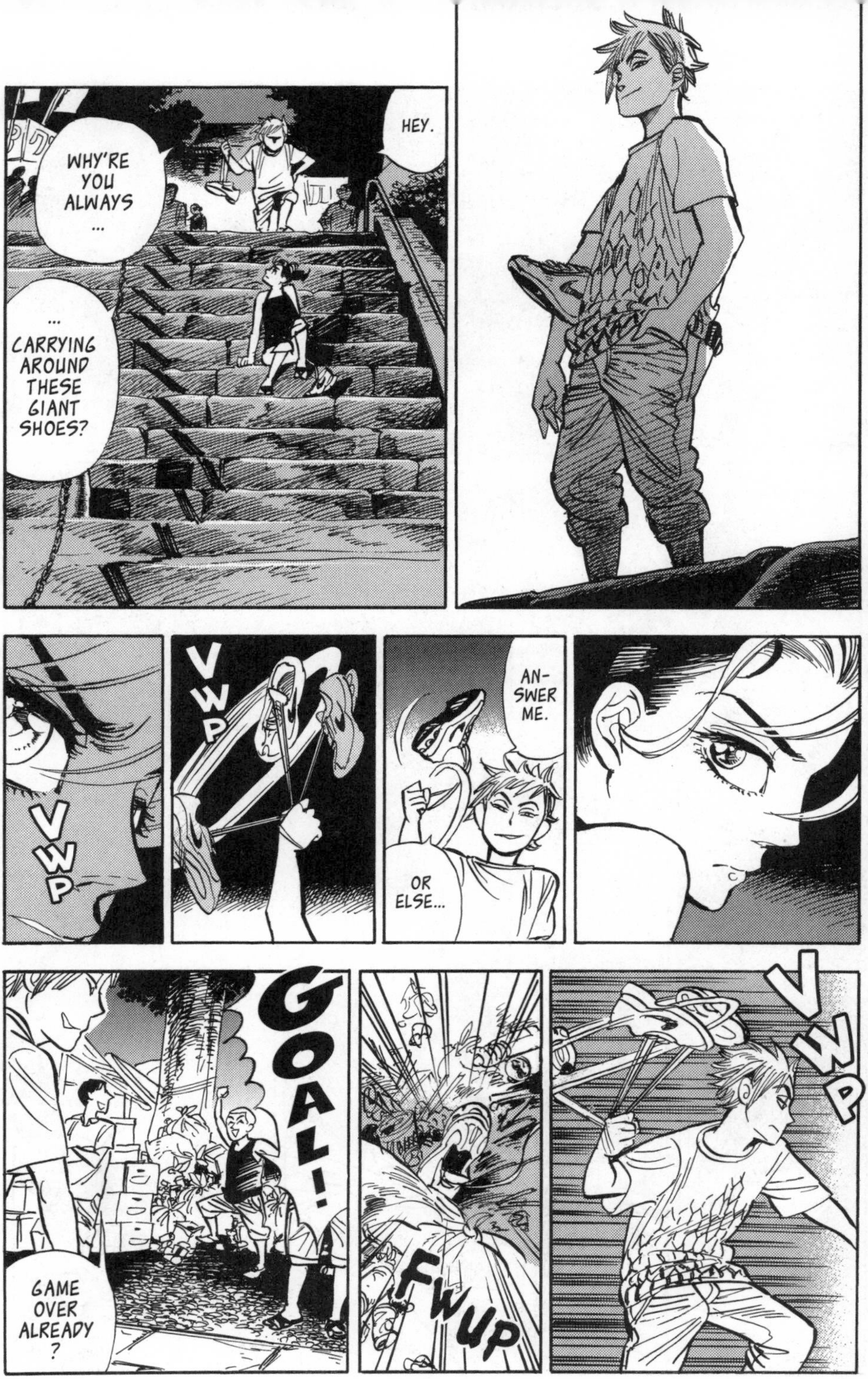
HEY.
WHY'RE YOU ALWAYS ...
... CARRYING AROUND THESE GIANT SHOES?
AN-SWER ME.
OR ELSE...
VWP
VWP
VWP
VWP
FWUP
GOAL!
GAME OVER ALREADY?

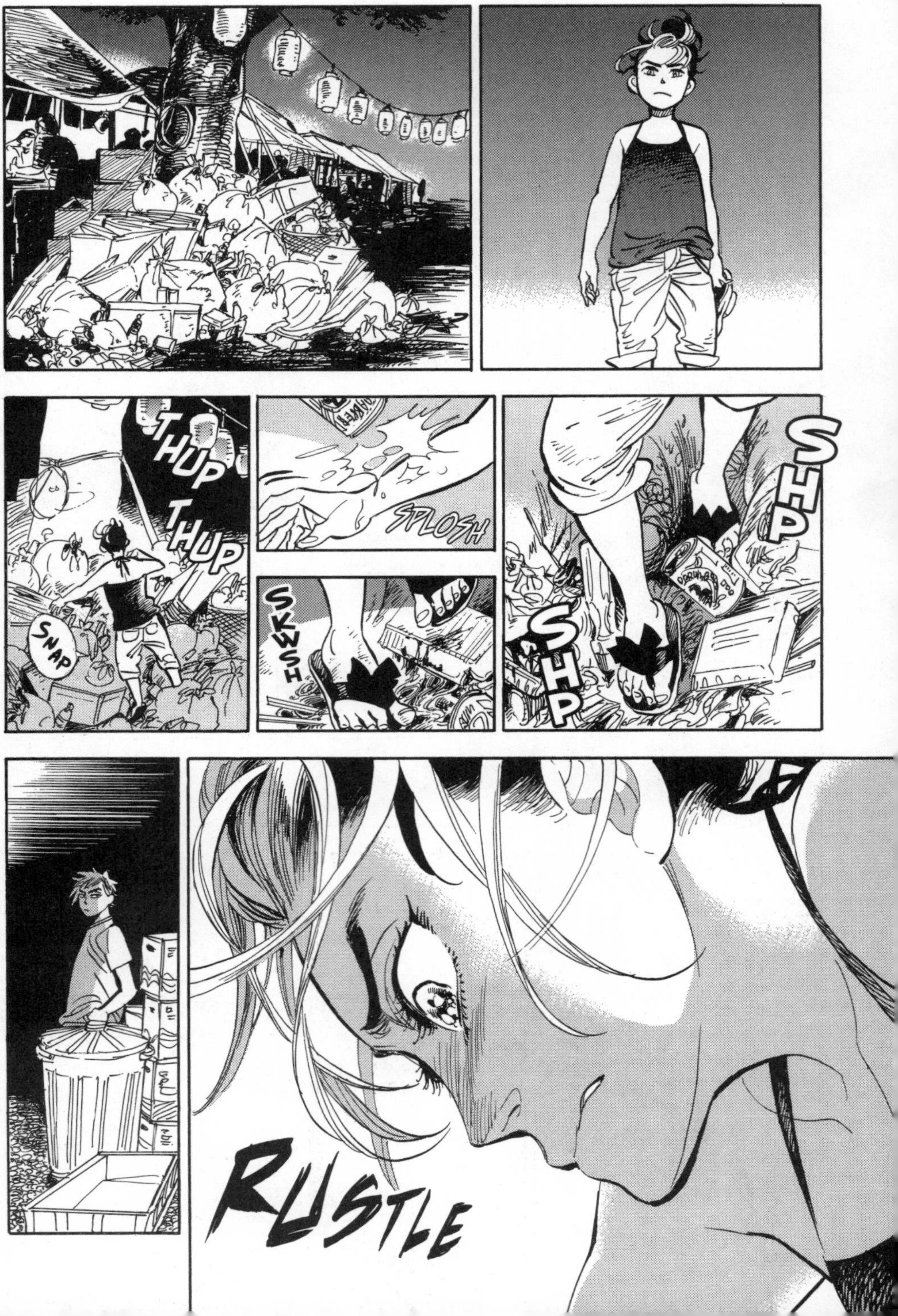
SHP
SHP
SPLOSH
SKWSH
THUP
THUP
SNAP
RUSTLE

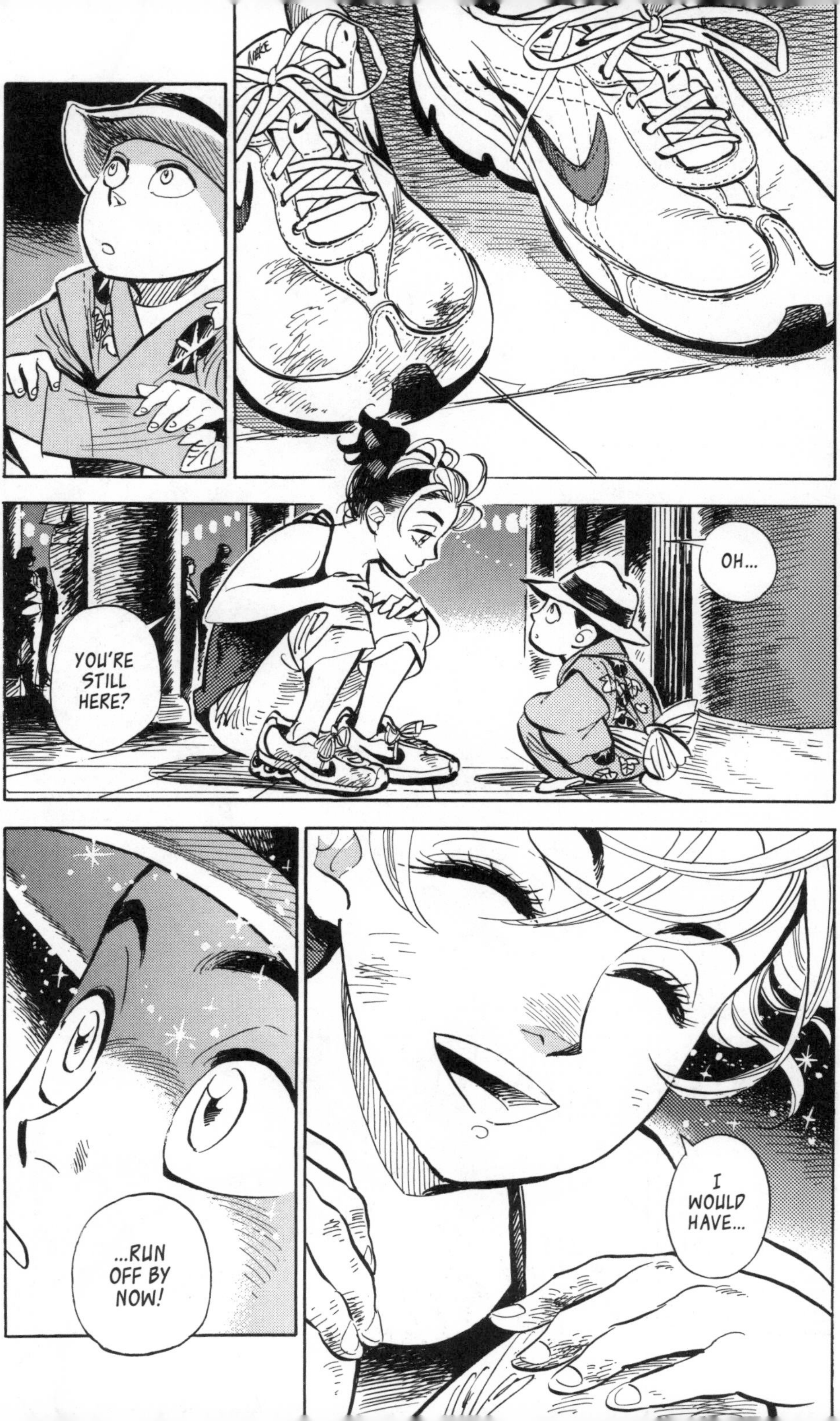
OH...
YOU'RE STILL HERE?
I WOULD HAVE...
...RUN OFF BY NOW!

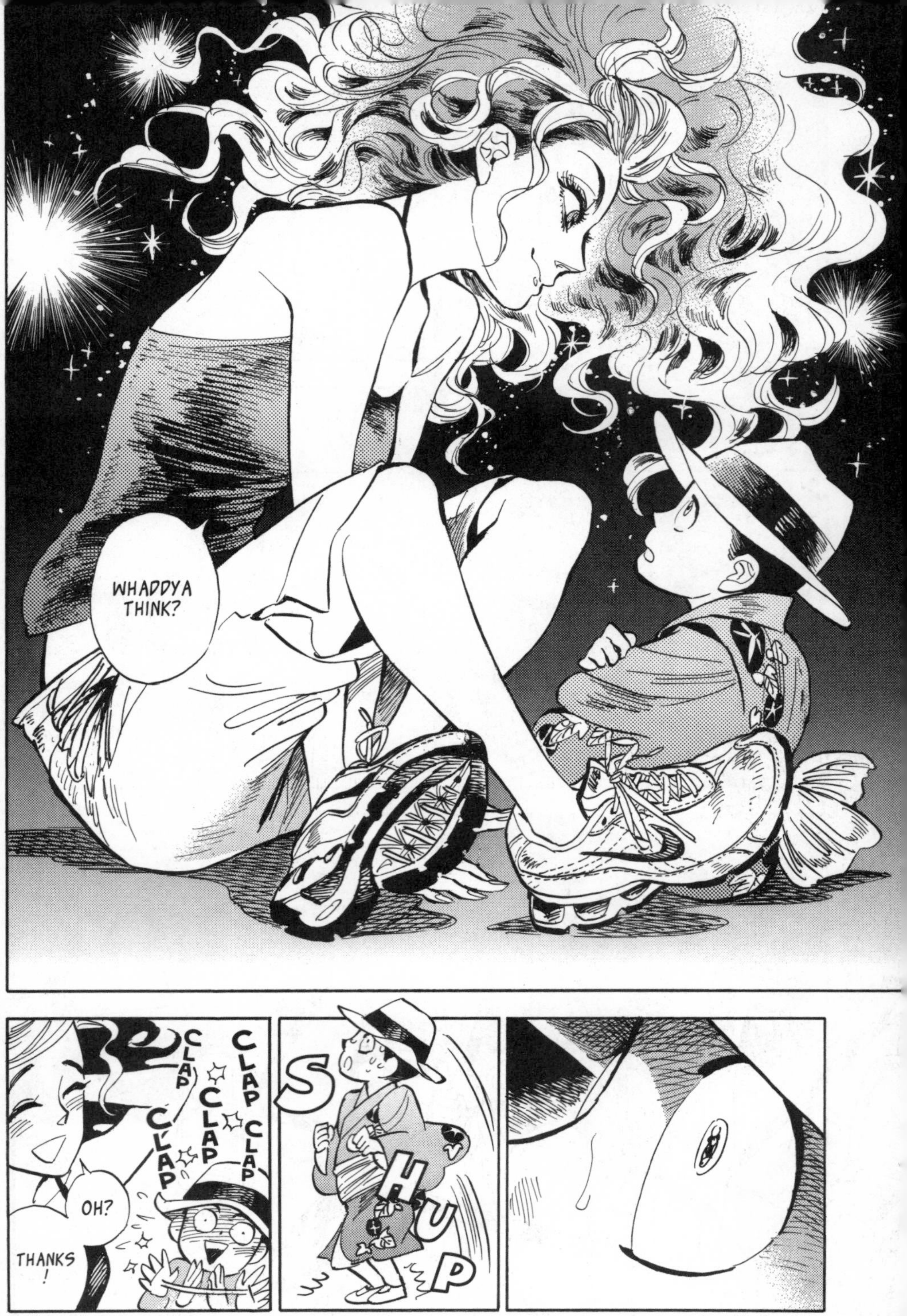
WHADDYA THINK?
SHUP
CLAP CLAP
CLAP CLAP
CLAP CLAP
OH?
THANKS!

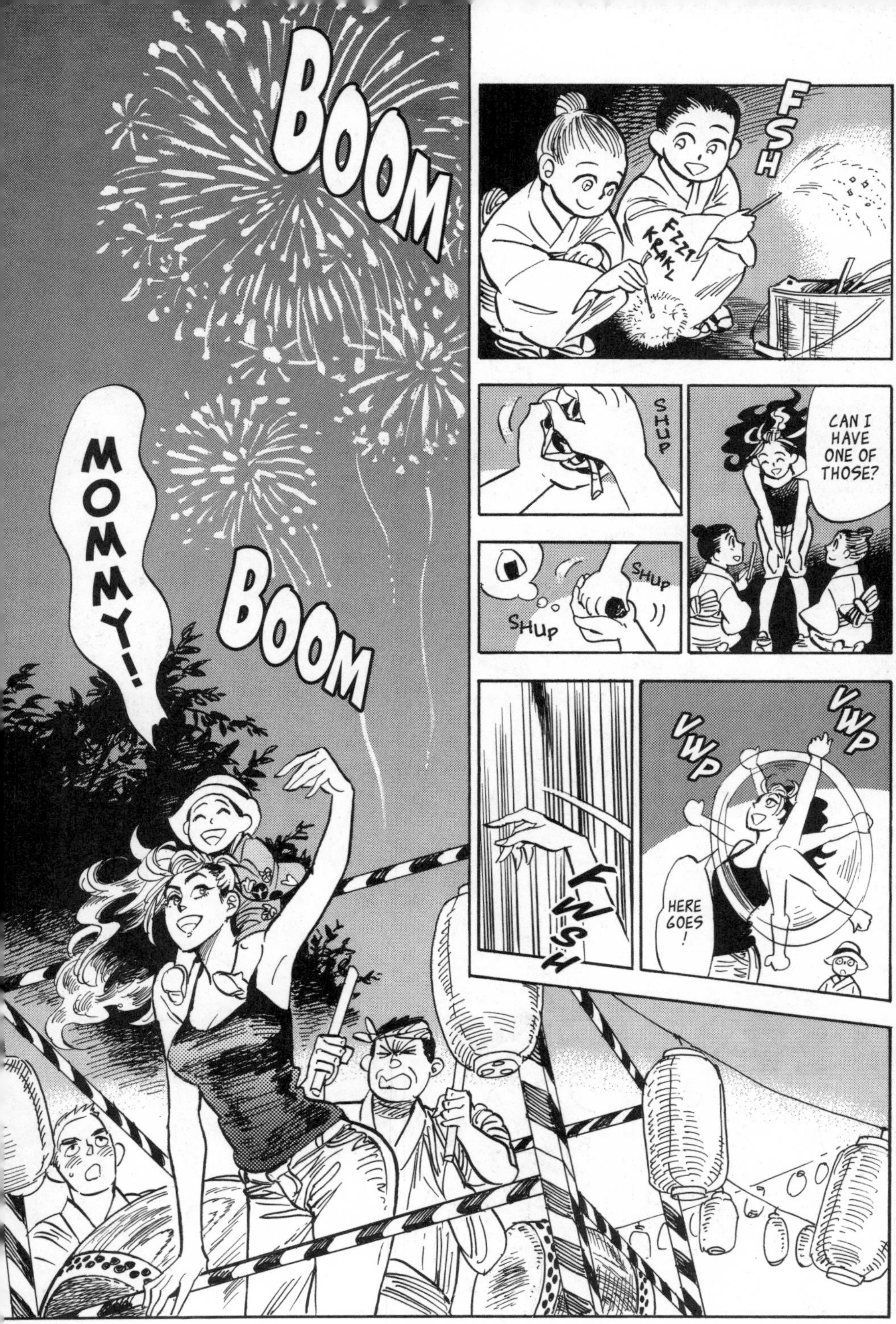
FSH
FZZZT
KRAKL
CAN I HAVE ONE OF THOSE?
SHUP
SHUP
SHUP
VWP
VWP
HERE GOES!
FWSH
BOOM
BOOM
MOMMY!!
BOOM

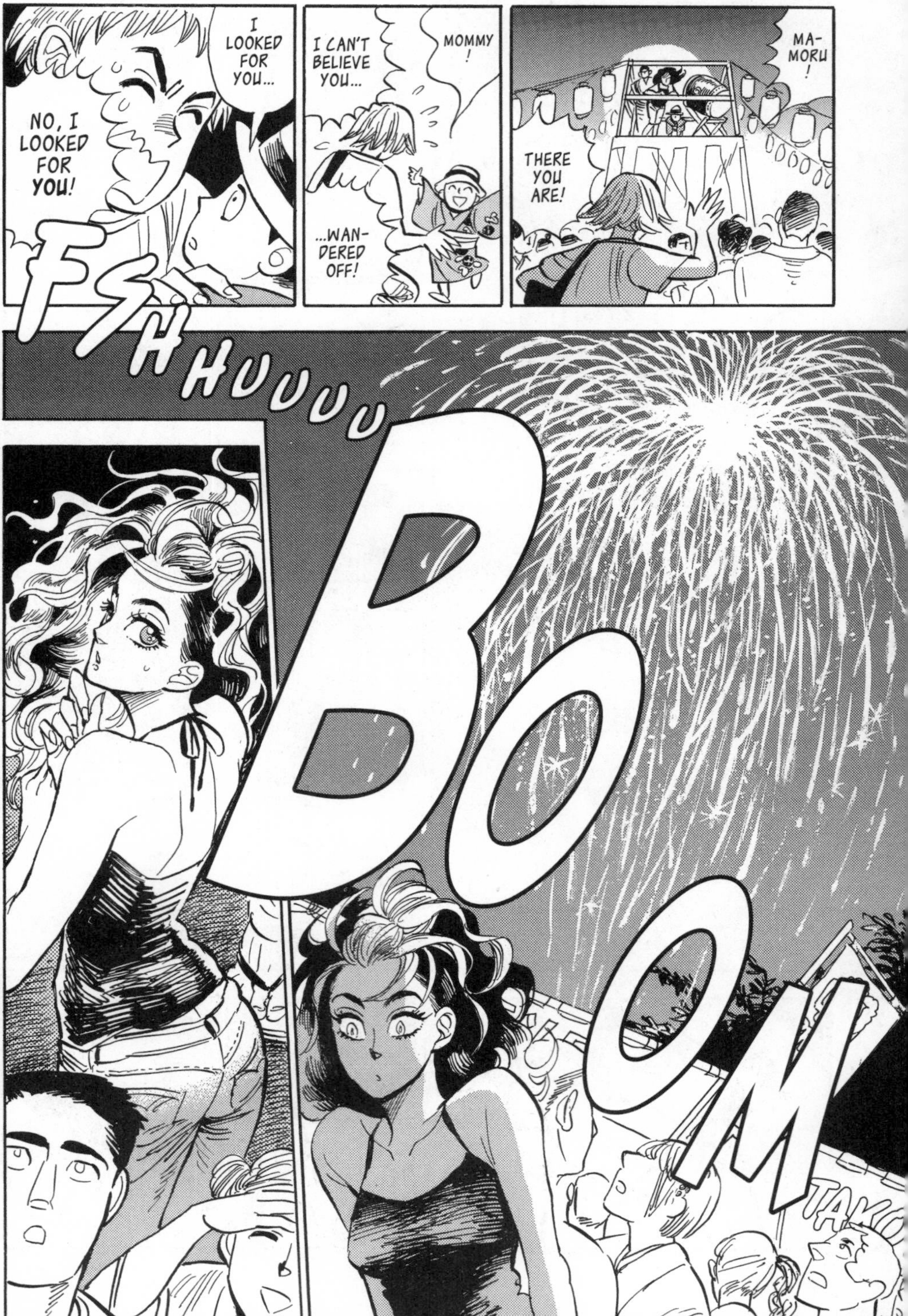
MA-MORU!
THERE YOU ARE!
MOMMY!
I CAN'T BELIEVE YOU...
...WAN-DERED OFF!
I LOOKED FOR YOU...
NO, I LOOKED FOR **YOU**!
FSHHUUUUU
BOOOM
TAKO

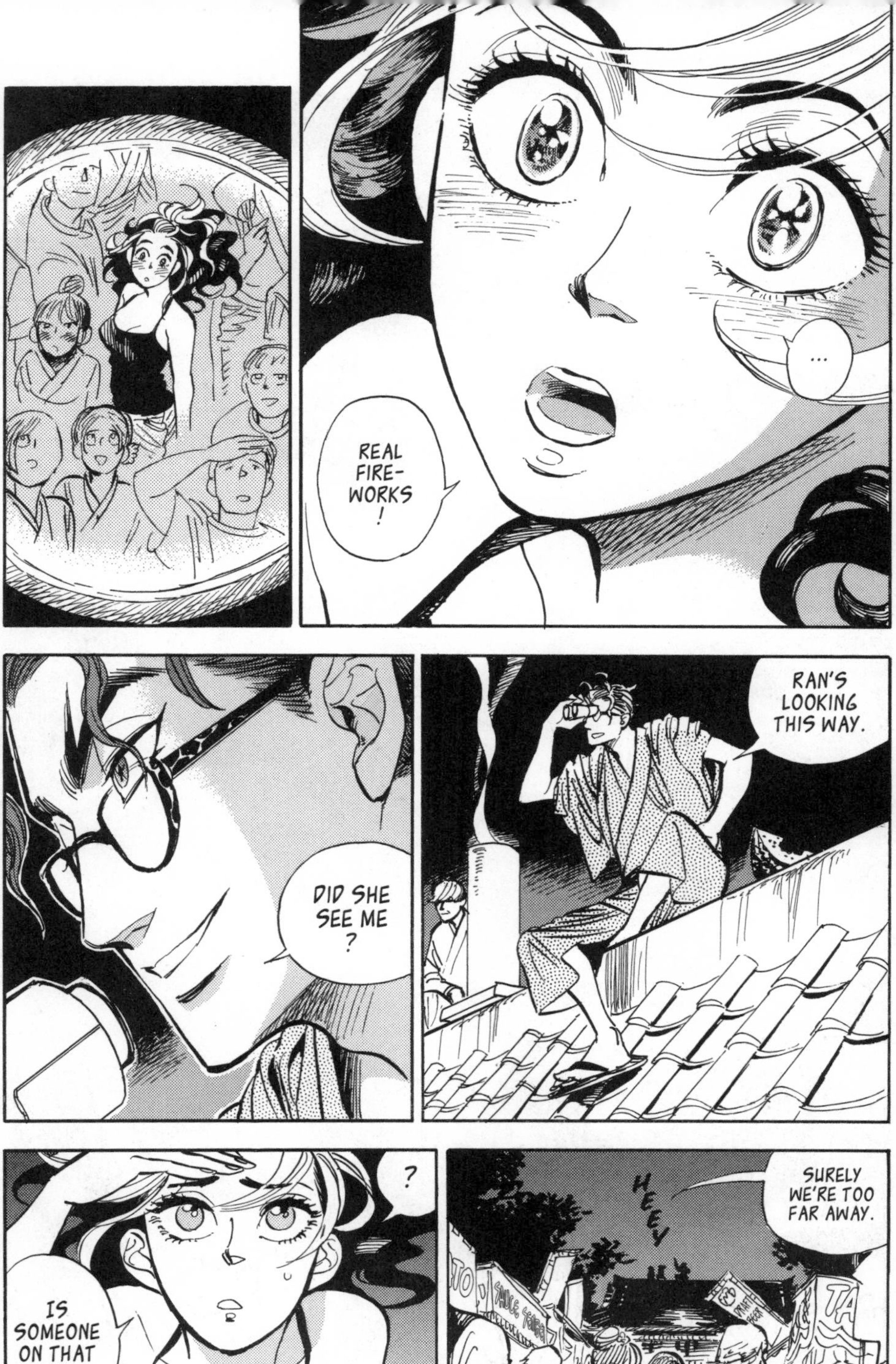
...
REAL FIRE-WORKS!
RAN'S LOOKING THIS WAY.
DID SHE SEE ME?
SURELY WE'RE TOO FAR AWAY.
HEEV
?
IS SOMEONE ON THAT ROOF?

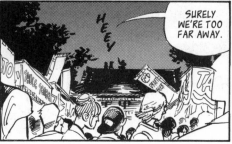

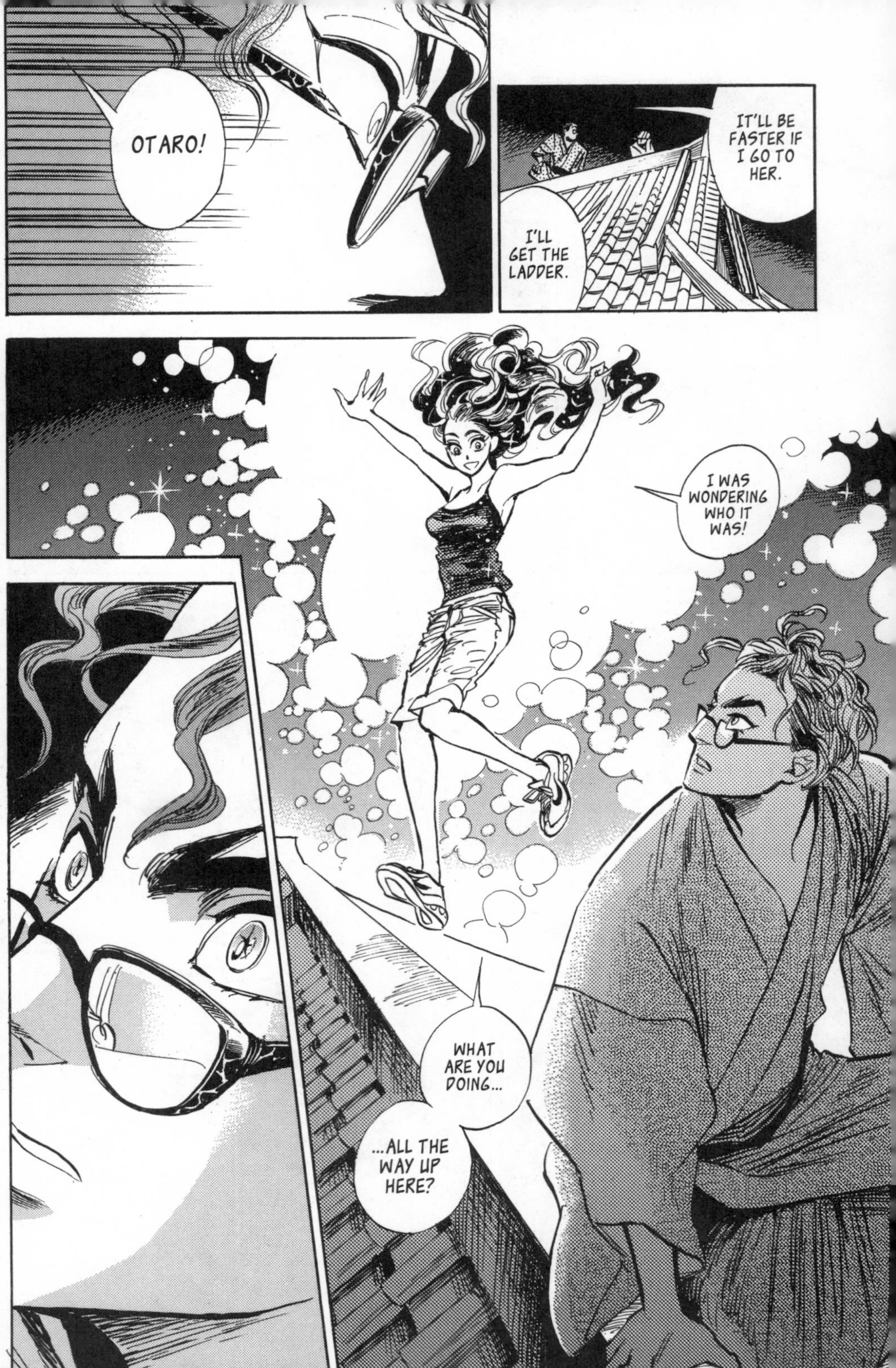
IT'LL BE FASTER IF I GO TO HER.
I'LL GET THE LADDER.
OTARO!
I WAS WONDERING WHO IT WAS!
WHAT ARE YOU DOING...
...ALL THE WAY UP HERE?

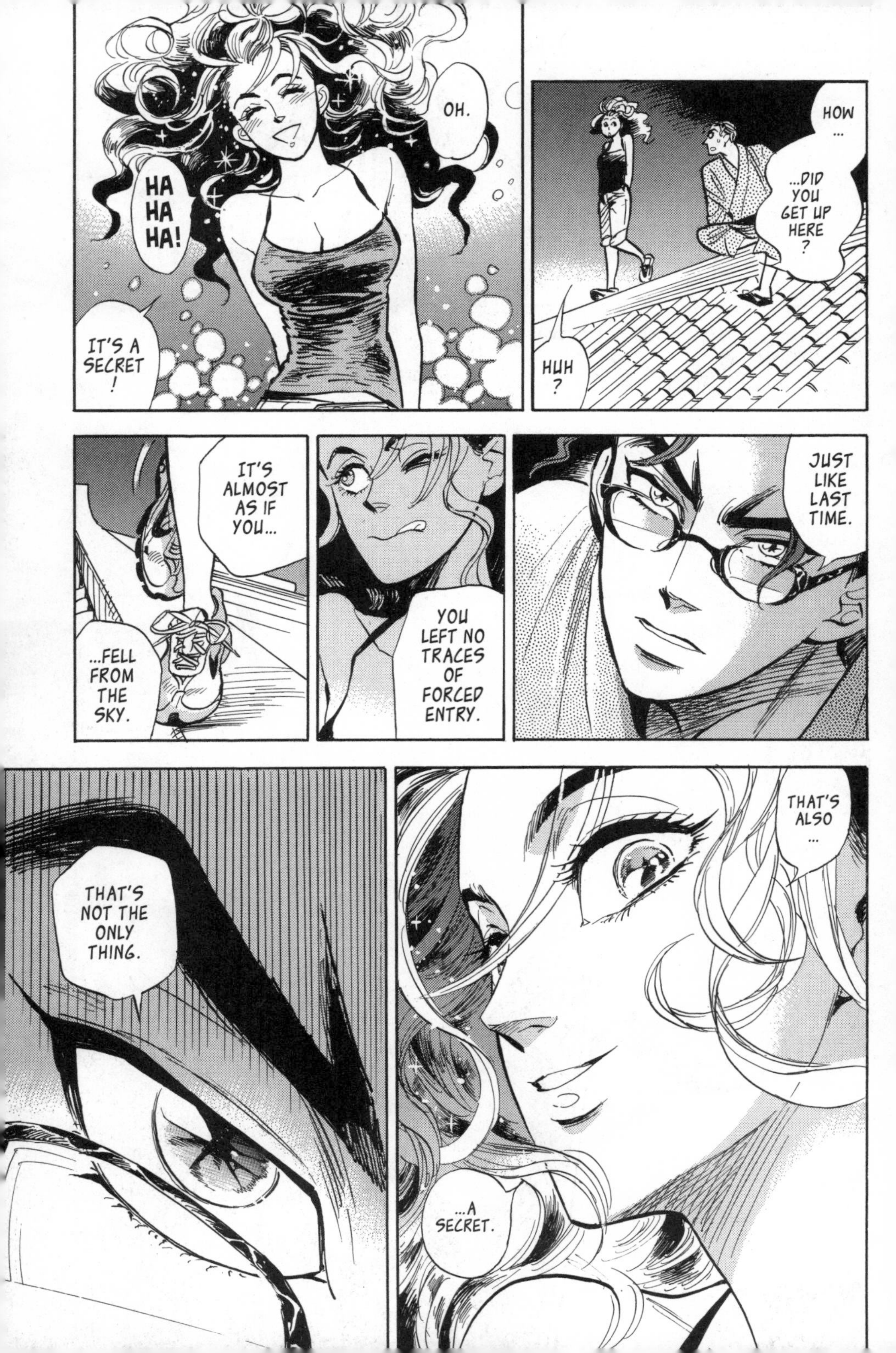
HOW ...
...DID YOU GET UP HERE ?
HUH ?
OH.
HA HA HA!
IT'S A SECRET !
JUST LIKE LAST TIME.
YOU LEFT NO TRACES OF FORCED ENTRY.
IT'S ALMOST AS IF YOU...
...FELL FROM THE SKY.
THAT'S ALSO ...
...A SECRET.
THAT'S NOT THE ONLY THING.

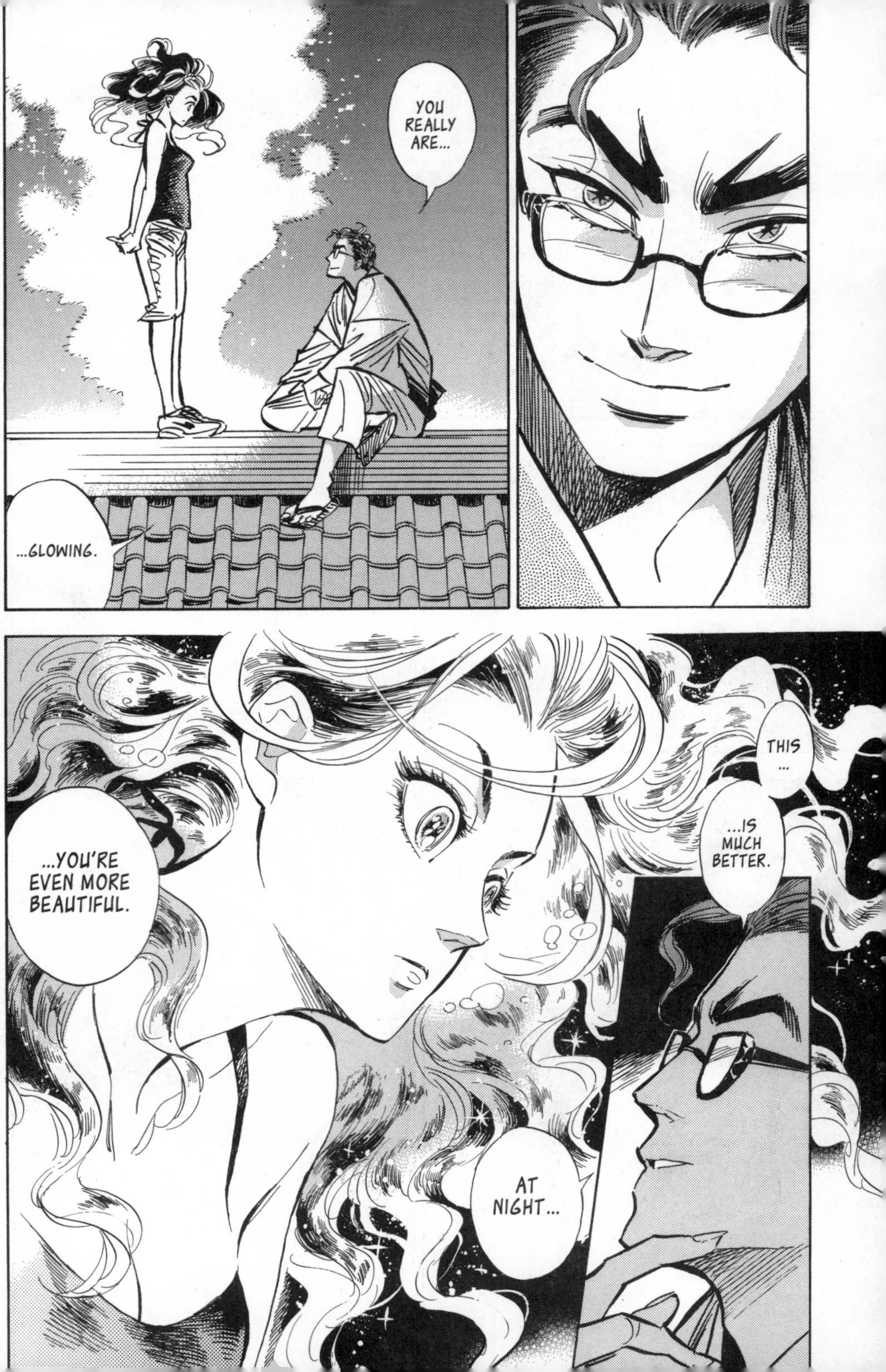
YOU REALLY ARE...
...GLOWING.
THIS...
...IS MUCH BETTER.
AT NIGHT...
...YOU'RE EVEN MORE BEAUTIFUL.

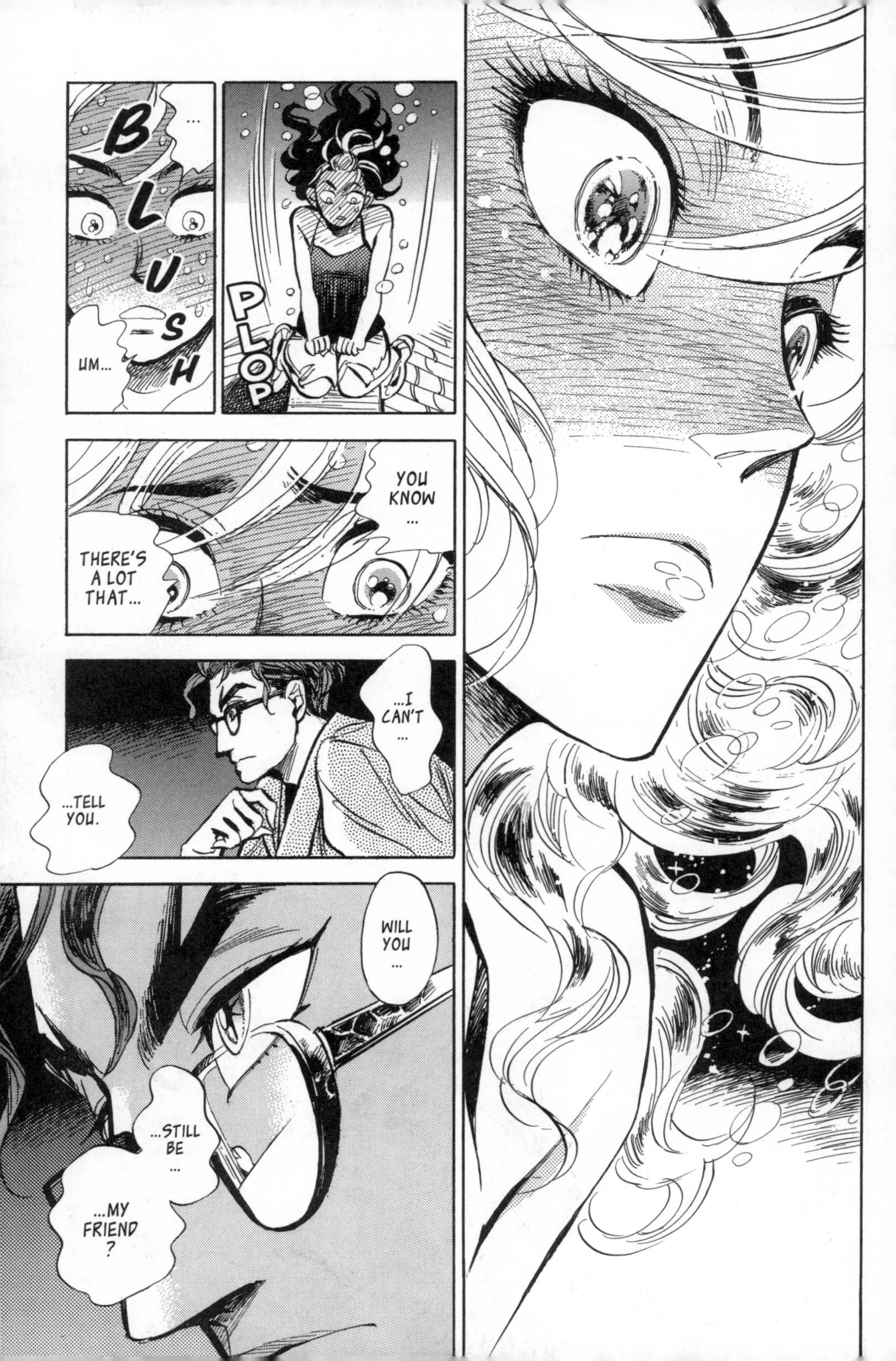
PLOP
BLUSH
...
UM...
YOU KNOW ...
THERE'S A LOT THAT...
...I CAN'T ...
...TELL YOU.
WILL YOU ...
...STILL BE ...
...MY FRIEND ?

...A LITTLE CLOSER.

RAN.

COME ...

CLOSER.

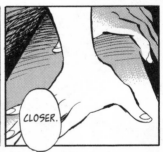

CLOSER.

EVEN CLOSER.

UM...

UH ...

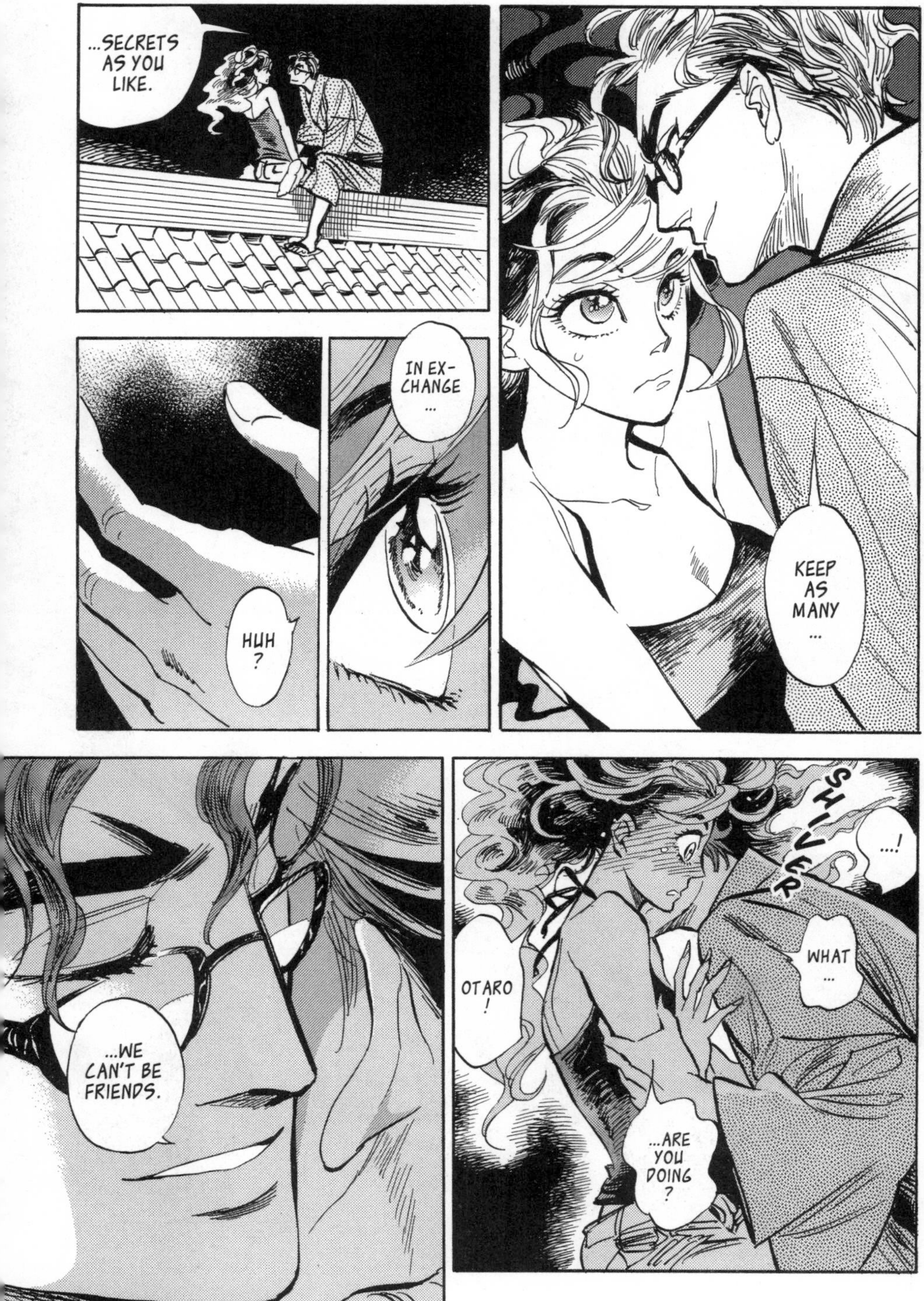
KEEP AS MANY ...
...SECRETS AS YOU LIKE.
IN EX-CHANGE ...
HUH ?
SHIVER
...!
WHAT ...
OTARO !
...ARE YOU DOING ?
...WE CAN'T BE FRIENDS.

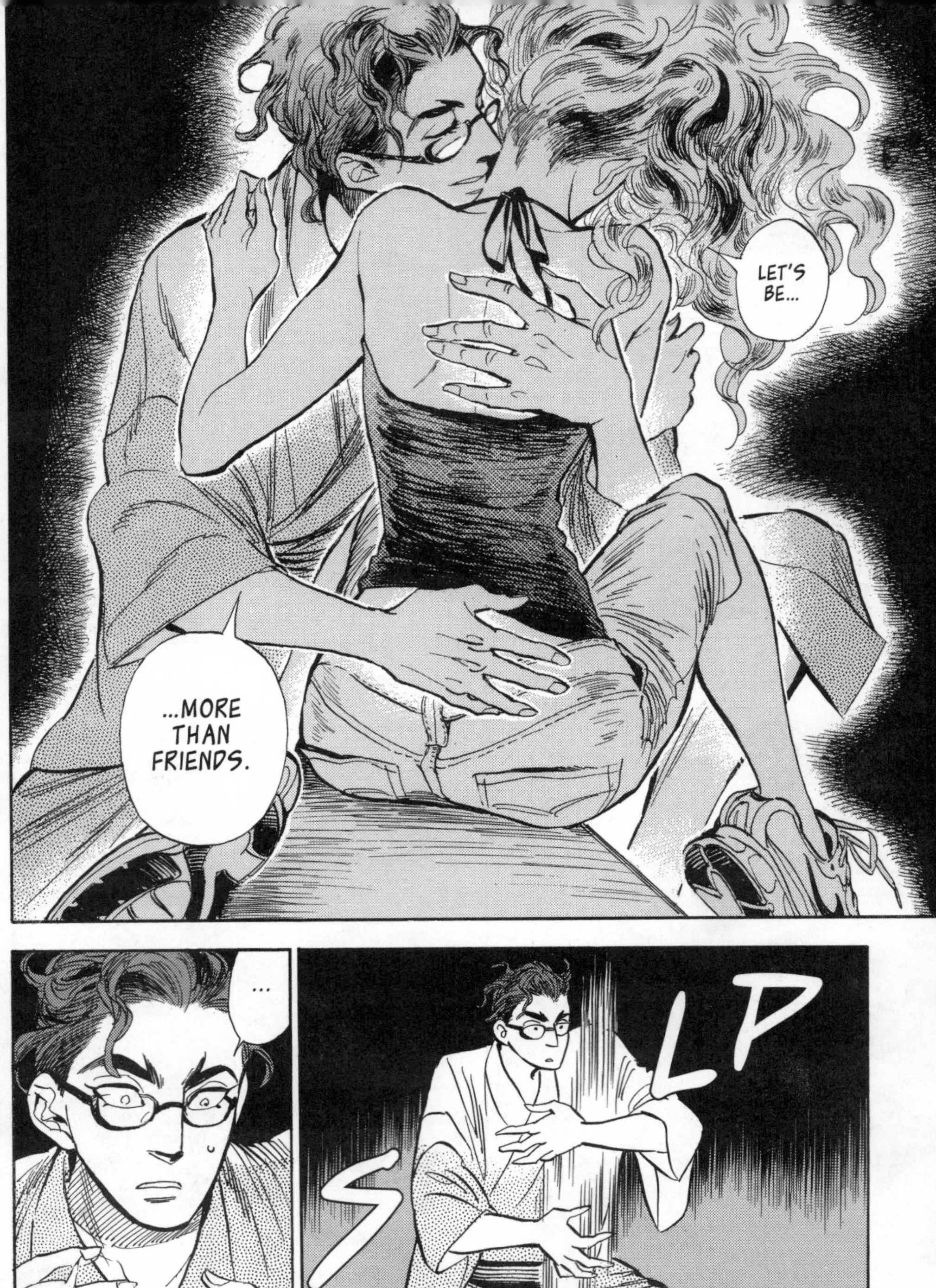
LET'S BE...
...MORE THAN FRIENDS.
SLP
...
HUH?

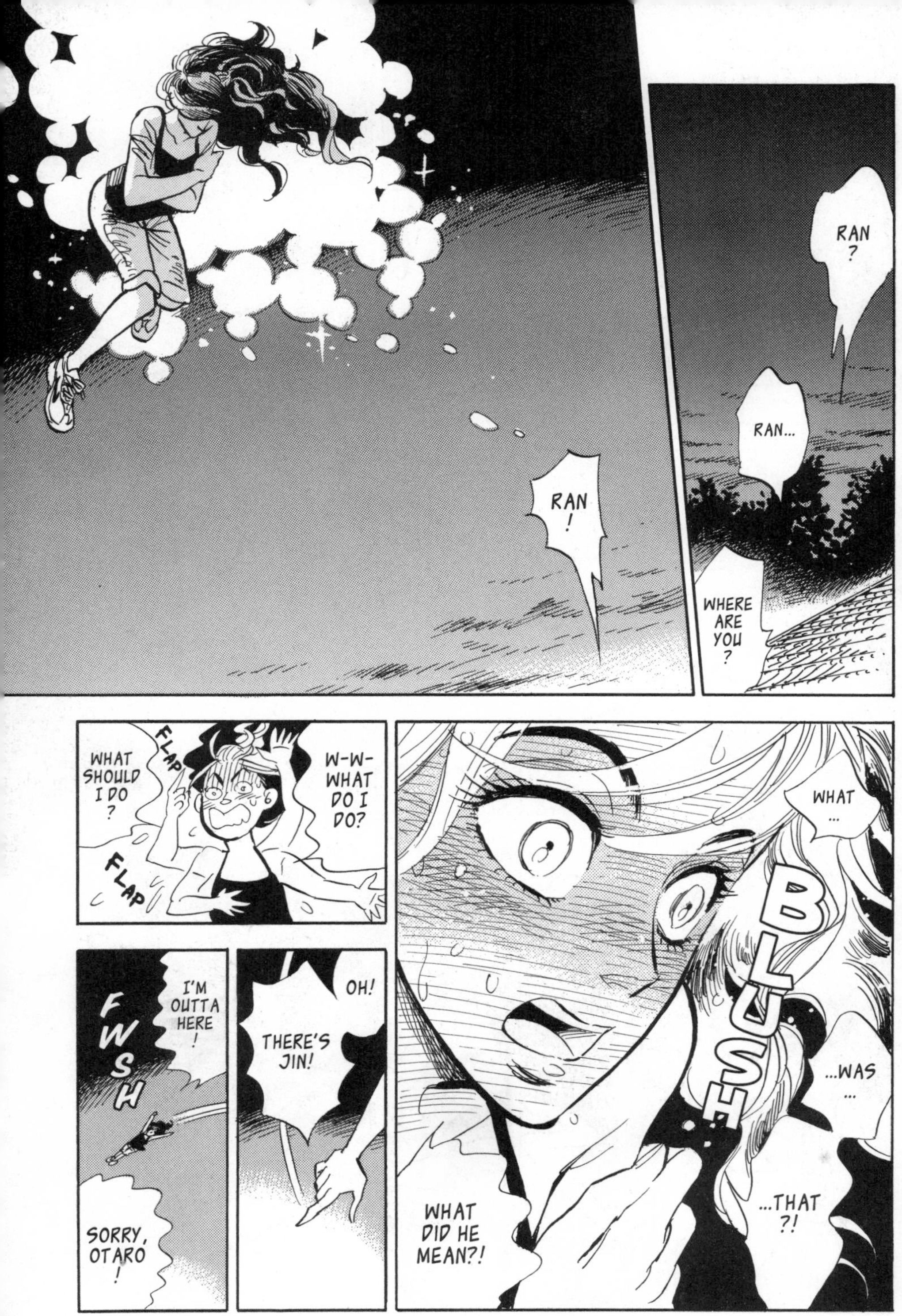
RAN?
RAN...
WHERE ARE YOU?
RAN!
WHAT...
BLUSH
...WAS...
...THAT?!
WHAT DID HE MEAN?!
W-W-WHAT DO I DO?
FLAP
WHAT SHOULD I DO?
FLAP
OH!
THERE'S JIN!
I'M OUTTA HERE!
FWSH
SORRY, OTARO!

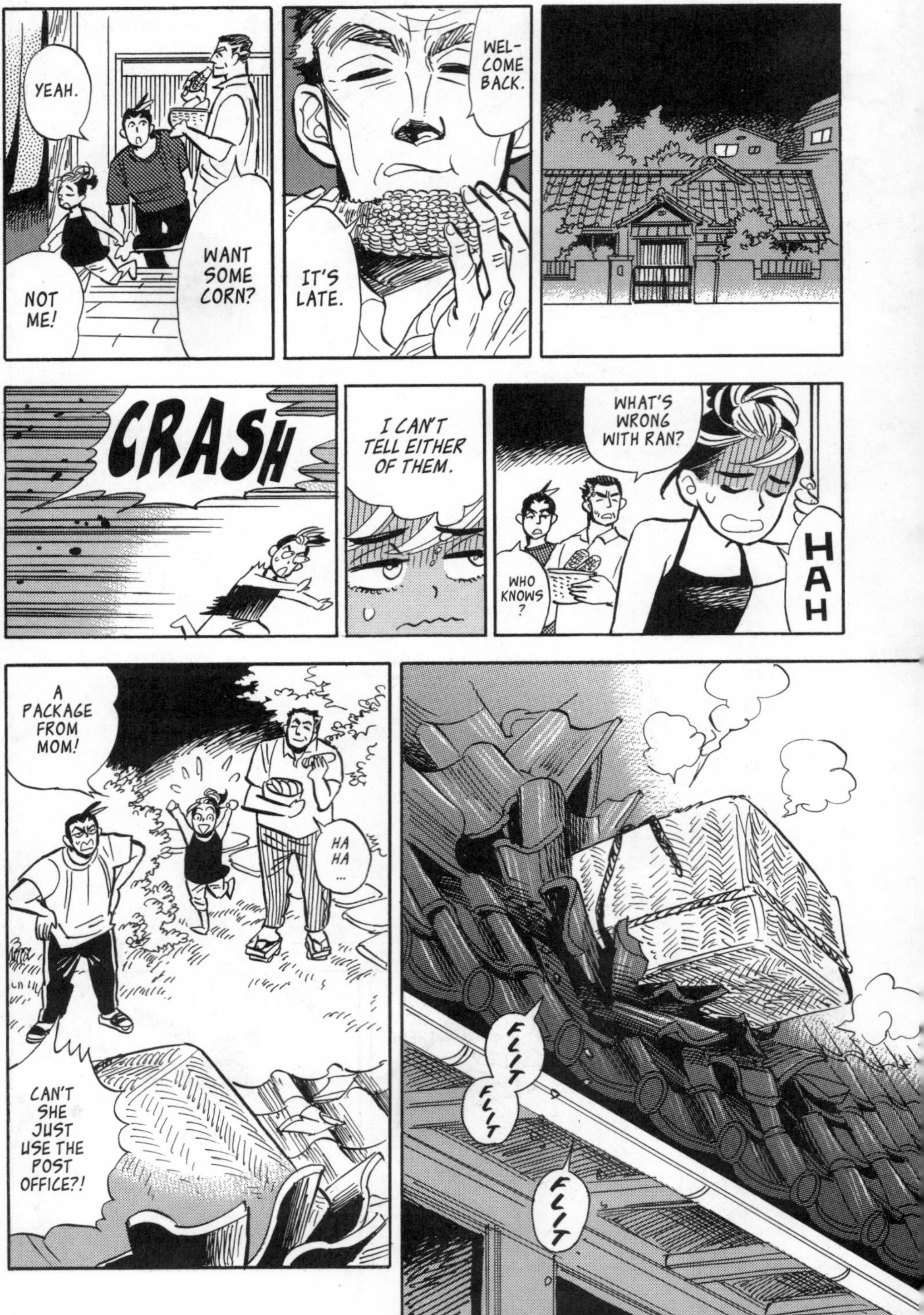
WEL-COME BACK.
IT'S LATE.
YEAH.
WANT SOME CORN?
NOT ME!
WHAT'S WRONG WITH RAN?
HAH
WHO KNOWS?
I CAN'T TELL EITHER OF THEM.
CRASH
FLIT FLIT
FLIT
A PACKAGE FROM MOM!
HA HA...
CAN'T SHE JUST USE THE POST OFFICE?!

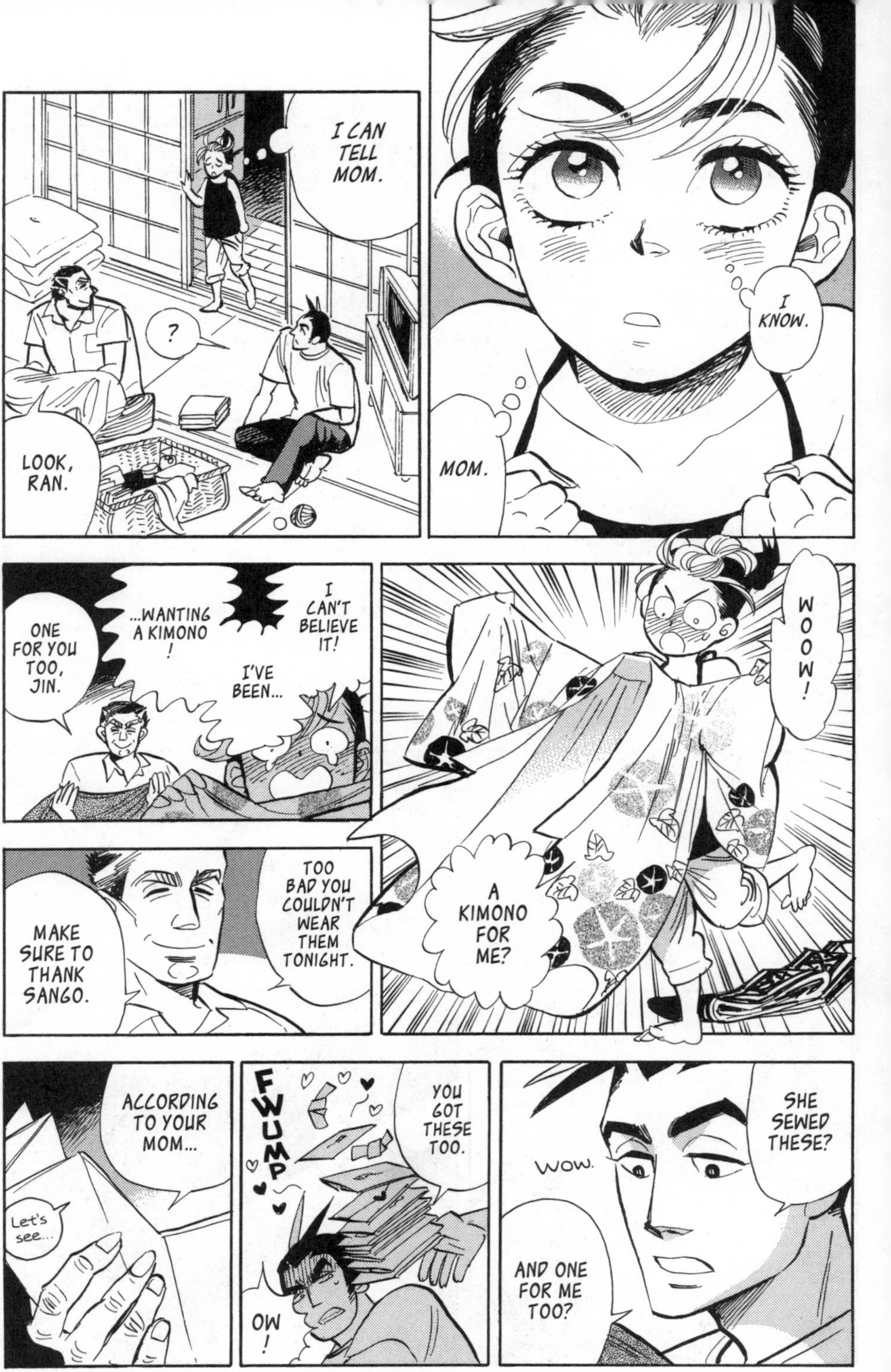
I KNOW.
MOM.
I CAN TELL MOM.
?
LOOK, RAN.
WOOOW!
A KIMONO FOR ME?
I CAN'T BELIEVE IT!
I'VE BEEN...
...WANTING A KIMONO!
ONE FOR YOU TOO, JIN.
TOO BAD YOU COULDN'T WEAR THEM TONIGHT.
MAKE SURE TO THANK SANGO.
SHE SEWED THESE?
WOW.
AND ONE FOR ME TOO?
YOU GOT THESE TOO.
FWUMP
OW!
ACCORDING TO YOUR MOM...
Let's see...

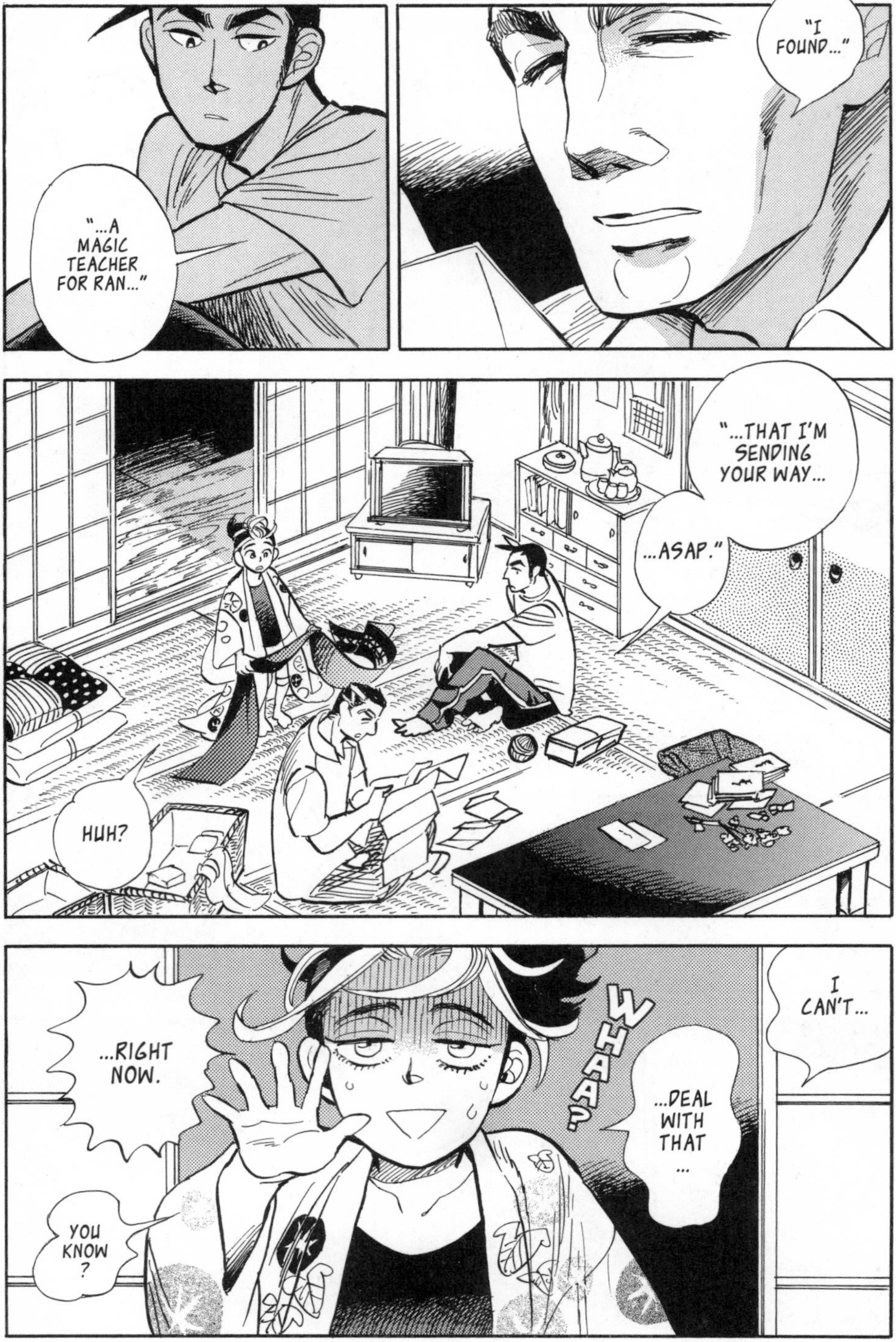
"I FOUND..."
"...A MAGIC TEACHER FOR RAN..."
"...THAT I'M SENDING YOUR WAY...
...ASAP."
HUH?
I CAN'T...
WHAAA?
...DEAL WITH THAT ...
...RIGHT NOW.
YOU KNOW ?

Chapter 6 / The End

Aki Irie was born in Kagawa Prefecture, Japan. She began her professional career as a manga artist in 2002 with the short story "Fuku-chan Tabi Mata Tabi" (Fuku-chan on the Road Again), which was published in the monthly manga magazine *Papu*. *Ran and the Gray World*, her first full-length series, is also the first of her works to be released in English.

RAN AND THE GRAY WORLD

VOL. 1
VIZ Signature Edition

Story & Art by
AKI IRIE

English Translation & Adaptation / Emi Louie-Nishikawa
Touch-Up Art & Lettering / Joanna Estep
Design / Yukiko Whitley
Editor / Amy Yu

RAN TO HAIIRO NO SEKAI Vol. 1

First published in Japan in 2009 by KADOKAWA CORPORATION ENTERBRAIN
English translation rights arranged with KADOKAWA CORPORATION ENTERBRAIN

Printed in Canada

Published by VIZ Media, LLC
P.O. Box 77010
San Francisco, CA 94107

10 9 8 7 6 5 4 3 2 1
First printing, November 2018

Bonus comics!

VIZ MEDIA
viz.com

VIZ SIGNATURE
vizsignature.com

ratings.viz.com RATED T+ OLDER TEEN

PARENTAL ADVISORY
RAN AND THE GRAY WORLD is rated T+ for Older Teen and is recommended for ages 16 and up. This volume contains brief nudity and suggestive themes.

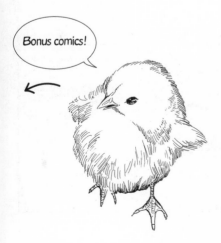

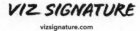

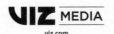

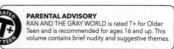

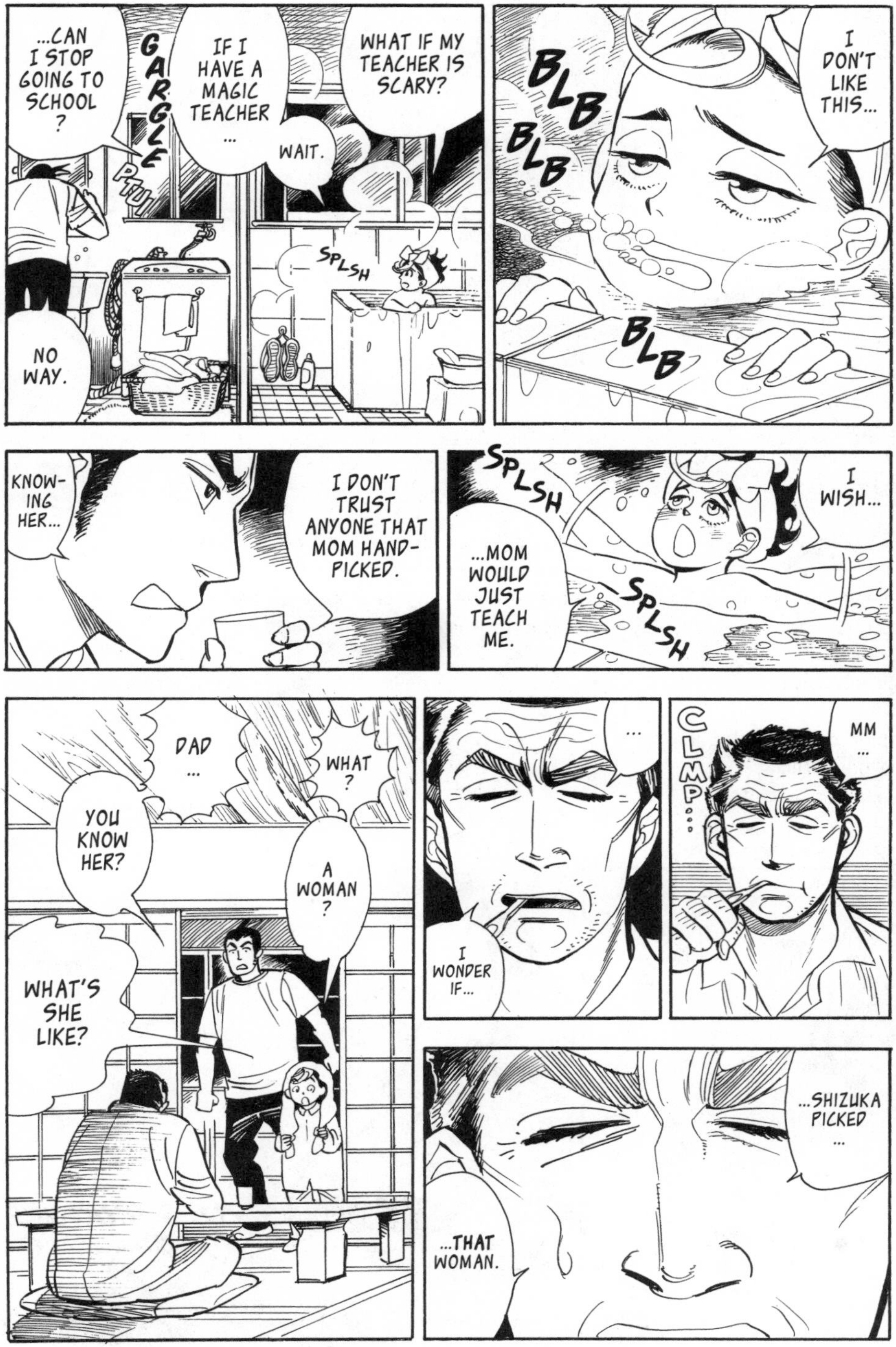

BLB
BLB
I DON'T LIKE THIS...
BLB
WHAT IF MY TEACHER IS SCARY?
IF I HAVE A MAGIC TEACHER...
WAIT.
...CAN I STOP GOING TO SCHOOL?
GARGLE
PTUI
SPLSH
NO WAY.
SPLSH
I WISH...
...MOM WOULD JUST TEACH ME.
SPLSH
I DON'T TRUST ANYONE THAT MOM HAND-PICKED.
KNOWING HER...
MM...
CLMP...
...
I WONDER IF...
...SHIZUKA PICKED...
...THAT WOMAN.
WHAT?
DAD...
A WOMAN?
YOU KNOW HER?
WHAT'S SHE LIKE?

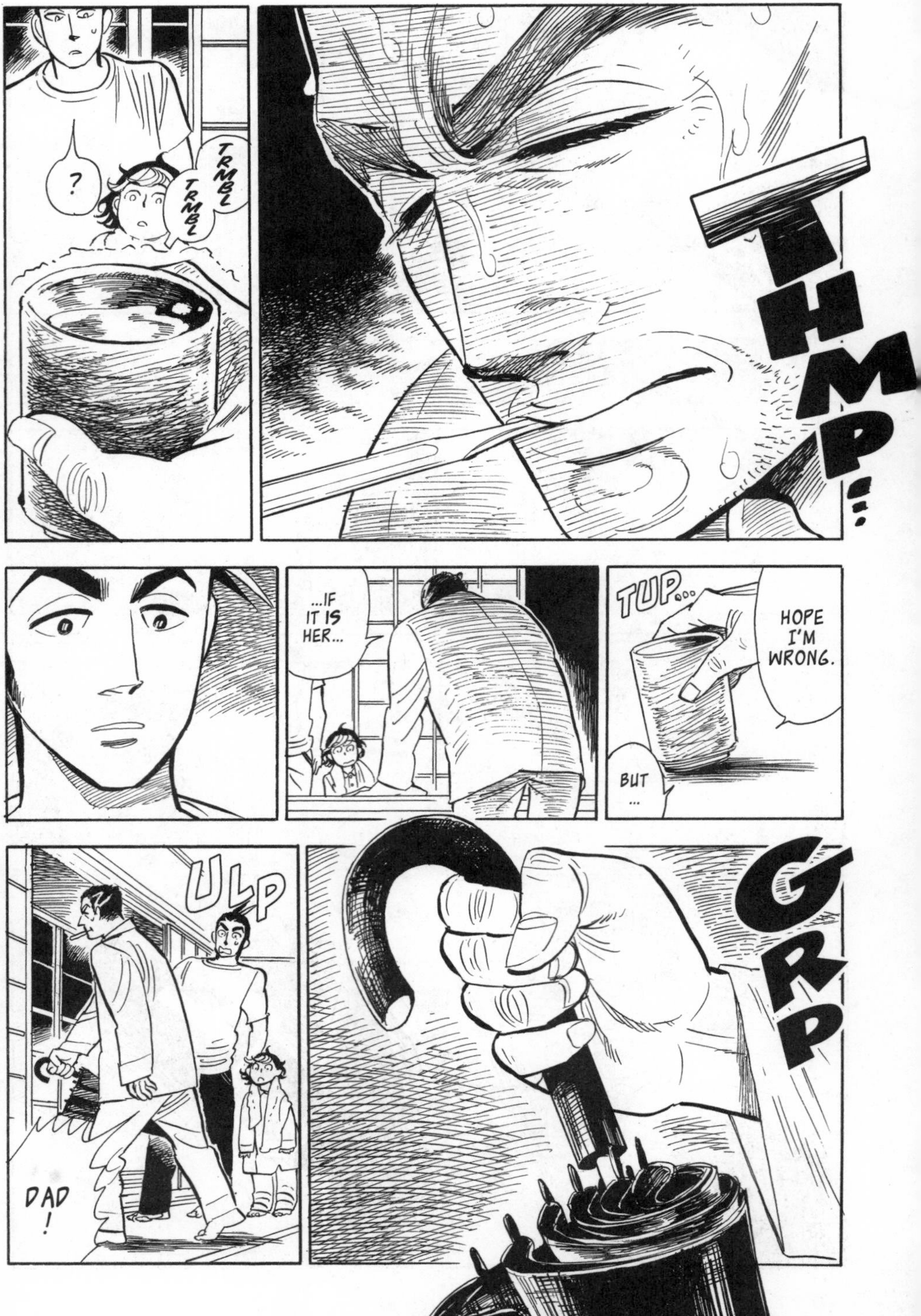

THMP!!
?
TRMBL TRMBL
TUP...
HOPE I'M WRONG.
BUT ...
...IF IT IS HER...
GRP
ULP
DAD!

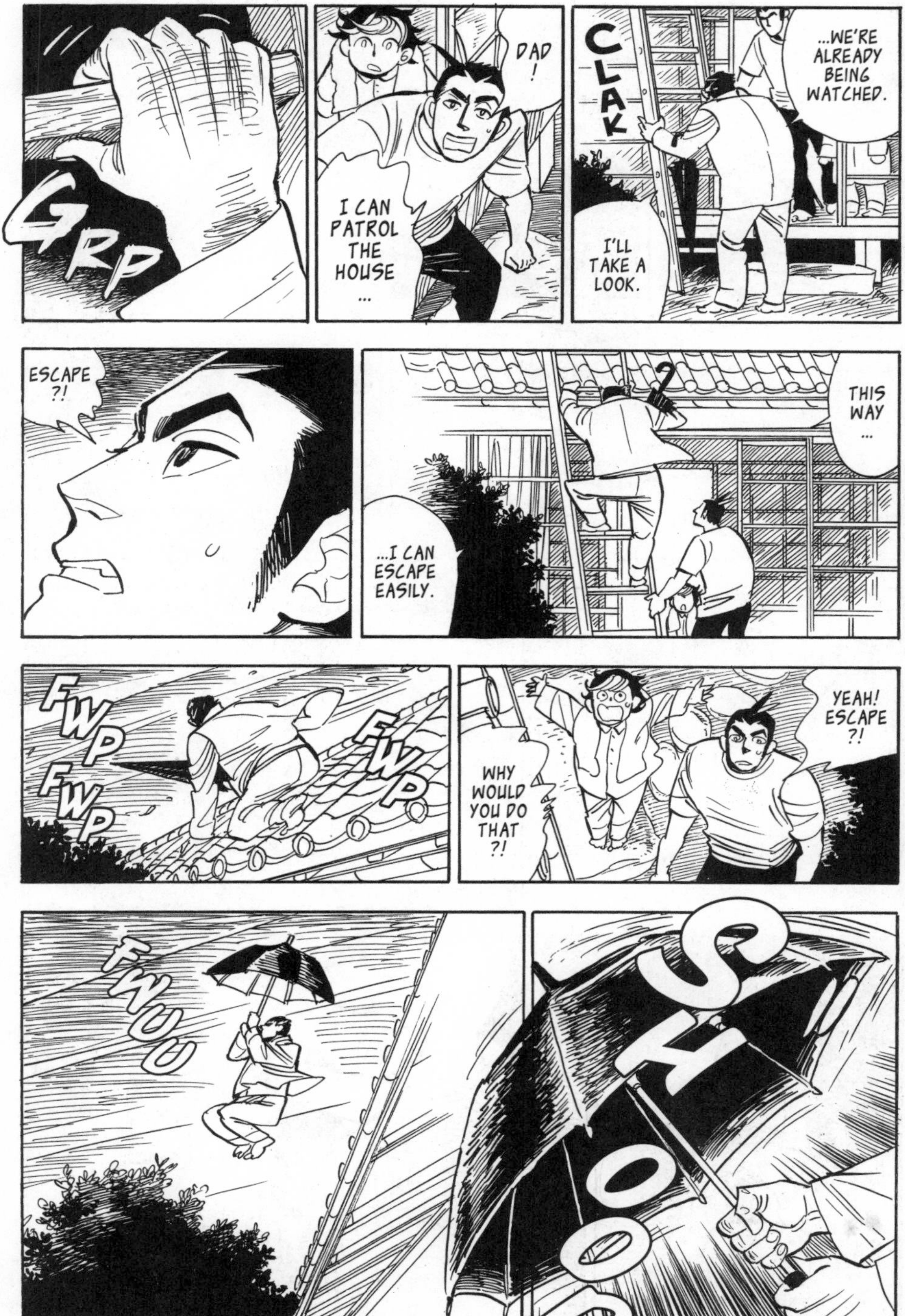

...WE'RE ALREADY BEING WATCHED.
CLAK
I'LL TAKE A LOOK.
DAD!
I CAN PATROL THE HOUSE ...
GRP
THIS WAY ...
...I CAN ESCAPE EASILY.
ESCAPE ?!
YEAH! ESCAPE ?!
WHY WOULD YOU DO THAT ?!
FWP
FWP
FWP
SHOOOP
FWUU

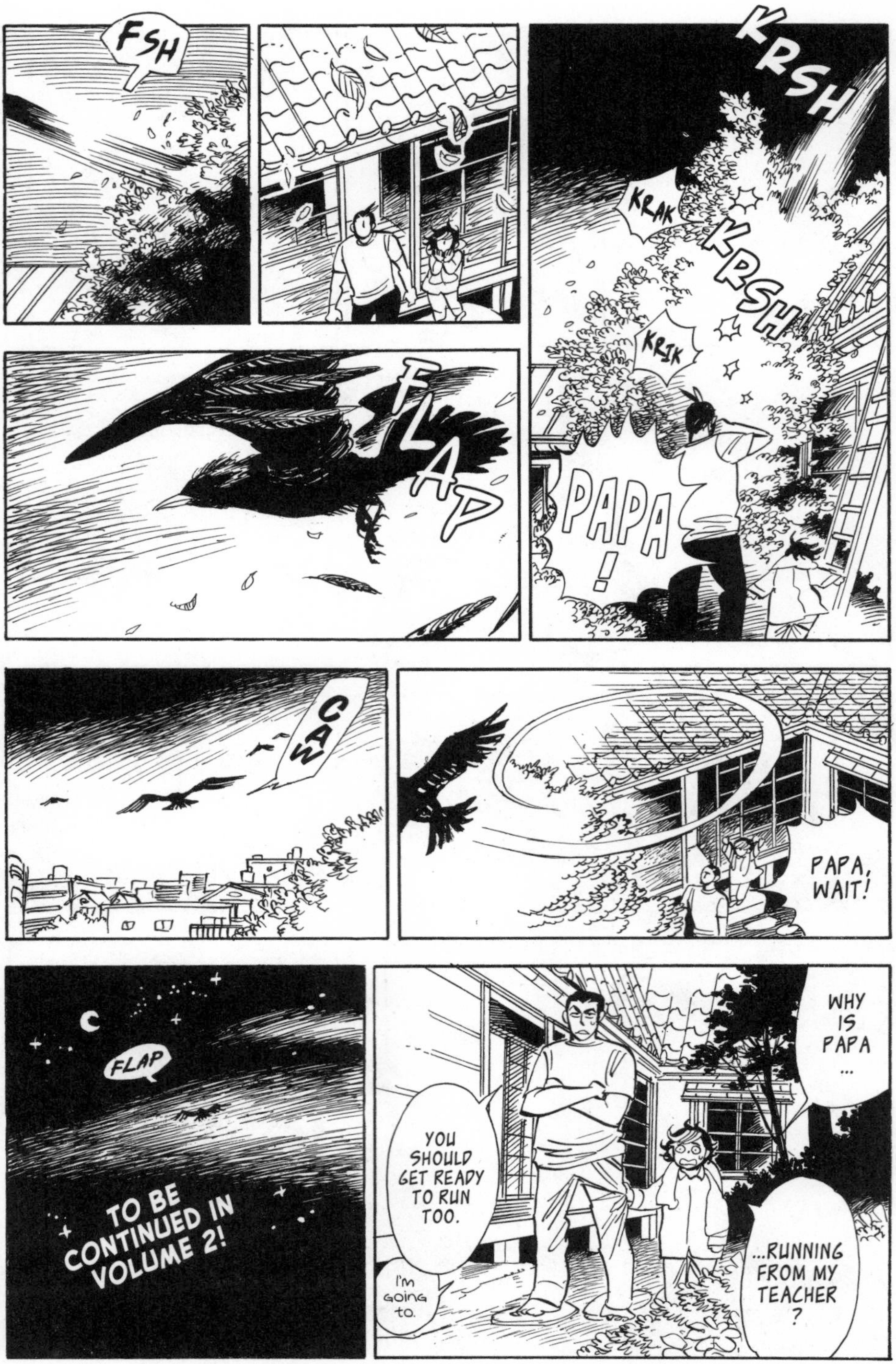
KRSH
KRAK
KRSH
KRIK
PAPA!
FSH
FLAP
PAPA, WAIT!
CAW
WHY IS PAPA ...
...RUNNING FROM MY TEACHER?
YOU SHOULD GET READY TO RUN TOO.
I'm going to.
FLAP
TO BE CONTINUED IN VOLUME 2!

Ran and the Gray World 1 / The End